Digital Transformation and Innovative Services for Business and Learning

Kamaljeet Sandhu
University of New England, Australia

IGI Global
DISSEMINATOR OF KNOWLEDGE

A volume in the Advances in Business Strategy and Competitive Advantage (ABSCA) Book Series

Published in the United States of America by
IGI Global
Business Science Reference (an imprint of IGI Global)
701 E. Chocolate Avenue
Hershey PA, USA 17033
Tel: 717-533-8845
Fax: 717-533-8661
E-mail: cust@igi-global.com
Web site: http://www.igi-global.com

Library of Congress Cataloging-in-Publication Data

Names: Sandhu, Kamaljeet, 1970- editor.
Title: Digital transformation and innovative services for business and learning / Kamaljeet Sandhu, editor.
Description: Hershey, PA : Business Science Reference, [2020] | Includes bibliographical references and index. | Summary: "This book is a collection of innovative research on the latest digital services and their role in supporting the digital transformation of businesses and education"-- Provided by publisher.
Identifiers: LCCN 2019060126 (print) | LCCN 2019060127 (ebook) | ISBN 9781799851752 (hardcover) | ISBN 9781799851769 (paperback) | ISBN 9781799851776 (ebook)
Subjects: LCSH: Technological innovations--Management. | Business enterprises--Technological innovations. | Educational innovations.
Classification: LCC HC79.T4 D54 2020 (print) | LCC HC79.T4 (ebook) | DDC 658/.05--dc23
LC record available at https://lccn.loc.gov/2019060126
LC ebook record available at https://lccn.loc.gov/2019060127

This book is published in the IGI Global book series Advances in Business Strategy and Competitive Advantage (ABSCA) (ISSN: 2327-3429; eISSN: 2327-3437)

British Cataloguing in Publication Data
A Cataloguing in Publication record for this book is available from the British Library.

I dedicate this book to the memory of my mother and father.

Editorial Advisory Board

Table of Contents

Detailed Table of Contents

Small and medium enterprises (SMEs) play an important role in the economic development of a country. On the other hand, one of the main factors that leads to organizational success is leadership effectiveness. In addition, many researchers argue that leadership effectiveness can improve organizational performance. Therefore, in order to contribute to economic growth, it is crucial to understand and evaluate the leadership effectiveness. Some researches carried out studies to introduce the dimensions of leadership effectiveness, although there is a lack of research to prioritize these dimensions to effectively guide leaders on how to improve their effectiveness. The chapter aims to prioritize dimensions of leadership effectiveness in SMEs, specifically Malaysia digital service SMEs. The applied research method in this chapter is a quantitative method using analytical hierarchy process (AHP) technique. Furthermore, in this chapter, leadership effectiveness dimensions have been evaluated by practitioner and academician experts in the Malaysia SME context.

In today's world, where technological developments and age-related consumption tendencies differ, entrepreneurship is a subject that needs to be investigated in the context of gerontology. Consumption behaviors are influenced by the effects of decreases due to aging on technology and the environment. In this chapter, where the effects of differentiation of consumption behaviors on entrepreneurship and its process are discussed, a new concept, gerontrepreneurship, is introduced. With this concept, the authors a new idea to gerontology in the context of entrepreneurship, elderly-technology interaction, and digital service innovations. In this chapter, the consumption processes of the elderly and their relations with the gerontrepreneurship process are explained, and recommendations are made.

Traffic optimization at an intersection, using real-time traffic information, presents an important focus of research into intelligent transportation systems. Several studies have proposed adaptive traffic lights control, which concentrates on determining green light length and sequence of the phases for each cycle in accordance with the real-time traffic detected. In order to minimize the waiting time at the intersection, the authors propose an intelligent traffic light using the information collected by a wireless sensors network installed in the road. The proposed algorithm is essentially based on two parameters: the waiting time in each lane and the length of its queue. The simulations show that the algorithm applied at a network of intersections improves significantly the average waiting time, queue length, fuel consumption, and CO2 emissions.

Service quality has turned out to be the most important topic of consideration to academicians and practitioners. It has been proven that the influence of service quality on business performance, cost leadership, customer satisfaction, customer loyalty, and profitability. The accomplishment of quality in services has turned out to be a vital concern of all services organisations. Quality in services is mainly undefined and becomes the crucial issue. Increased competition and knowledge of customer satisfaction made the service organisations use new service parameters and implement quality management tools as competitive advantage. Service quality is hard to evaluate, as it is subjective in nature. Many researchers did explore and confirm the dimensions of service quality. This study focuses on various studies of service quality conducted by earlier researchers in an array of industries. The chapter details the development of service quality theory and different models hypothesised to measure service quality.

Internet has become an important tool to deliver products, information, and services. Thus, customer satisfaction is increasingly recognized as a significant aspect of online business activities and is considered as a key determinant for successful digital services. Furthermore, since keeping current customers is more profitable than acquiring new clients, it is vital to gain customer satisfaction to achieve organizational goals. This introduces a new requirement to measure customer satisfaction as a factor for continuous business improvement. Therefore, there is a clear need for a theoretical survey instrument that integrates all aspects of customer satisfaction in the digital environment. The chapter responds to this need by its exploratory nature. In the first step, exploratory analysis is used to extract all customer

Preface

The term “Digital and Digital Transformation” in recent times have a profound impact on many businesses, customers, employees, suppliers, and stakeholders. Organisations are categorised as Digitally-ready or Digitally-not ready. Leaders of organisations are fast steering companies towards where the business is Digitally-ready. For an organisation that is ‘not’ Digitally-ready and to become Digitally-ready is not an easy and straight forward task. Leadership and Management around the organisation have to deal with several issues simultaneously such as technical that is related to IT and non-technical that is related to people e.g. customers, employees, suppliers. Businesses that have adopted both technical and non-technical approach to Digital Service Innovation are successful, and many others are not successful. Main drivers of “Digital Business and Digital Transformation” are people.

The Digital Transformation empowers an organisation and its people, revolves around leadership and management and adoption techniques for digital service innovation. Digital transformation provides an organisation – private or public - to better leverage technology for the customer’s, employees, and suppliers benefit and far reaching digital social impact on society through social media. Content development and use is driven by data for digital systems and are created by people. Digital Enterprises seeks to integrate complex processes and functions such as management, marketing, production, manufacturing, accounting and finance, customer relationship management, human resources, logistics, information technology, and many other activities as a core aspect of digital systems. Large investment into digital systems are guided which is based on value for money, real time digital services delivery online, cost effectiveness, and competition among firms to be digitally superior than the others and becoming digitally compliant.

Many governments are also digitalising their core functions and services delivery. Smart phones are increasingly popular and have become the standard platform for digital services delivery for banking, utilities, hospitality, travel, education, healthcare, government, social media, and many more. Organisations that are leading the drive to digitalisation are highly empowering people, as the drivers of digital systems are people creating content and its use, when the digital transformation succeeds people are empowered. This book is a good example of digital research in which every author has used digital tools provided by the publisher to make this book a success. At universities teaching, learning, and research are transformed into essential digital tools that are successfully adopted.

Digital system is not restricted to a particular academic domain, or a geographic region, or a particular industry, rather it is globally widespread phenomenon and merged with many other domains creating a self-evolving digital ecosystem. From traditional mortar brick to new start-up business, are harnessing the power of digital business as a cost-effective model to deliver goods, and services online 24/7. Digital business strategy is adopted for transforming business, for streamline processes, and making best use of technologies to enhance interaction with customers and employees and deliver excellent customer experience in real time. This book covers a broad area of research for Digital business in which the core emphasis is to bind on important topics such as Leadership, Management, Adoption Techniques, and Service Innovation. These topics are considered important as it provides a clear and a forward-thinking direction for the readership on digital projects. Interesting case studies and empirical research are presented by the authors to demonstrate the importance of Digital Service Innovation.

THE DIGITAL RESEARCH, GLOBAL CHALLENGES, AND NEW DISCOVERIES

The key areas of digitalisation and global challenges are new and unique and requires new knowledge that is gained from a deep understanding of complex issues (technical e.g. technology related, and non-technical e.g. people related) that have been reported in this book. Digital business is not clearly understood at different levels of management and their leaderships (as many top leaders are not IT experts, and not many IT experts are not top leaders, the competencies required are very different), and there is incomplete information around it. The challenges become more complex when data that is required to power digital systems is either non-existent or digitally-not ready to provide useful solutions on a digital platform. The issues related to digital skills, software, hardware, data, internet connectivity, website interaction and access from different devices such as smartphones and tablets, and cybersecurity, also presents complex challenges for the leadership and management of digital service innovation.

The chapters in this book unravel important information, piece by piece, so that the readers can clearly understand, that is driving the requirements for digital transformation for healthcare, universities, banks, hospitality, computing, government and private sector institutions, new start-up, and many others. Prominent researchers have deeply examined areas of digital business models and strategy and have provided the readers with a clear understanding of important issues and challenges being studied, such as problems, literature and theory, research methodology, new research data findings, solutions and recommendations, and future research direction for Digital Service Innovation that adds to the discovery of new knowledge and direction for further research.

The journey for developing and completing this book is a long one in which all authors have made a valuable contribution to the body of new research knowledge, and adopted new research techniques to study the problems, and found innovative solutions to address those complicated problems. This study will be very useful for many researchers to build on new findings that have been reported in this book. This book will also serve as a valuable tool for many students, practitioners, government, managerial staff and other professionals to learn about new developments in digital transformation of business systems from a global perspective. International studies have been presented with important new findings from America, Australia, Asia, Europe, Africa and the Middle east, which demonstrates the far-reaching impact for Digital Service Innovation, and suggests that digital businesses are global and are continuously evolving online into new ecosystems in different parts of the world via internet.

ORGANIZATION OF THE BOOK

A brief description of each of the chapters follows.

Chapter 1 presents an empirical study on Small and Medium Enterprises (SMEs) playing an important role in the economic development of a country. One of the main factors that leads to organizational success is leadership effectiveness. Besides, many researchers argue that leadership effectiveness can improve organizational performance. Therefore, in order to contribute to economic growth, it is crucial to understand and evaluate the leadership effectiveness. Some researches carried out to introduce the dimensions of leadership effectiveness although there is a lack of research to priorities these dimensions to effectively guide leaders on how to improve their effectiveness. The current book chapter aims to prioritize dimensions of leadership effectiveness in SMEs, specifically, Malaysia Digital Service for SMEs.

Chapter 2 describes the technological developments and age-related consumption tendencies differ, entrepreneurship is a subject that needs to be investigated in the context of gerontology. Consumption behaviors are influenced by the effects of decreases due to aging on technology and the environment. In this chapter where the effects of differentiation of consumption behaviors on entrepreneurship and it's process are discussed, a new concept, gerontrepreneurship, is introduced. With this concept, it has been tried to contribute a new idea to gerontology in the context of entrepreneurship, elderly-technology interaction and digital service innovations. In this chapter, the consumption processes of the elderly and their relations with the gerontrepreneurship process are explained and recommendations are made.

Chapter 3 explores the role of Internet technologies which are recently being widely adopted across academic higher education for web-based digital learning systems. In this context Digital Learning Management Systems (DLMSs) are an important and necessary academic tool for learning activities. Many universities are using the Digital LMS (DLMS) tools that are unique to their environment. Different universities have different DLMS tools that are software driven and allow the users (management, instructors, and students) to use them for regular teaching and learning tasks. This research will examine the qualitative data collected using the case study methodology. In this research, case study design was selected for the qualitative methodology and semi-structured interviews were employed as the data collection method. The research findings provide deep analysis of the interviews, to gain insights into students' perspectives regarding the factors influencing the implementation of the digital learning management system at higher education sector such as the universities.

Chapter 4 is based on the primary research for services (banking) sector as a case of service branding with services extended marketing mix variables. A research model has been developed to identify the impact of services extended marketing variables on customer-based brand equity. Two components of customer-based brand have been taken into consideration such as brand awareness and brand association. For this purpose, structured questionnaire was prepared and a survey was conducted on 400 respondents and structural equation modeling technique has been applied in this research.

Chapter 5 reports that academic higher education has adopted the use of internet technologies such as web-based digital learning systems. Digital Learning Management Systems (DLMSs) has widely been utilized by many universities as a tool that fosters learning activities due to its prevailing unique environment. DLMS is software-driven tools with different features; hence, different universities adopt different DLMS that meet their expectations in terms of helping their administrators, instructors, and student's learning the process. The research aims to examine collected qualitative data through a case study methodology coupled with semi-structured interviews as the data collection method. The interviews are analyzed deeply based on the research findings to gain insights on how the implementation of the digital learning management systems influences the learning perspective of instructors as far as universities and the higher education sector is concerned.

Chapter 6 explains that corporations have been donating millions of dollars for non-profit organizations in order to fulfil their duty towards society and companies are engaging in many approaches in order to strengthen their relationship with consumers. One of these is Corporate Social Responsibility

(CSR). The purpose of this chapter is to consolidate an understanding of business real world practices with an academic research perspective, and to inform the reader on the developments in CSR practices in the digital environment. With this purpose, a descriptive research is adopted, which will include a content analysis of the companies which will be selected from the list of Fortune 500 in Turkey, and the data from the web pages of the top 100 companies will be analysed. The results indicate that large Turkish companies are lagging behind global companies with regards to digitalisation of CSR practices and institutionalisation of their CSR practices when compared to the corporations in developed countries.

Chapter 7 describes the process of Accounting software selection, implementation, and use, which have received close interest for business efficiency purposes in a fast-changing global digital environment. This study reports the results of a survey for small-medium accounting firms in Thailand which have focused on the factors used to select the accounting software. The researchers have examined whether different firms have different factors in selecting the accounting software and which factor is most influential for accounting and auditing firms for their decision to select accounting software. A structured questionnaire survey instrument was used to collect data from 49 accounting firms. New findings from this study suggest that, firstly, there are no significant difference between accounting and auditing firms in the factors used to select accounting software. Secondly, it was found that the accuracy of data processing, calculation, and reports is the most influential factor that accounting, and auditing firms will consider for using the accounting software.

Chapter 8 articulates that Blockchain is an emerging technology that serves as an immutable ledger and publicly available infrastructure for building decentralized applications. Blockchain-based applications ensure transparency and trust between all parties involved in the interaction. Nowadays, educational organizations focus on online education and propose to create a system based on educational smart contracts in a public ledger. This public ledger shall be shared between major online and offline educational institutes around the world. From a software architecture perspective, blockchain enables new forms of distributed software architectures across a large network of untrusted participants. The objective of this chapter is to propose a Blockchain architecture stack to Smart Education. The proposed architecture exploits the benefits of the blockchain and global ecosystem simplification, to create a globally trusted higher education credit system.

Chapter 9 demonstrates traffic optimization at an intersection, using real time traffic information, presents an important focus of research into intelligent transportation system. Several studies have proposed digital traffic lights control, which concentrates on determining green light length and sequence of the phases for each cycle in accordance with the real time traffic detected. In order to minimize the waiting time at the intersection, we propose an intelligent traffic light using the information collected by a wireless sensors network installed in the road. The proposed algorithm is essentially based on two parameters: the waiting time in each lane and the length of its queue. Our simulations show that our algorithm applied at a network of intersections improves significantly the average waiting time, queue length, fuel consumption and CO2 emissions.

Chapter 10 rationalises that service quality has turn out to be a most important topic of consideration to academicians and practitioners. It has been proven that the influence of service quality on business performance, cost leadership, customer satisfaction, customer loyalty, and profitability. The accomplishment of quality in services has turn out to be vital concern of all services organisations. Quality in services is mainly undefined and becomes the crucial issue. Increased competition and knowledge of customer satisfaction made the service organisations to use new service parameter and implement quality management tools as competitive advantage. Service quality is hard to evaluate, as it is subjective in nature. Many researchers did explore and confirm the dimensions of service quality. This study focuses on various studies of service quality conducted by earlier researchers in an array of industries. The paper details the development of service quality theory and different models hypothesised to measure service quality.

Chapter 11 explains the important elements in a survey for the evaluation of customer satisfaction in digital environment. Customer satisfaction is increasingly recognized as a significant aspect of online business activities and is considered as a key determinant for successful digital services. Furthermore, since keeping current customers is more profitable than acquiring new clients, it is vital to gain customer satisfaction to achieve organizations' goals. This introduces a new requirement to measure customer satisfaction as a factor for continuous business improvement. Therefore, there is a clear need for a theoretical survey instrument which integrates all aspects of customer satisfaction in digital environment. The current chapter responds to this need by its exploratory nature. In the first step, exploratory analysis used to extract all customer satisfaction dimensions. Then, the exploratory factor analysis used to cluster the factors effectively, thereby, further analysis including content validity, discriminate, and constructive testing used to test the proposed survey instrument.

Chapter 12 justifies the importance of communication skills research and reports that university graduates do not possess sufficient business communication skills. In this chapter the author explores what communication skills the graduate of today may require for the business world of tomorrow. Klaus Schwab (2016) refers to tomorrow's business world as the Fourth Industrial Revolution, where digital innovation will amalgamate nearly every aspect of human lives, and where demographic change, coupled with industrial transitions and changing consumer requirements, necessitate the need for today's business communication student to learn how to be a creative problem solver, have emotional intelligence, be able to communicate across borders and be able to persuasively communicate in a variety of written mediums. In light of Schwab's observations, this chapter explores why creativity, social skills, intercultural and written communication skills are so essential for today's business graduate.

Kamaljeet Sandhu
University of New England, Australia

Acknowledgment

I would like to acknowledge the help and contribution of all people, more specifically, to the authors and reviewers that took part in the review process. Without their support, this book would not have become a reality. All the authors have made valuable contribution by making many revisions to their chapters, presenting their interesting research to readers of this book.

Reviewers provided continuous and important feedbacks to the authors for improvements in their chapters, coherence, and content presentation of chapters.

I would like to personally thank all the authors and reviewers who have worked very hard to complete this book successfully. At every step we worked together as a highly coordinated and focused team.

In this journey we became very good and close colleagues, and this book has brought us all together from different parts of the world, and we have a valuable working relationship and I look forward to working with this great team again in another interesting book project to come soon.

I would like to personally thank staff at IGI-Global, development editors, who have provided the highest level of service. They continually and convincingly been very helpful & supportive in this research at every stage of the book development process, without their persistent help this publication would not have been possible.

I would like to thank my family, including my father and mother who passed away leaving beautiful memories and the importance for higher education and new learning that was ingrained in my very early life and which later was built into my ability to provide this advanced scholarly work to the advancement of new knowledge. This book is a tribute to my dear mum for all her love, support, belief, kindness, and trust, she had provided which transformed me into an author for scholarly research. I would not have achieved this book success without it.

Kamaljeet Sandhu
University of New England, Australia

Chapter 1
Prioritization of Leadership Effectiveness Dimensions Improving Organizational Performance via Analytical Hierarchy Process (AHP) Technique:
A Case Study for Malaysia's Digital Service SMEs

Hamed Taherdoost
https://orcid.org/0000-0002-6503-6739
Research Club, Hamta Group, Canada

Mitra Madanchian
Hamta Academy, Hamta Group, Canada

ABSTRACT

Small and medium enterprises (SMEs) play an important role in the economic development of a country. On the other hand, one of the main factors that leads to organizational success is leadership effectiveness. In addition, many researchers argue that leadership effectiveness can improve organizational performance. Therefore, in order to contribute to economic growth, it is crucial to understand and evaluate the leadership effectiveness. Some researches carried out studies to introduce the dimensions of leadership effectiveness, although there is a lack of research to prioritize these dimensions to effectively guide leaders on how to improve their effectiveness. The chapter aims to prioritize dimensions of leadership effectiveness in SMEs, specifically Malaysia digital service SMEs. The applied research method in this chapter is a quantitative method using analytical hierarchy process (AHP) technique. Furthermore, in this chapter, leadership effectiveness dimensions have been evaluated by practitioner and academician experts in the Malaysia SME context.

DOI: 10.4018/978-1-7998-5175-2.ch001

INTRODUCTION

Achieving business goals that sustain the high performance in organizations over time, have raised the challenges for leaders. According to Mumford, et al (2000), leadership becomes more vital when one has to develop and lead adaptive analysis to new or changing situations. Meanwhile, as leaders are responsible for the achievement of organizational goals to enhance organizational performance, leadership becomes a significant subject. Therefore, leaders are responsible to the stakeholders in their organizations for generating the best potential products and services over best operation of the available resources (Gul, et al. 2012a). According to Hashim, et al. (2012) leaders must focus on developing their effectiveness, to established them separately from their competitors. Effective leadership offers a strategic direction and inspires the motivation of employees (Madanchian, et al. 2017).

During the early of the twentieth century attention in leadership area increased (Madanchian, et al. 2015b). Leadership is considering as one of the greatest discussed and argued topics in the social sciences (Madanchian, et al. 2015b). As said by Bass and Stogdill (1990), after 40 years of researchers attempt to come out with the meaning of leadership, Bass (1985) recognized more than 3,500 definitions and concluded, 'There are almost as many definitions of leadership as those who have attempted to define the concept'.

According to Harms and Credé (2010), leadership is defined as "a process whereby an individual influences a group of individuals to achieve a common goal" (p. 3). To enhance organizational performance, leadership plays a crucial role, therefore, to make the best possible products and services through the best utilization of the available resources, leaders are responsible to the stakeholders of their organizations (Gul, et al. 2012b; Madanchian & Taherdoost, 2017b).

The main aim of any organization and Digital service SMEs as well is to sustain competitive advantage and considered to be effective between the demands of various stakeholders and the needs of the employees (Madanchian, et al. 2016). Based on the previous studies in related field, it has been demonstrated that an appropriate leadership style can influence the success and the economic growth of both the organizations and employees (Madanchian, et al. 2016). Besides, Madanchian, et al. (2016c) concluded that a good leader moves their followers to action and help them realize their potential to accomplish a better objective. According to Arslan and Staub (2013) with the aim of meet the needs of the highly competitive markets, organizations should increase their performance. As said by earlier researchers such as Peterson, et al. (2003) the role of leadership is critically important for achieving the performance of organizations.

On the other hand, it is considered that a digital service company's success is attributable to organizational performance, employee job satisfaction and employee affective commitment (Bass & Riggio, 2006; Drucker, 2007; Madanchian, et al. 2016).

Leadership is one of the vital factors for improving firm performance (Madanchian, et al. 2016). Leaders, as the key decision-makers, determine the acquisition, development, and deployment of organizational resources, the conversion of these resources into valuable products and services, and the delivery of value to organizational stakeholders (Madanchian, et al. 2016). Thus, they are strong sources of managerial and sustained competitive advantage (Avolio, et al. 1999; Madanchian, et al. 2016; Rowe, 2012; Rowe, 2001).

These days, SMEs play critical roles in the economic growth of a country. In this regards, research on SMEs in Malaysia has been increased and attracted researchers for further studies although it is still argued that studies in this field and context are still limited in terms of scope and fragmented in nature

(Arham, et al. 2013; Madanchian, et al., 2015c). To challenge and continue effective competitiveness in the worldwide economy, SMEs should have some essential changes such as having effective leadership as an important key element in a successful organization. While SMEs are to increase their cooperation to the country's economy as anticipated by government, their leaders should be able to improve their sense of direction, to identify the needs for innovation, to be prepared to create necessary changes within their organization and, most outstandingly, to improve organizational performance. Therefore, it is vital to understand the leadership effectiveness dimensions and particularly their priority in order to improve the organizational performance and sustain the business competitiveness. As there is a lack of research study in prioritization of leadership effectiveness dimensions in the literature, this book chapter aims to cover this era by prioritizing the dimensions of leadership effectiveness in Malaysia SMEs to provide a better understanding of the contributions of leader's effectiveness to the performance of digital service SMEs in Malaysia.

BACKGROUND OF THE PROBLEM

As stated by Hashim et al. (2012), leaders in the 21st century are faced with an increasingly challenge to lead their organizations effectively. Therefore, leaders must concentrate on developing their effectiveness and use it as a strategic direction to make them apart from their competitors (Madanchian & Taherdoost, 2017b). While examining the factors that lead to organizational success, researchers have argued that effective leadership is a key analyst of organizational success or failure (Madanchian et al., 2017). SMEs are always suffering by severe struggle from globally and inside their industries. There is sufficient evidence in the literature to suggest that the performance of SMEs is essentially related to the leadership of the leaders (Madanchian & Taherdoost, 2017b). As Avolio, et al. (2003) points out, the activities of the SMEs' leaders relate to leadership, the all-important, driving force of the organization. Leadership is needed to move an organization forward among a changing, competitive landscape by imagining, motivating, organizing, managing and leading employees to a higher level of performance (Guay, 2013).

According to Bass and Riggio (2006), leadership is made up of four main parts: charisma, inspiration, intellectual stimulation and individual consideration (Madanchian, et al. 2016). Amagoh (2009) and Chen (2013) pointed out that a successful leadership knowledge results from the key elements consist of changing attitudes, personnel development, and improved business and leadership skills.

Leadership is regarded as effective when it brings positive efficacy of performance, which relates to better organizational performance. Organizational performance, as a result of leadership effectiveness of the leaders, contributes to the firms' success or failure (Madanchian & Taherdoost, 2017b). In summary, the outcomes of leadership as a result of effective leadership influence the satisfaction, work effectiveness and efforts of the employees and leaders in their organizations (Madanchian & Taherdoost, 2017b).

Moreover, several researchers (Lacerda, 2015; Madanchian, et al.2015; Mihelic, et al. 2010; Ofori, 2009; Ogbonna & Harris, 2000; Ojokuku, et al. 2012) also have claimed that leadership has been receiving greater attention in the SMEs literature since it has been recognized that SMEs cannot successfully develop new small businesses without the presence of effective leadership (Madanchian & Taherdoost, 2019).

To drive the success of SMEs, good leadership has been recognized as the key elements. The literature (Arham et al., 2013; Razak, 2011), in SMEs shows that insufficient and weak leadership skills are main factors causes failure of SMEs. For that reason, SMEs to guide their firms through all situations either crisis times need to develop their leadership behavior. To avoid organization failure and have good organizational performance, the right leadership behavior is an important element. As Fiedler (2010) approved, due to the leaders contribution to the achievement or failure of an organization, effective leaders are significant.

On the other hand, as stated by Madanchian, et al. (2016a), leadership effectiveness has significant role for stakeholders and their organization to producing best services via efficient use of existing resources. When examining the factors that lead to organizational success, researchers have argued that effective leadership is a key predictor of organizational success or failure (Warren Bennis, 2007). The compelling question is, do leaders and effective leadership matter and positively impact organizational outcomes. Denison, et al. (1995) argued that effective leadership is important and does impact organizational outcomes. According to Madanchian, et al. (2016a), leadership effectiveness is the capability to influence the behavior of an individual or group in the direction of the achievement of a goal.

Small and Medium Enterprises (SMEs) play a significant role in a country's economy and social wellbeing (Madanchian & Taherdoost, 2017b). The literature highlights on the importance of effective leadership to organizations (Madanchian & Taherdoost, 2017b). On the other hand, the review of the literature indicates limited studies have attempted to empirically examine leadership effectiveness in the context of small and medium-sized enterprises (SMEs). In spite of the importance of leadership, a review of past studies suggests few studies have attempted to investigate leadership behavior adopted by leaders of SMEs (Madanchian & Taherdoost, 2017b). Small and Medium Enterprises (SMEs) play a significant role in a country's economy and social wellbeing (Madanchian & Taherdoost, 2017b). The literature highlights on the importance of leadership to organizations (Madanchian & Taherdoost, 2017b). On the other hand the review of the literature indicates limited studies have attempted to empirically examine leadership effectiveness in the context of digital service small and medium-sized enterprises (SMEs). Therefore, this book chapter focus on this gap by prioritizing the dimensions of leadership effectiveness.

LEADERSHIP EFFECTIVENESS

Leadership always plays a significant role in the growth and development of any organization. The field of leadership research is also very important for practitioners to understand the reasons for effective leadership (Madanchian & Taherdoost, 2017a). The overall process of leadership is similar to a black box that requires detailed investigation in order to reveal why leadership is important and how leaders can influence followers to achieve organizational goals (Chen, 2013; Madanchian, et al., 2015a).

Once examining the factors that guide to organisational success, researchers have discussed that effective leadership is a key predictor of organisational success or failure. It is claimed that effective leadership is important and does impact organisational outcomes. For decades, leadership researchers have worked and argued to define leadership and understand what components contribute to a leader being effective. To evaluate an effective leader examining the consequences of a leader's actions is the most common outcome measure. If a leader is able to influence his followers or organisation in such a way that positive outcomes are realised, this composes an effective leader. Some researchers have used a leader's ability to facilitate effective group processes, group cohesiveness, group cooperation, motivation and conflict resolution among group members, and quality and efficiency of decision makings an indicator of leader effectiveness.

According to Addison (1985), leadership effectiveness is defined as "the ability to influence the activities of an individual or group toward the achievement of a goal". When examining the factors that lead to organizational success, researchers have argued that effective leadership is a key predictor of organizational success or failure (Bennis & Nanus, 1985). Effective leadership can improve organizational outcomes including improved financial and group performance, employee citizenship, employee growth, and organizational commitment. According to the literature in the field of leadership in Malaysia (Arham, 2014b; Khairuddin, et al. 2012; Sam, et al. 2012), it is argued that studies in this field in comparison to Western countries is very little although some researches have been carried out by local and international academic researchers to address the significance of leadership role in organizational growth in Malaysia context (Madanchian, et al. 2016b).

For decades, leadership researchers have worked to define leadership and understand what components contribute to a leader being effective (Madanchian, et al. 2018). The puzzle is that the definition of a leader, as well as leader effectiveness, varies amongst researchers (Madanchian et al., 2018; Yukl, 2008). Furthermore, leadership effectiveness is the outcome when leaders are able to influence a group to perform their roles with positive organizational outcomes (Dhar & Mishra, 2001; Ha, et al. 2016; Madanchian & Taherdoost, 2019). According to Denison et al. (1995), effective leadership is significant and influence organizational outcomes. Therefore, effective leadership can has impact on organizational performance. To evaluate an effective leader examining the consequences of a leader's actions is the most common outcome measure (Bass, 1985; W. Bennis, 1995; Bennis, 2007; Dhar, 2016; Dhar & Mishra, 2001; Madanchian & Taherdoost, 2019). Leadership effectiveness consider as an outcome when the individuals in the positions of leadership are able to impact on a group to perform their roles with positive organizational outcomes (Madanchian et al., 2017).

In order to evaluate an effective leader, examining the outcomes of a leader's actions are the most common measure (Conger & Kanungo, 1998; Conger, 1998; Dhar, 2016; Dhar & Mishra, 2001; Madanchian et al., 2017). Effective leadership is recognized when the leader has ability to influence his/her followers or organizational unit in same way that obtains positive results (Madanchian et al., 2015). As said by (Dhar & Mishra, 2001), some researchers have used a leader's ability to make possible effective group processes, group cohesiveness, group collaboration, motivation and divergence declaration among group members, and quality and efficiency of decision making as an indicator of leader effectiveness (Madanchian et al., 2017).

In order to evaluate an effective leader, examining the outcomes of a leader's actions are the most common measure (Bass, 1986; Conger, 1998; Dhar & Mishra, 2001). If a leader has ability to influence his/her subordinates or organizational unit in the same way that obtain positive results, then an effective leadership is recognized. Measurement tools of leader effectiveness have been numerous and diverse. Many of the evaluations of leader effectiveness were developed based on the literature, the authors' review of the industry or profession, and the assessment of what made a leader effective in the specific industry or profession (Madanchian et al., 2017). Therefore, this book chapter, based on the service industries context applied Dhar and Mishra's (2001) measurement tool of leader effectiveness in service organizations. This assessment tool asks the leader's subordinate to evaluate the effectiveness of the leader based on the leader's ability to monitor, be accountable, motivate, inspire, influence, have a positive attitude, and to facilitate the performance of subordinates. Consequently, this study prioritizes these dimensions of leadership effectiveness in Malaysia' SMEs, specifically, digital service industry.

METHODOLOGY

This chapter employs quantitative approaches for data collection and analysis. Since the focus of this book chapter is to prioritize leadership effectiveness dimensions, the practitioner and academician experts in the field of leadership and SMEs in the digital service sector are the target population of the present research. To prioritize dimensions of leadership effectiveness, experts have been asked for the assessment tools of Dhar and Mishra for leaders in a service organization. As presented in Table 1, Dhar and Mishra assessment tool contains seven dimensions to assess leader effectiveness. Dimensions are:

1. Ability to monitor which indicates a leader monitors the performance of the subordinates and has an ability to analyze complex events;
2. To be accountable which indicates a leader's support and ability to explain responsibilities and assign work;
3. Ability to motivate which indicates a leader's ability to praise and give rewards to motivate subordinates;
4. Ability to inspire which indicates a leader's ability to inspire subordinates and encourage them also recognizes the importance of situational factors and understand the interpersonal behavior;
5. Ability to influence which indicates a leader's ability to influence subordinates with setting objectives and give rewards to a well-done task and promote group identity in an organization;
6. Have a positive attitude which indicates a leader's ability to have positive feedback and attitude to subordinates;
7. Ability to facilitate which indicates a leader's ability to provides clear role perception, manages time, inspires task commitments and able to negotiate.

Table 1. Leadership effectiveness dimensions

Dimensions of Leadership Effectiveness	
1	Ability to Monitor
2	To be Accountable
3	Ability to Motivate
4	Ability to Inspire
5	Ability to Influence
6	Positive Attitude
7	Ability to Facilitate

Source: Dhar and Mishra's (2001)

For prioritization of the leadership effectiveness dimensions, Analytic Hierarchy Process (AHP) technique is applied. AHP has been introduced by Saaty (1980) as a Multi Criteria Decision Making (MCDM) approach. AHP, as a decision support tool is a hierarchical structure base which includes multi-level hierarchical structure of objectives, criteria, sub-criteria, and alternatives. In order to apply the AHP, first, the hierarchy of the problem should be shaped. After that, a nominal value needs to be given to each level of the hierarchy and then a matrix of pairwise comparison judgment should be generated.

According to Taherdoost (2017), pairwise comparison is defined as "a system of evaluation to demonstrate which element is more significant". Likewise, pairwise comparison assesses the connection between two components that are identified through numerical representations. The scale ranges of AHP are 1 to 9 in which one indicates that two elements are equal or same in terms of their significance. And nine designates that one component is extremely more important than another one. Table two presents the pairwise scale and the significance value attributed to each number.

Table 2. AHP scores for the importance of variable

Importance Scale	Definition of the Importance Scale
1	*Equally important / preferred*
2	*Equally or moderately important / preferred*
3	*Moderately important / preferred*
4	*Moderately to strongly important / preferred*
5	*Strongly important / preferred*
6	*Strongly to very strongly important / preferred*
7	*Very strongly important / preferred*
8	*Very strongly to extremely important / preferred*
9	*Extremely important / preferred*

Source: Taherdoost (2017)

After data collection via structured interviews, for AHP data analysis, first, Matrix "A" which is a pairwise comparison matrix is extracted from the collected data. The principal right eigenvector of the Matrix "A" is computed as "w". After that, Formula (1) is applied to convert the raw data into meaningful absolute values and normalized weight w= $(w_1, w_2, w_3 \ldots w_n)$:

$$Aw = \lambda_{max} W, \lambda_{max}{}^{3} n \tag{1}$$

$$\lambda \max = \frac{\sum ajwj - n}{w1}$$

$A = \{a_{ij}\}$ with $a_{ij} = 1/a_{ij}$

A: Pairwise comparison
W: Normalized weight vector
λ_{max}: Maximum eigenvalue of Matrix "A"
a_{ij}: Numerical comparison between the values I and j

In the final step and in order to validate the obtained results, the Consistency Ration (CR) should be measured, in which CR lower than 0.10 veriðes that the results of the comparison are acceptable. CR is equal to Consistency Index (CI) divide to Random Consistency Index (RI); CR = CI/RI.

Consistency index (CI) is calculated via Formula (2):

$$CI = \frac{\lambda \max - n}{n - 1} \tag{2}$$

Furthermore, the value of RI is associated to the dimension of the matrix and is extracted from Table 3.

Table 3. The value of random consistency index

Dimension	1	2	3	4	5	6	7	8	9	10
RI	0	0	0.5799	0.8921	1.1159	1.2358	1.3322	1.3952	1.4537	1.4882

Source: Golden and Wang (1990)

RESULTS AND DISCUSSION

Creating a Hierarchal Structure

The prioritization of the dimensions of leadership effectiveness which affect SMEs performance is done through their measured weight. As mentioned earlier, the ðrst step is to create a hierarchy of the dimensions to evaluating and prioritizing. As shown in Figure 1, leadership effectiveness is categorized as the main criterion and its seven dimensions as sub-criterion.

Figure 1. Hierarchical model of leadership effectiveness

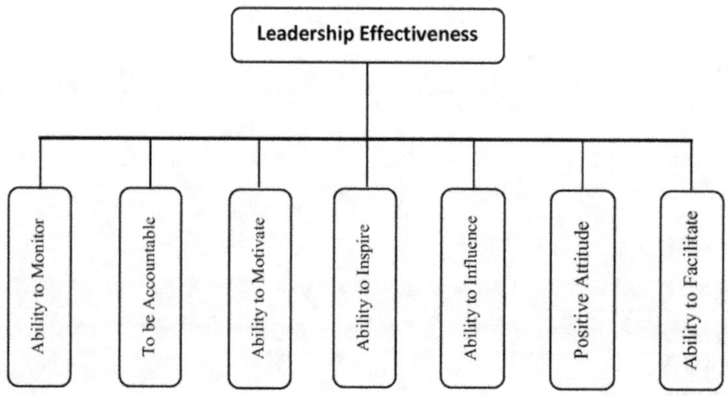

Creating Pairwise Comparison Matrix and Deriving Weights

The next step after creation of structure is to calculate the weight of each item. For this purpose, pairwise comparison strategy is applied. Hence, pairwise comparison matrix is made based on the importance attributed to each dimension by experts. In this regard, the questionnaire was distributed among 10 experts (practitioner and academician) in the field of leadership and SMEs. Table 4 shows the responses of the experts.

All these10 matrixes were transferred to a matrix using the calculation of geometric mean. Results are presented in Table 5. The geometric mean of a data set ($a_1, a_2,...,a_n$) is given by (Taherdoost, 2017b) as shown below:

$$\left(\prod_{i=1}^{n} a_i\right)^{1/n} = \sqrt[n]{a_1 a_2 \ldots a_n} \tag{3}$$

If the question $a_{ik} \times a_{kj} = a_{ij}$ for one of the k, j, i cannot be created, then matrix is inconsistence (Taherdoost, 2017a). Therefore:

$a_{12}= 1.99$, $a_{23}= 1.84 \rightarrow a_{13} \neq a_{12} \times a_{23} = 1.99 \times 1.84= 3.66$

thus, we have to use the eigenvector method to calculate the weight of each factor. The formula is as below:

$$e^T = (1,1,.....,1) \tag{4}$$

$$w = \lim_{k\to\infty} \frac{A^k \cdot e}{e^T \cdot A^k \cdot e}$$

In cases that the matrix is inconsistence, the calculation round should be repeated until the convergence among the results are achieved. Here, it is repeated five times. Results are shown in Tables 6-9.

Accordingly, $A^k \times e$ is calculated using Formula (5):

$$A^k . e = \begin{bmatrix} a_{11} & \cdots & a_{1n} \\ \vdots & \ddots & \vdots \\ a_{n1} & \cdots & a_{nn} \end{bmatrix} \times \begin{bmatrix} 1 \\ 1 \\ \vdots \\ 1 \end{bmatrix} = \begin{bmatrix} \sum_{j=1}^{n} a_{1j} \\ \sum_{j=1}^{n} a_{1j} \\ \vdots \\ \sum_{j=1}^{n} a_{nj} \end{bmatrix} \tag{5}$$

Table 4. Responses of experts to pairwise comparison

	Leadership Effectiveness Dimensions	Ability to Monitor	To be Accountable	Ability to Motivate	Ability to Inspire	Ability to Influence	Positive Attitude	Ability to Facilitate
Expert 1	Ability to Monitor	1	3	4	3	5	7	0.5
	To be Accountable	0.33	1	3	2	4	5	0.5
	Ability to Motivate	0.25	0.33	1	2	2	3	0.33
	Ability to Inspire	0.33	0.5	0.5	1	2	3	0.5
	Ability to Influence	0.2	0.25	0.5	0.5	1	2	0.5
	Positive Attitude	0.14	0.2	0.33	0.33	0.5	1	0.25
	Ability to Facilitate	2	2	3	2	2	4	1
Expert 2	Ability to Monitor	1	4	5	2	4	6	0.25
	To be Accountable	0.25	1	2	2	3	3	0.5
	Ability to Motivate	0.2	0.5	1	3	2	2	0.5
	Ability to Inspire	0.5	0.5	0.33	1	1	3	0.33
	Ability to Influence	0.25	0.33	0.5	1	1	1	0.33
	Positive Attitude	0.16	0.33	0.5	0.33	1	1	0.5
	Ability to Facilitate	4	2	2	3	3	2	1
Expert 3	Ability to Monitor	1	5	5	3	3	3	0.33
	To be Accountable	0.2	1	2	3	3	4	0.33
	Ability to Motivate	0.2	0.5	1	3	2	3	0.5
	Ability to Inspire	0.33	0.33	0.33	1	0.5	4	0.33
	Ability to Influence	0.33	0.33	0.5	2	1	0.5	0.33
	Positive Attitude	0.33	0.25	0.33	0.25	2	1	0.25
	Ability to Facilitate	3	3	2	3	3	4	1
Expert 4	Ability to Monitor	1	4	3	1	2	3	0.5
	To be Accountable	0.25	1	1	0.5	0.5	1	0.5
	Ability to Motivate	0.33	1	1	1	1	1	0.5
	Ability to Inspire	1	2	1	1	0.5	5	1
	Ability to Influence	0.5	2	1	2	1	2	1
	Positive Attitude	0.33	1	1	0.2	0.5	1	2
	Ability to Facilitate	2	2	2	1	1	0.5	1
Expert 5	Ability to Monitor	1	5	2	3	5	7	0.33
	To be Accountable	0.2	1	3	2	4	5	0.5
	Ability to Motivate	0.5	0.33	1	2	2	3	0.33
	Ability to Inspire	0.33	0.5	0.5	1	2	3	0.5
	Ability to Influence	0.2	0.25	0.5	0.5	1	2	0.5
	Positive Attitude	0.14	0.2	0.33	0.33	0.5	1	0.25
	Ability to Facilitate	3	2	3	2	2	4	1

continues on following page

Table 4. Continued

	Leadership Effectiveness Dimensions	Ability to Monitor	To be Accountable	Ability to Motivate	Ability to Inspire	Ability to Influence	Positive Attitude	Ability to Facilitate
Expert 6	Ability to Monitor	1	5	3	3	3	3	0.5
	To be Accountable	0.2	1	2	3	3	4	0.33
	Ability to Motivate	0.33	0.5	1	2	2	3	0.5
	Ability to Inspire	0.33	0.33	0.5	1	0.5	4	0.33
	Ability to Influence	0.33	0.33	0.5	2	1	0.5	0.33
	Positive Attitude	0.33	0.25	0.33	0.25	2	1	0.25
	Ability to Facilitate	2	3	2	3	3	4	1
Expert 7	Ability to Monitor	1	2	3	1	2	3	1
	To be Accountable	0.5	1	1	0.5	0.5	1	0.5
	Ability to Motivate	0.33	1	1	1	1	1	0.5
	Ability to Inspire	1	2	1	1	0.5	5	1
	Ability to Influence	0.5	2	1	2	1	2	1
	Positive Attitude	0.33	1	1	0.2	0.5	1	2
	Ability to Facilitate	1	2	2	1	1	0.5	1
Expert 8	Ability to Monitor	1	4	4	3	5	7	1
	To be Accountable	0.25	1	3	2	4	5	0.5
	Ability to Motivate	0.25	0.33	1	2	2	3	0.33
	Ability to Inspire	0.33	0.5	0.5	1	2	3	0.5
	Ability to Influence	0.2	0.25	0.5	0.5	1	2	0.5
	Positive Attitude	0.14	0.2	0.33	0.33	0.5	1	0.25
	Ability to Facilitate	1	2	3	2	2	4	1
Expert 9	Ability to Monitor	1	5	4	2	4	6	0.25
	To be Accountable	0.2	1	2	2	3	3	0.5
	Ability to Motivate	0.25	0.5	1	3	2	2	0.5
	Ability to Inspire	0.5	0.5	0.33	1	1	3	0.33
	Ability to Influence	0.25	0.33	0.5	1	1	1	0.33
	Positive Attitude	0.16	0.33	0.5	0.33	1	1	0.5
	Ability to Facilitate	4	2	2	3	3	2	1
Expert 10	Ability to Monitor	1	4	2	3	3	3	0.33
	To be Accountable	0.25	1	2	3	3	4	0.33
	Ability to Motivate	0.5	0.5	1	3	2	3	0.5
	Ability to Inspire	0.33	0.33	0.33	1	0.5	4	0.33
	Ability to Influence	0.33	0.33	0.5	2	1	0.5	0.33
	Positive Attitude	0.33	0.25	0.33	0.25	2	1	0.25
	Ability to Facilitate	3	3	2	3	3	4	1

Table 5. Result of pairwise comparison

Leadership Effectiveness' Dimensions	Ability to Monitor	To be Accountable	Ability to Motivate	Ability to Inspire	Ability to Influence	Positive Attitude	Ability to Facilitate
Ability to Monitor	1.000	3.965	3.340	2.221	3.415	4.443	0.441
To be Accountable	0.252	1.000	1.966	1.712	2.285	3.060	0.441
Ability to Motivate	0.298	0.507	1.000	2.048	1.741	2.221	0.441
Ability to Inspire	0.448	0.582	0.486	1.000	0.871	3.622	0.467
Ability to Influence	0.292	0.435	0.574	1.149	1.000	1.149	0.467
Positive Attitude	0.221	0.326	0.448	0.275	0.871	1.000	0.435
Ability to Facilitate	2.259	2.259	2.259	2.132	2.132	2.297	1.000

Table 6. A calculation round

<table>
<tr><td rowspan="7">D.D</td><td rowspan="7">=</td><td>1.000</td><td>3.965</td><td>3.340</td><td>2.221</td><td>3.415</td><td>4.443</td><td>0.441</td><td rowspan="7">*</td><td>1.000</td><td>3.965</td><td>3.340</td><td>2.221</td><td>3.415</td><td>4.443</td><td>0.441</td><td rowspan="7">=</td><td>6.965</td><td>14.850</td><td>20.504</td><td>24.153</td><td>28.450</td><td>41.418</td><td>8.671</td></tr>
<tr><td>0.252</td><td>1.000</td><td>1.966</td><td>1.712</td><td>2.285</td><td>3.060</td><td>0.441</td><td>0.252</td><td>1.000</td><td>1.966</td><td>1.712</td><td>2.285</td><td>3.060</td><td>0.441</td><td>4.197</td><td>6.983</td><td>9.286</td><td>12.417</td><td>13.950</td><td>21.446</td><td>5.059</td></tr>
<tr><td>0.298</td><td>0.507</td><td>1.000</td><td>2.048</td><td>1.741</td><td>2.221</td><td>0.441</td><td>0.298</td><td>0.507</td><td>1.000</td><td>2.048</td><td>1.741</td><td>2.221</td><td>0.441</td><td>3.637</td><td>5.869</td><td>6.981</td><td>9.177</td><td>10.318</td><td>17.750</td><td>3.973</td></tr>
<tr><td>0.448</td><td>0.582</td><td>0.486</td><td>1.000</td><td>0.871</td><td>3.622</td><td>0.467</td><td>0.448</td><td>0.582</td><td>0.486</td><td>1.000</td><td>0.871</td><td>3.622</td><td>0.467</td><td>3.295</td><td>5.800</td><td>6.788</td><td>6.977</td><td>9.596</td><td>14.168</td><td>3.585</td></tr>
<tr><td>0.292</td><td>0.435</td><td>0.574</td><td>1.149</td><td>1.000</td><td>1.149</td><td>0.467</td><td>0.292</td><td>0.435</td><td>0.574</td><td>1.149</td><td>1.000</td><td>1.149</td><td>0.467</td><td>2.687</td><td>4.417</td><td>5.107</td><td>6.177</td><td>6.987</td><td>11.435</td><td>2.544</td></tr>
<tr><td>0.221</td><td>0.326</td><td>0.448</td><td>0.275</td><td>0.871</td><td>1.000</td><td>0.435</td><td>0.221</td><td>0.326</td><td>0.448</td><td>0.275</td><td>0.871</td><td>1.000</td><td>0.435</td><td>2.018</td><td>3.277</td><td>3.891</td><td>4.443</td><td>5.187</td><td>6.968</td><td>1.844</td></tr>
<tr><td>2.259</td><td>2.259</td><td>2.259</td><td>2.132</td><td>2.132</td><td>2.297</td><td>1.000</td><td>2.259</td><td>2.259</td><td>2.259</td><td>2.132</td><td>2.132</td><td>2.297</td><td>1.000</td><td>7.845</td><td>17.538</td><td>19.793</td><td>20.853</td><td>24.930</td><td>36.732</td><td>6.981</td></tr>
</table>

Hence, $A^k . e = \begin{bmatrix} 59736.79 \\ 30907.54 \\ 24493.55 \\ 21787 \\ 16937.37 \\ 12211.27 \\ 56780.25 \end{bmatrix}$

After that $e^T \times A^k \times e$ is calculated using Formula (6):

Table 7. A calculation round

D.D.D						
=						
2.259	0.221	0.292	0.448	0.298	0.252	1.000
2.259	0.326	0.435	0.582	0.507	1.000	3.965
2.259	0.448	0.574	0.486	1.000	1.966	3.340
2.132	0.275	1.149	1.000	2.048	1.712	2.221
2.132	0.871	1.000	0.871	1.741	2.285	3.415
2.297	1.000	1.149	3.622	2.221	3.060	4.443
1.000	0.435	0.467	0.467	0.441	0.441	0.441
*						
7.845	2.018	2.687	3.295	3.637	4.197	6.965
17.538	3.277	4.417	5.800	5.869	6.983	14.850
19.793	3.891	5.107	6.788	6.981	9.286	20.504
20.853	4.443	6.177	6.977	9.177	12.417	24.153
24.930	5.187	6.987	9.596	10.318	13.950	28.450
36.732	6.968	11.435	14.168	17.750	21.446	41.418
6.981	1.844	2.544	3.585	3.973	5.059	8.671
=						
58.660	13.210	18.398	23.933	27.211	34.519	64.671
109.423	24.532	33.773	43.266	48.428	60.057	112.407
137.151	29.496	40.647	52.544	57.977	72.112	139.179
162.437	34.303	46.752	60.683	66.794	85.408	169.572
191.284	40.206	55.905	71.978	80.221	100.678	197.449
289.418	60.886	84.474	106.165	121.594	154.706	303.427
64.273	13.424	19.053	24.496	28.073	35.730	69.923

Table 8. A calculation round

D.D.D.D						
=						
2.259	0.221	0.292	0.448	0.298	0.252	1.000
2.259	0.326	0.435	0.582	0.507	1.000	3.965
2.259	0.448	0.574	0.486	1.000	1.966	3.340
2.132	0.275	1.149	1.000	2.048	1.712	2.221
2.132	0.871	1.000	0.871	1.741	2.285	3.415
2.297	1.000	1.149	3.622	2.221	3.060	4.443
1.000	0.435	0.467	0.467	0.441	0.441	0.441
*						
7.845	2.018	2.687	3.295	3.637	4.197	6.965
17.538	3.277	4.417	5.800	5.869	6.983	14.850
19.793	3.891	5.107	6.788	6.981	9.286	20.504
20.853	4.443	6.177	6.977	9.177	12.417	24.153
24.930	5.187	6.987	9.596	10.318	13.950	28.450
36.732	6.968	11.435	14.168	17.750	21.446	41.418
6.981	1.844	2.544	3.585	3.973	5.059	8.671
=						
464.7789	99.04886	137.9702	177.4588	200.2852	253.6521	492.9976
828.9869	179.5248	249.4822	321.4317	362.6036	458.2188	881.0069
1011.83	219.2072	304.2018	391.2632	440.4861	554.8191	1065.851
1197.13	257.5637	356.7016	459.5643	514.2492	646.8666	1249.856
1410.925	304.2382	421.5673	541.5723	608.6463	766.6125	1478.431
2145.243	461.4303	637.171	820.3551	918.0312	1159.107	2245.509
490.0268	104.3712	144.6927	185.4623	208.5759	263.4753	512.8474

Table 9. A calculation round

D.D.D.D.D						
=						
2.259	0.221	0.292	0.448	0.298	0.252	1.000
2.259	0.326	0.435	0.582	0.507	1.000	3.965
2.259	0.448	0.574	0.486	1.000	1.966	3.340
2.132	0.275	1.149	1.000	2.048	1.712	2.221
2.132	0.871	1.000	0.871	1.741	2.285	3.415
2.297	1.000	1.149	3.622	2.221	3.060	4.443
1.000	0.435	0.467	0.467	0.441	0.441	0.441
*						
464.7789	99.04886	137.9702	177.4588	200.2852	253.6521	492.9976
828.9869	179.5248	249.4822	321.4317	362.6036	458.2188	881.0069
1011.83	219.2072	304.2018	391.2632	440.4861	554.8191	1065.851
1197.13	257.5637	356.7016	459.5643	514.2492	646.8666	1249.856
1410.925	304.2382	421.5673	541.5723	608.6463	766.6125	1478.431
2145.243	461.4303	637.171	820.3551	918.0312	1159.107	2245.509
490.0268	104.3712	144.6927	185.4623	208.5759	263.4753	512.8474
=						
3503.792	751.4203	1041.834	1339.037	1504.757	1899.036	3678.228
6302.757	1352.08	1876.66	2413.303	2715.049	3428.863	6638.394
7653.969	1645.34	2283.238	2936.707	3304.179	4171.912	8065.372
8975.111	1932.476	2680.868	3447.961	3877.771	4891.43	9443.913
10609.3	2282.972	3166.381	4073.232	4579.992	5780.205	11167.98
16076.91	3459.898	4797.91	6174.166	6936.795	8749.436	16902.66
3658.418	787.0799	1090.477	1402.591	1575.01	1986.658	3840.244

$$e^T . A^k . e = e^T . (A^k . e) = [1\ 1\ \ldots\ 1\ ] \times \begin{bmatrix} \sum_{j=1}^{n} a_{1j} \\ \sum_{j=1}^{n} a_{1j} \\ \vdots \\ \sum_{j=1}^{n} a_{nj} \end{bmatrix} = \sum_{i=1}^{n} \sum_{j=1}^{n} a_{ij} \tag{6}$$

Thus, $e^T \times A^k \times e = 222853.8$.

Now, the maximum eigenvalue and the eigenvector of the matrix can be derived, which is $\lambda_{max} = 7.315$ and then the consistency test is implemented as CR = CI/RI = 0.039. Because the result is smaller than 0.1, the weights of each variable can be derived by normalizing the eigenvector. The ðnal weights are presented in Table 10.

As illustrated in Table 5, the prioritization of the leadership effectiveness dimensions are as follow; the positive attitude (w=0.263), ability to facilitated (w=0.254), positive influence (w=0.138), ability to motivate (w=0.109), ability to inspire (w=0.097), to be accountable (w=0.076) and ability to monitor (w=0.054).

The results showed that most of the experts are agreed respectively; the positive attitude, ability to facilitated, positive influence, ability to motivate, ability to inspire, to be accountable and ability to monitor dimensions has significant affect in an organization. For example, the leader's positive attitude has more significant affect and the leader's ability to monitor has less effect on organization's performance.

Table 10. Leadership effectiveness dimension' weight

Leadership Effectiveness' Dimensions	Weight
Ability to Monitor	0.054795
To be Accountable	0.076002
Ability to Motivate	0.109909
Ability to Inspire	0.097764
Ability to Influence	0.13869
Positive Attitude	0.268054
Ability to Facilitate	0.254787

SOLUTIONS AND RECOMMENDATIONS

Debate between experts and a review of organization and leadership literature reveals a vital need to address leadership development issues in small and medium sized enterprises (SMEs). At the present time, the purpose of any organizations is to endure and maintain its entity via improving their performance. Consequently, the role of leaders in ensuring excellent organizational performance cannot be over emphasized. Small and Medium Enterprises (SMEs) performance, as a topic, is generating numerous discussion between researchers, practitioner, academics and politicians. Leaders are important to all types of organizations and play different roles as well as perform various important functions in organization (Madanchian & Taherdoost, 2017b). Nowadays, the purpose of any organizations is to survive and maintain its entity by improving performance (Madanchian & Taherdoost, 2017b).

Organizations must always increase their performance to be highly competitive in markets (Arslan & Staub, 2013). Small and Medium Enterprises (SMEs) performance, as a topic, is generating numerous discussion between researchers, practitioner, academics and politicians (Arham, 2014a). Previous and to date literature suggest that to achieve good performance of organization, leadership is critically important factor (Boal & Hooijberg, 2001; Choudhary, et al. 2013; Danisman, et al. 2015; Peterson et al., 2003; Uchenwamgbe, 2013).

Leadership effectiveness can be outlined as the leader's ability to effectively influence followers and other organizational stakeholders to accomplish the goals of the organization. What constitutes influencing followers to accomplish the goals of the organization varies significantly from company to company, industry to industry, country to country, and so forth. In each scenario where leader effectiveness is being assessed it is necessary to examine the leader outcomes that represent a leader effectively leading subordinates to accomplish the goals of the particular organization, industry, and context.

The result of the study showed that the experts have identified the dimensions to be used as AHP criteria. The selected criteria respectively are the positive attitude, ability to facilitated, positive influence, ability to motivate, ability to inspire, to be accountable and ability to monitor. Experts have determined the importance of the AHP criteria and also the relationships between the criteria and alternatives.

Therefore, it is concluded that; (1) A leader should always be able to show direction to the followers, especially in times of distress; (2) A leader must possess the ability to improve objectives, inspire task commitment among followers and help followers in developing themselves; (3) A leader should also possess the ability to infuse energy and enthusiasm among followers towards task accomplishment; (4) A leader must exercise his/her authority to praise and reward people in order to motivate them; (5) A leader must be able to draw high degree of commitment and involvement from his/her followers; (6) A leader should be able to clearly describe the roles of followers and suitably reward them on their success in carrying out assigned activities; (7) A leader should have the ability to effectively monitor their subordinates' performance not only minimizes the possibilities of failure but also enhances the efficiency in performance.

FUTURE RESEARCH DIRECTIONS

The response to the challenges faced today by SMEs is only possible through adoption of leadership roles by the various people in charge. In the current business environment, besides factors such as finance, strategy and innovation, it becomes important to find out about SMEs' leaders, due to the increasing need to understand the road to success and the process of creating sustainable competitive advantages (Madanchian & Taherdoost, 2017b). In other words, SMEs must manage to find and adopt strategies that allow them to overcome their challenges.

The improvement of organizational performance requires the development of effective leadership (Avolio & Gardner, 2005; Avolio et al., 2003; Rowe, 2012; Rowe, 2001). Besides, Denison et al. (1995) argued that effective leadership is important and does impact on organization's outcomes. As said by Copeland (2013), effective leadership can result in enhanced organizational outcomes, particularly improved organizational profitability and growth. Therefore, there is a need to evaluate the dimensions of organizational performance and assess the effect of leadership effectiveness dimensions on organizational performance dimensions and find out how it can help to enhance the organizational goals.

CONCLUSION

This chapter presents a new approach to prioritize leadership effectiveness dimensions via an effective and reliable technique. The technique consists of the determining the dimension by using experts' opinion during decision making process and applying AHP to prioritize which dimension of the leadership effectiveness has more significant effect on organizational performance including growth and profitability.

The results showed that most of the experts are agreed respectively; the positive attitude, ability to facilitated, positive influence, ability to motivate, ability to inspire, to be accountable and ability to monitor dimensions has significant affect in an organization. For example, the leader's positive attitude has more significant affect and the leader's ability to monitor has less effect on organization's performance.

ACKNOWLEDGMENT

This research has been prepared and supported by Research Club, Research & Development Department of Ahoora Group | Management Consultation Group, Hamta Academy at Hamta Group | Hamta Business Solution Sdn Bhd and Tablokar Co | Switchgear Manufacturer.

REFERENCES

Addison, L. B. (1984). *Investigation of the leadership abilities of intellectually gifted students* (Unpublished dissertation). University of South Florida.

Amagoh, F. (2009). Leadership development and leadership effectiveness. *management. Decision (Washington, D.C.), 47*(6), 989–999.

Arham, A. F. (2014a). Leadership and Performance: The Case of Malaysian SMEs in the Services Sector. *International Journal of Asian Social Science, 4*(3), 343–355.

Arham, A. F. (2014b). *The Relationship between Leadership Behaviour, Entrepreneurial Orientation and Organisational Performance in Malaysian Small and Medium Enterprises (PhD)*. Royal Melbourne Institute of Technology University.

Arham, A. F., Boucher, C., & Muenjohn, N. (2013). Leadership and entrepreneurial success: A study of SMEs in Malaysia. *WORLD (Oakland, Calif.), 3*(5), 117–130.

Arslan, A., & Staub, S. (2013). Theory X and Theory Y Type Leadership Behavior and its Impact on Organizational Performance: Small Business Owners in the Şishane Lighting and Chandelier District. *Procedia: Social and Behavioral Sciences, 75*, 102–111. doi:10.1016/j.sbspro.2013.04.012

Avolio, B. J., Bass, B. M., & Jung, D. I. (1999). Re-examining the components of transformational and transactional leadership using the Multifactor Leadership. *Journal of Occupational and Organizational Psychology, 72*(4), 441–462. doi:10.1348/096317999166789

Avolio, B. J., & Gardner, W. L. (2005). Authentic leadership development: Getting to the root of positive forms of leadership. *The Leadership Quarterly, 16*(3), 315–338. doi:10.1016/j.leaqua.2005.03.001

Avolio, B. J., Sosik, J. J., Jung, D. I., & Berson, Y. (2003). *Leadership models, methods, and applications*. Handbook of psychology. doi:10.1002/0471264385.wei1212

Bass, B. M. (1985). *Leadership and performance beyond expectations*. Collier Macmillan.

Bass, B. M. (1985). Leadership: Good, better, best. *Organizational Dynamics, 13*(3), 26–40. doi:10.1016/0090-2616(85)90028-2

Bass, B. M. (1986). Leadership and performance beyond expectations (Vol. 25). New York: The Free Press.

Bass, B. M., & Riggio, R. E. (2006). *Transformational leadership*. Psychology Press. doi:10.4324/9781410617095

Bass, B. M., & Stogdill, R. M. (1990). *Bass & Stogdill's handbook of leadership: Theory, research, and managerial applications*. Simon and Schuster.

Bennis, W. (1995). *Nanus (1985) Leaders: The Strategies for Taking Charge*. New York: Harper and Row.

Bennis, W. (2007). The challenges of leadership in the modern world: Introduction to the special issue. *The American Psychologist, 62*(1), 2–5. doi:10.1037/0003-066X.62.1.2 PMID:17209674

Bennis, W., & Nanus, B. (1985). Leadership: The strategies for taking charge. New York.

Boal, K. B., & Hooijberg, R. (2001). Strategic leadership research: Moving on. *The Leadership Quarterly*, *11*(4), 515–549. doi:10.1016/S1048-9843(00)00057-6

Chen, Y. (2013). *Relationships Among Emotional Intelligence, Cultural Intelligence, Job Performance, and Leader Effectiveness: A Study of County Extension Directors in Ohio (Doctor of Philosophy)*. The Ohio State University.

Choudhary, A. I., Akhtar, S. A., & Zaheer, A. (2013). Impact of transformational and servant leadership on organizational performance: A comparative analysis. *Journal of Business Ethics*, *116*(2), 433–440. doi:10.100710551-012-1470-8

Conger, J., & Kanungo, R. (1998). *Charismatic leadership in organizations*. Sage Publications.

Conger, J. A. (1998). The dark side of leadership. *Leading organizations: Perspectives for a new era*, 250-260.

Copeland, M. K. (2013). *The Importance of Ethical Leadership in the Accounting Industry (Doctor of Philosophy in Organizational Leadership)*. Regent University.

Danisman, S., Tosuntas, S. B., & Karadag, E. (2015). The Effect of Leadership on Organizational Performance. *Leadership and Organizational Outcomes*, 143-168.

Denison, D. R., Hooijberg, R., & Quinn, R. E. (1995). Paradox and performance: Toward a theory of behavioral complexity in managerial leadership. *Organization Science*, *6*(5), 524–540. doi:10.1287/orsc.6.5.524

Dhar, R. L. (2016). Ethical leadership and its impact on service innovative behavior: The role of LMX and job autonomy. *Tourism Management*, *57*, 139–148. doi:10.1016/j.tourman.2016.05.011

Dhar, U., & Mishra, P. (2001). Leadership effectiveness: A study of constituent factors. *Journal of Management Research*, *1*(4), 254.

Drucker, P. F. (2007). *Management challenges for the 21st century*. Routledge.

Fiedler, S. (2010). Managing resistance in an organizational transformation: A case study from a mobile operator company. *International Journal of Project Management*, *28*, 370-383.

Guay, R. P. (2013). The relationship between leader fit and transformational leadership. *Journal of Managerial Psychology*, *28*(1), 55–73. doi:10.1108/02683941311298869

Gul, S., Ahmad, B., Rehman, S. U., Shabir, N., & Razzaq, N. (2012a). *Leadership styles, turnover intentions and the mediating role of organizational commitment*. Paper presented at the Information and Knowledge Management.

Gul, S., Ahmad, B., Rehman, S. U., Shabir, N., & Razzaq, N. (2012b). *Leadership styles, turnover intentions and the mediating role of organizational commitment*. Paper presented at the Information and Knowledge Management.

Ha, S.-T., Lo, M.-C., & Wang, Y.-C. (2016). Relationship between knowledge management and organizational performance: A test on SMEs in Malaysia. *Procedia: Social and Behavioral Sciences*, *224*, 184–189. doi:10.1016/j.sbspro.2016.05.438

Harms, P. D., & Credé, M. (2010). Emotional intelligence and transformational and transactional leadership: A meta-analysis. *Journal of Leadership & Organizational Studies*, *17*(1), 5–17. doi:10.1177/1548051809350894

Hashim, M. K., Ahmad, S. a., & Zakaria, M. (2012). *A Study on Leadership Styles in SMEs*. Academic Press.

Khairuddin, H. M., Sa'ari, A., & Zakaria, M. (2012). A Study on Leadership Styles in SMEs. In *Proceeding: International Conference on Islamic Leadership-2 (ICIL), Nilai, Negeri Sembilan*. Penerbit Universiti Sains Islam Malaysia

Lacerda, T. M. R. D. O. C. d. (2015). *Understanding Leadership Effectiveness in Organizational Settings: An Integrative Approach (PhD)*. Universidade De Lisboa.

Madanchian, M., Hussein, N., & Noordin, F. (2016). *Effects of Leadership on Organizational Performance*. Paper presented at the 12th International Conference on Educational Technologies (EDUTE '16), Barcelona, Spain.

Madanchian, M., Hussein, N., Noordin, F., & Taherdoost, H. (2015). The role of SMEs in economic development: Case study of Malaysia. *International Journal of Academic Research in Management*, *4*(3), 77–84.

Madanchian, M., Hussein, N., Noordin, F., & Taherdoost, H. (2015a). *Effects of Leadership on Organizational Performance*. Academic Press.

Madanchian, M., Hussein, N., Noordin, F., & Taherdoost, H. (2015b). *Leadership Theories; an Overview of Early Stages*. Paper presented at the 4th International Conference on Management, Marketing, Tourism, Retail, Finance and Computer Applications, Venice, Italy.

Madanchian, M., Hussein, N., Noordin, F., & Taherdoost, H. (2015c). The role of SMEs in economic development: Case study of Malaysia. *International Journal of Academic Research in Management*, *4*(3), 77–84.

Madanchian, M., Hussein, N., Noordin, F., & Taherdoost, H. (2016a). The Relationship between Ethical Leadership, Leadership Effectiveness and Organizational Performance: A Review of Literature in SMEs Context. *European Business & Management*, *2*(2), 17–21. doi:10.11648/j.ebm.20160202.11

Madanchian, M., Hussein, N., Noordin, F., & Taherdoost, H. (2016b). *The Relationship between Ethical Leadership, Leadership Effectiveness and Organizational Performance: A Review of Literature in SMEs Context*. Academic Press.

Madanchian, M., Hussein, N., Noordin, F., & Taherdoost, H. (2016c). *Review of Organizational Leadership Theories*. Paper presented at the 10th International Conference on Business Administration (ICBA '16), Barcelona, Spain.

Madanchian, M., Hussein, N., Noordin, F., & Taherdoost, H. (2017). Leadership Effectiveness Measurement and Its Effect on Organization Outcomes. *Procedia Engineering*, *181*, 1043–1048. doi:10.1016/j.proeng.2017.02.505

Madanchian, M., Hussein, N., Noordin, F., & Taherdoost, H. (2018). The Impact of Ethical Leadership on Leadership Effectiveness among SMES in Malaysia. *Procedia Manufacturing Journal, 22*, 968–974. doi:10.1016/j.promfg.2018.03.138

Madanchian, M., & Taherdoost, H. (2017a). Role of leadership in small and medium enterprises (SMEs). *Journal of Economics and Management Systems, 2*, 240–243.

Madanchian, M., & Taherdoost, H. (2017b). Role of Leadership in Small and Medium Enterprises (SMEs). *International Journal of Economics and Management Systems, 2*, 240–243.

Madanchian, M., & Taherdoost, H. (2019). Assessment of Leadership Effectiveness Dimensions in Small & Medium Enterprises (SMEs). *Procedia Manufacturing, 32*, 1035–1042. doi:10.1016/j.promfg.2019.02.318

Mihelic, K. K., Lipicnik, B., & Tekavcic, M. (2010). Ethical leadership. *International Journal of Management & Information Systems, 14*(5).

Mumford, M. D., Zaccaro, S. J., Harding, F. D., Jacobs, T. O., & Fleishman, E. A. (2000). Leadership skills for a changing world: Solving complex social problems. *The Leadership Quarterly, 11*(1), 11–35. doi:10.1016/S1048-9843(99)00041-7

Ofori, G. (2009). Ethical leadership: Examining the relationships with full range leadership model, employee outcomes, and organizational culture. *Journal of Business Ethics, 90*(4), 533–547. doi:10.100710551-009-0059-3

Ogbonna, E., & Harris, L. C. (2000). Leadership style, organizational culture and performance: Empirical evidence from UK companies. *International Journal of Human Resource Management, 11*(4), 766–788. doi:10.1080/09585190050075114

Ojokuku, R. M., Odetayo, T. A., & Sajuyigbe, A. S. (2012). Impact of leadership style on organizational performance: A case study of Nigerian Banks. *American Journal of Business and Management, 1*(4), 202–207.

Peterson, R. S., Smith, D. B., Martorana, P. V., & Owens, P. D. (2003). The impact of chief executive officer personality on top management team dynamics: One mechanism by which leadership affects organizational performance. *The Journal of Applied Psychology, 88*(5), 795–808. doi:10.1037/0021-9010.88.5.795 PMID:14516245

Razak, R. A. (2011). Entrepreneurial Orientation as a Universal Remedy for the Receding Productivity in Malaysian Small and Medium Enterprises: A Theoretical Perspective. *International Journal of Business and Social Science, 2*(19).

Rowe, G. (2012). Performance measurement. *Introduction to Nonprofit Management: Text and Cases*, 129.

Rowe, W. G. (2001). Creating wealth in organizations: The role of strategic leadership. *The Academy of Management Executive, 15*(1), 81–94. doi:10.5465/ame.2001.4251395

Saaty, T. L. (1980). *The Analytic Hierarchy Process: Planning, Priority Setting, Resources Allocation*. London: McGraw-Hill.

Sam, M., Fazli, M., Tahir, M. N. H., & Abu Bakar, K. (2012). Owner-managers of SMEs in it sector: Leadership and company performance. *International Journal of Business and Social Science, 3*(14), 1–11.

Taherdoost, H. (2017a). Decision Making Using the Analytic Hierarchy Process (AHP); A Step by Step Approach. *International Journal of Economics and Management Systems*, *2*, 244–246.

Taherdoost, H. (2017b). Understanding of e-service security dimensions and its effect on quality and intention to use. *Information & Computer Security*, *25*(5), 535–559. doi:10.1108/ICS-09-2016-0074

Uchenwamgbe, B. (2013). Effects of leadership style on organizational performance in small and medium scale enterprises (SMEs) in Nigeria. *European Journal of Business and Management*, *5*(23), 53–73.

Yukl, G. (2008). How leaders influence organizational effectiveness. *The Leadership Quarterly*, *19*(6), 708–722. doi:10.1016/j.leaqua.2008.09.008

Chapter 2
Gerontrepreneurship

Fahri Özsungur
https://orcid.org/0000-0001-6567-766X
Adana Alparslan Türkeş Science and Technology University, Turkey

ABSTRACT

In today's world, where technological developments and age-related consumption tendencies differ, entrepreneurship is a subject that needs to be investigated in the context of gerontology. Consumption behaviors are influenced by the effects of decreases due to aging on technology and the environment. In this chapter, where the effects of differentiation of consumption behaviors on entrepreneurship and its process are discussed, a new concept, gerontrepreneurship, is introduced. With this concept, the authors a new idea to gerontology in the context of entrepreneurship, elderly-technology interaction, and digital service innovations. In this chapter, the consumption processes of the elderly and their relations with the gerontrepreneurship process are explained, and recommendations are made.

INTRODUCTION

Technology is developing rapidly in today's world and taking its place in many fields. The Internet is compatible with many technological devices and facilitates daily work. Banking, recruitment, human resources management, product supply and management, rehabilitation services, health information systems, online shopping, and many other subjects can be realized on the internet and digital platform. The fact that technology started to help mainly in education, health, marketing, trade, and service sectors brought important innovations. These innovations reveal the importance of the process between the consumer-product / service provider.

Consumption is one of the precursors of innovation and varies depending on demographic characteristics. This is because consumption is a process that provides important information about the product/service after a behavior. This process provides information that needs to be improved, especially with the innovations of the digital world. This information can be derived from the interaction between consumers and the product/service. Experience in consumption helps to bring innovation. However, experience is a factor that varies depending on demographic characteristics. One of these features is age. Different experiences and needs of age-related changes shape consumption behaviors and innovations. Entrepre-

DOI: 10.4018/978-1-7998-5175-2.ch002

neurship is the transformation of opportunities into innovations inspired by experience and knowledge that vary depending on the characteristics of consumer behavior.

Changing needs due to increasing age also shape innovative behaviors related to products/services. Elderly individuals' physical, social, mental and physiological decline due to aging causes their needs to differ. The benefits that elderly people get with developing technology, assistive technology, internet applications that improve their social decline and social media offers innovative ideas for entrepreneurs. Assessing entrepreneurship in the context of gerontology due to the age-related decline of the elderly has become an important necessity in today's technology. This necessity raises an important and to be investigated question: What are the consumption and entrepreneurship processes in the context of digital service innovation, gerontology, and aging? In the context of this question, the study aims to determine the consumption processes of the elderly, who are consumers, and the entrepreneurship processes in the context of gerontology. A lack of study on these processes in the literature reveals the strength of the study. Therefore, in this chapter, gerontrepreneurship which expresses entrepreneurship in the context of gerontology, consumption behavior and consumption process in the elderly were examined. Gerontrepreneurship was introduced by considering the emergence of the idea of entrepreneurship, researching opportunities, and innovations, market research, transforming risks into opportunities, proactivity, adaptation to process, mobilization of resources, sustainability activities, post-purchase services.

Knowledge of entrepreneurship and consumption behaviors on medical technology, assistive technology, gerontechnology, use of technology in nursing homes, use of technology in elderly care centers, communication with smartphones, internet applications, digital service innovation issues can be obtained through this chapter. Furthermore, this chapter will provide important outputs, especially in the context of gerontology, related to digital service innovation.

RESEARCH METHODOLOGY

This study was prepared by a systematic review method (Robinson & Lowe, 2015; Uman et al., 2008). Identification, review, analysis, summarization, discussion, and presentation processes were followed respectively. First of all, the research question (What is the consumption and entrepreneurship processes in the context of digital service innovation, gerontology, and aging?) And its framework was determined. For this research, the concepts of entrepreneurship and gerontology were reviewed in the literature. The obtained information was categorized into subject headings and the identified framework was systematically organized (Uman, 2011). While constituting the titles, the framework and the obtained information were coded (Petticrew & Roberts, 2008). The concepts were chosen following the research topic. The chapter title was created by combining the new knowledge with the creative idea. During the creation of the chapter title, it was considered whether the representation of two concepts by one concept.

CONSUMPTION OF ELDERLY

Consumption Behavior of the Elderly

As individuals get older, they experience some physical, mental/cognitive, physiological, psychological and psychosocial changes.

Physical changes can be seen as a weakness in joints, weakness of bones, declines of strength, weakening of muscles, impaired balance, dexterity of hand and foot, tremor in the hand, decreased body fat, weight loss, reflex weakness, difficulty in breathing, visual impairment. Physical changes are age-related declines and weakening in the anatomical structure of the individual (Rogers & Evans, 1993).

Physiological changes include disruption of body oxygen balance, hypersensitivity to air temperatures, adaptation to environmental heat factors, blood pressure problems. Physiological changes are those that occur in a situation that facilitates daily physical activity. These changes can reduce the quality of life by increasing the risk of death and the likelihood of disease.

Psychosocial changes include social isolation, loneliness, a decrease in social activities, weakening relations with neighbors and friends, weakening family ties, avoiding social support, ageism. Psychosocial changes are changes caused by age-related changes in social interaction in an individual's life.

Psychological changes are related to stress, anxiety, depression, stress-related sleep disorders, high excitement, fear, panic, phobias, introvert. Psychological changes are those that occur with age-related psychological effects.

Mental/cognitive changes are regarding the difficulty in learning, weak perception, the problem of focus, forgetfulness. Mental changes are the changes related to the age-related difficulties and weaknesses at the cognitive level.

These problems are important phenomena that arise as the individual gets older and makes life difficult. These changes lead to the loss of skills required to perform daily activities. These losses can affect the consumption behavior of the individual to meet the needs of life. Weakness in physical abilities may make the use of products difficult. In this case, the products need to be harmonized to overcome this weakness. Improvement of products is possible with ergonomics (Neumann et al., 2006; Aalto & Saari, 2009). Some of the ergonomic solutions are to optimize the elevator for the elderly use who cannot climb the stairs, to design the keys for the elderly use of the phone, to make the smartphone applications suitable for the safety of the elderly, to make the seats and chairs suitable for the elderly, and to make the household goods suitable for the elderly use. Making traffic lights, public transportation and public vehicles suitable for the elderly is important for overcoming physical disability problems. Gerontechnological devices used in elderly care and rehabilitation centers for the elderly should also be suitable for elderly care (Chen & Chan, 2013).

Consumption Process in the Elderly

Elderly individuals may experience significant differences in consumer behavior due to cellular destruction and physical decline caused by advancing age. As long as the innovations brought about by the developing technology do not meet the needs of the elderly individual, it is not possible to improve consumption behavior. The consumption behavior of the elderly consists of the emergence of the need, the perception of the need, the tendency assessment for consumption, the research for consumption, the evaluation of the product/service according to internal factors, the consumption behavior, the post-consumption evaluation/feedback process.

The Emergence of Needs

This stage is essentially involved in the person's perception activity. Perception is the process of meaning-making that is different from the individual, which is affected by the person's life, goals, desires, and emotions, internal and external stimuli (Hershfield & Alter, 2019). The request arises as a result of these stimuli. Thus, in the process of emergence and awareness of the need, the problem is not the need or the desire, but the need and the desire (Klein & Hilbig, 2019). Because limiting the wishes and needs of the human being, which is a whole with the soul and body, in the context of the consumer will lead to making a distinction between soul and body (Melnyk et al., 2019). For instance; There is no difference between a person who is thirsty and wants to drink water from the first fountain to meet the need for water and a person who does not drink water from the fountain enters the market and drinks bottled water (Huck et al., 2018; Brecht et al., 2017; White; 2018; Brecht et al., 2017; White; et al., 2017). The need is water drinking and the fountain or bottled water does not affect this need. The need is not the first starting point of the desire of someone if someone drinks water because his friend drinks even though she/he is not thirsty. This request is automatically perceived as a need in terms of problem perception in the brain. Now this desire becomes a personal need without going into the decision-making process. This clearly shows that needs and desires are inseparably intertwined, so that it is not right to draw clear boundaries in the context of desires and needs in the emergence of a consumer's need.

Perceptual Evaluation of Needs

Consumption behavior in elderly individuals occurs under the influence of many factors. In particular, the decline in the elderly may have a negative effect on consumption behavior. Negative effects of physical, physiological, mental, psychological, social and psychosocial declines on the individual may affect perceptual tendencies and evaluations in consumption behavior. Gerontechnological devices that the individual has to use due to physical regression or disability should be appropriate and compatible with the current situation (Mitseva et al., 2012). Smartphones with medication reminders and special programs for emergencies must be suitable for the elderly's sense of sight, hearing, touch, and mental abilities. The predetermination of such conditions and the design of the product features accordingly enables the adaptation between the elderly with different characteristics and the product. Entrepreneurs and manufacturers are required to enact research and development works before introducing innovations, products, and services for older individuals.

The elderly person assesses their compulsory or voluntary consumption needs perceptively. Mandatory consumption needs are the products or services that are physically necessary for an individual's physical, physiological, mental, psychological, social and psychosocial regression, illness or disability. An individual's perceptual evaluation of mandatory products or services is important in terms of positive response to treatment. In prosthesis and orthosis applications, the psychological, social and mental abilities of the elderly should be determined in advance. Prosthetics suitable for active participation in social life is important for successful aging and quality of life. The design should be carried out considering the colors appropriate to the psychology of the elderly individuals and possible safety problems that may occur due to mental problems. The products produced for daily activities from voluntary consumption products should be suitable for static and dynamic anthropometric (dimensional) measurements of elderly individuals.

Tendency Assessment for Consumption

Consumption is subject to tendency assessment in older individuals. The individual evaluates consumption and needs by considering the experiences, ageism, social isolation and the current situation

(Beller & Wagner, 2018). Consumption stimulation that occurs as a result of the emergence of needs brings about an important cognitive assessment process. This process is different from the consumption assessment for the needs of a normal individual. It is essential that an individual consumes based on needs under normal conditions. However, consumption is perceived as a need in the elderly individual, and a lot of information is filtered for consumption behavior. For instance, an elderly person exposed to ageism may reactively reject to use a computer or smartphone (Barber, & Tan, 2018). This individual is isolated from social environments and rejects to cooperate. In an elderly person whose physical and physiological abilities have declined, the tendency to give up is higher than the normal individual and the resistance is lower. The experience gained with the advancement of age is subjected to a significant comparative assessment for consumption. When the negative experiences of the past are dominant, the elderly individual may give up the consumption behavior. The elderly person attaches importance to the tendency when the needs arise. The individual tendency is determined by the elderly and it is decided whether consumption will be realized or not.

Research for Consumption

When the belief that consumers should be realized as a result of the evaluation of tendencies prevails, the elderly individual begins to research the needs (Schewe, 1984). The studies are aimed at meeting the needs and individual satisfaction. The individual may fall into error in his / her research for his / her compulsory or voluntary needs. They may not be able to determine whether the products and services needed due to their physical and physiological decline are appropriate for the current situation of the elderly individual. In such a case, information is needed for the products or services. Information should be provided by entrepreneurs, non-governmental organizations and/or government. Public spots need to provide information for older people to choose the right products. When a product/service that meets the need is identified, it is evaluated for internal and external factors.

Evaluation of Product / Service According to Internal Factors

After the necessary researches for consumption, the individual assesses according to the effect of aging (Roedder John & Cole, 1986). Compares the current situation and the product/service it determines in the cognitive process. An elderly individual who feels that he/she is discriminated against can give up the consumption of products/services when he/she thinks that consumption is related to young people. Emotions are more effective in this evaluation. This process is different from the tendency assessment for consumption. Experience is predominantly important in tendency assessment for consumption (Yoon, Feinberg & Schwarz, 2010). Emotional factors are predominant since evaluations after the selection of products and services are final assessments for consumption. Decision making in the elderly individual is sophisticated and needs to be investigated in detail. The urgency of the need does not affect this situation much. The important thing is to make the right decision. However, regressions brought about by older age may cause misperceptions and emotional reactions. Therefore, although the choice is made for the consumption of a product or service, the realization of the consumption behavior depends on the final emotional evaluation in the cognitive process. The individual whose emotional characteristics increase with age can review the consumption decision several times. An elderly person whose final assessment is in a positive direction performs consumption behavior.

Consumption Behavior

Consumption is a condition for individual acceptance beyond the need for older individuals. Consumption is related to resistance, reactive action, self-assertion, self-realization, loneliness, psychological acceptance. Once the need arises, the individual can try to demonstrate that he/she applies his / her own decisions after reviewing the benefits to be achieved by realizing consumption (Park, Iyer & Smith, 1989). This happens as a reaction and a message to the environment. The emergence of consumer behavior in the elderly is possible by measuring the effect level of age-related declines affecting the cognitive process. Although the process mainly depends on these effects, mental and psychological problems can often lead to errors in decision-making behavior. Symptoms such as anxiety, stress, depression, and burnout may cause the individual to feel that they need it even if they do not. Such psychological syndromes cause an individual to make wrong decisions. Thus, the individual may become aware of the wrong decisions he/she makes very later. The emergence of consumer behavior as a result of wrong decisions can trigger a sense of regret and cause larger psychological problems. For example, anxiety leads to the idea that if consumption does not occur, trouble will occur. The individual acting with this idea can make a consumption decision and perform the consumption behavior with a sudden decision. This consumption can cause stress if it does not benefit the elderly and / or causes harm. Repeated misbehavior and harm can lead to depression. Psychological sensitivities that arise with increasing age cause differences in reactions to events. For this reason, it is important to consider all factors related to elderly individuals that affect consumer behavior in terms of post-consumption satisfaction and sustainability of consumption. Information regarding the decline in elderly individuals, consumption trends, real needs related to the product/service, social position, geographical and cultural characteristics, ageism perception should be determined in advance and the products/services should be designed with these factors in mind.

Post-Consumption Assessment / Feedback

Consumption is a type of behavior that is experienced by the consumers and has effects on the individual. Each consumption behavior has positive or negative effects on the individual (Lumpkin, & Festervand, 1988). These effects can be revealed by feedbacks as a result of consumption behavior (Mata, Schoole, & Rieskamp, 2007). As a result of the consumption behavior experienced by the elderly individual, meeting the needs, obtained benefits and risk factors are evaluated together. Feedback is the disclosure of these assessments. The individual can convey the level of benefit or satisfaction obtained by consumption behavior to the social environment, nursing homes, hospitals, elderly care nurses or his/her family. Feedbacks provide important information about the product/service delivery, quality, ergonomics, and the level of meeting the needs (Burt, & Gabbott, 1995). The entrepreneur/manufacturer/ service provider should receive this feedbacks. Every information to be obtained helps prevent potential problems for elderly individuals with the same characteristics.

GERONTREPRENEURSHIP

Gerontology

Gerontology is an emerging and interdisciplinary field that sheds light on today's aging process. This field is an important science that investigates the social and physical needs of elderly individuals, whether their difficulties in cognitive processes arise due to age progression or the effect of cellular destruction (Eismann, Verbeij & Henkens, 2019). Physiological, biological, psychological, cultural and social effects of aging have created a field of study in different disciplines in the context of gerontology (Saryazdi, Bannon, & Chambers, 2019). One of these areas is social gerontology. Social gerontology is a sub-science of gerontology which examines the aging process in terms of social aspects, aims to improve the lives of elderly individuals and bring them to the society in the light of social needs, and evaluates aging within the framework of macro and micro-economy. The theories developed with social gerontology focus on practical results and aim to realize the necessary initiatives for the development of social policies. A country's social policy, aging policy, social security, and social work are shaped by social gerontology. How the effects of cultural influences on human beings are transferred in the aging process leads to socially important consequences (Zahodne et al., 2019; Gonçalves et al., 2019; Kochhann, & Wilson, 2019).

Gerontology and Entrepreneurship

An important aspect of gerontology, which tries to explain the aging process, is entrepreneurship and innovation. Aging is not just a total of physical, biological and cognitive processes. Aging is the process in which the individual is the subject of the individual and is considered as a whole with the individual. When examining this process, social gerontology also deals with the individual and the environment in which the individual interacts. Family, work environment, friends, neighbors constitute the social environment. The municipality, state, governorate, ministries, public institutions are the legal environment. Examples of support groups are international organizations, voluntary organizations, foundations, and associations. Companies that produce products for consumers, manufacturers of hand products, designers and organizations providing services are consumption-oriented groups. These groups are communities around elderly individuals that affect the aging process. These social formations may contribute to the individual and social needs of the individual as the age progresses, or may cause social isolation and loneliness of the individual. Physical, mental and psychological declines that occur with aging may make it difficult to perform daily activities.

Consumption, like every individual, is a behavior and need that holds an important place in the life of elderly individuals. Consumption behavior occurs as a result of a specific need. In elderly individuals, this need may vary depending on some age-related declines. Feedback on ergonomics and consumer behavior is one of the most important of these needs (Shinar, 2017; Ismaila & Samuel, 2014). To understand Gerontrepreneurship, consumer behavior in the elderly should be examined first.

Conceptual Framework

Gerontrepreneurship consists of the words gerontology and entrepreneurship. This type of entrepreneurship examines the pre- and post-consumption processes that take place under factors that arise from age-related advances. Consumption tendencies and consumption needs of elderly individuals, satisfaction levels, tendencies related to products/services, factors affecting consumption related to aging affect entrepreneurship. Gerontrepreneurs take risks, act proactively and enact innovative behaviors by evaluating these factors together (Sandberg, 2007). Gerontrepreneurs turn the risks into opportunities in elderly consumption. Spirit, empathy and R & D are important in this type of entrepreneurship. Considering the consumption needs of elderly individuals in advance, evaluating the results of medical research, measuring the tendencies of the elderly with R & D, conducting the necessary researches about ergonomics are important for the products and services to be produced in the future (Dino, 2015; Nicholls & Gad Mohsen, 2015). Gerentrepreneurship is related to the production of new products/providing new services, forming new service/product processes, researching and entering new markets, ensuring organizational sustainability, creating new strategies and organizational forms, efficient use of resources (Schumpeter, 1965; Joern et al., 2017). Interactions of elderly people with communication and assistive technology, important opportunities, and innovations in gerontechnology issues are proactively evaluated in the entrepreneurship process (Schoon, & Duckworth, 2012; Obschonka et al., 2013). Social, economic, physical, psychological, mental, physiological, psychosocial, political and cultural conditions of the elderly are the subjects that should be investigated during the entrepreneurship process.

Gerontrepreneurship Process

Entrepreneurship requires a specific process. This process includes the following elements: the emergence of problem/emergence of an idea, researching opportunities and innovations, market research, transforming risks into opportunities, and proactivity, adaptation to process, resource research / mobilization of resources, producing-providing new products / services, and ensuring the adaptation by the elderly to existing-new products / services, promotion strategies / sustainability activities / feedback, post-purchase services.

The Emergence of Problem / Emergence of an Idea

The realization of innovations in entrepreneurship, the production of products or providing services depends on perceiving a problem that will give rise to an idea of innovation (Hisrich, 1990). The problems that arise can be revealed by individuals or organizations. A problem in the care of the elderly, difficulties in the communication of elderly people with technology can lead to the emergence of new ideas. These innovations can improve an existing product with ergonomics and design, develop a new product/technology, and create a new service (Axelrod et al., 2009; Aldrich, Smith & Dong, 1998). Improvement or creation of products and services is possible through ideas or feedback from older individuals or elderly care centers. The solution to the emerging problems is an important step in gerontrepreneurship. Every problem is important for the adaptation of technology, product or service to the elderly.

Researching Opportunities and Innovations

Another important process in entrepreneurship after the emergence of an idea is the research for opportunities and innovations (Cummings, 2000; Meyer, Walker & Litwin, 1961). The research process involves obtaining information from older individuals or from individuals or organizations with which older individuals interact. Feedback on the interactions of older individuals with current technology, product/service provides important ideas. Patient care centers, elderly rehabilitation centers, nursing homes, families or neighbors of elderly individuals, elderly care nurses are the elements from which this information and ideas can be obtained. Risks to be transformed into opportunities during the research, possible benefit and loss costs, cultural and demographic characteristics of elderly individuals in the geography lived, social responsibility should be considered together. When considering innovations, the difference between the total benefit for the elderly and the total benefit for the entrepreneur should not be great. The profit margin should be considered in the cost calculation. However, this profit margin is not sufficient for the decisions to be made as a result of the research. To provide a sustainable competitive advantage in entrepreneurship, the difference between the total benefit for the elderly and the total benefit for the entrepreneur must be minimum.

Market Research

Market research is necessary for the region or the innovations or processes in the society where the product/service will be provided (Gummesson, 1979). The level of competition in the market, sectoral risks, state / social policies, number of competitors, national and international factors, product/service characteristics, customer potential, sustainability, future customers, organizational infrastructure, technological opportunities, the network should be considered together (Noh & Fitzsimmons, 1999; Hua et al., 1994; St- Hilaire & Boisselier, 2018; Kirk-Smith & Gault, 1995). Technology related to the elderly, rehabilitation services, care services for palliative patients, gerontechnology, services for elderly care, assistive technology for the elderly can be the subject of market research. In these innovations, sectoral risks may arise from the cultural characteristics of the geography where the market is located. Consumption habits, mandatory needs of elderly individuals, low ratio of elderly individuals to the total population, low or decreasing rate of elderly population growth may be among high-risk factors. Lack of government incentives, difficulties in entering the market and high tax liabilities are other risk factors. These risks should be evaluated together when entering the market.

Transforming Risks into Opportunities, and Proactivity

Risks in entrepreneurship include important opportunities such as first-mover advantage, products to be produced by receiving feedback from elderly individuals and entering international markets. Entrepreneurs are individuals/organizations that transform risks into opportunities and act proactively (Chang et al., 2005; Kam Sing Wong, 2012; Dickel, 2017). Every entrepreneur contributes to the innovation process by considering risks. Risks should be considered with the difference between minimum-maximum loss. The cost of the product to be produced/the service to be provided, the competitiveness in the market and future customer forecasts should be considered together in the risk factor. Estimates are based on a specific strategy. Foreseen for the first time in the market or sector, an estimated target audience of an organization/individual should be identified. The national or international field of activity of the organization should be determined in advance and the growth rates should be compared with the current financial/legal status of the organization.

Adaptation to Process

Adaptation to the entrepreneurial process of the organization or enterprise should be ensured upon entry into the market or sector (Griffith et al., 2014). Adaptation requires collaboration with all units of the organization. Internal and external environment needs to be determined for cooperation. It is important that the internal environment of the organization is compatible with itself and the internal environment is compatible with the external environment (Filipe Lages & Montgomery, 2004). Identifying the environment in which information flow is related to innovation helps to achieve the set goal. The harmonious flow of information enables adaptation. Providing communication and information flow with the company where the parts of a new product will be supplied can significantly affect the success of entrepreneurship. Likewise, the flow of information and compliance between the employees who will provide a new service and the leader of the enterprise can affect the success of entrepreneurship. For this reason, the relationships between leader-follower, employee-employee, supplier-business, business-government, business-customer and harmony within the organization are important key points in entrepreneurship.

Resource Research / Mobilization of Resources

Innovations as a result of research on elderly needs require a specific resource. Activation of the entrepreneurship process, market research, R & D activities, research on the needs of elderly individuals require labor and financial resources (Casanueva, Gallego & Revilla, 2015). Human resources, technology, budget, process planning are among the main issues that need to be investigated in entrepreneurship (Orr, 2019). Organizational and individual entrepreneurship depends on the efficient use of human resources (Batistic & Tymon, 2017). The necessary budget should be set according to the sector and market to be undertaken and the resources should be provided accordingly. Support factors such as government incentives, organizational supports, non-governmental organizations, and financial institutions should be considered in resource research. Furthermore, the supply of human resources required for innovation in production and service is necessary for the entrepreneurial process (Wasiuzzaman, 2019). Gerontrepreneurship can be implemented with an effective human resources strategy related to innovation. The technology required for entrepreneurship can be provided by technology transfer. Researching and mobilizing the resources required for entrepreneurship depends on an adaptive management strategy. Families, friends, banks, government incentives are important financial resources for entrepreneurs.

Producing-Providing New Products / Services, and Ensuring the Adaptation by the Elderly to Existing-New Products / Services

New products are produced and new services are provided after the resources are mobilized in the process of entrepreneurship. Innovations in the form of production or providing the existing product/service are also within the scope of entrepreneurship. The output after this production and providing process has some impact on the customer. In the entrepreneurship examples to be carried out to meet the needs of the elderly, the adaptation of the product/service in the interaction with the elderly provides important information about the efficiency of innovation. For this reason, gerontrepreneurs should learn about the adaptation of innovation to the elderly. The information obtained from the elderly experiences provides new knowledge about the benefits of entrepreneurship. Providing the necessary agents and tools for the right flow of information is one of the most important issues in entrepreneurship. Providing information on product/service evaluations over the internet, telephone, and e-mail, and providing information from elderly care centers, elderly care nurses and nursing homes provide information about the suitability of entrepreneurship for its purpose. The information to be obtained is used by means of samples or for promotional purposes before the production or service is fully communicated to the target customer. Promotional activities to be performed before mass production will provide the necessary benefit about the efficiency and suitability of the entrepreneurship. In elderly individuals, these activities can be realized through intergenerational cooperation programs, evaluation of the use of voluntary elderly individuals and participation in social responsibility projects.

Promotion Strategies / Sustainability Activities / Feedback

Promotion strategies are the strategies that ensure the sustainability of innovation in the product/service in the process from the production of a product to the post-sale (Petit & McEnally, 1985; Lin, 2017). Advertising, communication, social responsibility, creativity, ergonomics, security, sales development, cooperation, public relations are important issues in the promotion (Empen, Loy & Weiss, 2015; Efanny et al., 2018). The development of communication ways with the elderly individual is the main factor in promotion. How communication should take place depends on the demographic and cultural characteristics of older individuals. Creating innovation in entrepreneurship according to the anthropometric measurements of elderly individuals and ergonomics is the priority element of gerontrepreneurship (Roper & Yeh, 2007; Gupta et al., 2013). Elderly feedback on products/services is possible through an effective communication policy. The impression left by the entrepreneur on elderly individuals is important for the perception of the product/service. For this reason, the entrepreneur's social responsibility, environmental policies and activities related to the elderly affect the perception of innovations with entrepreneurial output. Advertising, trainings, individual sales can be less effective than other elements in the promotion of the gerontrepreneurship. Therefore, the promotion strategy should be realized in the order of priority in the form of communication, interaction, cooperation, and feedback. For promotion, communication should be established with the target audience, communication should be turned into interaction, and necessary information should be presented or obtained in cooperation. This cycle provides promotion as well as important information for new entrepreneurs. However, the process is not limited to interaction with older individuals. This process should also be carried out together with the environment of older individuals. Examples of the environment of elderly individuals include family, neighbors, friends, nursing homes, elderly care centers, nurses, retirement homes, doctors.

Post-Purchase Services

Gerontrepreneurship does not end with the production and presentation of the product/service. Entrepreneurship involves increasing customer satisfaction to capture new opportunities. Improvements should be initiated after the problems, satisfaction, creative ideas, requests, and perceptions experienced by the elderly after purchasing the product or service are obtained through feedback. Improving the product/service according to the feedback received can create new examples and inspiration for entrepreneurship. Elimination of dissatisfaction with the use of a gerontechnological device with an innovation creates entrepreneurship. As long as the entrepreneur evaluates this process well, she/he can carry out new initiatives.

CONCLUSION

Although the study has introduced the concept of "gerontrepreneurship" to the literature for the first time, the fact that the study was carried out by the systematic review method revealed some limitations. The fact that the results are not supported by an empirical study and the problem of generalizability are important limitations of the study. Therefore, this area should be enriched with qualitative and quantitative research.

Gerontrepreneurship is a type of entrepreneurship, a set of innovative actions performed in the product/service, aimed at responding to the needs of the growing elderly population. This entrepreneurship type is inspired by developing technology, varying consumption needs by age-changing, and elderly-technology interactions. The increasing number of the elderly population, the development of technology, and the increasing research on aging make it necessary to examine entrepreneurship in the context of the elderly. The differentiation of elderly consumption compared to young consumers in the perceptual process necessitates the investigation of consumption trends of the elderly. It is recommended that factors such as ageism, social isolation, stress, depression that affect the consumption behavior of elderly individuals should be examined in the context of perception and decision-making behavior. Identifying the problems and trends experienced in this process is important for the efficiency of entrepreneurship.

Interactions of elderly people with technology are important for consumption behaviors and entrepreneurs. The increasing importance of technology in nursing homes, elderly care centers, medical, social and many other areas provides important information for entrepreneurship and innovation. Information about the experience gained from the interaction of elderly individuals with many technologies such as digital technology, communication technology, assistive technology, and gerontechnology can lead to the production of new products/services. Besides, harmonization of existing products/services with the internet and new technology depends on the information to be obtained from elderly individual-technology interactions. It is recommended to research the problems caused by progressive age-related setbacks and to reveal innovations related to digital service and smart technologies following the gerontrepreneurship process. These processes and innovations should be revealed by considering the consumption behavior and processes of elderly individuals. Besides, the contribution of digital service innovations to social isolation, ageism, Alzheimer's disease, dementia, palliative diseases related to elderly individuals should be investigated. It should be kept in mind that aging is an age-related change and it is recommended that the gerontrepreneurship be encouraged through social policies for quality of elderly life.

ACKNOWLEDGMENT

This research received no specific grant from any funding agency in the public, commercial, or not-for-profit sectors.

REFERENCES

Aalto, L., & Saari, A. (2009). Reengineering of the meal logistics in a sheltered house for elderly people. *Facilities*, *27*(3/4), 120–137. doi:10.1108/02632770910933143

Aldrich, W., Smith, B., & Dong, F. (1998). Obtaining repeatability of natural extended upper body positions: Its use in comparisons of the functional comfort of garments. *Journal of Fashion Marketing and Management*, *2*(4), 329–351. doi:10.1108/eb022538

Axelrod, L., Fitzpatrick, G., Burridge, J., Mawson, S., Smith, P., Rodden, T., & Ricketts, I. (2009). The reality of homes fit for heroes: Design challenges for rehabilitation technology at home. *Journal of Assistive Technologies*, *3*(2), 35–43. doi:10.1108/17549450200900014

Barber, S. J., & Tan, S. C. (2018). Ageism affects the future time perspective of older adults. *GeroPsych*, *31*(3), 115–126. doi:10.1024/1662-9647/a000189

Batistic, S., & Tymon, A. (2017). Networking behaviour, graduate employability: A social capital perspective. *Education + Training*, *59*(4), 374–388. doi:10.1108/ET-06-2016-0100

Beller, J., & Wagner, A. (2018). Loneliness, social isolation, their synergistic interaction, and mortality. *Health Psychology*, *37*(9), 808–813. doi:10.1037/hea0000605 PMID:30138019

Block, J. H., Fisch, C. O., & van Praag, M. (2017). The Schumpeterian entrepreneur: A review of the empirical evidence on the antecedents, behaviour and consequences of innovative entrepreneurship. *Industry and Innovation*, *24*(1), 61–95. doi:10.1080/13662716.2016.1216397

Brach, J. S., FitzGerald, S., Newman, A. B., Kelsey, S., Kuller, L., VanSwearingen, J. M., & Kriska, A. M. (2003). Physical activity and functional status in community-dwelling older women: A 14-year prospective study. *Archives of Internal Medicine*, *163*(21), 2565–2571. doi:10.1001/archinte.163.21.2565 PMID:14638556

Brecht, K., Swift, J. K., Worrall, J. M., & Parkin, S. R. (2017). A randomized controlled test of direct-to-consumer marketing using the American Psychological Association psychotherapy works videos. *Professional Psychology, Research and Practice*, *48*(6), 421–428. doi:10.1037/pro0000167

Burt, S., & Gabbott, M. (1995). The elderly consumer and non-food purchase behaviour. *European Journal of Marketing*, *29*(2), 43–57. doi:10.1108/03090569510080941

Casanueva, C., Gallego, A., & Revilla, M. (2015). Access and mobilization of network resources and competitive advantage in hotels. *International Journal of Contemporary Hospitality Management*, *27*(6), 1279–1300. doi:10.1108/IJCHM-03-2013-0144

Chang, S., Lin, R., Chen, J., & Huang, L. (2005). Manufacturing flexibility and manufacturing proactiveness. *Industrial Management & Data Systems*, *105*(8), 1115–1132. doi:10.1108/02635570510624482

Chen, K., & Chan, A. H. (2013). Use or Non-Use of Gerontechnology—A Qualitative Study. *International Journal of Environmental Research and Public Health*, *10*(10), 4645–4666. doi:10.3390/ijerph10104645

Cummings, N. A. (2000). Psychology and the new entrepreneurship: Possibilities and opportunities. *The Psychologist Manager Journal*, *4*(1), 27–43. doi:10.1037/h0095877

Dickel, P. (2017). The impact of protectability and proactiveness on the environmental performance of new ventures. *Corporate Governance*, *17*(1), 117–133. doi:10.1108/CG-03-2016-0055

Dino, R. N. (2015). Crossing boundaries: Toward integrating creativity, innovation, and entrepreneurship research through practice. *Psychology of Aesthetics, Creativity, and the Arts*, *9*(2), 139–146. doi:10.1037/aca0000015

Efanny, W., Haryanto, J., Kashif, M., & Widyanto, H. (2018). The relationship between marketing mix and retailer-perceived brand equity. *IMP Journal*, *12*(1), 192–208. doi:10.1108/IMP-12-2016-0019

Eismann, M., Verbeij, T., & Henkens, K. (2019). Older workers' plans for activities in retirement: The role of opportunities, spousal support, and time perception. *Psychology and Aging*, *34*(5), 738–749. doi:10.1037/pag0000377 PMID:31305089

Empen, J., Loy, J., & Weiss, C. (2015). Price promotions and brand loyalty. *European Journal of Marketing*, *49*(5/6), 736–759. doi:10.1108/EJM-08-2013-0433

Filipe Lages, L., & Montgomery, D. (2004). Export performance as an antecedent of export commitment and marketing strategy adaptation. *European Journal of Marketing*, *38*(9/10), 1186–1214. doi:10.1108/03090560410548933

Goldspink, D. F. (2005). Ageing and activity: Their effects on the functional reserve capacities of the heart and vascular smooth and skeletal muscles. *Ergonomics*, *48*(11–14), 1334–1351. doi:10.1080/00140130500101247 PMID:16338704

Gonçalves, A. P. B., Tarrasconi, M. A., Holz, M. R., Kochhann, R., & Paz Fonseca, R. (2019). Cognitive flexibility and inhibition in single-versus multiple-domain mild cognitive impairment: A comparative and discriminative analysis. *Psychology & Neuroscience*, *12*(2), 209–223. doi:10.1037/pne0000160

Griffith, D. A., Lee, S., Seob, H., Yeo, C., & Calantone, R. (2014). Marketing process adaptation. *International Marketing Review*, *31*(3), 308–334. doi:10.1108/IMR-06-2013-0113

Gummesson, E. (1979). The Marketing of Professional Services— An Organizational Dilemma. *European Journal of Marketing*, *13*(5), 308–318. doi:10.1108/EUM0000000004951

Gupta, D., Das, A., Jain, V., Soneja, T., Dang, P., & Srivastava, P. (2013). Design of Ergonomic Garment for Elderly Indian Women. *Research Journal of Textile and Apparel*, *17*(3), 118–127. doi:10.1108/RJTA-17-03-2013-B012

Hershfield, H. E., & Alter, A. L. (2019). On the naturalistic relationship between mood and entertainment choice. *Journal of Experimental Psychology. Applied*, *25*(3), 458–476. doi:10.1037/xap0000220 PMID:31120264

Himann, J. E., Cunningham, D. A., Rechnitzer, P. A., & Paterson, D. H. (1988). Age-related changes in speed of walking. *Medicine and Science in Sports and Exercise*, *20*(2), 161–166. doi:10.1249/00005768-198820020-00010 PMID:3367751

Hisrich, R. D. (1990). Entrepreneurship/intrapreneurship. *The American Psychologist*, *45*(2), 209–222. doi:10.1037/0003-066X.45.2.209

Hua Lu, M., Madu, C., Kuei, C., & Winokur, D. (1994). Integrating QFD, AHP and Benchmarking in Strategic Marketing. *Journal of Business and Industrial Marketing*, *9*(1), 41–50. doi:10.1108/08858629410053470

Huck, G. E., Finnicum, C., Morrison, B., Kaseroff, A., & Umucu, E. (2018). Consumer perspectives on physical activity interventions within assertive community treatment programs. *Psychiatric Rehabilitation Journal*, *41*(4), 312–318. doi:10.1037/prj0000311 PMID:29999334

Ismaila, S., & Samuel, T. (2014). Human-centered engineering: The challenges of Nigerian engineer. *Journal of Engineering. Design and Technology*, *12*(2), 195–208. doi:10.1108/JEDT-02-2011-0013

Joyner, M. J. (1993). Physiological limiting factors and distance running: Influence of gender and age on record performances. *Exercise and Sport Sciences Reviews*, *21*(1), 103–133. doi:10.1249/00003677-199301000-00004 PMID:8504840

Kallman, D. A., Plato, C. C., & Tobin, J. D. (1990). The role of muscle loss in the age-related decline of grip strength: Cross-sectional and longitudinal perspectives. *Journal of Gerontology*, *45*(3), 82–88. doi:10.1093/geronj/45.3.M82 PMID:2335723

Kam Sing Wong, S. (2012). The influences of entrepreneurial orientation on product advantage and new product success. *Journal of Chinese Entrepreneurship*, *4*(3), 243–262. doi:10.1108/17561391211262175

Kirk-Smith, M., & Gault, W. (1995). Marketing Local Enterprise Agencies. *Journal of Small Business and Enterprise Development*, *2*(3), 142–148. doi:10.1108/eb020956

Klein, S. A., & Hilbig, B. E. (2019). On the lack of real consequences in consumer choice research: And its consequences. *Experimental Psychology*, *66*(1), 68–76. doi:10.1027/1618-3169/a000420 PMID:30777510

Kochhann, R., & Wilson, M. A. (2019). Introduction: Special issue on neuropsychology of aging. *Psychology & Neuroscience*, *12*(2), 141–143. doi:10.1037/pne0000176

Larsson, L., Grimby, G., & Karlsson, J. (1979). Muscle strength and speed of movement in relation to age and muscle morphology. *Journal of Applied Physiology*, *46*(3), 451–456. doi:10.1152/jappl.1979.46.3.451 PMID:438011

Lexell, J., Taylor, C. C., & Sjöström, M. (1988). What is the cause of the ageing atrophy? Total number, size and proportion of different fiber types studied in whole vastus lateralis muscle from 15- to 83-year-old men. *Journal of the Neurological Sciences*, *84*(2–3), 275–294. doi:10.1016/0022-510X(88)90132-3 PMID:3379447

Lin, C. (2017). A multi-level test for social regulatory focus and team member creativity. *Leadership and Organization Development Journal*, *38*(8), 1057–1077. doi:10.1108/LODJ-05-2016-0125

Lumpkin, J. R., & Festervand, T. A. (1988). Purchase information sources of the elderly. *Journal of Advertising Research*, *27*, 31–43.

Mata, R., Schooler, L. J., & Rieskamp, J. (2007). The aging decision maker: Cognitive aging and the adaptive selection of decision strategies. *Psychology and Aging*, *22*(4), 796–810. doi:10.1037/0882-7974.22.4.796 PMID:18179298

Melnyk, V., van Herpen, E., Jak, S., & van Trijp, H. C. M. (2019). The mechanisms of social norms' influence on consumer decision making: A meta-analysis. *Zeitschrift fur Psychologie mit Zeitschrift fur Angewandte Psychologie, 227*(1), 4–17. doi:10.1027/2151-2604/a000352

Meyer, H. H., Walker, W. B., & Litwin, G. H. (1961). Motive patterns and risk preferences associated with entrepreneurship. *Journal of Abnormal and Social Psychology, 63*(3), 570–574. doi:10.1037/h0043698 PMID:14473104

Mitseva, A. P., Peterson, C. B., Karamberi, C., Oikonomou, L. C., Ballis, A., Giannakakos, C., & Dafoulas, G. E. (2012). Gerontechnology: Providing a Helping Hand When Caring for Cognitively Impaired Older Adults—Intermediate Results from a Controlled Study on the Satisfaction and Acceptance of Informal Caregivers. *Current Gerontology and Geriatrics Research*, 1–19.

Narici, M. V., Bordini, M., & Cerretelli, P. (1991). Effect of aging on human adductor pollicis muscle function. *Journal of Applied Physiology, 71*(4), 1277–1281. doi:10.1152/jappl.1991.71.4.1277 PMID:1757349

Neumann, W., Winkel, J., Medbo, L., Magneberg, R., & Mathiassen, S. (2006). Production system design elements influencing productivity and ergonomics. *International Journal of Operations & Production Management, 26*(8), 904–923. doi:10.1108/01443570610678666

Nicholls, R., & Gad Mohsen, M. (2015). Other customer age: Exploring customer age-difference related CCI. *Journal of Services Marketing, 29*(4), 255–267. doi:10.1108/JSM-04-2014-0144

Noh, J., & Fitzsimmons, J. (1999). Effect of information technology on marketing performance of Korean service firms. *International Journal of Service Industry Management, 10*(3), 307–321. doi:10.1108/09564239910276908

Obschonka, M., Schmitt-Rodermund, E., Silbereisen, R. K., Gosling, S. D., & Potter, J. (2013). The regional distribution and correlates of an entrepreneurship-prone personality profile in the United States, Germany, and the United Kingdom: A socioecological perspective. *Journal of Personality and Social Psychology, 105*(1), 104–122. doi:10.1037/a0032275 PMID:23586410

Orr, S. (2019). Daring to tap external strategic resources: Competitive advantage in global industries. *The Journal of Business Strategy, 40*(3), 25–35. doi:10.1108/JBS-03-2018-0032

Park, C. W., Iyer, E. S., & Smith, D. C. (1989). The effects of situational factors on in-store grocery shopping behavior: The role of store environment and time available for shopping. *The Journal of Consumer Research, 15*(4), 422–433. doi:10.1086/209182

Petit, T., & McEnally, M. (1985). Putting Strategy Into Promotion Mix Decisions. *Journal of Consumer Marketing, 2*(1), 41–47. doi:10.1108/eb038819

Petticrew, M., & Roberts, H. (2008). *Systematic reviews in the social sciences: A practical guide*. John Wiley & Sons.

Phillips, S. K., Rook, K. M., Siddle, N. C., Bruce, S. A., & Woledge, R. C. (1993). Muscle weakness in women occurs at an earlier age than in men, but strength is preserved by hormone replacement therapy. *Clinical Science, 84*(1), 95–98. doi:10.1042/cs0840095 PMID:8382141

Porter, M. M., Vandervoort, A. A., & Lexell, J. (1995). Aging of human muscle: Structure, function, and adaptability. *Scandinavian Journal of Medicine & Science in Sports*, *5*(3), 129–142. doi:10.1111/j.1600-0838.1995.tb00026.x PMID:7552755

Riebe, D., Blissmer, B. J., Greaney, M. L., Garber, C. E., Lees, F. D., & Clark, P. G. (2009). The relationship between obesity, physical activity, and physical function in older adults. *Journal of Aging and Health*, *21*(8), 1159–1178. doi:10.1177/0898264309350076 PMID:19897781

Robinson, P., & Lowe, J. (2015). Literature reviews vs systematic reviews. *Australian and New Zealand Journal of Public Health*, *39*(2), 103–103. doi:10.1111/1753-6405.12393 PMID:25827181

Roedder John, D., & Cole, C. A. (1986). Age differences in information processing: Understanding deficits in young and elderly consumers. *The Journal of Consumer Research*, *13*(3), 297–315. doi:10.1086/209070

Rogers, M. A., & Evans, W. J. (1993). Changes in skeletal muscle with aging: Effects of exercise training. *Exercise and Sport Sciences Reviews*, *21*(1), 65–102. doi:10.1249/00003677-199301000-00003 PMID:8504850

Roper, K., & Yeh, D. (2007). Ergonomic solutions for an aging workforce. *Journal of Facilities Management*, *5*(3), 172–178. doi:10.1108/14725960710775054

Rowe, J. W., & Kahn, R. L. (1987). Human aging: Usual and successful. *Science*, *237*(4811), 143–149. doi:10.1126cience.3299702 PMID:3299702

Sandberg, B. (2007). Customer-related proactiveness in the radical innovation development process. *European Journal of Innovation Management*, *10*(2), 252–267. doi:10.1108/14601060710745288

Saryazdi, R., Bannon, J., & Chambers, C. G. (2019). Age-related differences in referential production: A multiple-measures study. *Psychology and Aging*, *34*(6), 791–804. doi:10.1037/pag0000372 PMID:31204834

Schewe, C. D. (1984). Buying and Consuming Behavior of the Elderly Findings From Behavioral Research. NA - Advances in Consumer Research, 11, 558-562.

Schoon, I., & Duckworth, K. (2012). Who becomes an entrepreneur? Early life experiences as predictors of entrepreneurship. *Developmental Psychology*, *48*(6), 1719–1726. doi:10.1037/a0029168 PMID:22746220

Schumpeter, J. A. (1965). Economic Theory and Entrepreneurial History. In H. G. Aitken (Ed.), *Explorations in enterprise*. Cambridge, MA: Harvard University Press. doi:10.4159/harvard.9780674594470.c5

Shinar, D. (2017). Driver Information Processing: Attention, Perception, Reaction Time, and Comprehension. *Traffic Safety and Human Behavior*, 189-256.

Skelton, D. A., Greig, C. A., Davies, J. M., & Young, A. (1994). Strength, power and related functional ability of healthy people aged 65–89 years. *Age and Ageing*, *23*(5), 371–377. doi:10.1093/ageing/23.5.371 PMID:7825481

St-Hilaire, W., & Boisselier, P. (2018). Evaluating profitability strategies and the determinants of the risk performance of sectoral and banking institutions. *Journal of Economic and Administrative Sciences*, *34*(3), 174–186. doi:10.1108/JEAS-08-2017-0078

Steffens, N. K., Yang, J., Jetten, J., Haslam, S. A., & Lipponen, J. (2018). The unfolding impact of leader identity entrepreneurship on burnout, work engagement, and turnover intentions. *Journal of Occupational Health Psychology, 23*(3), 373–387. doi:10.1037/ocp0000090 PMID:28749160

Tanaka, H., & Higuchi, M. (1998). Age, exercise performance, and physiological functional capacities. *Advances in Exercise and Sports Physiology, 4*, 51–56.

Tanaka, H., & Seals, D. R. (1997). Age and gender interactions in physiological functional capacity: Insight from swimming performance. *Journal of Applied Physiology, 82*(3), 846–851. doi:10.1152/jappl.1997.82.3.846 PMID:9074973

Tuna, H. D., Edeer, A. O., Malkoc, M., & Aksakoglu, G. (2009). Effect of age and physical activity level on functional fitness in older adults. *European Review of Aging and Physical Activity, 6*(2), 99–106. doi:10.100711556-009-0051-z

Uman L. S. (2011). Systematic reviews and meta-analyses. *Journal of the Canadian Academy of Child and Adolescent Psychiatry = Journal de l'Academie canadienne de psychiatrie de l'enfant et de l'adolescent, 20*(1), 57–59.

Uman, L. S., Chambers, C. T., McGrath, P. J., & Kisely, S. (2008). A systematic review of randomized controlled trials examining psychological interventions for needle-related procedural pain and distress in children and adolescents: An abbreviated Cochrane review. *Journal of Pediatric Psychology, 33*(8), 842–854. doi:10.1093/jpepsy/jsn031 PMID:18387963

Wasiuzzaman, S. (2019). Resource sharing in interfirm alliances between SMEs and large firms and SME access to finance. *Management Research Review, 42*(12), 1375–1399. doi:10.1108/MRR-10-2018-0369

Westerterp, K. R. (2000). Daily physical activity and ageing. *Current Opinion in Clinical Nutrition and Metabolic Care, 3*(6), 485–488. doi:10.1097/00075197-200011000-00011 PMID:11085835

White, D. A., McGuire, A. B., Luther, L., Anderson, A. I., Phalen, P., & McGrew, J. H. (2017). Consumer factors predicting level of treatment response to illness management and recovery. *Psychiatric Rehabilitation Journal, 40*(4), 344–353. doi:10.1037/prj0000284 PMID:28910123

Yoon, C., Feinberg, F., & Schwarz, N. (2010). Older consumers and satisfaction. In A. Drolet, N. Schwarz, & C. Yoon (Eds.), *The Aging Consumer: Perspectives from Psychology and Economics* (pp. 209–227). London: Taylor and Francis.

Zahodne, L. B., Ajrouch, K. J., Sharifian, N., & Antonucci, T. C. (2019). Social relations and age-related change in memory. *Psychology and Aging, 34*(6), 751–765. doi:10.1037/pag0000369 PMID:31180697

ADDITIONAL READING

Amarya, S., Singh, K., & Sabharwal, M. (2018). *Ageing Process and Physiological Changes*, Gerontology, Grazia D'Onofrio, Antonio Greco and Daniele Sancarlo, IntechOpen, DOI: . Available from: https://www.intechopen.com/books/gerontology/ageing-process-and-physiological-changes doi:10.5772/intechopen.76249

Bonnar, S. P. (2016). Consumption Patterns of the Elderly. (Unpublished doctoral dissertation), McMaster University, Hamilton, Ontario.

Börsch-Supan, A. (1992). Saving and consumption patterns of the elderly: The German Case. *Journal of Population Economics*, *5*(4), 289–303. doi:10.1007/BF00163062 PMID:12285681

Hurd, M. (1990). Research on the Elderly: Economic Status, Retirement, and Consumption and Saving. *Journal of Economic Literature*, *28*(2), 565–637.

Mcnamara, R. (1998). *Social Gerontology*. London: Greenwood Publishing Group.

Mok, C. F. J., Wang, H., & Hanna, S. D. (1994). Are Consumption Patterns of Elderly Households Consistent With a Life-Cycle Model? In J. A. Cote & S. M. Leong (Eds.), *AP - Asia Pacific Advances in Consumer Research* (Vol. 1, pp. 237–245). Provo, UT: Association for Consumer Research.

Torres-Collado, L., García-de la Hera, M., Navarrete-Muñoz, E. M., Compañ-Gabucio, L. M., Gonzalez-Palacios, S., & Vioque, J. (2018). Coffee Drinking and Associated Factors in an Elderly Population in Spain. *International Journal of Environmental Research and Public Health*, *15*(8), 1508–1661. doi:10.3390/ijerph15081661 PMID:30082581

Wilmoth, J., & Ferraro, K. (2013). *Gerontology: Perspectives and Issues* (4th ed.). New York: Springer.

KEY TERMS AND DEFINITIONS

Consumption: A type of behavior that is experienced by the consumers and has effects on the individual. The act of benefiting from services, drinking, using, eating.

Entrepreneurship: The production of new products/providing new services, forming new service/product processes, researching and entering new markets, ensuring organizational sustainability, creating new strategies and organizational forms, efficient use of resources.

Gerontology: An emerging and interdisciplinary field regarding the aging process.

Gerontrepreneur: An entrepreneur in gerontology. Gerontrepreneurs take risks, act proactively and enact innovative behaviors by evaluating the aging factors, turn the risks into opportunities in elderly consumption.

Gerontrepreneurship: The combination of the words of gerontology and entrepreneurship. It is a type of entrepreneurship that examines the pre- and post-consumption processes that take place under factors that arise from age-related advances.

Social Gerontology: A sub-science of gerontology which examines the aging process in terms of social aspects, aims to improve the lives of elderly individuals and bring them to the society in the light of social needs and evaluates aging within the framework of macro and micro-economy.

Chapter 3
Digital Transformation of Learning Management Systems at Universities:
Case Analysis for Student Perspectives

Abdeleh Bassam Al Amoush
University of New England, Australia

Kamaljeet Sandhu
https://orcid.org/0000-0003-4624-6834
University of New England, Australia

ABSTRACT

Internet technologies are recently being more utilised in the field of higher education in distance digital learning systems. Digital learning management systems (DLMSs) are an important and necessary educational tool for learning activities. The universities are using the digital LMS (DLMS) tools that are unique to their environment. Different universities have different DLMS tools that are software driven and allow the users (management, instructors, and students) to use them for regular tasks. This research discusses the qualitative data collected using the case study methodology. In this research, case study design was selected for the qualitative methodology, and semi-structured interviews were employed as the data collection method. The case study is based in a deanship of a university implementing a digital learning management system in Jordan. The research provides an analysis of the interviews to gain insights into students' perspectives regarding the factors influencing the implementation of the digital learning management system in the higher education sector.

DOI: 10.4018/978-1-7998-5175-2.ch003

INTRODUCTION

Digital Learning Management Systems (DLMSs) are widely adopted (Rogers, 1995) and used at universities for streamlining teaching and learning tasks, as they effectively manage learning tools and resources for user participants (students and teachers) (Kats, 2010; Orr, 2003; Rogers, 1995; Unwin et al., 2010). Research suggests that innovation within the university education over the past decade as a result of digital learning management systems, which have been found to significantly benefit students' understanding and academic progress (Alnsour, Muhsen, Dababnah, Eljinini, & Barhoum, 2011; Orr, 2003; Rogers, 1995). In this study DLMSs refers to Digital Learning Management Systems. DLMS applications are multifunctional, enabling students to have ubiquitous access to systems, watch lectures, download course materials and upload assignments online (AlQudah, 2014).

The latter provides convenience to students as never before and is conducive to study. To have efficient functioning of a DLMS, it is necessary to enable well-established links between data that is indexed by search engines, and web bots that connect and bind information together (Babić, 2012). DLMS empowers users and offers a greatly enhanced user experience overall (McIntosh & Torres, 2014; Phillipo & Krongard, 2012).

A DLMS greatly simplifies learning and deliverables, such as tests, assignments and other forms of assessment, with the use of multimedia applications that incorporate team learning through dynamic, real time, documented collaboration (Potter & Thompson, 2019). Some examples include the use of chat, file transfer and assessment applications. A DLMS creates new platforms for the active learner and results in greatly expanding the learning curve. To fully understand the nature and implications of different DLMSs, it is vital to explore exactly what the DLMS context is (Ahmad, Chinade, Gambaki, Ibrahim, & Ala, 2012). This study is based on the most recent and related literature explaining various scenarios where DLMSs address learning issues in the digital environment in a way that was not possible in the previous confines of print logics.

The research contribution is based on the higher educational sector at Jordanian universities. Research zone has applied in Jordanian universities, which are an educational institutions with a good reputation and each university has several branches across Jordan. The university management recognises the importance of IT for educational purposes; in its initial stages, it created an Information Technology Centre for supporting and train the users on DLMS.

This research study aims to identify the factors that impact on the acceptance of the DLMS at Jordanian universities. This research also investigate the acceptance and use of DLMS at Jordanian universities. It also focuses on the factors influencing acceptance of the DLMS at these Jordanian universities. However, the university management seeks, through related parties, to achieve the following goals:

- Provide all possible means of modern machine technologies (servers- information centre-operation centre-computer workshops-television digital learning management system such as Blackboard or Moodle) and necessary operating systems;
- Guarantee the application of information systems;
- Automate (machines of procedures and models) all information tasks;
- Take advantage of networks affiliated with the university, such as email services, banner system and television transmission of lectures and activities;
- Provide an environment suitable for spreading digital learning management system and applications and related training;

- Achieve high levels of information security from the source to the users;
- Safety of procedures and policies that guarantee the provision of electronic services.

STUDY OF FACTORS FOR THE ACCEPTANCE OF DLMS AT JORDANIAN UNIVERSITIES

The Technology Acceptance Model (TAM) (Davis, 1989; Venkatesh, 1999) has usually been used to examine the acceptance of a new technology. In this study, a research model is based on the TAM to investigate the acceptance of using DLMSs at Jordanian universities. The component of technical support will be incorporated through the TAM model, and serves as an extension to TAM. This is conducted in order to measure the acceptance of using DLMSs at Jordanian universities. The research model explains the system usage of applying DLMSs at Jordanian universities. It consists of concepts that will be refined in relation to the Digital Learning Management System (DLMS) and include technical support, perceived usefulness (PU) and perceived ease of use (PEOU) (Venkatesh & Davis, 2000).

Information Technology (IT) Infrastructure for DLMSs at Jordanian Universities

IT infrastructure for DLMSs in Jordan refers to the availability of technology in the country in general, and in universities in particular, such Internet connections, computers and DLMS tools (AlQudah, 2014). Many developing countries are still struggling with lack of IT infrastructure, and this research will highlight this factor as being one of the main factors influencing the acceptance of the DLMS in Jordan universities. According to Samak and Tawfik (2017), the Jordanian Ministry of Education made a five-year plan to establish IT infrastructure for public schools. This plan will be useful to identify the amount, methods and types of infrastructure used in the schools.

According to Khwaldeh, Al-Hadid, and Masa'deh (2017), the infrastructure for DLMS in Jordanian universities needs to improve and suit the demands of users (students, instructors and administration users). The study highlighted some users' infrastructure needs, such as deaf and the blind users, which means there is a gap in the IT infrastructure that needs to be identified and improved to be usable for all users (students and stuff).

According to (Wimpenny, Adefila, & DeWinter, 2018), Jordanian academic staff plan around the existing technology. As some interviewers stated, *access to technology appears to be limited in certain organisations, and there is also evidence of unequal provision around the country. This could therefore justifiably explain why relatively few respondents (10.8%) feel that they can draw from a range of activities to meet their learner needs* (Wimpenny et al., 2018, pp. 33-48).

Donation from developed countries and organisations are being used to help upgrade the IT infrastructure for DLMSs in Jordanian universities from the old infrastructure to a new platform infrastructure; however, because of other obstacles like refugees from the border country and Jordan's lack of financial resources, the improvement is slow, which means that there is a lack of infrastructure, especially in the education sectors.

IT infrastructure for DLMSs in Jordanian universities positively affects the acceptance of DLMS through perceived use and perceived ease of use. Two hypotheses (H) were formulated regarding IT infrastructure for DLMSs as follows:

H1: IT infrastructure for DLMSs has a positive effect on perceived usefulness for the DLMS.
H3: IT infrastructure for DLMSs has a positive effect on perceived ease of use for the DLMS.

Culture in Jordan

Cultural factors affect the use of DLMS tools in Jordanian universities. The unique culture in Jordan is a very important factor that influences the use of DLMSs in different ways, and this research will focus on this factor through perceived use and perceived ease of use (Al-Shaikh, 2003). According to Cho and Berge (2002), the most influential factors regarding the adoption and deployment of a DLMS are the culture and norms of those working in higher education faculties. Therefore, pedagogical issues and the lack of technology professional training are affecting the acceptance of a DLMS.

Many researchers highlight culture as one of the most significant factors affecting the acceptance of using DLMSs in Jordanian universities. A limitation in the studies done in Jordan universities is that they do not reflect the real number of users, and to be accurate, the sample size should represent all types of users (Abdullateef, Elias, Mohamed, Zaidan, & Zaidan, 2016; M. Al-Shboul, 2013; Al-Zoubi & Ali, 2019; Al Musawi, Ambusaidi, Al-Balushi, & Al-Balushi, 2015; Atoum, Otoom, & Ali, 2017; Hofstede, 1983; Khwaldeh et al., 2017). On the other hand, *emotions play a significant part in students' learning experiences within complex educational environments* (Arguel, Lockyer, Kennedy, Lodge, & Pachman, 2019, pp. 44-56).

According to M. Al-Shboul (2013, pp. 13-28), *We need to spread the culture of using e-Learning technology to enhance the quality of learning*. The university management advised that more focus on user training is needed and the university culture needs to be more open to new technology to improve the quality of teaching and learning. With reference to Abbad, Morris, and De Nahlik (2009, p. 19) *Cultures that are more focused on oral traditions may be less engaged with e-learning*. Management should work more on user training so the users can accept and enjoy the new technology and look forward to new updates. According to Varis and Al-Agtash (2008, p. 74) *As a relevant factor in the dissemination of values and in the formation of society's thinking, the media are responsible for disseminating local culture and the events that occur in the world*. The media today is a very important player in local social life and improving the use of any new technology. It's the key player in changing user culture and improving positively any new technology.

In this research, a significant relationship exists between the influence of culture and the perceived usefulness and perceived ease of use of adopting a DLMS in Jordanian universities. There is a need to confirm this prediction with respect to the location (Jordanian universities) through this research. The relationship between cultural influence and the use of a DLMS is hypothesised in this research as follows:

H2: Culture has a positive effect on perceived ease of use for the DLMS.
H4: Culture has a positive effect on perceived usefulness for the DLMS.

Perceived Usefulness of a DLMS

The perceived usefulness of a DLMS is defined as the degree to which the user believes that using the DLMS would improve their learning performance (Davis, 1989). It is *the degree to which a person believes that using a particular system could enhance their job performance and it is the extent to which an individual believes that using the system enhances his/her performance* (Saadé & Bahli, 2005, pp. 217-

240). According to Davis (1989, p. 320) People *tend to use or not use an application to the extent they believe it will help them perform their job better. We refer to this first variable as perceived usefulness.*

The benefits of the hypotheses of IT infrastructure and culture are to encourage users (students, instructors and management) to accept any new technology and work on it to gain all the advantages and improve the quality of learning. The IT infrastructure and culture in Jordan are very important factors affecting the acceptance of any new technology to accept, including the use of DLMSs in Jordanian universities (M. Al-Shboul, 2011; M. A. Al-Shboul & Alsmadi, 2010; Alnsour et al., 2011; AlQudah, 2014).

This research highlights the perceived usefulness on DLMS tools from the IT infrastructure and the culture in Jordan context to show the attention of acceptance using DLMS in Jordan universities. The relationship between perceived usefulness and the acceptance of DLMS to adopt DLMS is hypothesised as follows:

H5: Perceived usefulness in accepting a DLMS has a positive effect on acceptance of the DLMS.

Perceived Ease of Use of a DLMS

The perceived ease of use of a DLMS is defined as the degree to which the user believes that using the DLMS will be free of effort (Davis, 1989). It can be described as *the degree to which a person believes that using a particular system is free of effort. Previous research has demonstrated that individuals are more likely to use a new technology if they perceive that it is easy to use* (Saadé & Bahli, 2005, pp. 101-132).

Davis (1989) shows that ease of use had a direct effect on perceived usefulness. Many studies on the TAM also provided strong experimental support for a positive relationship between perceived usefulness and perceived ease of use. The TAM shows that perceived ease of use and perceived usefulness have a direct effect on acceptance of using a new technology (Adams, Nelson, & Todd, 1992; Szajna, 1996; Venkatesh & Davis, 2000). Venkatesh (1999) discovered that *facilitating conditions and external control served as anchors that users employ to inform perceived ease of use about information technology* as cited in (Abbad et al., 2009, p. 167). According to Williams (2002), an important factor in determining the acceptance of technology such as a DLMS is the availability of "technical support".

Both IT infrastructure and culture are very important factors that affect ease of use of a DLMS. According to M. Al-Shboul (2013) IT infrastructure and culture are key players in enhancing the quality of learning. IT infrastructure should be able to support and accept any technology and software tools without obstacles. Poor infrastructure will cost any organisation money and time in activating the new tools or new technology software.

It is hypothesised that IT infrastructure and culture affect the perceived ease of use a DLMS positively and negatively. Good infrastructure makes any new software easy to apply and use. With regard to culture, knowledge of the culture where a new software will be applied will allow the new technology to be easy for the uses to use for the users to use (students, instructors and managements) (Al-Dmour, 2014; AlQudah, 2014).

Perceived ease of use of a DLMS shows the intention a user has to make use of a technology under a given behaviour. It was predicted that users' behavioural intention to adopt DLMS has an encouraging influence on acceptance of the DLMS.

H6: Perceived ease of use of a DLMS has a positive effect on acceptance for the DLMS.

Acceptance and Continued Use of DLMS

The Technology Acceptance Model (TAM) *has become well-established as a robust, powerful, and parsimonious model for predicting user acceptance* (Venkatesh & Davis, 2000, p. 19). A large number of researchers have adopted the TAM to test and examine the acceptance of new technologies like personal computers (Igbaria, Zinatelli, Cragg, & Cavaye, 1997).

Davis (1989, p. 335) indicates that: *the possibility of dysfunctional impacts generated by information technology emphasizes that user acceptance is not a universal goal and is actually undesirable in cases where systems fail to provide true performance gains. Although there has been a growing pessimism in the field about the ability to identify measures that are robustly linked to user acceptance, the view taken here is much more optimistic. User reactions to computers are complex and multifaceted. But if the field continues to systematically investigate fundamental mechanisms driving user behaviour, cultivating better and well measures and critically examining alternative theoretical models, sustainable progress is within reach.*

To accept a new system, hypotheses for both perceived usefulness and perceived ease of use should be examined (Davis, 1989). The model reflects these hypotheses to measure the acceptance of new software for any organisation, especially Jordanian universities, and it will then be possible to see if it is appropriate to use this new software in these universities. The model can then be used for all universities in Jordan. The outcome will influence the continued use of DLMS software in Jordanian universities in general (Almarabeh, 2014).

Acceptance of a DLMS shows the perceived usefulness and perceived ease of use of a DLMS under a given behaviour for continued use of DLMSs in Jordanian universities.

H7: Acceptance of a DLMS has a positive effect on continued use of the DLMS.

CONCEPTUAL CONSTRUCTS AND THE RESEARCH MODEL

The research utilises the Technology Acceptance Model (TAM) as a framework to address all the relevant issues around the DLMS context. In this research, the proposed model based on the extension of the Technology Acceptance Model (TAM) (Davis, 1989) that has been applied, tested and examined for the discovery of new information and understanding of the Digital Learning Management System model (DLMS). The following is a review and definition of this framework with critical perspectives.

A number of issues can affect users' decision to accept DLMS tools of choice, and Jordan is one of the developing countries that experience problems such as lack of network connectivity, slow system response and social cultural issues. In this research, the many factors that affect acceptance and rate of adoption are used to understand how they influence the diffusion rate of DLMS tools as innovative instructional delivery tools. Therefore, we investigate behavioural intent to use DLMS tools by employees, based on attitude, relative advantage, complexity and compatibility (Mkhize, Mtsweni, & Buthelezi, 2016). Table 1 shows definition of the latent variable for this study.

In the TAM, Davis (1989) suggests two determinants of computer usage: PU (perceived usefulness) and PEOU (perceived ease of use). Later, other investigators and researchers extended the TAM model to combine additional variables that could account for extra variance in computer usage technology (Gefen

Figure 1. Conceptual framework for Digital Learning Management System Model at Jordan universities (DLMS)

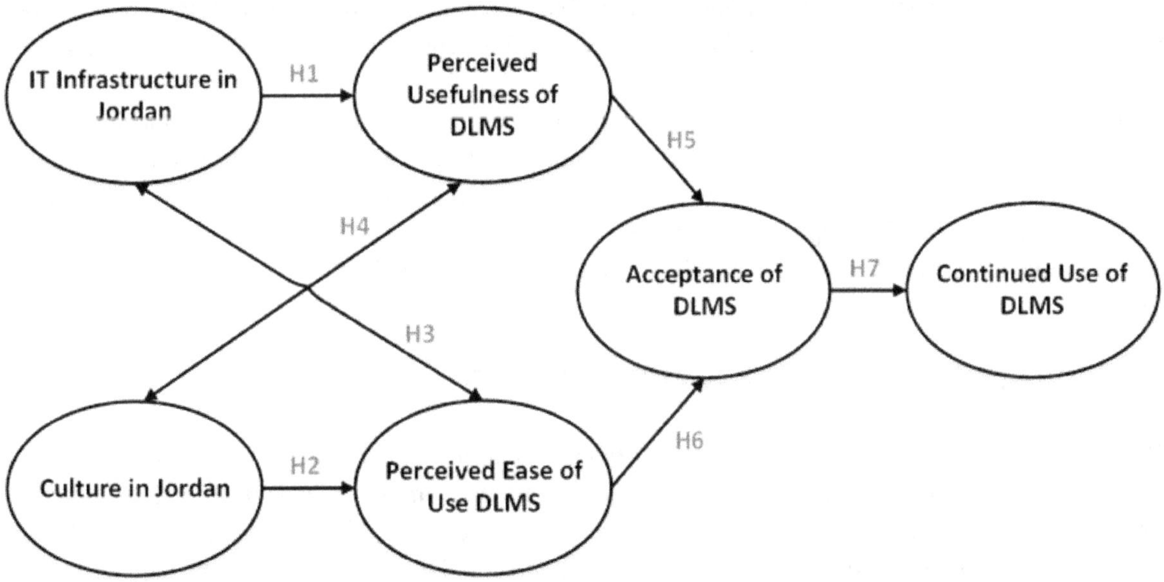

& Straub, 1997; Venkatesh & Davis, 2000). The advantage paradigm from behavioural decision theory is relevant to perceived usefulness and perceived ease of use (Beach & Mitchell, 1978).

METHODOLOGICAL APPROACH

The methodological approach considered the requirements for this study in order to find the values related to the research problems & aims and also to constitute ethical behaviour in the research (Ridder, 2017). The researchers conducted several interviews with the participants at Jordanian universities (six universities) to extract research data. The researchers collected qualitative data from interviews and then

Table 1. Definition of the latent variable

Latent Variable	Definitions
IT infrastructure	The availability of technology in the country in general, and in universities in particular, such Internet connections, computers and DLMS tools (AlQudah, 2014).
Jordanian Culture	The unique culture in Jordan is a very important factor that influences the use of DLMSs in different ways, and this research will focus on this factor through perceived use and perceived ease of use.
Perceived ease of use (PEOU)	Perceived ease of use refers to *the degree to which a person believes that using a particular system would be free of effort* (Davis, 1989, p. 320).
Perceived usefulness (PU)	the degree to which the user believes that using the DLMS would improve their learning performance (Davis, 1989).
Acceptance of an DLMS	The perceived usefulness and perceived ease of use of a DLMS under a given behaviour for continued use of DLMSs in Jordanian universities.

refine the quantitative data questionnaire. It also adopted to obtain qualitative and quantitative data in order to develop and refine concepts identified from the literature for inclusion in the conceptual model and examine the acceptance of the Digital Learning Management System Model (DLMS) at Jordanian universities. It will formulate the quantitative survey questions and discover the findings obtained from the survey (Creswell, 2013; Yin, 1981).

A semi-structured interviews method and questionnaires were adopted and built from the aims of the research, in order to examine and test the DMLS model and to evaluate qualitative data for this study (Rowley, 2002; Yin, 2012). The interviews method can be critical, positivist or interpretive, depending on the researcher's philosophical assumptions. In this research, the researcher adopted a positivist interview method for the qualitative data phase (Gupta & Rao, 2018; Yin, 2015).

RESEARCH DATA COLLECTION AND ANALYSIS

The interviews conducted among the research participants within Jordanian universities (six universities) to extract evidence. The researchers collected qualitative data from interviews. It has been adopted to obtain qualitative data in order to develop and refine concepts identified from the literature for inclusion in the conceptual model and to examine the acceptance of the Digital Learning Management System Model (DLMS) at Jordanian universities (Creswell, 2013; Yin, 1981).

The research conducted in the academic context of Jordanian universities. Altogether 37 interviews conducted for the DLMS users (Instructors, Administrators and Students) from six universities (refer to Table 2). In that category, there are 22 instructors interviews are conducted, 8 administrators interviews are conducted, and 7 students' interviews are conducted to assess the DLMS. This chapter reports on the data from the students' perceptions to analyse DLMS. In particular it has focused on six main universities at Jordan: the University of Jordan (UJ), which is the oldest and reputed government university at Jordan, Princess Sumaya University for Technology (PSUT), which has a mixed model of a university system (government and private), and Philadelphia University (PU), which is one of the private university at Jordan. Jordan University of Science and Technology (JUST), which is another public university at Jordan. The final university is the Applied Science Private University (ASU), which is a private university at Jordan. These six different academic institutions are represented as major universities at Jordan. According to (Rank, 2019), Table 2 shows some important data for these universities from which the research evidence was collected.

Students' Perceptions on the Digital Learning Management System

This section explores students' perceptions on the factors affecting the acceptance and continuance usage of digital learning management systems in Jordanian universities on the basis of qualitative data collected using the case study methodology. This is significant as students give more attention to discuss digital learning management systems from a pedagogical perspective, as opposed to IT staff, who are more concerned with the technological features of the system. The following are the students' perceptions on the IT infrastructure, Jordanian culture, perceived usefulness, perceived ease of use, acceptance of DLMS and continuance usage of the digital learning management system.

It was clear from the students' interviewees that the digital learning management system encourages cooperative learning among students themselves and/or between instructors, administrators and students.

Table 2. Research context for Jordanian universities

University	World Rank	Country Rank	Type	Enrollment Range Students	Location
UJ	1643	1	non-profit public	35,000-39,999	Large city Amman
PSUT	6452	11	non-profit private	3,000-3,999	Amman
JUST	2315	2	non-profit public	20,000-24,999	Irbid
PU	2528	3	profit private	5,000-5,999	North Amman
ASU	7342	16	profit private	8,000-8,999	Amman
AABU	5362	9	non-profit public	15,000-19,999	Mafraq

Note. UJ = University of Jordan; PSUT = Princess Sumaya University of Technology; JUST = Jordan University of Science and Technology; PU = Philadelphia University; ASU = Applied Science Private University; AABU = Al al-Bayt University (Rank, 2019).

This cooperative practice shows to extend users (instructors', administrators' and students') prospects and add value, by giving them to look at same topic from another perspectives. Student 3 agreed, stating:

The essential way my experience of the digital system has evolved my learning is by encouraging cooperative practices. When instructors and students cooperate among themselves and/or between groups, it delivers more possibility to consider learning materials and study topics from different perspectives and to find more learning styles.

Student also painted that digital learning management system provides a better and new communication experience with users. Students believed that the digital systems open more places for bi-directional communication and collaboration with their users (instructors, administrators and students), as users can rate different recommended courses based on their experiences, which is helpful for all users they use the digital learning management system. With digital learning management systems, students should be more confident about the efficacy of the topic to their special study area. There is an advantage for students as they become more expert and aware when they keep using the digital learning management system continuously. For instance, student 3 pointed:

The digital system offers a better experience in relation to the communication pathways between users (instructors, administrators and students). It is more meaningful as the instructors can make recommendations to use learning topics and the students can provide feedback, and even provide their own recommendations if they want. This assistances to involve the students in the education process.

Students' Perceptions on the IT Infrastructure of Using the Digital Learning Management System

From the interviews, it was clear that the digital learning management system is still not fully utilised by users (instructors, administrators and students). According to student 2:

We know that most of students still do not realise the full capacity of the digital learning management system.

Student 4 agreed with student 2, saying:

Still we need large efforts to get users (instructors, administrators and students) use the digital learning management system frequently.

Nevertheless, although the digital learning management system is in its early stages of adoption, some users (instructors, administrators and students) demonstrated sound knowledge of the system and held positive perceptions about the importance of implementing the system. The interviewees stressed the importance of adopting innovative systems to deliver high quality educational services to users (instructors, administrators and students). For instance, student 3 stated:

The university management is trying to increase its information technology infrastructure to provide better education quality to the users. To be competitive, you must have a good quality of IT infrastructure and we always try hard to make the IT services accessible for everyone, and I think the university management is supporting us to present innovative service to both users (instructors, administrators and students).

Student 2, who is one of e-learning user, concurred, and highlighted the importance of the digital learning management system for connecting users (instructors, administrators and students) in a virtual community infrastructure, saying:

The university uses the digital learning management system to help students, instructors, etc. choose and use quality content of IT infrastructure. It is being used to create an e-university environment whereby instructors and students can be better connected with each other and also the global learning community infrastructure.

Similarly, student 3 showed that he had knowledge of the features of the digital learning management system. He mentioned some of these features of DLMS, and linked them to students' learning performance:

The digital learning management system combines content-based filtering and learner ratings to provide recommendations on learning materials. It gives me an easier way to upload documents related to the lecture like guidelines. The aim at the university is to increase the students' learning performance, and the system used at the university I think it combines some very useful platforms.

Moreover, digital learning management system provides students with personalised content based on their needs, which enables them to make choices without prior experience of the alternatives, and it is noticeably required to reduce the information overload. Students 4 and 5 explicitly noted this, stating:

The university is using the learning system to provide instructors and students with better quality digital learning platforms. These types of systems help to personalise the information retrieval and management process. The university is aiming to deliver a better infrastructure tool to help personalise the education experience.

Nonetheless, the implementation of the digital learning management system was challenging and required much effort in IT infrastructure. The concept itself is still new in the education domain. Additionally, users (instructors, administrators and students) were unfamiliar with the digital learning management system, which makes them perceive it as a complex technology. Student 1 clarified:

I would like to mention that the implementation process of the digital learning management system was not an easy task. We faced many challenges including the old IT infrastructure, the unfamiliarity of our users with the system and the complexity of the concept itself.

Moreover, students indicated that the university management needs to provide a mandatory adequate training programmes on the topic especially for the new instructors' and students'. In this regard, students2, 3 and 5 mentioned:

We believe it's really high important to train students and instructors on the digital learning management system to fully utilise its valuable services, and it should be a mandatory for both users (instructors, administrators and students) and especially for new users (instructors, administrators and students).

Students' Perceptions on the Jordanian Cultural of Using the Digital Learning Management System

Cultural factors affect the use of DLMS tools in Jordanian universities. The unique culture in Jordan is a very important factor that influences the use of DLMSs in different ways, and this research focuses on this factor through perceived use and perceived ease of use. According to Cho and Berge (2002), the most influential factors regarding the adoption and deployment of a DLMS are the culture and norms of those working in higher education faculties. Therefore, pedagogical issues and the lack of technology professional training are affecting the acceptance of a DLMS.

It was reported, that the university management were aware of the cultural issues. However, as technical people, it is evident that their focus was on the system quality, and little attention has been paid to the Jordanian culture. Interviewees mentioned culture and its dimensions several times during interviews, from different perspectives. For example, student 1 mentioned Jordanian culture and how the culture affect using digital learning management system at Jordanian universities when he said:

Jordanian culture affect using digital learning management system (DLMS) tool in both side (positive and negative), and not only for DLMS tool, it can affect any new application to use. The culture is a main factor effect using DLMS tool in the university, and it determines the acceptance of using DLMS tool.

Student 4 mentioned cultural from another perspective, when she noted the relationship between culture and age:

Most of the old fashion users they lost desire to use a new software and that maybe because the age, or the way that they learned. On the other hand, the fresh users (instructors, administrators and students) are so excited to learn and use new software's especially if that software helps them in their daily works.

As mentioned earlier in this section, the main focus of interviewees was on the acceptance of using digital learning management system in higher education sector at Jordanian universities. The implementation of the digital learning management system has some difficulties and required much effort. As for accessibility, student 5 stated:

I do not know if the cultural implications of using a digital learning management system software is a problem or that the problem is that some users are rickety to use digital learning management system, it's very difficult to say. In my opinion, there is no problem from students wise to use the DLMS software but it should be driven by management, like the assessments, material, assignments and exams can be online. The problem here is the cheating, and that's not for specific culture only, it can be anywhere. That's why the main exams are still paper based.

Student 4 indicated that the students prefer using social media to communicate with instructors and with themselves instead of digital system. This is due to constant use of my social media so some users prefer to use social media instead of any other system, and also for the ease of use of social media, especially since our existing digital learning system does not help users to easily use it:

From my opinion, I don't think the culture is affecting using digital learning management system, because in these days most of the students can use the social media to share their information, and they prefer to use social media instead of other system.

Student 7 also highlighted the role of culture in predicting the usage of the digital learning management system. Most of new and novel IT technologies are developed and designed in developed countries. However, it was evident in the literature that differences in cultures systematically influence whether and for what reasons users adopt—or fail to adopt—new technologies (Al-Hujran, Al-Debei, Chatfield, & Migdadi, 2015; Steers, Meyer, & Sanchez-Runde, 2008). The culture must be considered when designing and developing new systems. Student 7 said:

Most of the digital learning management systems are developed and designed in the Western world. Developers and designers usually forget to take the differences in culture into consideration. This is become as a serious matter that needs to be taken into consideration when designing and implementing emerging technologies in our country.

Students' Perceptions on Perceived Usefulness of the Digital Learning Management System

Perceived Usefulness (PU) affect directly the acceptance of technology. Indeed, if the user perceives the digital learning management system to be useful in terms of increase or improvement in work productivity, then the user will have a favorable perception of accepting the digital learning management system. Institutions of higher education around the globe implemented digital learning management systems as a channel to effective deliver educational material to users. The use of digital learning management systems can be considered as a gain to develop teaching and learning processes (Hsbollah & Idris, 2009). In this research, it was revealed that perceived usefulness of the digital learning management system was known by students'. Most interviewees admitted sufficient knowledge of the perceived usefulness of the system. In this context, student 1 believed that the digital learning management system would help both users (instructors, administrators and students), saying:

I know that a lot of students find the system useful so I suppose it works for them. The university students would like to have a centralised platform with all the information needed to locate people or course materials. I believe that the students think it helps them.

Student 4 agreed with his colleague, saying:

It is not easy to argue against the fact that technology is fundamental for learning and teaching in the new world. Student needs to be able to manage information and learning materials properly and instructor wants to be able to apply the latest teaching techniques. Most of universities have digital learning platforms, and digital systems are becoming more and more important.

Moreover, student 5 indicates the value of the digital learning management system compared with the traditional learning systems, commenting:

Digital learning management system makes our daily work easier, instead of printing and talk to each one in the classes, it gives us more flexibility to communication with other. We can do our daily works by using DLMS software processes in efficient time (save time). We can save the lecture time instead of paper work.

According to the interviews, students were also fully aware of the personalisation features of the digital learning management system, such as collaborative filtering and rating. Student 3 noted that:

From my side, I use digital learning management system software in my daily base and there are many benefit for me as a student. I uploaded and downloaded all my assignments, guidelines, materials and study plans.

Similarly, student 7 agreed on the role of the digital learning management system for personalising the educational materials, stating:

These types of software's help to personalise the information retrieval and management process. The university is aiming to offer a tool to help personalise the education experience.

The student also advised of the usefulness of the digital system to build a collaborative learning environment. Student 6 mentioned:

A digital learning management system is becoming an important tool. The more that the system supports users to identify interesting content, the more it will play a key role in learning and teaching. As the filtering systems become more elaborate for identifying content and generating collaborative learning, students' will use them more and more.

Besides that, some users expected more from the system, and indicted that the implemented digital learning management system needs improvement. They recommended extra features to improve to the current system. Students 2, 4 and 6 provided examples of useful features:

We think the university management could improve the way of the digital learning management system is used. The way technology is advancing at the moment, there are always new systems to embed within the IT infrastructure framework, such as examination systems, digital learning management systems and learner directory platforms. We would like to see the university continue to grow the system.

Students' Perceptions on Perceived Ease of Use of the Digital Learning Management System

Perceived ease of use concurrently pretended a strong direct effect on behavioural to use any new technologies, and previous research has found a positive relationship between PEOU and continuance usage. Thus, it is essential for designer and developer to design and develop an easy to use tool, which would lead to better user engagement and motivation. Although the system reduces users' efforts by showing them personalised material according to their needs, student presented real concern about the complexity of the digital learning management system. For instance, student 4 stated:

The feedback from students regarding the DLMS, I can tell the system is complicated for the new user and they need orientation workshops and training to assist them to react with the system. This exemplifies a real concern for me.

To bypass this essential issue, he proposed that the institute needs to provide orientation workshops and training programmes especially for the new users' on the system. Student 3, 5 & 6 agreed on the complexity of the digital learning management system for new users', they seeing it as a new system that was rarely used by users':

The digital learning management system is new technology adopted in the high education field and many users' may not be familiar with it yet. It's not easy to ask users' to use advanced technology without adequate knowledge.

Student 7 highlighted some features in using DLMS in daily base. Saving time and effort are an important feature for all the system users'. It makes them (users') happy and comfortable to use it in any time. Student 5 stated:

... This tool is easy to use, and it makes my daily job easier. When I uploaded the assignments to DLMS tool, this will make interaction easier to access their need, so student don't have to visit instructors in the office and asking them for a copy of anything like assignments, and that makes instructors and students happy to use in any time.

Students' Perceptions on Acceptance and Continuance Usage of the Digital Learning Management System

It was obvious that the usage regularity of the digital learning management system was the ultimate goal of university management. During the interviews, students frequently commented that the value of implementing new system will not be known without usage regularity of the system by users' (instructors, administrators and students). Some Jordanian universities invested extensive finances into deploying the digital system to improve users' (instructors, administrators and students) education process. Nevertheless, higher university management assumed that the return on this investment would be the effective use of the digital system. Student 1 stated:

In theory, the value of the digital system comes from the usage regularity of the system by both users' (educators and learners). In another words, the system that becomes enhanced the more people are using it because this means there is more data go into the system to direct the recommendation. If users (instructors) can use platforms to store and deliver information, and if users (students) can access what they need to for the course they are needing, then it has got to make a contribution to more effective learning.

University management indicated that they understand that the digital learning management system needs to store more contents and learning materials to work efficiently and effectively. If instructors and students do not effectively involve with the system, the usefulness of the system will be restricted. Thus, university management thought often about how to rise the usage regularity by both instructors and students to fully utilise the valuable facilities provided by the digital system. Student 2 noted:

I consider it's highly significant to train instructors and students on the digital learning management system to fully utilise its valuable facilities. We stated that the majority of users still do not understand the full capacity of the digital system. The challenge is to get more instructors and students to use the system regularly in order to recognise its benefits for efficient and effective learning.

To rise the usage levels of the digital learning management system, users (instructors, administrators and students) must perceive its ease of use, usefulness and quality. Improved user experience by training and workshops was also an important factor. As regards the user experience and the quality, student 4 stated:

The existing digital system model is good, but there is always need to improve IT infrastructure and cultural behaviour to rise usage knowledge levels.

SOLUTIONS AND RECOMMENDATIONS

DLMS's are managed by the administrators to restrict access to some or all documents stored (depends on the permissions for each user). However, in some cases the administrators can override the safeguard to access information in order to provide the best services. It is particularly important that Jordanian universities use one learning system for culturally and linguistically diverse. This also requires everyone to have access to smart phones, laptop and internet connections. On the other hand, it is essential for the users (instructors, administrators and students) to also embrace, access and manage the privacy of their profile's to enhance their practice and provide positive outcome to the daily works.

The challenge is to strike a balance between the qualities of using and managing the online digital learning management system by the users is very important in partnership with each other's. Following recommendations can be taken to improve using of digital learning management system as well as e-learning so that users can use 'DLMS' to empower them for their goal benefit in best and professional way:

- Promoting using digital learning management system is essential, as DLMS facilitates and motivates users to self-manage and empower themselves that determine their daily processes with other users or with themselves;
- It is essential for users to not just have access, know how to use their digital learning system records, but foremost how to use the basics computer skills, as a minimum requirement. In each university at Jordan has a specialised computer centre can be run one semester digital/computer literacy units to teach how to use the computer and internet search engine skills to users with low-computer literacy and non-English speaking background;
- All key stakeholders such as the Ministry of Higher Education at Jordan, Jordanian university management (public and private) must work together for the adoption, safety, security, privacy of the digital learning management system, for beneficial usage of electronic educational system to empower the users to manage themselves and to improve using DLMS;
- It's obvious that DLMS must be improved and changed to suit users. Many users have complained about the complexity of use the digital learning management system due to the difficulty of accessing the information. Further, they propose improving the DLMS system through improving the notifications system, so they can access and know any updates on the DLMS instead of using unprofessional tools such as social media between each other.

FUTURE RESEARCH DIRECTIONS

Future research could collect interview data with the instructors and the administrators to test the validity of the qualitative findings, followed by quantitative survey with the users' (instructors', students' and administrators'). Studies can also survey users satisfaction with the use of 'DLMS' by purposeful sampling of diverse population belonging to different demographic groups, education, gender characteristics and rural urban setting, due to digital divide. Such as youth, middle age. The hypothesised relationship between digital literacy, improves communication and enhances using DLMA can be explored and empirically tested with different groups of people in developed countries such as Australia, USA, UK…

CONCLUSION

To sum up, university management fully understand that digital system use and continued use are significant factors for the fruitful implementing of the digital learning management system. Users should use the digital system efficiently and effectively to get the fully value and advantages of system. Nevertheless, to rise up usage levels, users (instructors, administrators and students) need to realise the advantages of using the digital system. This is believed to be a respectable indication, as university management perception was that increased ease of use, usefulness and quality of the digital system would lead to advanced usage by instructors and students.

Case study (qualitative analysis) showed that university management's main objective in deploying the digital learning management system was to deliver better quality education to users (instructors, administrators and students). University management is fully recognise the expected benefits of such a system. Depend on interviews, students clearly showed the value of using the digital learning management system in terms of suggesting personalised contents and learning materials according to users' need and preferences, building a digital collaborative learning environment, saving money and time, which may stimulate collaboration among users (instructors, administrators and students) and conclusively evolve higher learning efficiency and effectiveness of users.

Universities management notified a number of challenges facing the application and use of the digital learning management system, which are the limited use of the digital system by users (instructors, administrators and students), some complexity of the digital system and the inelastic to satisfy and support users' needs.

Interviewers (students) showed a serious intention to raise the usage level of the digital system as to raise the significance of the system for users (instructors, administrators and students). Users' believed that the system significance will not be recognised without efficiently and effectively using it. Nevertheless, to encourage the acceptance process of DMLS, each university management is required to conduct regular orientation programmes and awareness campaigns especially for the fresh users, to clarify the expected features of the digital system. Furthermore, the university management should offer tutorials and training to increase the user experience with the digital system.

In summary, the university management recognised that the developed and increased of IT infrastructure, cultural, ease of use and usefulness would lead to better acceptance and usage by instructors, administrators and students. Hence, it is substantial for the university management to think seriously about developing and implementing a strategy and action plan to meet these strategic goals.

REFERENCES

Abbad, M. M., Morris, D., & De Nahlik, C. (2009). Looking under the bonnet: Factors affecting student adoption of e-learning systems in Jordan. *The International Review of Research in Open and Distributed Learning*, *10*(2). doi:10.19173/irrodl.v10i2.596

Abdullateef, B. N., Elias, N. F., Mohamed, H., Zaidan, A., & Zaidan, B. (2016). An evaluation and selection problems of OSS-LMS packages. *SpringerPlus*, *5*(1), 1. doi:10.118640064-016-1828-y PMID:27064567

Adams, D. A., Nelson, R. R., & Todd, P. A. (1992). Perceived usefulness, ease of use, and usage of information technology: A replication. *Management Information Systems Quarterly*, *16*(2), 227–247. doi:10.2307/249577

Ahmad, S. A., Chinade, U. B., Gambaki, A. M., Ibrahim, S., & Ala, N. A. (2012). The need for MOODLE as a learning management system in Nigerian Universities: Digesting University Utara Malaysia Learning Zone as a case study. *Academic Research International*, *2*(3), 444.

Al Amoush, A. B., & Sandhu, K. (2019). *A New Model for Acceptance of Analytics in Learning Management Systems at Jordanian Universities (JLMS). In Modern Technologies for Teaching and Learning in Socio-Humanitarian Disciplines* (pp. 138–161). IGI Global.

Al-Dmour, R. (2014). *An integration model for identifying the determinants of the adoption and implementation level of HRIS applications and Its effectiveness in business organisations in Jordan* (Doctor of Philosophy). Brunel University. Retrieved from http://bura.brunel.ac.uk/handle/2438/9222

Al-Hujran, O., Al-Debei, M. M., Chatfield, A., & Migdadi, M. (2015). The imperative of influencing citizen attitude toward e-government adoption and use. *Computers in Human Behavior, 53*, 189–203. doi:10.1016/j.chb.2015.06.025

Al Musawi, A., Ambusaidi, A., Al-Balushi, S., & Al-Balushi, K. (2015). Effectiveness of E-Lab Use in Science Teaching at the Omani Schools. *TOJET: The Turkish Online Journal of Educational Technology, 14*(1).

Al-Shaikh, F. N. (2003). The practical reality theory and business ethics in non-Western context: Evidence from Jordan. *Journal of Management Development, 22*(8), 679–693. doi:10.1108/02621710310487855

Al-Shboul, M. (2011). Potential Use of Course Management Systems in Higher Education Institutions in Jordan. *Online Submission, 8*(2), 220–232.

Al-Shboul, M. (2013). The Level of E-Learning Integration at the University of Jordan: Challenges and Opportunities. *International Education Studies, 6*(4). doi:10.5539/ies.v6n4p93

Al-Shboul, M. A., & Alsmadi, I. (2010). Challenges of Utilizing E-Learning Systems in Public Universities in Jordan. *iJET, 5*(1), 4-10.

Al-Zoubi, S. I., & Ali, M. (2019). *The Bearing of Culture upon Intention to Utilize D-learning Amongst Jordanian University Students: Modernizing with Emerging Technologies.* Paper presented at the International Conference for Emerging Technologies in Computing. 10.1007/978-3-030-23943-5_21

Almarabeh, T. (2014). Students' Perceptions of E-learning at the University of Jordan. *iJET, 9*(3), 31-35.

Alnsour, A., Muhsen, Z., Dababnah, M., Eljinini, M. A., & Barhoum, K. A. (2011). Implementing Moodle as a Tool to develop the Isra University e-learn system. *IJCSNS International Journal of Computer Science and Network Security, 11*, 120–124.

AlQudah, A. A. (2014). Accepting Moodle by academic staff at the University of Jordan: Applying and extending TAM in technical support factors. *European Scientific Journal, 10*(18).

Arguel, A., Lockyer, L., Kennedy, G., Lodge, J. M., & Pachman, M. (2019). Seeking optimal confusion: A review on epistemic emotion management in interactive digital learning environments. *Interactive Learning Environments, 27*(2), 200–210. doi:10.1080/10494820.2018.1457544

Atoum, I., Otoom, A., & Ali, A. A. (2017). Holistic Cyber Security Implementation Frameworks: A Case Study of Jordan. *International Journal of Information. Business and Management, 9*(1), 108.

Babić, S. (2012). Factors that influence academic teacher's acceptance of e-learning technology in blended learning environment. *E-Learning-Organizational Infrastructure and Tools for Specific Areas*, 3-18.

Beach, L. R., & Mitchell, T. R. (1978). A contingency model for the selection of decision strategies. *Academy of Management Review, 3*(3), 439–449. doi:10.5465/amr.1978.4305717

Cho, S. K., & Berge, Z. L. (2002). Overcoming barriers to distance training and education. *USDLA Journal, 16*(1), 16–34.

Creswell, J. W. (2013). *Research design: Qualitative, quantitative, and mixed methods approaches.* Sage Publications.

Davis, F. D. (1989). Perceived usefulness, perceived ease of use, and user acceptance of information technology. *Management Information Systems Quarterly*, *13*(3), 319–340. doi:10.2307/249008

Gefen, D., & Straub, D. W. (1997). Gender differences in the perception and use of e-mail: An extension to the technology acceptance model. *Management Information Systems Quarterly*, *21*(4), 389–400. doi:10.2307/249720

Gupta, S. K., & Rao, D. (2018). A case study on contemporary water management innovation (CWMI) in sustainable agriculture: Farmers joined hands for mutual survival and prosperity: The case of Kummarvandlapalli. *IJCS*, *6*(6), 2283–2287.

Hofstede, G. (1983). National cultures in four dimensions: A research-based theory of cultural differences among nations. *International Studies of Management & Organization*, *13*(1-2), 46–74. doi:10.1080/00208825.1983.11656358

Hsbollah, H. M., & Idris, K. M. (2009). E-learning adoption: The role of relative advantages, trialability and academic specialisation. *Campus-Wide Information Systems*, *26*(1), 54–70. doi:10.1108/10650740910921564

Igbaria, M., Zinatelli, N., Cragg, P., & Cavaye, A. L. (1997). Personal computing acceptance factors in small firms: A structural equation model. *Management Information Systems Quarterly*, *21*(3), 279–305. doi:10.2307/249498

Kats, Y. (2010). *Learning Management System Technologies and Software Solutions for Online Teaching: Tools and Applications: Tools and Applications*. IGI Global.

Khwaldeh, S. M., Al-Hadid, I., Masa'deh, R. e., & Alrowwad, A. (2017). The Association between E-Services Web Portals Information Quality and ICT Competence in the Jordanian Universities. *Asian Social Science*, *13*(3), 156. doi:10.5539/ass.v13n3p156

McIntosh, J., & Torres, M. I. (2014). *Learning Management Systems: Revisiting Learning Management Systems at the University Level*. The University of Tampa.

Mkhize, P., Mtsweni, E. S., & Buthelezi, P. (2016). Diffusion of Innovations Approach to the Evaluation of Learning Management System Usage in an Open Distance Learning Institution. *The International Review of Research in Open and Distributed Learning*, *17*(3). doi:10.19173/irrodl.v17i3.2191

Mutlag, A. A., Ghani, M. K. A., Arunkumar, N., Mohamed, M. A., & Mohd, O. (2019). Enabling technologies for fog computing in healthcare IoT systems. *Future Generation Computer Systems*, *90*, 62–78. doi:10.1016/j.future.2018.07.049

Orr, G. (2003). *Diffusion of innovations*. Everett Rogers.

Phillipo, J., & Krongard, S. (2012). *Learning Management System*. LMS.

Potter, L. E., & Thompson, A. (2019). Engaging with STEM Students: Successes and Challenges in Course Design. *Blended Learning Designs in STEM Higher Education*, 231–248.

Rank, u. U. (2019). *Jordanian University Ranking 2019*. Retrieved from https://www.4icu.org/jo/

Ridder, H.-G. (2017). The theory contribution of case study research designs. *Business Research, 10*(2), 281–305. doi:10.100740685-017-0045-z

Rogers, E. (1995). *Diffusion of Innovations*. The Free Press.

Rowley, J. (2002). Using case studies in research. *Management Research News, 25*(1), 16–27. doi:10.1108/01409170210782990

Saadé, R., & Bahli, B. (2005). The impact of cognitive absorption on perceived usefulness and perceived ease of use in on-line learning: An extension of the technology acceptance model. *Information & Management, 42*(2), 317–327. doi:10.1016/j.im.2003.12.013

Samak, A., & Tawfik, Z. (2017). *Exploration of Jordanian English Language Teachers' Attitudes*. Skills, and Access as Indicator of Information and Communication Technology Integration in Jordan.

Steers, R. M., Meyer, A. D., & Sanchez-Runde, C. J. (2008). National culture and the adoption of new technologies. *Journal of World Business, 43*(3), 255–260. doi:10.1016/j.jwb.2008.03.007

Szajna, B. (1996). Empirical evaluation of the revised technology acceptance model. *Management Science, 42*(1), 85–92. doi:10.1287/mnsc.42.1.85

Unwin, T., Kleessen, B., Hollow, D., Williams, J. B., Oloo, L. M., Alwala, J., . . . Muianga, X. (2010). Digital learning management systems in Africa: myths and realities. *Open Learning: The Journal of Open, Distance and e-Learning, 25*(1), 5-23.

Varis, T., & Al-Agtash, S. (2008). *Ubiquitous ICT for sustainable education and cultural literacy*. Citeseer.

Venkatesh, V. (1999). Creation of favorable user perceptions: Exploring the role of intrinsic motivation. *Management Information Systems Quarterly, 23*(2), 239–260. doi:10.2307/249753

Venkatesh, V., & Davis, F. D. (2000). A theoretical extension of the technology acceptance model: Four longitudinal field studies. *Management Science, 46*(2), 186–204. doi:10.1287/mnsc.46.2.186.11926

Williams, P. (2002). The learning web: The development, implementation and evaluation of internet-based undergraduate materials for the teaching of key skills. *Active Learning in Higher Education, 3*(1), 40–53. doi:10.1177/1469787402003001004

Wimpenny, K., Adefila, A., & DeWinter, A. (2018). *Jordan Opportunity for Virtual Innovative Teaching and Learning: A Needs Analysis Report Contextualising the State of the Art in International Online Teaching and Learning, with Particular Attention to the Jordanian Case*. Academic Press.

Yin, R. K. (1981). The case study crisis: Some answers. *Administrative Science Quarterly, 26*(1), 58–65. doi:10.2307/2392599

Yin, R. K. (2012). A (very) brief refresher on the case study method. *Applications of Case Study Research*, 3-20.

Yin, R. K. (2015). *Qualitative research from start to finish*. Guilford Publications.

ADDITIONAL READING

Al Amoush, A. B., & Sandhu, K. (2018b). Learning Management Systems in Jordan Context. Australasian Journal of Business. *Social Science and Information Technology*, *4*(2), 46–54.

Al Amoush, A. B., & Sandhu, K. (2019a). *Discovery of New Knowledge for an LMS at Jordanian Universities Open and Social Learning in Impact Communities and Smart Territories* (pp. 187–214). IGI Global.

Al Amoush, A. B., & Sandhu, K. (2019b). *LMS Tools and Data Analysis Approaches: Similarities and Differences Educational and Social Dimensions of Digital Transformation in Organizations* (pp. 65–76). IGI Global. doi:10.4018/978-1-5225-6261-0.ch004

Al Amoush, A. B., & Sandhu, K. (2019c). *A New Model for Acceptance of Analytics in Learning Management Systems at Jordanian Universities (JLMS) Modern Technologies for Teaching and Learning in Socio-Humanitarian Disciplines* (pp. 138–161). IGI Global.

Al Amoush, A. B., & Sandhu, K. (2020). *A New Paradigm for Acceptance of Analytics in Learning Management Systems at Jordanian Universities (JLMS) Revolutionizing Education in the Age of AI and Machine Learning* (pp. 173–195). IGI Global.

KEY TERMS AND DEFINITIONS

Acceptance of a DLMS: The perceived usefulness and perceived ease of use of a DLMS under a given behaviour for continued use of DLMSs in Jordanian universities.

DLMS: Digital learning management systems (DLMSs) are a necessary educational tools for learning activities (Al Amoush & Sandhu, 2019).

Information Technology: The technology involving the development, maintenance, and use of computer systems, software, and networks for the processing and distribution of data (Mutlag, Ghani, Arunkumar, Mohamed, & Mohd, 2019).

IT Infrastructure: The availability of technology in the country in general, and in universities in particular, such Internet connections, computers and DLMS tools (AlQudah, 2014).

Jordanian Culture: The unique culture in Jordan is a very important factor that influences the use of DLMSs in different ways, and this research will focus on this factor through perceived use.

Perceived Ease of Use: Perceived ease of use refers to the degree to which a person believes that using a particular system would be free of effort (Davis, 1989, p. 320).

Perceived Usefulness: The degree to which the user believes that using the DLMS would improve their learning performance (Davis, 1989).

Technology Acceptance Model (TAM): It has become well-established as a robust, powerful, and parsimonious model for predicting user acceptance (Venkatesh & Davis, 2000, p. 19).

Chapter 4
Innovations in Digital Banking Service Brand Equity and Millennial Consumerism

Subhankar Das
https://orcid.org/0000-0001-7344-4583
Duy Tan University, Vietnam

ABSTRACT

In the goods industry, the product is considered the primary brand with various attributes. However, in the case of the services industry, the company itself is a primary brand. This chapter is based upon primary research of the services (banking) sector as a case of service branding with services extended marketing mix variables. A model has been developed to identify the impact of services extended marketing variables on customer-based brand equity. Two components of customer-based brand have been given consideration such as brand awareness and brand association. For this purpose, a structured questionnaire was prepared, and a survey was conducted on 400 respondents, and a structural equation model has been applied.

INTRODUCTION

Brand equity can be studied with the help of three different aspects. i.e. Cognitive Psychology Perspective, Economics Perspective & Financial Perspective. Cognitive Psychology Perspective is related with customer response to brand's marketing mix (Aaker 1991, Keller 1993). Customers who have more considerable brand associations, will produce more significant marketing mix response. Economics Perspective is considered as increased utility that a brand name gives to a product. Brand name which played vital role in identifying the quality of the product and it was related with perceived firm investment and quality, directly lead to reduce the information cost for the customer. Hence it increased utility. Financial Perspective is a measure that was related with firm market value subtracting the tangible asset value (Simon & Sullivan, 1993).

DOI: 10.4018/978-1-7998-5175-2.ch004

For every organization, brand name has become very important in today's competitive era. A brand can simply be termed as a unique identity of a product or service offered by a particular organization. It enables both, the organization as well as the consumer to differentiate between similar products or services offered by competitors. However, in light of competition, brand name is not just a unique identity. It has assumed a broader meaning. According to Keller, a brand, which is powerful, will be able to create a meaningful image in consumers' mind as compared to a weaker brand. A strong brand image and powerful reputation will be able to enhance the differentiation capability of a product or service and it will have a positive influence on the buying behavior of consumers. Further, branding is important for all kinds of products and services. Branding of an offering in consumer markets could result in enhancing the financial performance and competitive position of a firm. Brand can be defined as a bundle of functional, economic and psychological benefits for the end user. According to the American Marketing Association (AMA), brand is a name, term, sign, symbol, or design, or a combination of them which is intended to identify the goods or services of one seller or a group of sellers and to differentiate them from those of competitors. Brand equity refers to the marketing effects and outcomes that build up to a good or service with its brand name. The power of brand equity can be seen in the form of consumers' willingness to pay a premium price for a preferred brand in comparison to others. Not only that, brand equity is reflected in the way consumers recommend it to their peers. The domain of brand relationships is extremely complex. There are numerous types of brand relationships and multiple dimensions that characterize them. They involve varying types and intensities of emotions and normative processes. They vary in the motivations that drive them, the strength of the connection bonding the consumer with the brand, and the role of various meaning makers in creating, establishing, and expanding the brand's relationship to the self. Moreover, the psychological and behavioral outcomes of brand relationships are also numerous and complex. When customers are emotionally attached to a brand (brand feeling), they go on to create strong association with the brand. The quality of the services of a brand, its credibility, and its presence in the choice set of customers (together what is called Brand Judgment) also lead to customers' strong association with a brand. On the other hand, some of the building blocks of the CBBE model were not found to be strongly contributing for the creation of brand association in the banking sector of Bangladesh. Brand recognition and brand recall (together called brand salience) were found not contributing significantly in creating strong association with the brand. Banking institutions may place less emphasis on them in creating brand awareness. As we know the development of brand is the process which includes identity, meaning, response and relationship but if helps to attachment of consumers towards brand. The studies on brand relationship reveal that strong brand relationship is important factor for promoting tolerance in the face of negative brand information. Past research shows that if marketers wants to convert negative brand information to positive then consumer brand relationship is the best competent to transform this information. Consumer viewed brand as a relationship partner. There is different way to achieve this understanding of consumers about brand, one way is to brand are animated, humanized or personalized. She also explained the brand animated process through which the spirit of past or present other, by using brand-person associations, and through a complete anthropomorphising of the brand. Brand relationship also depends on the consumers lived experience, this define level of brand relationship. These relationships offer meanings to the consumer, some being functional and utilitarian, while others are psychological or emotional.

Brand Equity Perspective of the Study

This study focuses on the Customer based brand equity (CBBE). Farquhar (1989) defined Brand equity as "The added value with which a given brand endows a product" According to Lassar, Mittal, and Sharma (1995), brand equity has been examined from a financial perspective. Keller (1993) defined the brand equity in terms of customer based perspective. Brand equity has also been defined as "the enhancement in the perceived utility and desirability a brand name confers on a product" (Lassar, 1995).

Lassar (1995) have given five dimension of brand equity: performance, value, social image, trustworthiness, and commitment. Aaker (1996) proposed brand equity Ten point for measuring brand equity across market and products. And these were structured by four dimensions of brand equity (a) loyalty (b) perceived quality (c) awareness (d) association.

Keller (1993) introduced new model for measuring customer based brand equity. The model was based upon the premises of "that the power of a brand lies in what customers have learned, felt, seen and heard about the brand as a result of their experiences over time". Mainly the model was consisted of two dimensions: brand awareness and brand image. Brand awareness is related with brand recognition means "consumer's ability to confirm prior exposure to the brand when given a brand as a cue" and brand recall refers to how frequently a brand can be retrieved from the memory of the consumer when different product category is given to them.

The changing trend towards embracing marketing philosophy and the extent of the banks' performance level in response to changing expectations of customers. Theoretical issues relating marketing, customer philosophy, financial marketing, customer loyalty, satisfaction, and brand equity were explored to establish the key performance variables and the existing relationships amongst them (Alao, A. E., Diyaolu, G. O., & Afuape, A. M. (2014).

Attitude dimension underlying the variable Brand equity of Spanish banks suffered more influence than the Awareness dimension. Furthermore, it was found that the country of origin image positively influences the brand equity of Spanish banks. The technical aspects, in general, influence more than friendly aspects, thus implying a direction for the Spain brand development strategy focused on these aspects Prado, M. A., & Giraldi, J. D. M. E. (2015).

REVIEW OF LITERATURE

The term brand equity can be studied from two different perspectives i.e. financial and customer based. The first perspective is related with the financial asset value that creates to the business, but in this study, there will be no focus on financial perspective. The second perspective is customer baser based, in which customer response to brand name is evaluated. (Lassar,1995). Brand equity is considered as value which the consumer associates with the brand. (Aaker 1991). Aaker has developed the conceptual framework for measuring customer based brand equity with the help of four dimensions: Brand awareness, brand loyalty, perceived quality of brand and brand associations. Brand awareness includes whether the organization is able to create that position which may take place position of the product on the top of mind. Brand awareness also represents customer ability to identify a brand in their memory, and this concept is considered as brand recall. (Aaker, 1991). Besides this Aaker and Keller also identified some of the other important aspects in brand awareness: brand dominance, brand knowledge and brand opinion. (Aaker, 1991) (Keller,1996). Brand knowledge and brand opinion can be used to explore the concept of brand recall. (Keller,1993) stated that brand recognition is most important aspect of brand awareness and customer based brand equity occurs when the customer is fully aware about the product and holds some strong association in the memory. Brand recall refers to when consumer can correctly generate the brand from memory. The importance of brand recognition and brand recall is totally dependent upon the decision taken by the customer at the time of purchase. (Keller, 1993) Brand loyalty is considered as one of the important concept of brand equity. Aaker, (1991) defined loyalty the attachment that a customer has to a brand. Behavioural loyalty is directly linked with consumer behaviour in market place. Cognitive loyalty comes into mind of the customer when the actual purchase is made. The "loyalty" a commitment from the consumer to purchase again product near the future, despite situational influences and marketing efforts that could change the mindset of the customer. The loyal customer is one whose purchase decision is insensitive to pricing and shows their loyalty toward the organization.

Perceived quality is also one of the most important component of brand equity (Aaker,1991) perceived quality does not mean only the actual quality of the product but more related with evaluation parameters assumes by the consumer to the product quality (Zeithaml, 1988). Perceived quality also deals with customer perception of the brand of total quality. The combination of quality of service and product is crucial in determining the brand equity. Zeithmal (1988) has broken down the concept into two parts i.e. Intrinsic attributes and Extrinsic attributes. Intrinsic attributes are related with the physical attributes of the product and extrinsic attributes is related with the indispensable branding attributes such as brand name, quality, stamp of quality etc. Brand association is also one of the most integral as well as accepted component of brand equity. Association represents the basis for purchase as well as brand loyalty. (Aaker, 1991, 1992). Brand association is related with product related thoughts, feelings perception, images, beliefs, attitude etc (Keller, 2006). It has categorized brand association into two categories such as product association and organization association. Product association includes functional as well as non-functional attributes (intangible attributes) are as follows: social image, perceived value, trustworthiness, differentiation, country of origin. Organization association includes corporate ability association, corporate social responsibility etc.

The literature review on customer brand equity dimensions and services marketing mix elements in banking sector was carried out in Table 1.

RESEARCH METHODOLOGY

Objective of the Study

The primary objectives of the study is as follows; To investigate the Relationship between Extended services marketing mix 3P's: People, Process and Physical Evidence and customer based brand equity components: Brand Awareness and Brand Association in banking sector.

Design of Survey Constructs and Items

For measuring Customer based brand equity, 22 items were included under different constructs. Such as Brand Association, Brand Awareness, People, Process, Physical Evidence and construct was evaluated on Five point Likert scale Such as Highly Dissatisfied, Dissatisfied, Somewhat satisfied, Satisfied and Highly Satisfied.

Table 1. Reviews related to brand equity dimension

Sl.No.	Researcher	Brand Equity Dimension Given
1	**Makasi (2015)**	Brand awareness, brand loyalty, brand association and perceived quality, Brand Assets. This research has managed to extend the body of knowledge on brand equity by exploring the role of advertising.
2	**Makasi (2014)**	Brand awareness, brand loyalty, brand association and perceived quality. He concludes rebranding has positive effects on consumers' perceptions and can be used as a marketing tool in order gain competitive advantage and has an impact on the financial performance of an organization.
3	**Dua (2013)**	Brand awareness, brand loyalty, brand association and perceived quality. Customer based brand equity dimensions in banking sector.
4	**Taylor (2007)**	Loyalty. The majority of research in marketing now represents loyalty as a multi-dimensional construct; however, agreement on whether it has two or three dimensions is lacking, and measurement of these dimensions has been inconsistent.
5	**Atilgan (2005)**	Brand awareness, brand loyalty, brand association and perceived quality. Examine the practicality and application of a customer-based brand equity model, based on Aaker's well-known conceptual framework of brand equity. Brand loyalty is the most influential dimension of brand equity. Weak support is found for the brand awareness and perceived quality dimensions.
6	**Yoo & Donthu (2001)**	(a) Brand loyalty (b) Perceived quality (c) Brand awareness (d) Brand associations. Little systematic research has been done to develop a scale to measure consumer-based brand equity. The authors report the results of a multistep study to develop and validate a multidimensional consumer-based brand equity scale (MBE) drawn from Aaker's and Keller's conceptualizations of brand equity.
7	**Mackay (2001)**	Brand awareness, brand recall and familiarity. Presents further empirical results on the convergent and predictive ability of a selection of consumer based brand equity measures. An underlying assumption in this study was that choice was an indicator of brand equity.Managers should have more confidence in selecting from a range of brand equity measures, many of which can be collected easily and at minimal cost. More empirical studies, however, need to be carried out in a range of different markets to assess the wider performance of these brand equity measures.
8	**Krishnan (2001)**	Services Branding. While the brand equity associated with tangible goods has received a great deal of attention in the literature, a basic understanding of the nature of brand equity for services has yet to emerge.
9	**Keller (1993)**	(a) Brand Awareness (b) Brand Image. Rather than taking the more traditional approach of measuring brand equity for accounting or strategic reasons, the approach taken here is concerned with optimizing brand equity through parsimonious manipulation of the marketing mix.
10	**Churchill (1979)**	Developed procedure for marketing constructs. A critical element in the evolution of a fundamental body of knowledge in marketing, as well as for improved marketing practice, is the development of better measures of the variables with which marketers work. In this article an approach is outlined by which this goal can be achieved and portions of the approach are illustrated in terms of a job satisfaction measure.

Table 2. Reviews related to different P's studied by researchers

Sl.No.	Researcher	Brand Equity Dimension Given
1	**Mohammadi (2016)**	Product, Price, Promotion, Distribution Marketing network is very much depending on 4Ps of marketing and it is the important structure of any company.
2	**Dmour (2013)**	Services Nature, Price, Distribution, promotion, Physical Evidence, processes The effect of services marketing mix elements on customer-based brand equity through empirical study of mobile telecommunication service recipients. It also aims to determine the influence of such elements on customer-based brand equity and to reveal which is the most influential.
3	**Das (2012)**	People, Process, Physical Evidence Effective service marketing is a complex activity that involves many different strategies, skills, tasks and activities. Customers perceive services in terms of quality of the service and how satisfied they are overall with their experiences. It will be easier for the marketers if they know what their present or potential customers think about their services in terms of the service specific 3Ps (People, Process, Physical Evidence). If the relationship between customer satisfaction and the customers' perception of the 3Ps can be identified, it would be much easier to close the providers' gaps described by the GAP Model of service marketing. Opinions of customers in and around Kolkata have been collected on some pre-defined variables linked with the 3Ps & statistical analysis has been used to identify key factors on which the customer satisfaction regarding the banking services depends. Thereafter a quantitative relationship among the key factors & customer satisfaction has been established to provide a guideline to close service providers' gap in the context of banking & financial service sector.
4	**Martensen (2003)**	The most successful companies today are said to have strong brands. But what is a strong brand? What makes a brand strong? How do we build a strong brand? This paper develops a customer-based brand equity model to help address these important questions. The developed model is a cause-and-effect model linking customer-brand relationships to rational and emotional brand associations, as well as rational and emotional brand evaluations. The customer-brand relationships are characterized by loyalty, based on both behaviour and attitude. As branding is a very complex concept, it is important to determine which of the many branding elements should be included in the model. This paper discusses why a given aspect is important for a brand's equity and which relations exist between the included variables from a theoretical perspective. The model provides insight into the creation of a brand's equity and can thus be used in the brand management process to achieve brand excellence.
5	**Wang (2009)**	Staff, Process, Service escape Explored relationships among resilience characteristics, background variables, and adjustment problem areas, and to gauge the effects of resilience and background variables on adjustment. Statistical analyses revealed that resilience characteristics were moderately associated with background variables, highly negatively correlated with adjustment problem areas, better correlated with adjustment problem areas than were background variables, and resilience had the greatest effect on adjustment.
6	**Nath (2011)**	Results showed that country of origin image had a positive and significant effect on components of brand equity, i.e. brand strength and brand awareness, derived from factor analysis conducted on brand equity components. The result also showed that country of origin image of branded generics significantly, but indirectly, affected brand equity through the mediating variables, brand strength and brand awareness.
7	**Che-Ha (2016)**	The elements of country branding from the perspectives of a country's citizens. In this exploration, the study constructs their views toward the country using both emotion (affect) and perceptions of competitive advantage and subsequently conceptualizes and tests a framework of internal country-branding elements. While some elements (human capital, culture and heritage, and politics) are important to foster positive emotions among its citizens, others (export, human capital, and politics) are considered as key tools to build competitive advantage. Implications exist for tourism marketers and policy makers, as the study highlights the importance of branding toward a country's citizens and revealing the specific preferences affecting the citizens' emotions and perceptions toward competitive advantage.
8	**Yoo (2002)**	A two-step approach is introduced and used to test the factorial invariance of the model cross-culturally. The results reveal which marketing efforts and brand equity dimensions have invariant effects on brand equity across the US and Korean samples. Specifically, brand loyalty and perceived product quality do not have an invariant effect on brand equity, while brand awareness/associations have an equivalent effect. Price and store image show an equivalent, positive effect on perceived quality; distribution intensity has an equivalent, positive effect on both perceived quality and brand loyalty; and price deals have an equivalent, negative effect on both perceived quality and brand awareness/associations. But advertising has a quite different effect on brand equity. The between-group differences in the brand equity formation process are explained from a cultural perspective.

Pilot Testing

A pilot test was undertaken with sample size of 100 customers. And with the help of results, those items whose factor loading was below 0.50 were out rightly rejected (Heir, 1998).

Figure 1. Conceptual model for measuring customer based brand equity

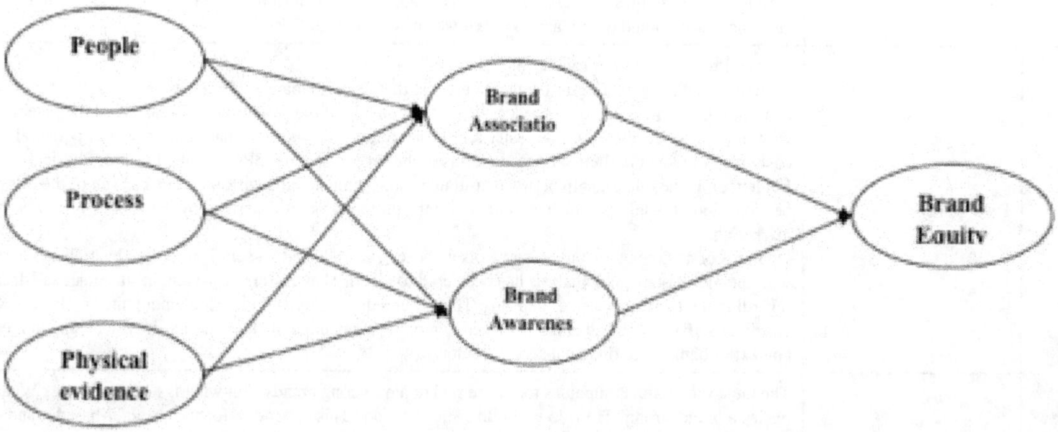

Data Collection

The data was collected with the help of structured questionnaire. Convenient sampling technique was used to collect the data from the respondents. A survey was conducted on 459 respondents, out which 400 responses were fully completed. The demographics characteristics of the customer are shown in Table 3.

DATA ANALYSIS

The procedure consist of two steps: Validating and fitting the structural model.

(A) Conducting CFA

The *reliability analysis* of all the constructs are shown in Table 4.

The results shown in Table 4 explain a higher level of reliability, that is an acceptable statistical indicator for the reliability analysis of the constructs being studied.

Exploratory Factor Analysis

Principal Component Analysis method was applied for verifying various Constructs/dimensions and eight factors were retained, in which the Eigen values were greater than one. Accordingly, seven factors were extracted that together accounted for 66.757% of the total variance. The results of the rotated factor loadings along with the percentage of variance and Eigen values have been shown in Table 5.

Table 3. Demographic characteristics of respondents

No.	Respondents Characteristics	% of Respondents
Age Group		
1	<20	5
	21-30	20
	31-40	25
	41-50	30
	51-60	15
	60 & >	5
Gender		
2	Male	70
	Female	30
Education		
3	10 + 2	10
	Graduation	35
	Post Graduation	40
	Ph.D	5
	Professional	5
	Other	5
Income		
4	>10000	5
	10001-20000	10
	20001-30000	30
	30001-40000	20
	40001-50000	20
	50001 & >	10
	No Income	5
Family		
5	Joint Family	60
	Nuclear Family	40

Table 4. Reliability analysis of constructs

S. No	Constructs	Cronbach's α
1	Brand awareness (BAA)	0.77
2	Brand association (BASS)	0.85
3	Brand Equity (BEE)	0.82
4	People (PEE)	0.74
5	Process (PRR)	0.86
6	Physical Evidence (PHH)	0.81

Source. Output Generated from SPSS 16.0

Table 5. Factor extraction and Eigen value

Factors	1 (BAA)	2 (BAS)	3 (BEE)	4 (PEE)	5 (PRR)	6 (PHH)
Factor Loadings	0.674	0.885	0.730	0.93	0.814	0.781
	0.875	0.858	0.799	0.880	0.826	0.832
	0.852	0.729	0.836	0.873	0.777	0.30
	0.852	0.861	0.793	0.821	0.763	—
	—	—	—	—	0.854	—
	—	—	—	—	—	—
Eigen Value	3.603	3.267	2.909	2.534	2.303	1.406
% of variance	15.014	13.611	12.121	10.557	9.598	5.857
Cumulative Variance	15.014	28.625	40.745	51.302	60.899	66.757

Source. Output Generated from SPSS 16.0

Confirmatory Factor Analysis

This analysis is generally used to test the hypotheses pertaining to unmeasured source of variability which is highly responsible for commonality among the set of scores. In other terms, it is related with study of relationships between indicators and constructs for which they were designed to measure.

Validity Analysis: Discriminant Validity

Discriminant validity referred to the score of a measure are unique in nature as compared to the score of other construct (Schwab 2005). In Discriminant analysis, two major issues were taken into consideration while performing the structural equation modeling. A) AVE of each construct must be greater than MSV. B) AVE of each construct must be greater than ASV.

Table 6. Comparison of AVE, MSV, ASV and Alpha value

Construct	AVE	MSV	ASV	Alpha Value
Process (PRR)	0.868	0.570	0.011	0.86
Brand Equity (BEE)	0.824	0.539	0.225	0.82
People (PEE)	0.794	0.542	0.013	0.74
Brand awareness (BAA)	0.797	0.508	0.014	0.77
Brand association (BASS)	0.859	0.607	0.006	0.85
Physical Evidence (PHH)	0.817	0.598	0.225	0.81

Source. Output Generated from SPSS 16.0

From Table 6, it was concluded that (AVE) of Process (PRR): 0.868 was greater than (MSV) i.e. 0.570. Similarly (AVE) of Brand Equity (BEE) was 0.824, People (PEE): 0.794, Brand Awareness (BAA): 0.797, Brand Association (BAS): 0.859, Physical Evidence (PHH): 0.817 were greater than the (MSV) of Brand Equity (BEE) 0.539, People (PEE): 0.542, Brand Awareness (BAA): 0.508, Brand Association (BAS): 0.607 and Physical Evidence (PHH): 0.598.

From Table 6, it was explained that (AVE) of Process (PRR): 0.868 was greater than (ASV) i.e. 0.011. Similarly (AVE) of Brand Equity (BEE) was 0.824, People (PEE): 0.794, Brand Awareness (BAA): 0.797, Brand Association (BAS): 0.859, Physical Evidence (PHH): 0.817 were greater than the (ASV) of Brand Equity (BEE) 0.225, People (PEE): 0.013, Brand Awareness (BAA): 0.014, Brand Association (BAS): 0.006 and Physical Evidence (PHH): 0.225.

Convergent Validity

Table 6 revealed that Cronbach's alpha value of each construct Process (PRR): 0.86, Brand Equity (BEE): 0.82, People (PEE): 0.74, Brand Awareness (BAA): 0.77, Brand Association (BAS): 0.85, Physical Evidence (PHH): 0.81 were higher than (0.70). The other issue can also be concluded from Table 6 that AVE of all constructs have loaded higher than (0.50). Similarly, from Table 6 it was also revealed that the third issue for alpha values of each constructs was greater than AVE of each construct.

As reported in Table 7, the factor loadings of each statement i.e. Physical Evidence (PHH1: 0.781, PHH2: 0.832, PHH3: 0.861), People (PEE1: 0.93, PEE2: 0.880, PEE3: 0.873, PEE4: 0.821), Process (PRR1: 0.814, PRR2: 0.826, PRR3: 0.777, PRR4: 0.763, PRR5: 0.854), Brand Equity (BEE1: 0.730, BEE2: 0.799, BEE3: 0.836, BEE4: 0.793), Brand Association (BAS1:0.885, BAS2: 0.858, BAS3: 0.729, BAS4: 0.861), Brand Awareness (BAA1: 0.674, BAA2: 0.875, BAA3: 0.852, BAA4:0.852) were significantly high as compare to the cut off limit i.e. 0.5 levels, similarly the KMO of factor analysis was 0.82. Lastly the composite reliability of each construct Physical Evidence (0.81), People (0.74), Process (0.86), Brand Equity (0.82), Brand Association (0.85) and Brand Awareness (0.77) were also significantly high.

Examining the Data Analysis

As suggested by Anderson and Gerbing (1988), after confirming the various conditions such as convergent validity, Discriminant validity and nomological validity for measurement model, then to test the hypothesized relations between the predictor and outcome variables, structural model with maximum likelihood estimation was employed.

After testing reliability and validity of the constructs, the next step was related with path analysis reported in Table 8, which helped in examining the overall fit measures.

HYPOTHESIS TESTING AND VALIDATION PROCESS

The results showed in Table 9 explain higher levels of support for various hypotheses by examining the direct effects of extended services marketing mix variable on Brand equity. Overall the result suggested that services extended marketing mix variable had positive and significant impact on brand equity. From the above results, it was found that Brand equity dimensions have strong support as a predictor of Brand equity. Important findings that are discovered as follows:

Table 7. CFA result

Construct	Items	Factor Loadings	Composite Reliability
Physical Evidence	PHH1	0.781	0.81
	PHH2	0.832	
	PHH3	0.861	
People	PEE1	0.93	0.74
	PEE2	0.880	
	PEE3	0.873	
	PEE4	0.821	
Process	PRR1	0.814	0.86
	PRR2	0.826	
	PRR3	0.777	
	PRR4	0.763	
	PRR5	0.854	
Brand Equity	BEE1	0.730	0.82
	BEE2	0.799	
	BEE3	0.836	
	BEE4	0.793	
Brand Association	BAS1	0.885	0.85
	BAS2	0.858	
	BAS3	0.729	
	BAS4	0.861	
Brand Awareness	BAA1	0.674	0.77
	BAA2	0.875	
	BAA3	0.852	
	BAA4	0.852	

Source. Output Generated from AMOS 20.0 and SPSS 16.0

Table 8. Goodness of fit indices for analysis

S. No	Name of Index	Results
1	Chi-square Value	419.6
2	DF	237
3	Chi-square Value/ DF	1.771
4	(CFI)	0.954
5	(GFI)	0.921
6	(AGFI)	0.901
7	(NFI)	0.942
8	(IFI)	0.931
9	(RMEA)	0.04
10	(RMR)	0.02

Source. Output Generated from AMOS 20.0

1. The variable People positively & significantly affected the brand equity;
2. The variable Process positively & significantly affected the brand equity;
3. The variable Physical Evidence positively & significantly affected the brand equity;
4. Brand Awareness mediates the relationship between brand equity & extended services marketing mix variable;
5. Brand Association mediates the relationship between extended services marketing mix variable and brand equity;
6. The extended services marketing mix variable (i.e. People) positively and significantly affected the brand Awareness;
7. The variable People positively & significantly affected the brand Association;
8. The variable Process positively & significantly affected the brand Awareness;
9. The variable Process positively & significantly affected the brand Association;
10. The variable Physical Evidence positively & significantly affected the brand Awareness;
11. The extended services marketing mix variable (i.e. Physical Evidence) positively and significantly affected the brand Association.

Table 9. Results of hypothesis testing

Sl. No	Hypothesis	Validation: Accepted/ Rejected	Beta Value	P Value
1	People ⇨ Brand Equity	Accepted	0.524	0.001
2	Process ⇨ Brand Equity	Accepted	0.422	0.001
3	Physical Evidence ⇨ Brand Equity	Accepted	0.498	0.001
4	People ⇨ Brand Awareness	Accepted	0.466	0.001
5	Process ⇨ Brand Awareness	Accepted	0.577	0.001
6	Physical Evidence ⇨ Brand Awareness	Accepted	0.328	0.03
7	People ⇨ Brand Association	Accepted	0.523	0.001
8	Process ⇨ Brand Association	Accepted	0.333	0.02
9	Physical Evidence ⇨ Brand Awareness	Accepted	0.445	0.001
10	Brand Awareness ⇨ Brand Equity	Accepted	0.658	0.001
11	Brand Association ⇨ Brand Equity	Accepted	0.598	0.001

The drivers of brand equity for high-tech industrial products (where technology embedded within a product has traditionally assumed a higher profile) is likely to affect the purchase at various stages in the process. The key determinants of brand equity were identified as perceived value and trust. The drivers of perceived value were identified as performance indicators and tangibles, and the drivers of trust as credibility of company, market acceptance of the product and reputation of alliance partners.

SOLUTIONS AND RECOMMENDATIONS

Theoretically, the research framework of this study holds relevance as it has introduced extended services marketing mix as important marketing activities for brand equity dimensions as mediator to brand equity itself. With new technologies like internet banking banks are looking to enhance their brand equity (Singh, 2019). With mergers of smaller banks, govt. is also bringing the brand value of banks high (Singh, 2018). However, the latest review study of Das (2012) only suggested three extended services marketing variables, but it did not provide any empirical support pertaining to the role extended services marketing mix as important marketing activities for brand equity dimensions as mediator to brand equity itself. Customer loyalty can also be a measure force for brand equity (Das, 2019). Loyalty helps in customer satisfaction and increases the brand equity (Singh, 2019). The employee morale and working environment also contributes to brand equity of bank (Gupta, 2019). Customer satisfaction enhances brand equity (Mondal, 2017). The significant amount of studies *(Nath,2007;* Hosseini,2015;) have examined all the marketing mix variables and extended services marketing mix variable as important marketing activities for brand equity dimensions as mediator to brand equity itself, but in different sectors. Emotional intelligence and employee's swift action also contribute immensely to brand equity (Jain, 2018). Digital sustainability also has a vital role in increasing brand equity (Das, 2019).

Brand equity learning in B-schools has a significant impact on services marketing mix as a strategic management function and opening new avenues for the budding managers. This study will persuade the management educators to introduce brand equity as a specialized or at least an elective course in MBA program like it is done in Harvard Business School. So, the service-branding model that underscores the salient role of customers' service experiences in brand formation. Four primary strategies that excellent service firms use to cultivate brand equity are discussed and illustrated. Branding is not just for tangible goods; it is a principal success driver for service organizations as well.

FUTURE RESEARCH DIRECTIONS

While arriving at the above conclusions and inferences, it was important to be aware of some of the limitations of this study. The study has the potential to be improved further by addressing the following limitations:

1. This study has been done mainly in Punjab and Chandigarh only. Further researches could be done at some other places of India to examine the relationship between service extended marketing mix and brand equity dimensions;
2. Secondly this study was confined only in banking sector. Further researches could be done in insurance, retail, Telecom sector also;

3. This study was included only the variables of services extended marketing mix i.e. People, Process and Physical evidence. Further it could be explored in all seven P's of marketing mix. i.e. Product, Price, Place, Promotion, People, Process and Physical evidence;
4. As per the condition of the model of this study, the sample size was appropriate. But further researches could be done with large representative size.

Recent writings on brand equity indicate that brand equity is the current marketing focus of many leading companies today. The usefulness of brand equity in the business world is undeniably important. It is not only important to businesses that offer tangible products but also to service organizations. Recent trends in marketing are creating global brands that compete across countries and cultures. With the efforts of many companies to have their service brands become more internationally recognized it is increasingly important to understand service brand equity and to become more sophisticated in managing services. Although branding is often associated with tangible goods, it is just as relevant for intangible goods such as services. With tangible goods, the physical product is the primary brand. For services, the service organization or the service provider is the primary brand. There are fundamental differences between goods and services, which may have implications for brand equity. For example, the branding efforts for tangible products can be materialized through the product, packaging, labelling, and logo design. On the other hand, services lack the tangibility that allows packaging, labelling and displaying.

CONCLUSION

This chapter is initiated to solve the several queries like role of Brand equity dimensions in banking sector in respect to most widely applicable extended services marketing mix variable in service industry specifically related to emerging banking sector.

Several keys points have emerged from the findings of the study, which were also supported by several reviews. According to the conceptual model, there should be positive and direct effect of extended services marketing mix variable on brand equity. And the results also revealed positive and direct effects of extended services marketing mix variable on brand equity. Brand awareness was one of the relevant dimensions of brand equity, which also affected directly and indirectly by influencing customer association to make with the brand. The results were statistically significant with other reviews (Yoo, Donthu 2013). Several others reviews (Keller, 2003) considered brand awareness as corner stone of brand equity, which acted as foundation for creating brand equity. The importance of brand awareness was more important in initial stages of brand development, but in later stages, the importance of brand awareness declined because consumers were fully aware about the brand. But in later stages, more spending were required for creating an image to get more customer base for longer period of time. In case banking sector, where several brands were emerging in Indian sector, for those the brand awareness dimensions will be the key factor for creating an image in the market. Brand Association again one of the relevant factors of brand equity, but in this study it didn't support either directly or indirectly to the brand equity, which also affected directly and indirectly to the brand equity. Brand equity is very important to marketers of consumer goods and services. Brand equity facilitates in the effectiveness of brand extensions and brand introductions. This is because consumers who trust and display loyalty toward a brand are willing to try to adopt brand extensions. While there have been methods to measure the financial value of brand equity, measurement of customer-based brand equity has been lacking. Presents a scale to measure customer-based brand equity. The customer-based brand equity scale is developed based on the five underlying dimensions of brand equity: performance, value, social image, trustworthiness and commitment. In empirical tests, brands that scored higher on the customer-based brand equity scale generally had higher prices.

REFERENCES

Aaker, D. A. (1991). *Managing Brand Equity*. New York: Maxweel Macmillan-Canada.

Aaker, D. A. (1996). Measuring brand equity across products and markets. *California Management Review*, *38*(3), 102–120. doi:10.2307/41165845

Al-Dmour, H., Zu'bi, M. F., & Kakeesh, D. (2013). The effect of services marketing mix elements on customer-based brand equity: An empirical study on mobile telecom service recipients in Jordan. *International Journal of Business and Management*, *8*(11), 13. doi:10.5539/ijbm.v8n11p13

Alao, A. E., Diyaolu, G. O., & Afuape, A. M. (2014). The changing trend in marketing of financial services: An empirical study on bank performance in Nigeria. *International Journal of Business and Economic Development*, *2*(2).

Anderson, E. W., & Sullivan, M. W. (1993). The antecedents and consequences of customer satisfaction for firms. *Marketing Science*, *12*(2), 125–143. doi:10.1287/mksc.12.2.125

Anderson, J. C., & Gerbing, D. W. (1988). Structural equation modeling in practice: A review and recommended two-step approach. *Psychological Bulletin*, *103*(3), 411–423. doi:10.1037/0033-2909.103.3.411

Atilgan, E., Aksoy, Ş., & Akinci, S. (2005). Determinants of the brand equity: A verification approach in the beverage industry in Turkey. *Marketing Intelligence & Planning*, *23*(3), 237–248. doi:10.1108/02634500510597283

Bentler, P. M. (1995). EQS structural equations program manual (Vol. 6). Encino, CA: Multivariate Software.

Carmines, E. G., & Zeller, R. A. (1979). *Reliability and validity assessment* (Vol. 17). Sage publications. doi:10.4135/9781412985642

Che-Ha, N., & Hashim, S. (2007). Brand equity, customer satisfaction and loyalty: Malaysian banking sector. *International Review of Business Research Papers, 3*(5), 123-133.

Che-Ha, N., Nguyen, B., Yahya, W. K., Melewar, T. C., & Chen, Y. P. (2016). Country branding emerging from citizens' emotions and the perceptions of competitive advantage: The case of Malaysia. *Journal of Vacation Marketing*, *22*(1), 13–28. doi:10.1177/1356766715586454

Churchill, G. A. Jr. (1979). A paradigm for developing better measures of marketing constructs. *JMR, Journal of Marketing Research*, *16*(1), 64–73. doi:10.1177/002224377901600110

Churchill, G. A. Jr, & Surprenant, C. (1982). An investigation into the determinants of customer satisfaction. *JMR, Journal of Marketing Research*, *19*(4), 491–504. doi:10.1177/002224378201900410

Das, D. (2011). An Empirical Study To Build A Theoretical Framework That Can Determine Customer Satisfaction In Terms Of People, Process & Physical Evidence. *Service Marketing Practices in India: Changing Paradigms*, 135-143.

Das, S., Nayyar, A., & Singh, I. (2019). *An assessment of forerunners for customer loyalty in the selected financial sector by SEM approach toward their effect on business*. Data Technologies and Applications. doi:10.1108/DTA-04-2019-0059

De Chernatony, L., & Harris, F. J. (2001). *Measuring the consumer-based equity of financial services brands. Birminghan Business Scholl*. The University of Birmingham.

Dua, S., Chahal, R., & Sharma, A. (2013). Interrelationship of Aaker's customer based brand equity dimensions: Offering a model to banking sector. *Asian Journal of Management Research*, *4*(2), 297–307.

Farjam, S., & Hongyi, X. (2015). Reviewing the concept of brand equity and evaluating consumer-based brand equity (CBBE) models. *International Journal of Management Science and Business Administration*, *1*(8), 14–29. doi:10.18775/ijmsba.1849-5664-5419.2014.18.1002

Farquhar, P. H. (1989). *Managing Brand Equity Marketing Research*. Academic Press.

Gandhi, S., & Kang, L. S. (2011). Customer satisfaction, its antecedents and linkage between employee satisfaction and customer satisfaction: A study. *Asian Journal of Business and Management Sciences*, *1*(1), 129–137.

Ghost, F. H., & Gnanadhas, M. E. (2011). Impact of service quality in commercial banks on the customers satisfaction: An empirical study. *International Journal of Multidisciplinary Research*, *1*(6), 19–37.

Gupta, D. K., Jena, D., Samantaray, A. K., & Das, S. (2019). HRD climate in selected public sector banks in India. *Revista ESPACIOS, 40*(11).

Hair, J. F., Anderson, R. E., Tatham, R. L., & Black, W. C. (1998). *Multivariate Data Analysis*. Upper Saddle River, NJ: Prentice Hall.

Hattie, J. (1985). Methodology review: Assessing unidimensionality of tests and ltenls. *Applied Psychological Measurement*, *9*(2), 139–164. doi:10.1177/014662168500900204

Hattie, J., & Fraser, C. (1988). The constraining of parameters in restricted factor analysis. *Applied Psychological Measurement*, *12*(2), 155–162. doi:10.1177/014662168801200204

Hu, L. T., & Bentler, P. M. (1999). Cutoff criteria for fit indexes in covariance structure analysis: Conventional criteria versus new alternatives. *Structural Equation Modeling*, *6*(1), 1–55. doi:10.1080/10705519909540118

Jain, S., Jain, V., & Das, S. (2018). Relationship analysis between emotional intelligence and service quality with special evidences from Indian banking sector. *Revista ESPACIOS, 39*(33).

Jain, S. K., & Gupta, G. (2004). Measuring service quality: SERVQUAL vs. SERVPERF scales. *Vikalpa*, *29*(2), 25–38. doi:10.1177/0256090920040203

Jalilvand, M. R., Esfahani, S. S., & Samiei, N. (2011). Electronic word-of-mouth: Challenges and opportunities. *Procedia Computer Science*, *3*, 42–46. doi:10.1016/j.procs.2010.12.008

Jones, T., & Taylor, S. F. (2007). The conceptual domain of service loyalty: How many dimensions? *Journal of Services Marketing*, *21*(1), 36–51. doi:10.1108/08876040710726284

Kapferer, J. N. (2015). *Kapferer on luxury: How luxury brands can grow yet remain rare*. Kogan Page Publishers.

Keller, K. L., Parameswaran, M. G., & Jacob, I. (2011). *Strategic brand management: Building, measuring, and managing brand equity*. Pearson Education India.

Khorsandi, H., Mohammadi, A., Karimzadeh, S., & Khorsandi, J. (2016). Evaluation of corrosion and scaling potential in rural water distribution network of Urmia, Iran. *Desalination and Water Treatment*, *57*(23), 10585–10592. doi:10.1080/19443994.2015.1042058

Kirmani, A., & Zeithaml, V. (1993). Advertising, perceived quality, and brand image. *Brand equity & advertising: Advertising's role in building strong brands*, 143-161.

Kotler, P., Hayes, T., & Bloom, P. N. (2002). *Marketing professional services*. Prentice Hall.

Kotler, P., & Keller, K. L. (2006). *Marketing Management*. Twelefth Edition.

Krishnan, B. C., & Hartline, M. D. (2001). Brand equity: Is it more important in services? *Journal of Services Marketing*, *15*(5), 328–342. doi:10.1108/EUM0000000005654

Lassar, W., Mittal, B., & Sharma, A. (1995). Measuring customer-based brand equity. *Journal of Consumer Marketing*, *12*(4), 11–19. doi:10.1108/07363769510095270

Maio Mackay, M. (2001). Evaluation of brand equity measures: Further empirical results. *Journal of Product and Brand Management*, *10*(1), 38–51. doi:10.1108/10610420110382812

Makasi, A., Govender, K., & Madzorera, N. (2014). Re-branding and its effects on consumer perceptions: A case study of a Zimbabwean bank. *Mediterranean Journal of Social Sciences*, *5*(20), 2582.

Makasi, A., Govender, K., & Rukweza, C. (2015). Building brand equity through advertising. *Mediterranean Journal of Social Sciences*, *5*(20), 2613.

Malhotra, N. K., Mukhopadhyay, S., Liu, X., & Dash, S. (2012). One, few or many?: An integrated framework for identifying the items in measurement scales. *International Journal of Market Research*, *54*(6), 835–862. doi:10.2501/IJMR-54-6-835-862

Martensen, A., & Grønholdt, L. (2003). Understanding and modelling brand equity. *Asian Journal on Quality*, *4*(2), 73-100.

Mathwick, C., Malhotra, N., & Rigdon, E. (2001). Experiential value: Conceptualization, measurement and application in the catalog and Internet shopping environment. *Journal of Retailing*, *77*(1), 39–56. doi:10.1016/S0022-4359(00)00045-2

Mondal, S., Mall, M., Mishra, U. S., & Sahoo, K. (2017). Investigating the factors affecting customer purchase activity in retail stores. *Revista ESPACIOS*, *38*(57).

Nath Sanyal, S., & Datta, S. K. (2011). The effect of country of origin on brand equity: An empirical study on generic drugs. *Journal of Product and Brand Management*, *20*(2), 130–140. doi:10.1108/10610421111121125

Oliver, R. L. (2014). *Satisfaction: A behavioral perspective on the consumer: A behavioral perspective on the consumer*. Routledge. doi:10.4324/9781315700892

Oly Ndubisi, N. (2006). Effect of gender on customer loyalty: A relationship marketing approach. *Marketing Intelligence & Planning*, *24*(1), 48–61. doi:10.1108/02634500610641552

Parasuraman, A., Zeithaml, V. A., & Berry, L. L. (1988). Servqual: A multiple-item scale for measuring consumer perc. *Journal of Retailing*, *64*(1), 12.

Pinar, M., Girard, T., & Eser, Z. (2012). Consumer-based brand equity in banking industry: A comparison of local and global banks in Turkey. *International Journal of Bank Marketing*, *30*(5), 359–375. doi:10.1108/02652321211247417

Prado, M. A., & Giraldi, J. D. M. E. (2015). A Influência da Imagem do País de Origem no Brand Equity: Um Estudo com Bancos Espanhóis. *Revista Brasileira de Marketing*, *14*(3), 407–420. doi:10.5585/remark.v14i3.2890

Rios, R. (2007). *Sources and antecedents of brand equity for online companies*. Academic Press.

Singh, I., Nayyar, A., & Das, S. (2019). A study of antecedents of customer loyalty in banking & insurance sector and their impact on business performance. *Revista ESPACIOS, 40*(6).

Singh, I., Nayyar, A., Le, D. H., & Das, S. (2019). A conceptual analysis of internet banking users' perceptions. An Indian perceptive. *Revista ESPACIOS, 40*(14).

Singh, S., & Das, S. (2018). Impact of post-merger and acquisition activities on the financial performance of banks: A study of Indian private sector and public sector banks. *Revista Espacios Magazine*, *39*(26), 25.

Subhankar, D., & Anand, N. (2019, May). Digital sustainability in social media innovation: a microscopic analysis of Instagram advertising & its demographic reflection for buying activity with R. In *1st International Scientific Conference" Modern Management Trends and the Digital Economy: from Regional Development to Global Economic Growth"(MTDE 2019)*. Atlantis Press. 10.2991/mtde-19.2019.72

Tahseen Arshi, A., & Al Lawati Jassim, M. (2013). *Customer satisfaction in banking sector in Oman: what do they care for?* Advances in Management.

Wang, J. (2009). A study of resiliency characteristics in the adjustment of international graduate students at American universities. *Journal of Studies in International Education*, *13*(1), 22–45. doi:10.1177/1028315307308139

Yoo, B., & Donthu, N. (2001). Developing and validating a multidimensional consumer-based brand equity scale. *Journal of Business Research*, *52*(1), 1–14. doi:10.1016/S0148-2963(99)00098-3

Yoo, B., & Donthu, N. (2002). Testing cross-cultural invariance of the brand equity creation process. *Journal of Product and Brand Management*, *11*(6), 380–398. doi:10.1108/10610420210445505

Chapter 5
A Study of Digital Learning Management Systems in Developing Countries:
Instructors' Perspectives

Abdeleh Bassam Al Amoush
University of New England, Australia

Kamaljeet Sandhu
https://orcid.org/0000-0003-4624-6834
University of New England, Australia

ABSTRACT

Academic higher education has adopted the use of internet technologies such as web-based digital learning systems. Digital learning management systems (DLMSs) have widely been utilized by many universities as a tool that fosters learning activities due to its prevailing unique environment. DLMS is a software-driven tool with different features; hence, different universities adopt different DLMSs that meet their expectations in terms of helping their administrators, instructors, and students learning the processes. The research aims to examine collected qualitative data through a case study methodology coupled with semi-structured interviews as the data collection method. The interviews are analyzed deeply based on the research findings to gain insights on how the implementation of the digital learning management systems influences the learning perspective of instructors as far as universities and the higher education sector is concerned.

INTRODUCTION

The adoption and use of Digital Learning Management Systems (DLMSs) by various universities help in effectively managing learning resources and tools for user participants as well as streamlining learning and teaching tasks (Kats, 2010; Orr, 2003; Rogers, 1995; Unwin et al., 2010). Research shows that

DOI: 10.4018/978-1-7998-5175-2.ch005

instructors benefit when universities improve their innovations through the utilisation of DLMS since it becomes easier for them to understand all that is needed for academic progress (Alnsour, Muhsen, Dababnah, Eljinini, & Barhoum, 2011; Orr, 2003; Rogers, 1995). One important aspect of DLMSs is that the applications are multifunctional with the ability for instructors to access the system, watch lectures, download course materials, and hand over assignments online (AlQudah, 2014).

Adoption of DLMS systems in universities provide instructors with an environment that is conducive as well as a convenience based on the study and learning environment. However, DLMS functions efficiently when there is a well-established link between indexed data by search engines and information that has been connected and bind by web bots (Babić, 2012). The use of DLMS empowers users through enhanced user experience (McIntosh & Torres, 2014; Phillipo & Krongard, 2012).

A DLMS through the amalgamation of multimedia applications takes into account real-time and dynamic team learning as well as documented collaboration simplifies learning and deliverables (Potter & Thompson, 2019). School assignments, tests, and other forms of assessment are part of learning deliverables students are subjected to achieve learning objectives. The use of assessment applications, chat, and file transfer has simplified the learning process in learning institutions. Expansion on the learning curve happens when an active learner has access to new platforms created by a DLMS. However, the context of how DLMS works and what it is can be understood through a reflection on nature and implications associated with different DLMSs (Ahmad, Chinade, Gambaki, Ibrahim, & Ala, 2012). Hence, the study takes into account recent literature that offers case scenarios on how learning issues within the digital environment has been addressed as compared to previous print logics confines.

The research is based on Jordanian Universities under the higher education sector with several branches across Jordan. The reputation of the Jordanian universities makes it desirable for the research given that university management acknowledges information technology as a tool that streamlines the education framework. Additionally, the university supports the DLMS system, opting to train users through its Information Technology Centre it has created.

The main aim of the study is to identify factors impacting the acceptance of the DLMS at Jordanian universities. Additionally, the study intends to investigate the use and acceptance of DLMS at Jordanian universities with a focus on factors influencing DLMS acceptance. However, the following are goals that the university management through related parties intends to achieve:

- Ensure that the universities have access to all modern machine technologies, including necessary operating systems, servers, and computer workshops, and information centres, television digital learning management systems such as Moodle or Blackboard and operation centre;
- Ensure that the application of information systems are guaranteed;
- Ensure that all information tasks from machines of models and procedures are automated;
- Make use of networks such as banner system, email services and television transmission of lectures and activities that are affiliated with the university;
- Offer an environment that is conducive to spread digital learning management systems based on an available application with related training;
- Achieve end to end information security between the source and the users;
- Ensure that the provision of electronic services are safety from policies and related procedures.

LITERATURE REVIEW

This study examines the existing literature about DLMSs, the functionality of a DLMS, the strengths and weaknesses of a DLMS, and the status of the DLMS in higher education. Iskander (2008) and Whelan and Bhartu (2007) identify DLMS as a macro level term that refers to facilitating and managing the online learning process for all user profiles. These user types are students, administrators or instructors. The services facilitated by the LMS include interactive strategies and organising and monitoring control among learning groups.

This approach was used to identify important factors that could or do affect the acceptance of using a DLMS at Jordanian universities. The existing literature provides substantial evidence of what these factors might be and how they might be modelled in terms of their effect on LMS use at Jordanian universities. These insights are used to develop research propositions about the relationships between the factors and to build a conceptual framework of the acceptance of LMS practices.

The study uses a research model known as the Technology Acceptance Model (TAM), to examine and investigate how the use of DLMSs at Jordanian universities is accepted (Davis, 1989; Venkatesh, 1999). TAM is a technology with the ability to examine any new technology acceptance. Application of DLMSs at Jordanian universities through TAM research model helps us understand how the systems work in terms of technical support, perceived ease of use (PEOU) and perceived usefulness (PU) (Venkatesh & Davis, 2000).

ADOPTION OF A CONCEPTUAL FRAMEWORK FOR DIGITAL LEARNING MANAGEMENT SYSTEMS (DLMSs)

The following section explores the important concepts for a Digital Learning Management Systems (DLMSs) at Jordanian universities for the development and adoption of a conceptual framework. A number of Hypotheses have been proposed from instructors' perspective that have been reported in this study for developing a conceptual framework.

Important Role of DLMSs at Jordanian Universities

The availability of technology in Jordan and particularly in universities is defined by IT infrastructure for DLMSs that incur the use of computers and DLMS tools to run the education systems via internet connections (AlQudah, 2014; Imlawi, Gregg, & Karimi, 2015). Lack of IT infrastructure affects most developing countries, and this is the main factor that influences DLMS acceptance in Jordanian universities, given that Jordan, as a country, has heavily invested in IT infrastructure to foster its economy. Samak and Tawfik (2017) indicate that the Jordanian Ministry of Education has accepted to invest and establish an IT infrastructure plan for public schools, a plan that will last for five consecutive years. The plan aims to identify methods, amount, and type of infrastructure suitable for public schools as far as quality education is Jordan is concerned.

Khwaldeh, Al-Hadid, and Masa'deh (2017) suggests that the high demand of users (students, instructors and users) at Jordanian universities prompt for upgrade and improvement of the infrastructure for DLMS systems. User's infrastructure needs such as blind and deaf users require attention, and therefore the study intends to highlight these needs that provide a gap in the IT infrastructure. The study also has to state recommendations on how these needs can be identified as well as improved to carter to the needs of all users, who include students and staff.

All plans of Jordanian academic staff revolve around the existing technology (Wimpenny, Adefila, & DeWinter, 2018). The view on the existing technology has to be reflected based on some interviewer's sentiment that:

Access to technology appears to be limited in certain organisations, and there is also evidence of unequal provision around the country. This could therefore justifiably explain why relatively few respondents (10.8%) feel that they can draw from a range of activities to meet their learner needs. (Wimpenny et al., 2018, pp. 33-48)

Jordanian universities have utilized donations from developed organizations and countries to upgrade their old infrastructure to a new platform infrastructure for DLMSs. However, the improvement has been slow due to a lack of financial resources and obstacles like refugees from Jordan bordering countries. This is an indication that Jordan still has an issue with its infrastructure and therefore needs to put more resources in investing heavily in IT infrastructure that would foster education sectors at large.

The acceptance of DLMS via perceived use and ease of use is positively affected by IT infrastructure for DLMS, and as far as operation within Jordanian universities is concerned. The study, therefore, has formulated two hypotheses (H) regarding IT infrastructure for DLMSs which are from instructor's perspective as indicated below:

H1: IT infrastructure for DLMSs has a positive effect on perceived usefulness for the DLMS.
H3: IT infrastructure for DLMSs has a positive effect on perceived ease of use for the DLMS.

Important Role of Culture on DLMSs in Jordan

The use of DLMS tools in Jordanian universities is also affected by cultural factors. This research intends to focus on various cultural factors based on perceived use and ease of use on account that Jordan has a unique culture that influences the use of DLMSs (Al-Shaikh, 2003). As per Cho and Berge (2002), the culture and norms of those working in higher education faculties are perceived to influence the adoption as well as the deployment of DLMS in Jordanian universities. Therefore, the acceptance of a DLMS is highly affected by a lack of professional technology training and pedagogical issues.

Various research have highlighted culture as a significant factor affecting DLMS acceptance in Jordanian universities, but there are limitation in the prevailing studies given that all research have failed to reflect on the accuracy of the sample size, and real number of all type of users (Abdullateef, Elias, Mohamed, Zaidan, & Zaidan, 2016; M. Al-Shboul, 2013; Al-Zoubi & Ali, 2019; Al Musawi, Ambusaidi, Al-Balushi, & Al-Balushi, 2015; Atoum, Otoom, & Ali, 2017; Hofstede, 1983; Khwaldeh et al., 2017). However, the researchers perceives that instructor's emotions play a significant part in learning experiences as far as complex education environments is concerned (Arguel, Lockyer, Kennedy, Lodge, & Pachman, 2019).

Quality learning can be achieved if the culture of using e-Learning technology is embraced and spread across the board (M. Al-Shboul, 2013). The university management has to put more focus on user training regarding a culture that is open to new technology to deliver quality teaching and learning environment. Abbad, Morris, and De Nahlik (2009) posit that less engagement on e-Learning technology is supported by cultures that focus on oral traditions. More training of users by management team through e-Learning technology creates a culture that embraces and accepts new technology without a second thought and open to a new challenge as well as updates. Media is an important player that fosters local culture dissemination based on the world occurrence events, and therefore utilizing media will disseminate values and transform the formation of society's thinking (Varis & Al-Agtash, 2008). An improvement in the use of new technology can be channelled through the use of media, which is an important player in local social life in terms of positive new technology improvement and change in user culture.

There is a relationship between perceived usefulness and ease of use when adopting a DLMS and culture influence regarding Jordanian universities. This research intends to confirm how this relationship exists concerning the case of Jordanian universities. Below is the hypothesis which are from instructor's perspective reflecting on the coexisting relationship between the use of a DLMS and cultural influence as far as Jordanian universities are concerned:

H2: Culture has a positive effect on perceived ease of use for the DLMS.
H4: Culture has a positive effect on perceived usefulness for the DLMS.

Important Role of Perceived Usefulness on DLMSs in Jordan

From the definition point of view, the perceived usefulness of a DLMS is a measure under which users have faith that using DLMS will have a positive impact on their learning performance (Davis, 1989). Saadé and Bahli (2005) add that perceived usefulness of a DLMS is a measure with which an individual has faith using a particular system that has a positive influence on their job performance. Davis (1989) notes that perceived usefulness is a variable that people opt to choose or not to choose based on the help associated with the application.

IT infrastructure and culture hypotheses are important since they encourage, students, instructors, and management who are part of users in accepting new technology that will enhance quality service and provide a working environment that is conducive and desirable as far learning process is concerned. Culture and IT infrastructure form the core values and factors that define acceptance of new technology, and therefore the use of DLMSs in Jordanian universities is defined by the two factors (M. Al-Shboul, 2011; M. A. Al-Shboul & Alsmadi, 2010; Alnsour et al., 2011; AlQudah, 2014).

The culture and perceived usefulness on DLMS tools from the IT infrastructure in Jordan context are two highlights this research has taken into consideration. The highlights reflect on the theme of DLMS acceptance in Jordan universities. Below is a hypothesis which is from instructor's perspective that reflects on the relationship between acceptance as well as the adoption of DLMS and perceived usefulness associated with DLMSs:

H5: Perceived usefulness in accepting a DLMS has a positive effect on acceptance of the DLMS.

Important Role of Perceived Ease of Use on DLMSs in Jordan

Davis (1989) defines perceived ease of use of a DLMS as a measure under which users have faith in embracing DLMS on the fact that the tools offer support that is free of effort. However, Saadé and Bahli (2005) believe that perceived ease of use of a DLMS is a perception that people tend to believe using a particular system eases their effort to accomplish certain tasks in line of duty. Various researches show that easy use of new technology attracts the attention of individuals who are perceived to try and make use of its usefulness.

There is a direct effect of ease of use on perceived usefulness Davis (1989). There is strong experimental support from many studies on how TAM exhibits a positive relationship between perceived usefulness and ease of use. Both perceived usefulness and ease of use affect the use of new technology based on its acceptance and as far as TAM is taken into consideration (Adams, Nelson, & Todd, 1992; Szajna, 1996; Venkatesh & Davis, 2000). As cited in Abbad et al. (2009); Venkatesh (1999), attribute on external control and facilitating conditions trigger the effort of users employing perceived ease of use as far as information technology is concerned. However, the availability of technical support acts as an important factor that determines the degree under which technology such as a DLMS has been accepted (Williams, 2002).

Ease of use of DLMS depends on the culture and IT infrastructure as the two defining factors to acceptance of new technology by users. Both culture and IT infrastructure enhance quality learning as well as support and accept software tolls and any new technology, respectively, without a hitch (M. Al-Shboul, 2013). However, an organization may incur losses and lag in terms of new technology software and tools activation if there is poor infrastructure.

Through a hypothesis, both culture and IT infrastructure are believed to affect positively and negatively the perceived ease of using a DLMS. Easy application and use of a new software depend on good infrastructure and the surrounding culture since knowledge of culture offer ease utilisation of new technology by users (Students, instructors, and students) (Al-Dmour, 2014; AlQudah, 2014).

The intention of users on how to utilize technology and associated behaviors is realized easily when perceived ease of use of a DLMS is used. The research predicted that the acceptance of the DLMS is triggered by the user's behavioral intention to adopt DLMS, and following is a hypothesis which is from instructor's perspective:

H6: Perceived ease of use of a DLMS has a positive effect on acceptance for the DLMS.

Important Role of Acceptance and Continued Use of DLMS in Jordan

According to Venkatesh and Davis (2000) the prediction of user acceptance is on point when the Technology Acceptance Model (TAM) is used given that the model has established, powerful, robust and parsimonious traits for the correct prediction of acceptance perception. TAM has widely been adopted by many researchers as they examine new technology acceptance, such as personal computers, and confirm that it is a desirable model in predicting user acceptance (Igbaria, Zinatelli, Cragg, & Cavaye, 1997).

As per Davis (1989) user acceptance has no universal goal and therefore, there are dysfunctional impacts associated with an emphasis on using information technology to give that cases of system failure have been there in terms of true performance gain. It is optimistic rather than pessimism on attributes of identifying measures that are linked to user acceptance. Complexity, as well as multifaceted reactions, are realized when computers are used by users. However, factors such as fundamental mechanisms that drive behaviors need to be investigated to cultivate better and measure alternative theoretical models that are sustainable in terms of progress.

Examining both perceived usefulness and perceived ease of use hypothesis based on new system acceptance is important (Davis, 1989). The model reflection through these hypotheses helps in measuring how an organization has accepted a new software with regards to Jordanian universities, as the study contemplates on how new software can be adopted by these universities. If the outcome of the study proves positive, then the model can be adopted by all universities in Jordan as far as it incorporates the use of DLMS software (Almarabeh, 2014).

Given behaviors have an influence on the acceptance of a DLMS and therefore perceived usefulness and perceived ease of use under DLMS in Jordanian university depends on the behavioral factors, and following is a hypothesis which is from instructor's perspective:

H7: Acceptance of a DLMS has a positive effect on continued use of the DLMS.

RESEARCH METHODOLOGY ADOPTED FOR THIS STUDY

Finding the values related to aims and research problems as well as the constitution of ethical behavior in the research solely depend on the methodological approached considered by this research (Ridder, 2017). Several interviews were conducted involving participants from six Jordanian universities, where both qualitative and quantitative data methods were utilised. Qualitative data was collected from the interviews and later refining quantitative data questionnaires done to develop concepts identified from the literature. A conceptual model was used to examine ho Digital Learning Management System Model can be accepted in Jordanian universities. The research, however, formulated quantitative survey questions to discover findings related an obtained from the survey (Creswell, 2013; Yin, 1981).

The research adopted questionnaires and semi-structured interview methods to work on the aims of the research, as well as examine and test the DMLS model. The two methods were also adopted to evaluate qualitative data for this study (Rowley, 2002; Yin, 2012). The use of interviews depends on the researcher's philosophical assumptions and therefore adopted as a critical positivist or interpretive. This research therefore adopted a positivist interview method given that the researcher had to work on the qualitative data phase (Gupta & Rao, 2018; Yin, 2015).

CASE ANALYSIS FOR DEEPER INSIGHTs INTO dlms AT JORDANIAN UNCIVERSITIES

The research participants were from six Jordanian universities, where evidence and qualitative data were collected from the interviews. Interviews were utilized to obtain qualitative data and be able to refine and develop concepts identified from the literature as far as conceptual model inclusion and acceptance of DLMS at the Jordanian universities are concerned (Creswell, 2013; Yin, 1981).

The research adopted six universities with a total of 37 interviews done by DLMS users (Students, instructors, and administrators) based in Jordanian universities (refer to table 2). Out of 37 users, 22 were instructors, 8 were administrators, and 7 were students. The interviews aimed to assess DLMS. This chapter utilises student's data to analyse the perception of DLMS in Jordanian universities. Six different Jordanian universities have been reflected in this research and they include the University of Jordan (UJ), which is the oldest and reputed government university at Jordan, Princess Sumaya University for Technology (PSUT), which has a mixed model of a university system (government and private), and Philadelphia University (PU), which is one of the private university at Jordan, Jordan University of Science and Technology (JUST), which is another public university at Jordan and Applied Science Private

University (ASU), which is a private university at Jordan The six universities are top-ranked universities in Jordan with reflection on public domain data and academic perception (Rank, 2019).

Exploring Instructors' Perceptions on the Digital Learning Management System

This section takes into account instructor's perceptions of continuance use of digital learning management systems as well as factors that affect DLMS acceptance as far as Jordanian universities are concerned. The case study methodology adopted the use of qualitative data methods as instructors gave their views on the subject matters. The adoption of the methodology was to enhance and capture instructor's attention to fully discuss DLMS from a pedagogical perspective. The idea of qualitative data collection was to get information on how DLMS affects their learning environment, and therefore the views from IT staff did not count given that their perceptions reflected on the technological features of the systems and IT infrastructure rather than its impacts and acceptance to the learning process. The following are the perceptions of instructors on the Jordanian culture, PEOE, PU, DLMS acceptance, IT infrastructure, and DLMS continuance usage.

The interviews from instructors indicated that learning cooperation between students, administrators, and instructors is encouraged by the digital learning management system. Users (instructors, administrators, and students) through cooperative practice can understand more on the topics at hand and realize the value and prospect of using DLMS in terms of efficiency, easy access, and quality learning as agreed by instructor 3 with the below statement:

My learning and experience on the digital system has evolved through encouragement from cooperative practices. More learning styles as well as consideration of study topics with different learning materials for cross-references are considered when students and instructors cooperate among them or between groups.

The instructor also added that there is new communication between users when digital learning management system is utilised. Additionally, digital systems as per the instructors are channel for user's collaboration and offer bi-directional communication. Using digital management system in learning institutions helps students, administrators and instructors to collaborate and use well recommended courses with confidence and topic efficacy based on the area of specialisation. Use of digital learning management system has advantage over instructors who are able to become more expert and aware of the emerging issues as indicated by instructor below:

There is a better experience when digital system is used since it improves communication pathways between users (instructors, administrators and students). Better experience from the digital systems gives an opportunity instructors to make recommendations to use learning topics and receive feedback from students with their academic preferences. The digital learning management system assists users in the education process.

Exploring Instructors' Perceptions on the IT Infrastructure for Using the Digital Learning Management System

It is clear from the interview that the digital learning management system fails to be utilised by instructor as per instructor 2 who posit:

Current literature and research indicate that most of instructors don't have adequate knowledge regarding full capacity of the digital learning management system.

The sentiment from instructor 2 was agreed by instructor 4, indicating that:

A large effort is required to help users embrace the digital learning management system frequently.

Despite the adoption of the digital learning management system being in its early stage, some users knew the system with positive perception regarding the associated importance as far as its implementation process is concerned. High-quality educational services to users were the main reason as to why interviewee believed that adopting innovative systems is paramount to educational institutions. For instance, instructor 3 stated:

The University management has adopted the use of information technology infrastructure as a framework that will enhance education quality to the users. Competition among educational institutions is paramount, and therefore University opts to improve its education quality through heavy investment in the IT infrastructure with easy access to IT services for everyone. I think the University management has full support to all students and supports us through the presentation of innovative services that cater to both users (instructors, administrators, and students).

Instructor 2 is based on e-learning user and believes that digital learning management system connects all user through a virtual community infrastructure, hence indicating that:

The aim of the University to utilize digital learning management system is to help users have access to quality content powered by IT infrastructure. Additionally, the digital system creates an e-university environment where students and instructors interact and have knowledge about global learning community infrastructure.

Similarly, instructor 3 knew the features of the digital learning management system through his perception that the instructors learning performance is linked by DLMS:

A combination of learner ratings and content-based filtering comes into place when a digital learning management system is adopted and, therefore, a recommendation drew on learning materials. It is easier for me to upload documents related to the lecture as per the guideline, and therefore as an institution with the ambition to increase instructors learning performance, the university has no option but to adopt the digital system at all stake.

Digital learning management systems help instructors to meet their needs through personalized content, make proper choices without considering alternatives, and reduce information overload. As per instructor 4 and 5:

The aim of the University to use the learning system is to provide better quality digital learning platforms to instructors and students. The systems can personalize the management process and information retrieval. Hence the university will be able to deliver a better infrastructure to facilitate better education experience.

Nonetheless, a challenge was exhibited during the implementation of the digital learning management system with much effort needed in IT infrastructure. One reason is that the concept is still new within the education domain with users (instructors, administrators, and students) unfamiliar with the digital system due to the perceived notion that it is complex technology. Instructor 1 notes that:

I want to stress that the implementation process of the digital learning management system was tricky and coupled with challenges such as users' unfamiliarity with the system, its complexity based on the involved concept, and the existing old IT infrastructure that needed an upgrade to enable easy implementation process.

The instructors believed that mandatory and adequate training programmes are paramount as the university management seeks to meet the needs of the new as well as old students and instructors. Instructor 2, 3 and 5 noted that:

We understand how it is important to train instructors and students on the digital learning management system since it will help them to utilise its services fully. All users, both new and old, have to undergo regular mandatory training to validate their experience with a new and existing feature within the digital learning management system.

Exploring Instructors' Perceptions on the Jordanian Cultural Aspects for Using the Digital Learning Management System

The use of DLMS in Jordanian Universities is affected by cultural factors. Jordan has a unique culture that has had an impact on the use of DLMS in different ways. As per Cho and Berge (2002), culture and norms of people working in higher education faculties are the most influential factors affecting the rate under which DLMS is deployed and adopted. Therefore, it is paramount to work on the pedagogical issues and embrace technology through professional training for easy acceptance of a DLMS.

A report indicates that the University management has knowledge of the impact associated with cultural issues, but it has reflected solely to the system quality with little attention to the Jordanian culture. It was mentioned by the interviewee that culture and its dimensions play a vital role as instructor 1 posits that the impact of Jordanian culture in the utilisation of the digital learning management system at Jordanian universities cannot be overlooked. The instructor 1 adds that:

Jordanian culture offers both positive and negative impacts on the implementation and use of the digital learning management system (DLMS). The culture not only affects DLMS tool, but the new application used becomes tricky. Culture determines the acceptance of using DLMS and therefore becomes a vital aspect the university management has not to overlook.

However, instructor 4 reflects the culture from a different perspective point of view based on the relationship between age and culture. He notes that:

Elderly users find it difficult to use the newly implemented software with a lack of desire to learn more about the system due to their age. However, it was excitement and desire for new users to learn more about the software and be able to accomplish their day to day activities and works effectively.

As mentioned earlier in this section, acceptance of using DLMS in the higher education sector within Jordanian universities was a focus on administering the interview. However, it is confirmed that it is not easy to implement the digital learning management system, and therefore, much effort is required. Instructor 5 reflects on the accessibility of DLMS by stating that:

It is not clear to me if cultural implications of using a digital learning management system software is a problem or if users are perceived that using DLMS is hard or attached to complexity. My opinion is that the use of the DLMS system should be management driven for well adoption. However, delivery of assignments, learning materials and exams can be done through the DLMS system, but the issue of the exam cheating becomes paramount, given that cheating is not for specific culture only. This is the reason main exams will be paper-based orientated rather than solely delivered through DLMS system.

As per instructor 4, the use of social media as a communication tool is embraced and the most preferred method by most instructors as compared to a digital system. I use my social media to reach my friend easily, and therefore, it is difficult for other systems for convenience and easy access. The issue with our existing digital learning systems has no support for users with less or no knowledge of how to use them:

From my point of view, the modern world has adopted the use of social media in sharing information, and therefore, culture has less impact on the use of digital learning management systems. People prefer using social media rather than other systems since social media is user-friendly and easy to access and use.

Instructor 7 reflected on how culture predicts the usage of the digital learning management system. From the literature, the adoption of the digital learning management system may fail or be accepted due to differences in cultures. Most IT technology's origins are from developed countries and adoption depends on the surrounding culture and norm of the users (Al-Hujran, Al-Debei, Chatfield, & Migdadi, 2015; Steers, Meyer, & Sanchez-Runde, 2008). Therefore, it is paramount to consider culture during the development and design of the new systems. Instructor 7 indicates that:

Most of DLMS are designed and developed in Western countries with failure to consider culture differences. This is an issue that needs to be addressed before and during designing and implementation of the emerging technology for every country with its unique cultures.

Exploring Instructors' Perceptions on Perceived Usefulness for the Digital Learning Management System

Technology acceptance is also affected directly by Perceived Usefulness (PU). User has favourable perception regarding the acceptance of the digital learning management system if they are perceived that the digital system with improving and increase their work output and productivity. Most higher education institutions around the globe implement digital learning management system as a channel to the effective delivery of educational materials to users. Additionally, higher education institutions embrace DLMS to develop their teaching and learning processes (Hsbollah & Idris, 2009). This research reveals that perceived usefulness of the DLMS has a positive impact on both users, with all interviewees admitting to knowing the perceived usefulness of the system. As per Instructor 1, DLMS help both users (Instructors, Administrators, and students) in that:

From my knowledge of understanding, the instructors are well articulated on the usefulness of the system. The University instructor believes that a centralized platform coupled with needed information that locates easing course materials and people is paramount. I believe that the recommendation of universal centralized platform is the base to effective learning environment as far as the implementation of the DLMS system is concerned.

On perceived usefulness, Instructor 4 was in agreement with instructor 1, who said that:

Technology plays a vital role in effective learning and teaching of education curriculum and therefore instructors require a system that will make their work easier when it comes to managing information and locating learning materials. The latest techniques and technology serves all instructors well and therefore it is paramount all universities to implement digital learning platforms and digital systems that will impacts its operations positively.

However, instructor 5 believed that there is value when a comparison between traditional learning systems and digital learning management system is made. He states that:

Work becomes easy when digital learning management systems are adopted instead of traditional learning systems such as one on one talk and prints during class time. Adopting DLMS enhances communication with a flexible approach to the educational approach. Time efficiency is a by-product of utilizing DLMS since DLMS software saves time for lecture and paperwork delivery.

The interview took into consideration the personalisation of features with instructors knowing the perceived digital learning management system, such as rating and collaborative filtering. As per instructor 3:

My opinion is that using digital learning management system is paramount as it eases my workload with so many benefits associated as far as my daily activities are concerned. I am able to upload and download all my assignment guidelines, study plans and materials with ease, saving my time to deliver quality lectures to my students and understand the progress of the course work.

This notion was well articulated and accepted by instructor 7 based on the role of DLMS for personalizing the educational materials. He noted that:

DLMS software help to personalize the information retrieval and management process of an institution. The university is aiming to offer a tool to help personalise the education experience.

The instructor had advice on the usefulness of the digital system as it is a tool that build a collaborative learning environment. Instructor 6 indicates that:

Adoption of DLMS tool is important since users are able to identify interesting contents with key role to the outcomes associated with learning and teaching goals. Instructors will use the DLMS system occasionally since the existence of an elaborate system coupled with filtered feature makes the identification of content easy with collaborative learning between instructors and students.

However, some users have more expectations from the system as they believe that the digital system and its implementation require regular improvement to meet the demand and needs of the users (Instructors, Administrators, and students). Extra features that would improve the current system were recommended with examples of useful features given by instructor 2, 4, and 6 as follows:

We anticipate that the University management will have to improve on how DLMS is utilised. The rates at which technologies changes require progressive system upgrade and updates within the IT infrastructure framework. Aspect such as DLMS, examination systems and learner directory platforms has to be embedded well in order to foster proper implementation and acceptance of digital learning and associated learning environment. It is the sole responsibility of the university management to grow the system and keep up with current technology and associated upgrade to do away with system vulnerabilities.

Exploring Instructors' Perceptions on Perceived Ease of Use for the Digital Learning Management System

Previous research has found that there is a strong relationship between continuance usage of DLMS and PEOU since perceived ease of use concurrently offers a strong direct effect on behavioral use of new technologies. Therefore, the developer and designer need to come up with a system that has easy tools to use for the sake of better user engagement and motivation. Despite the system reducing user's efforts for service delivery through personalized materials that meet their needs, instructors have a real concern about the associated complexity within the digital learning management system. For instance, instructor 2 noted that:

From my perspective point of view I can say that the system is complicated especially for new users who need workshop orientation for proper use. The training will oversee new users to react positively to the system and therefore without proper orientation and training the system will create issues in terms of acceptance.

Institutions need to provide training programmes and orientation workshops for new users to do away with prevailing issues on system usage and acceptability. Instructor 3, 5, and 6 agreed that new users find it difficult to use a DLMS system that is complex since they perceive a new system with rare use of it:

Many users are not familiar with the digital learning management system since the system is a new technology to have adopted by the higher education sector. Adequate knowledge is therefore required to help a new user to use and adopt well-advanced technology with ease and desire.

Some features, when using DLMS in daily activities and works, were highlighted by instructor 7. He believed that users get happy and comfortable using a system they have the knowledge and mastered all associated features. He adds that:

...My daily job has been easy due to easy use of this tool. I am able to interact with other users easily since the DLMS tool makes it easier to upload assignments and students access their needs without struggling. Earlier on I used to visit in person to the office of other instructor and ask them for a copy of assignments they have at disposal but now am happy it is a click away from the DLMS system to interact with my fellow instructors and students as well hence effective communication that foster better learning environment.

Exploring Instructors' Perceptions on Acceptance and Continuance Usage of the Digital Learning Management System

The ultimate goal of the university management was to ensure that there is regular usage of the digital learning management systems in its management process. The instructors during the interview had frequent commendation on the value of new system implementation and therefore became paramount if system usage regularity by users is known. Most of the Jordanian universities have invested heavily in digital systems to improve users (Instructors, Administrators, and students) education process and enhance education into a modernity perspective. The university management invested heavily in DLMS with the expectation that return investment of using the digital system will be high as compared to the current one. Instructor 1 indicated that:

Theoretically, regular usage of the system by instructors and students define and show the value of the digital system. This is an indication that the more people use the system, the more it is enhanced and an organization is able to make changes and upgrade systems based on the users recommendation to the prevailing vulnerability as far as associated system features are concerned. An effective learning is realised when the system meet the demand of the users such as effective delivery of information for instructors and effective access to the information for students.

The university management believed that the role of DLMS is to store more content as well as learning materials in one domain with easy access and an effective and efficient working environment for all users (Instructors, Administrators, and Students). However, system usefulness restrictions are exhibited if there is no effective involvement of instructors and students with the system. Thus, the reflection of the university management was to raise the usage regularity of instructors and students and foster fully utilization of valuable facilities provided by DLMS. Instructor 2 posits that:

Training instructors and students on the DLMS is one way of utilising associated valuable facilities of the system. It is evident that the majority of the users have less knowledge on how the digital system works and therefore becomes a challenge getting more instructors and students accept using the system on a regular basis. The benefits, efficiency and effectiveness associated with system is only recognised through regular exposure when using the DLMS.

Users (Instructors, Administrators, and students) have to perceive its ease of use, quality, and usefulness to raise the usage levels of the digital learning management system. As per instructor 4:

Despite the existing digital system model working well, an improvement in IT infrastructure, as well as cultural behaviours, is paramount since it raises the usage knowledge levels and offers digital system acceptance.

SUMMARY OF THE IMPORTANT FINDINGS FROM THE CASE STUDY ANALYSIS

The decision of users to accept DLMS tools can be affected by many issues. Slow system response, lack of network connectivity, and social-cultural issues are issues that are affecting Jordanian university users with the decision to accept DLMS tools. The research, however, adopt these factors affecting acceptance and rate of adoption of DLMS to give an understanding aspect how the diffusion of DLMS tools by employees are influenced by these factors with regards to their relative advantage, attitude, compatibility and complexity (Mkhize, Mtsweni, & Buthelezi, 2016).

The availability of technology in the country in general, and in universities in particular, such Internet connections, computers and DLMS tools (AlQudah, 2014) called IT infrastructure. The unique culture in Jordan is a very important factor that influences the use of DLMSs in different ways, and this research will focus on this factor through perceived use and perceived ease of use. Perceived ease of use refers to *the degree to which a person believes that using a particular system would be free of effort* (Davis, 1989, p. 320). The degree to which the user believes that using the DLMS would improve their learning performance (Davis, 1989). The perceived usefulness and perceived ease of use of a DLMS under a given behaviour for continued use of DLMSs in Jordanian universities.

TAM - Technology Acceptance Model is a framework that this research has utilized to address all relevant issues surrounding the DLMS context. The reason why TAM is proposed by this research is that the model is based on the extension of TAM that has been tested and examined through an application on the discovery of new information as well as an understanding of DLMS (Davis, 1989).

Two determinants of computer use have been suggested through TAM, which includes PEOU (Perceived ease of use) and PU (Perceived usefulness) (Davis, 1989). However, other researchers, as well as investigators, have come up with an extension of the TAM model that accommodates additional variables to account for extra computer usage technology variance (Gefen & Straub, 1997; Venkatesh & Davis, 2000). Behavioral decision theory is perceived to have an advantage paradigm that is relevant to PU and PEOU (Beach & Mitchell, 1978).

SOLUTIONS AND RECOMMENDATIONS

Administrators are the sole manager to DLMSs who have access to restricted documentation stored within the server and school database. However, safeguarding and overriding all documents is overridden by administrators lead to the provision of the best service. Jordanian universities need to consider using one learning system for linguistic and cultural diversity. However, the recommendation means that everyone needs to have access to the laptop, smart phones as well as internet connections. It is, therefore, the work of users to embrace access and manage profile privacy to get positive outcomes on their daily work schedules.

FUTURE RESEARCH DIRECTIONS

There is a challenge when users partner with each other in terms of creating a balance between the qualities of managing and using an online digital learning management system. However, the following recommendations can be utilized for future research directions to improve the adoption and acceptance of DLMS as perceived by users based on their goals:

- Future research needs to dissect data from multiple sources to make meaningful sense of DLMS from users and technical perspectives;
- DLMS motivates, empowers, and facilitates the self-image of users, and therefore, it is essential to promote well DLMS to help users meet their daily process easily without hustle;
- Knowing how to use DLMS records, using basic computer skills as well as easy remote access becomes essential in terms of acceptance and adoption of DLMS. It will be wise if all Jordan universities utilize the available specialized computer centres and run one semester that teaches all users, especially those users from non-English speaking backgrounds or with low-computer literacy, basic computer skills to enhance the rate of acceptance and adoption of DLMS;
- Working as a team between stakeholders from the higher education ministry and Jordanian universities management help in adopting the safety, privacy, and security of DLMS, hence offering benefits associated with the use of electronic educational systems to users;
- The system seems complex for users with difficulties accessing information easily, and therefore awareness and basic knowledge of DLMS are paramount. Additionally, the DLMS system must be improved so that we have a real-time notification system that helps users to access and have progressive updates on DLMS instead of utilizing unprofessional tools such as the use of media between each other.

CONCLUSION

As a summary, it is essential for university management to fully understand and continue using a digital system since the implementation of the digital learning management system is paramount to effective service delivery. Effective and efficient use of the digital system by users is paramount since the value and advantages of the system are realized and fully utilized. However, when users (instructors, administrators, and students) realize the advantages associated with a digital system, the usage levels automatically rises. For instance, 90 percent of the interview responses from the six Jordanian universities show that advanced usage by instructors and students results from the adoption of university management utilizing DLMS systems in their learning process.

Through a qualitative case study analysis, the main objective of the university management in the deployment of DLMS was to deliver better as well as quality education to users. Adoption of the system had the benefit from university management, and it is evident from the instructor's interview responses that the use of DLMS has value in terms of personalized contents and availability of learning materials that meet personal preferences and needs through a digitalized collaborative learning environment. Collaboration among users can be achieved when money and time are saved by efficient as well as effective DLMS implementation.

There are challenges faced by university management when using and implementing DLMS tools and associated applications. These challenges include limited use of the digital system by users, digital system complexity, and inelastic to support and satisfy the needs of the users.

Interviews from the instructors indicated that it is important to raise the levels and awareness of using the DLMS system for users to maximize the merits of the system without exhibiting operations vulnerabilities. The efficient and effective use of the system as per the users raises the recognition of significance associated with the implementation and use of DLMS in university management. Therefore, it is the mandate of the university management to clarify the features of the digital system and associated functions as far as the efficient learning process is concerned.

To sum up, it is recognized by the university management that increased development and use of cultural, IT infrastructure, usefulness, and ease of use better usage and acceptance rate of DLMS by users (instructors, administrators, and students). Therefore, development and implementation strategy, as well as an action plan, should be prioritized by university management to meet their strategic goals.

REFERENCES

Abbad, M. M., Morris, D., & De Nahlik, C. (2009). Looking under the bonnet: Factors affecting student adoption of e-learning systems in Jordan. *The International Review of Research in Open and Distributed Learning*, *10*(2). doi:10.19173/irrodl.v10i2.596

Abdullateef, B. N., Elias, N. F., Mohamed, H., Zaidan, A., & Zaidan, B. (2016). An evaluation and selection problems of OSS-LMS packages. *SpringerPlus*, *5*(1), 1. doi:10.118640064-016-1828-y PMID:27064567

Adams, D. A., Nelson, R. R., & Todd, P. A. (1992). Perceived usefulness, ease of use, and usage of information technology: A replication. *Management Information Systems Quarterly*, *16*(2), 227–247. doi:10.2307/249577

Ahmad, S. A., Chinade, U. B., Gambaki, A. M., Ibrahim, S., & Ala, N. A. (2012). The need for MOODLE as a learning management system in Nigerian Universities: Digesting University Utara Malaysia Learning Zone as a case study. *Academic Research International*, *2*(3), 444.

Al Amoush, A. B., & Sandhu, K. (2019). *A New Model for Acceptance of Analytics in Learning Management Systems at Jordanian Universities (JLMS). In Modern Technologies for Teaching and Learning in Socio-Humanitarian Disciplines* (pp. 138–161). IGI Global.

Al-Dmour, R. (2014). *An integration model for identifying the determinants of the adoption and implementation level of HRIS applications and Its effectiveness in business organisations in Jordan* (Doctor of Philosophy). Brunel University. Retrieved from http://bura.brunel.ac.uk/handle/2438/9222

Al-Hujran, O., Al-Debei, M. M., Chatfield, A., & Migdadi, M. (2015). The imperative of influencing citizen attitude toward e-government adoption and use. *Computers in Human Behavior, 53*, 189–203. doi:10.1016/j.chb.2015.06.025

Al Musawi, A., Ambusaidi, A., Al-Balushi, S., & Al-Balushi, K. (2015). Effectiveness of E-Lab Use in Science Teaching at the Omani Schools. *TOJET: The Turkish Online Journal of Educational Technology, 14*(1).

Al-Shaikh, F. N. (2003). The practical reality theory and business ethics in non-Western context: Evidence from Jordan. *Journal of Management Development, 22*(8), 679–693. doi:10.1108/02621710310487855

Al-Shboul, M. (2011). Potential Use of Course Management Systems in Higher Education Institutions in Jordan. *Online Submission, 8*(2), 220–232.

Al-Shboul, M. (2013). The Level of E-Learning Integration at the University of Jordan: Challenges and Opportunities. *International Education Studies, 6*(4). doi:10.5539/ies.v6n4p93

Al-Shboul, M. A., & Alsmadi, I. (2010). Challenges of Utilizing E-Learning Systems in Public Universities in Jordan. *iJET, 5*(1), 4-10.

Al-Zoubi, S. I., & Ali, M. (2019). *The Bearing of Culture upon Intention to Utilize D-learning Amongst Jordanian University Students: Modernizing with Emerging Technologies.* Paper presented at the International Conference for Emerging Technologies in Computing. 10.1007/978-3-030-23943-5_21

Almarabch, T. (2014). Students' Perceptions of E-learning at the University of Jordan. *iJET, 9*(3), 31-35.

Alnsour, A., Muhsen, Z., Dababnah, M., Eljinini, M. A., & Barhoum, K. A. (2011). Implementing Moodle as a Tool to develop the Isra University e-learn system. *IJCSNS International Journal of Computer Science and Network Security, 11*, 120–124.

AlQudah, A. A. (2014). Accepting Moodle by academic staff at the University of Jordan: Applying and extending TAM in technical support factors. *European Scientific Journal, 10*(18).

Arguel, A., Lockyer, L., Kennedy, G., Lodge, J. M., & Pachman, M. (2019). Seeking optimal confusion: A review on epistemic emotion management in interactive digital learning environments. *Interactive Learning Environments, 27*(2), 200–210. doi:10.1080/10494820.2018.1457544

Atoum, I., Otoom, A., & Ali, A. A. (2017). Holistic Cyber Security Implementation Frameworks: A Case Study of Jordan. *International Journal of Information. Business and Management, 9*(1), 108.

Babić, S. (2012). Factors that influence academic teacher's acceptance of e-learning technology in blended learning environment. *E-Learning-Organizational Infrastructure and Tools for Specific Areas*, 3-18.

Beach, L. R., & Mitchell, T. R. (1978). A contingency model for the selection of decision strategies. *Academy of Management Review, 3*(3), 439–449. doi:10.5465/amr.1978.4305717

Cho, S. K., & Berge, Z. L. (2002). Overcoming barriers to distance training and education. *USDLA Journal, 16*(1), 16–34.

Creswell, J. W. (2013). *Research design: Qualitative, quantitative, and mixed methods approaches*. Sage publications.

Davis, F. D. (1989). Perceived usefulness, perceived ease of use, and user acceptance of information technology. *Management Information Systems Quarterly, 13*(3), 319–340. doi:10.2307/249008

Gefen, D., & Straub, D. W. (1997). Gender differences in the perception and use of e-mail: An extension to the technology acceptance model. *Management Information Systems Quarterly, 21*(4), 389–400. doi:10.2307/249720

Gupta, S. K., & Rao, D. (2018). A case study on contemporary water management innovation (CWMI) in sustainable agriculture: Farmers joined hands for mutual survival and prosperity: The case of Kummarvandlapalli. *IJCS, 6*(6), 2283–2287.

Hofstede, G. (1983). National cultures in four dimensions: A research-based theory of cultural differences among nations. *International Studies of Management & Organization, 13*(1-2), 46–74. doi:10.1080/00208825.1983.11656358

Hsbollah, H. M., & Idris, K. M. (2009). E-learning adoption: The role of relative advantages, trialability and academic specialisation. *Campus-Wide Information Systems, 26*(1), 54–70. doi:10.1108/10650740910921564

Igbaria, M., Zinatelli, N., Cragg, P., & Cavaye, A. L. (1997). Personal computing acceptance factors in small firms: A structural equation model. *Management Information Systems Quarterly, 21*(3), 279–305. doi:10.2307/249498

Imlawi, J., Gregg, D., & Karimi, J. (2015). Student engagement in course-based social networks: The impact of instructor credibility and use of communication. *Computers & Education, 88*, 84–96. doi:10.1016/j.compedu.2015.04.015

Iskander, M. (2008). *Innovative techniques in instruction technology, e-learning, e-assessment and education*. Springer Science & Business Media. doi:10.1007/978-1-4020-8739-4

Kats, Y. (2010). *Learning Management System Technologies and Software Solutions for Online Teaching: Tools and Applications: Tools and Applications*. IGI Global.

Khwaldeh, S. M., Al-Hadid, I., Masa'deh, R. e., & Alrowwad, A. (2017). The Association between E-Services Web Portals Information Quality and ICT Competence in the Jordanian Universities. *Asian Social Science, 13*(3), 156. doi:10.5539/ass.v13n3p156

McIntosh, J., & Torres, M. I. (2014). *Learning Management Systems: Revisiting Learning Management Systems at the University Level*. The University of Tampa.

Mkhize, P., Mtsweni, E. S., & Buthelezi, P. (2016). Diffusion of Innovations Approach to the Evaluation of Learning Management System Usage in an Open Distance Learning Institution. *The International Review of Research in Open and Distributed Learning, 17*(3). doi:10.19173/irrodl.v17i3.2191

Mutlag, A. A., Ghani, M. K. A., Arunkumar, N., Mohamed, M. A., & Mohd, O. (2019). Enabling technologies for fog computing in healthcare IoT systems. *Future Generation Computer Systems, 90*, 62–78. doi:10.1016/j.future.2018.07.049

Orr, G. (2003). *Diffusion of innovations*. Everett Rogers.

Phillipo, J., & Krongard, S. (2012). *Learning Management System*. LMS.

Potter, L. E., & Thompson, A. (2019). Engaging with STEM Students: Successes and Challenges in Course Design. *Blended Learning Designs in STEM Higher Education*, 231–248.

Rank, u. U. (2019). *Jordanian University Ranking 2019*. Retrieved from https://www.4icu.org/jo/

Ridder, H.-G. (2017). The theory contribution of case study research designs. *Business Research, 10*(2), 281–305. doi:10.100740685-017-0045-z

Rogers, E. (1995). *Diffusion of Innovations*. The Free Press.

Rowley, J. (2002). Using case studies in research. *Management Research News, 25*(1), 16–27. doi:10.1108/01409170210782990

Saadé, R., & Bahli, B. (2005). The impact of cognitive absorption on perceived usefulness and perceived ease of use in on-line learning: An extension of the technology acceptance model. *Information & Management, 42*(2), 317–327. doi:10.1016/j.im.2003.12.013

Samak, A., & Tawfik, Z. (2017). *Exploration of Jordanian English Language Teachers' Attitudes*. Skills, and Access as Indicator of Information and Communication Technology Integration in Jordan.

Steers, R. M., Meyer, A. D., & Sanchez-Runde, C. J. (2008). National culture and the adoption of new technologies. *Journal of World Business, 43*(3), 255–260. doi:10.1016/j.jwb.2008.03.007

Szajna, B. (1996). Empirical evaluation of the revised technology acceptance model. *Management Science, 42*(1), 85–92. doi:10.1287/mnsc.42.1.85

Unwin, T., Kleessen, B., Hollow, D., Williams, J. B., Oloo, L. M., Alwala, J., . . . Muianga, X. (2010). Digital learning management systems in Africa: myths and realities. *Open Learning: The Journal of Open, Distance and e-Learning, 25*(1), 5-23.

Varis, T., & Al-Agtash, S. (2008). *Ubiquitous ICT for sustainable education and cultural literacy*. Citeseer.

Venkatesh, V. (1999). Creation of favorable user perceptions: Exploring the role of intrinsic motivation. *Management Information Systems Quarterly, 23*(2), 239–260. doi:10.2307/249753

Venkatesh, V., & Davis, F. D. (2000). A theoretical extension of the technology acceptance model: Four longitudinal field studies. *Management Science, 46*(2), 186–204. doi:10.1287/mnsc.46.2.186.11926

Whelan, R., & Bhartu, D. (2007). Factors in the deployment of a learning management system at the University of the South Pacific. *Proceedings Ascilite Singapore*, 1053-1062.

Williams, P. (2002). The learning web: The development, implementation and evaluation of internet-based undergraduate materials for the teaching of key skills. *Active Learning in Higher Education, 3*(1), 40–53. doi:10.1177/1469787402003001004

Wimpenny, K., Adefila, A., & DeWinter, A. (2018). *Jordan Opportunity for Virtual Innovative Teaching and Learning: A Needs Analysis Report Contextualising the State of the Art in International Online Teaching and Learning, with Particular Attention to the Jordanian Case*. Academic Press.

Yin, R. K. (1981). The case study crisis: Some answers. *Administrative Science Quarterly*, *26*(1), 58–65. doi:10.2307/2392599

Yin, R. K. (2012). A (very) brief refresher on the case study method. *Applications of Case Study Research*, 3-20.

Yin, R. K. (2015). *Qualitative research from start to finish*. Guilford Publications.

ADDITIONAL READING

Al Amoush, A. B., & Sandhu, K. (2018b). Learning Management Systems in Jordan Context. Australasian Journal of Business. *Social Science and Information Technology*, *4*(2), 46–54.

Al Amoush, A. B., & Sandhu, K. (2019a). *Discovery of New Knowledge for an LMS at Jordanian Universities Open and Social Learning in Impact Communities and Smart Territories* (pp. 187–214). IGI Global.

Al Amoush, A. B., & Sandhu, K. (2019b). *LMS Tools and Data Analysis Approaches: Similarities and Differences Educational and Social Dimensions of Digital Transformation in Organizations* (pp. 65–76). IGI Global. doi:10.4018/978-1-5225-6261-0.ch004

Al Amoush, A. B., & Sandhu, K. (2019c). *A New Model for Acceptance of Analytics in Learning Management Systems at Jordanian Universities (JLMS) Modern Technologies for Teaching and Learning in Socio-Humanitarian Disciplines* (pp. 138–161). IGI Global.

Al Amoush, A. B., & Sandhu, K. (2020). *A New Paradigm for Acceptance of Analytics in Learning Management Systems at Jordanian Universities (JLMS) Revolutionizing Education in the Age of AI and Machine Learning* (pp. 173–195). IGI Global.

KEY TERMS AND DEFINITIONS

Acceptance of a DLMS: The perceived usefulness and perceived ease of use of a DLMS under a given behaviour for continued use of DLMSs in Jordanian universities.

DLMS: Digital learning management systems (DLMSs) are a necessary educational tools for learning activities (Al Amoush & Sandhu, 2019).

Information Technology: The technology involving the development, maintenance, and use of computer systems, software, and networks for the processing and distribution of data (Mutlag, Ghani, Arunkumar, Mohamed, & Mohd, 2019).

IT Infrastructure: The availability of technology in the country in general, and in universities in particular, such Internet connections, computers and DLMS tools (AlQudah, 2014).

Jordanian Culture: The unique culture in Jordan is a very important factor that influences the use of DLMSs in different ways, and this research will focus on this factor through perceived use.

Perceived Ease of Use: Perceived ease of use refers to the degree to which a person believes that using a particular system would be free of effort (Davis, 1989, p. 320).

Perceived Usefulness: The degree to which the user believes that using the DLMS would improve their learning performance (Davis, 1989).

Technology Acceptance Model (TAM): It has become well-established as a robust, powerful, and parsimonious model for predicting user acceptance (Venkatesh & Davis, 2000, p. 19).

Chapter 6
Impact of Digital Transformations on Corporate Social Responsibility (CSR) Practices in Turkey:
A Study of the Current Environment

Aslıhan Kıymalıoğlu
Akdeniz University, Turkey

ABSTRACT

Each year, corporations have been donating millions of dollars for non-profit organizations in order to fulfil their duty towards society, and companies are engaging in many approaches in order to strengthen their relationship with consumers. One of these is corporate social responsibility (CSR). The purpose of this chapter is to consolidate an understanding of real-world business practices with an academic research perspective and to inform the reader on the developments in CSR practices in the digital environment. With this purpose, a descriptive research is adopted that will include a content analysis of the companies that will be selected from the list of Fortune 500 in Turkey, and the data from the web pages of the top 100 companies will be analysed. The results indicate that large Turkish companies are lagging behind global companies with regards to digitalisation of CSR practices and institutionalisation of their CSR practices when compared to the corporations in developed countries.

INTRODUCTION

Each year, corporations have been donating millions of dollars for non-profit organizations in order to fulfil their duty towards society. The rapid changes in especially the technology have altered the classical rules of the business.

Together with the financial responsibilities of the firms towards its shareholders, societal responsibility has become as much important. Consumers, who used to be concerned with only the product,

DOI: 10.4018/978-1-7998-5175-2.ch006

now turned their attention to the company. It is no longer preferred by consumers to be a loved-brand, but instead being a loving-brand is more reputable, where CSR plays a crucial role. In addition to the company's prominence in business issues, sensitivity towards issues related to the society has become an emphasized matter. The social consequences of consumers' purchase behaviour have become a major concern for them. They expect a behavioural change by being a part of the campaigns raised by the company. It allows development of society through solving social problems and raising awareness besides changing attitudes (Elden, Yeygel Cakir & Bakir, 2011). The prevalence of the concept can be explained by repeating a search by Idowu (2017) where he has googled the concept and obtained a result of 77,000,000 in 48 seconds; whereas it was 318,000,000 in 55 seconds at the time of the current study, increasing in more than 4 times in the two-year period.

This change has been fostered with the digital revolution where consumers are going through a completely different journey. Digital revolution started in 1980s and refers to the improvements in use of technology. Its impact is listed as the effects on business and revenue models, new digital channels and media, and the penetration of data (Leeflang et al., 2014) and is reflected not only on business practices, but also on education, society, politics and government.

Corporate social responsibility (CSR) practices of the companies are one of these areas which have been transformed as a result of digital revolution. It has become easier to collect and share the information worldwide, to receive feedback from stakeholders rapidly and easily, and to turn CSR communication into an interactive process (Antal, Dierkes, MacMillan & Marz, 2002; Orbik & Zozul'akova, 2019). The digital age has transformed the way corporations communicate with the society. This "dynamization of communication" (Castello, Morsing & Schultz, 2013) enabled democratization of society as all the issues pertaining to the society could be discussed from diverse perspectives by reducing the barriers. Despite the prevalent dominance of digitalization, only limited number of businesses could go beyond using internet only for reporting the CSR practices. The number of digital CSR practices does not reflect the pace of digital transformation experienced.

The aims of this study are to investigate the CSR environment in Turkey, which is an important destination for business, commerce, and trade, and strategically located between Europe, Asia, & Africa. And analysing the data from top 100 companies from Fortune 500 list will provide a valuable information about the impact of Digital Transformations on Corporate Social Responsibility (CSR) Practices in Turkey. Findings will reveal the current situation with regards to integration of digital developments with CSR practice in Turkey.

WHAT IS CSR?

Companies are engaging in many approaches in order to strengthen their relationship with consumers. One of these efforts is Corporate Social Responsibility (CSR). Acting as a social contract between consumer and company, CSR has been defined as "a term describing a company's obligations to be accountable to all of its stakeholders in all its operations and activities. Socially responsible companies consider the full scope of their impact on communities and the environment when making decisions, balancing the needs of stakeholders with their need to make a profit" (Doane, 2005, pp. 217). The early approach to the concept was considering it as a part of company obligation to increase its profits only, which was acknowledged as the sole responsibility of the company. However, thanks to the discussions over the role of businesses with regards to the welfare of all its stakeholders, perception of CSR has changed. It has become a management concept which "is generally understood as being the way through which a company achieves a balance of economic, environmental and social imperatives, while at the same time addressing the expectations of shareholders and stakeholders" (UNIDO, 2019). Since first mentioned in Sheldon's (1923) work until the present day, the scope of CSR has evolved, which led to various definitions. The lack of consensus on CSR indicates the broad scope and complexity of the concept (Castro-Gonzales, Bande, Fernandez-Ferrin & Kimura, 2019).

Although no standard definition of CSR yet exists, various authors have proposed alternative classifications for its developmental stages (Zadek, 2004; Visser, 2014), a comprehensive review of which was provided by Maon, Lindgreen & Swaen (2010). Zadek (2004) explained the five stages that businesses go through by using the Nike example, stating that all of them experience the same "metamorphosis". According to the author, there are two interrelated dimensions about corporate responsibility, organizational and societal learning. Organisational learning has five stages, which are defensive ('It's not our job to fix that'), compliance ('We'll do just as much as we have to'), managerial ('It's the business'), strategic ('It gives us a competitive edge') and civil ('We need to make sure everybody does it'). These stages should be aligned with the changing awareness of the society towards certain issues in order to respond to their demands.

Visser (2014) also suggested five stages of CSR, which are defensive, charitable, promotional, strategic, transformative. According to the author, the stages represent the evolution of business responsibility. In the defensive stage, the dominant paradigm is greed, whose focal point is the shareholder value. The paradigm of charitable stage is philanthropy which supports the idea of earning money first, then sharing it. The third stage of a business in CSR evolution is promotional CSR, whose paradigm is represented by marketing. Businesses start to benefit from public relations in order to increase their reputation. And for this, they use media as their tool. Strategic CSR is the fourth stage with its dominant paradigm of management. It is based on management systems that enable improvement of business processes through relating the CSR activities to the company business. The fifth and last stage of CSR is transformative CSR with the paradigm of responsibility. This stage focuses on the macro level system and works for the welfare of the larger human and ecosystem.

Lee (2008) has detailed the evolution of CSR theories in order to reflect the conceptual shifts. The author has defined the 50s – 60s period as "social responsibility of businessmen" when the businesses are obliged to consider the social consequences of their acts. This period also witnessed the acts protecting the rights of consumers and employees. One of the most important objections to the business responsibility idea developed in this period was raised by Milton Friedman (1962). He suggested that the only responsibility of a company is to make profits for its shareholders. The second period is the "enlightened self-interest" that took place in 1970s. This approach supported the idea that CSR would benefit the business itself in the long run, therefore they should also work for the well-being of their environment. The author cited CSR in 1980s as experiencing corporate social performance model, which was built on the seminal work by Carroll (1979), integrating economic, legal, ethical and discretionary responsibility of corporations under the social responsibility title. For each of these categories, corporations can employ reaction, defence, accommodation or pro-action strategy. The fourth phase following is named as strategic management which span through 1990s. Stakeholder analysis of the management research is applied to CSR in this period. The level of analysis narrowed down to the organisation with a managerial orientation. This period represents unification of social and economic performance of corporations, together with the competitive edge. Therefore, CSR starts to mean more than just social activities a company engages in, but the financial performance of it also comes to the foreground. It is suggested that corporations considering the welfare of society will also do better financially. The display of Lee (2008) indicated the evolution of CSR theories where the macro level analysis gave their way to organizational level with a managerial orientation instead of an ethical one. The developments in CSR approach also has resulted in *tight coupling* – as stated by Lee (2008) – between CSR and corporate financial performance.

A comprehensive review of the theories on CSR has been proposed by Garriga and Mele (2004). The authors have "mapped the territory" by clarifying the unclear and complex situation caused by different perspectives dominating the concept. They have grouped CSR theories under four titles, namely instrumental, political, integrative and ethical theories. Each of these groups represents an important aspect of social responsibility issue. The instrumental theories are concerned with profits and wealth creation, and thus, their expected output is related to economic results. The political theories, as the authors suggest, are focused on the power and role of corporations in society and represent the political performance that arises as a result. Integrative theories deal with the social demands and their satisfaction. The theories in this group suggest that society is vital for the existence of businesses and therefore, its activities should be operated in line with social demands. The final group is named as ethical theories that focus on ethical responsibilities of the businesses towards society. The approaches are based on the premise of doing what is right for the society. However, the authors posit that each group has its own limitations and a new theory that comprises the four approaches should be developed in order to better understand and apply corporate social responsibility.

Studies on CSR

The interest towards CSR has risen recently although the effects of corporations on nature and society have not been a recent topic. Since the landmark book written by Bowen (1953), where the responsibilities of a business are discussed, there is a large volume of published studies on the role of CSR debated from diverse perspectives. A comprehensive review by Aguinis and Glavas (2012) draw a picture of the relevant studies on CSR. The authors have grouped the studies on institutional, organisational and individual level and determined the predictors, mediators, moderators and outcomes of CSR in the studies of each group. They have come up with numerous conclusions, such as stakeholders are an important determinant in CSR practices of corporations; CSR increases firm reputation, customer loyalty and positive evaluation; financial performance is an important motivator for engaging in CSR; personal values acts as a significant predictor of CSR success; employees are positively affected from CSR initiatives, their engagement, commitment and identification with the firm increases (Aguinis & Glavas, 2012).

Similar studies have also supported the positive effect of CSR on various topics, some of which are firm performance (McGuire, Sundgren & Schneeweis, 1988; Mishra & Suar, 2010; Wang, Chen, Yu & Hsiao, 2015), customer satisfaction (Luo & Bhattacharya, 2006; Galbreath & Shum, 2012; Sun & Price, 2016), brand related concepts (Klein & Dawar, 2004; Martinez & Nishiyama, 2017; Kang & Namkung, 2018) and firm image (Mohr & Webb, 2005; Lee & Shin, 2010; Kim, Youn & Lee, 2019).

CSR represents the shift from the compelled donations of corporations to voluntary philanthropic activities and both firms and non-profit organizations need it for success and finding resources, respectively (Buyukkupcu et al., 2007). It has become a 'must', instead of a 'would better'. Not only customers and society are the addressee of CSR activities, but also the shareholders, employees, competitors and state are within the sphere of influence of these activities. Consumers are more sensitive to the negative effects of corporations on various aspects of life (Sheikh & Beise-Zee, 2011). Thus, using the products of a socially responsible company makes consumers feel better. Increased social responsibility from corporations results in more support from consumers and the community. Therefore, transparent and proactive communication is a critical issue for CSR (Chaudri and Wang, 2007) which is a model satisfying economic, social and environmental responsibilities simultaneously.

Facilitating the performance improvement and positive social impact efforts of corporations is the digital transformation. Organisations are now integrating their strategy and identity with digital innovations thanks to what it has become easier and more rapid to communicate corporate activities with stakeholders. The speed, transparency and adaptability of this tool have changed the rules of the game for the benefit of all parties. The digital change, thus, is an important milestone in the way CSR is practiced and perceived.

Digital Change and CSR

Besides the changes that CSR has undergone with respect to the developments in business approaches, digital transformation has also changed corporate philanthropic activities. Similar to the value chain activities, CSR practices have undergone digitalisation in order to enact the positive change required in the era we are in. The global environment compelled businesses to be responsible, accountable and transparent as technology has enabled the information to be collected and shared worldwide quickly. Thus, the instruments we use in the business need to be remodelled in order to meet the needs of modern global citizens (Idowu, 2018). The increasing use of the Internet in all activities has provided organisations with new mediums and patterns to communicate with their stakeholders, CSR receiving its share. It will not be wrong to state that the crucial advantage of the Internet for CSR practices is that "[it] can become an ongoing and interactive process rather than a static annual report" (Antal et al., 2002, pp. 34). Through this proactive communication with stakeholders, companies can involve them in strategy planning and CSR practices, and thus, establish long-term relationships with them by effectively responding to their influence (Roşca, Sarău & Vonţea, 2015).

Visser (2014) explained this shift from the notion of corporate social responsibility (CSR 1.0) to a novel concept as CSR 2.0, which he coined as 'corporate sustainability and responsibility', similar to the shift from Web 1.0 to Web 2.0 (see Table 1 and Table 2).

Table 1. Similarities between Web 1.0 and CSR 1.0

Web 1.0	CSR 1.0
A flat world just beginning to connect itself and finding a new medium to push out information and plug advertising	A vehicle for companies to establish relationships with communities, channel philanthropic contributions and manage their image
Saw the rise to prominence of innovators like Netscape, but these were quickly outmuscled by giants like Microsoft with its Internet Explorer	Included many start-up pioneers like Traidcraft, but has ultimately turned into a product for large multinationals like Wal-Mart
Focused largely on the standardized hardware and software of the PC as its delivery platform, rather than multi-level applications	Travelled down the road of 'one size fits all' standardization, through codes, standards and guidelines to shape its offering

Source: Visser, 2014, pp. 37

Table 2. Similarities between Web 2.0 and CSR 2.0

Web 2.0	CSR 2.0
Being defined by watchwords like 'collective intelligence', 'collaborative networks' and 'user participation	Being defined by 'global commons', 'innovative partnerships' and 'stakeholder involvement'
Tools include social media, knowledge syndication and beta testing	Mechanisms include diverse stakeholder panels, real-time transparent reporting and new-wave social entrepreneurship
Is as much a state of being as a technical advance—it is a new philosophy or way of seeing the world differently	Is recognising a shift in power from centralized to decentralised; a change in scale from few and big to many and small; and a change in application from single and exclusive to multiple and shared

Source: Visser, 2014, pp. 38

The author states the similarity by saying that "[t]he transformation of the internet through the emergence of social media networks, user-generated content and open source approaches is a fitting metaphor for the changes business is experiencing as it begins to redefine its role in society" (Visser, 2014, pp. 37). It is clear that not only the businesses that are lagging in embracing a corporate social responsibility approach, but also the ones that still practice classical CSR notion cannot keep up with their competitive counterparts. The world is becoming more connected. And the business practices that use CSR 1.0 (just like Web 1.0) will be left behind; and the corporations that can find innovative ways to deal with the challenges the global era has brought, who use CSR 2.0, will be successful and competitive. Visser (2014) has also provided an "acid test" for the CSR practices and defines the ontological shift in CSR (Table 3).

Table 3. Shift of CSR features

CSR 1.0	CSR 2.0
Philanthropic	Collaborative
Risk-based	Reward-based
Image-driven	Performance-driven
Specialised	Integrated
Standardised	Diversified
Marginal	Scalable
Western	Global

Source: Visser, 2014, pp. 41

What can be clearly deduced from the above lists and comparisons is that CSR is passing through a new phase, which goes parallel with the developments in the digital world. Therefore, businesses need to embrace the new mentality which integrates digital innovations into its practices, acts in cooperation with its stakeholders and finds creative solutions to global challenges by using technology.

Communicating CSR in Digital World

Recently, most of the companies have started to publish their social responsibility efforts through corporate web pages or social media, which enables uniting CSR efforts in one platform, maintaining transparency, and maximising stakeholder engagement and collaboration. CSR communication turned into an important tool in conveying the message and image of the company. Corporations start to use digital tools as leverage because social media and web site publications allow active participation and information gathering for participants. For businesses, the rise of digital technologies and social media provides endless opportunities that enable public awareness (Kaplan & Haenlein, 2010). Furthermore, digital media is crucial thanks to uniting various interest groups, allowing corporations to announce their practices to a wider public and incorporate relevant stakeholders. Thus, digital tools are increasingly preferred over traditional media. With regards to communicating CSR practices, companies prefer publishing through their web pages or social media accounts. Recently, CSR campaigns that are carried out via social media have emerged.

This new media has three characteristics that shape business – public relationship (Lee, Oh & Kim, 2013). Social media is *dialogic*. This type of communication is built on constituting and maintaining relationship instead of managing audiences. Second, social media is *uncontrollable*. There is not a single entity controlling the inputs. There is a multidirectional information sharing. And last, all content in social media is *searchable and accessible* to anyone. Hence, anyone having a negative experience can find a social support instead of suffering from that experience alone.

Digital and social media tools, which are used increasingly more for CSR communication, have provided a trade-off between CSR controllability and credibility as the stakeholders consider a less controllable communicator as more credible (Du, Bhattacharya & Sen, 2010). Corporations are generally considered as self-interested communicators and stakeholders are sceptical towards the CSR communication. Digital developments have decreased this skepticism. Traditional media tools could easily be manipulated by the corporations yet social and digital media allows open dialogues. To put it another way, public-engaged CSR programmes provides an optimal level of self-disclosure for businesses and an opportunity of avoiding activities that can result in stakeholder skepticism (Illia et al., 2017).

In today's digital world, traditional communication channels are no longer preferred and are not as efficient. Companies are required to communicate with consumers instead of just listening. Consumers need to express themselves, and social media and Internet provide the best tool for this (Ali, Jimenez-Zarco & Bicho, 2015). Communicating CSR practices through the Internet and social media has been "a direct offshoot of the digital revolution" (Chaudhri & Wang, 2007). Via these communications in Internet and social media, corporations are expecting to have the positive considerations of their stakeholders.

Studies on Digital CSR

The findings of previous studies on CSR communication indicate that most of the global companies shift from traditional reporting to digital, through websites and social channels. Taking advantage of technological innovations would strengthen the business-society relationship. However, it is also expected that, though it is more suitable to publicize CSR activities through the corporate web pages and social media accounts in this digital age, it is not sufficient. Corporations should commence carrying out their CSR activities through digital channels. Initial seeds of this approach are planted by some global companies that practice digital CSR campaigns.

Internet and social media has provided a perfect tool for businesses to spread information, display their corporate image, and communicate their social responsibility with their stakeholders and the public. When businesses communicate their CSR actions effectively, stakeholder involvement increases and they become advocates of the company (Ali et al., 2015).

Research comparing a three-year difference in displaying CSR activities on websites of a thousand Canadian companies revealed a 40% increase (Basil and Erlandson, 2008). On the other hand, the study of Coluccia, Fontana and Solimene (2016) indicated that online reporting of CSR activities is still limited in Italy. In addition to the studies analysing the use of digital CSR, some papers discuss the digitalisation process of it (Crisan & Zbuchea, 2015; Grigore, Molesworth & Watkins, 2016; Knaut, 2017) and reveal the ambiguity over the definition and the framework of CSR in the digital age. Besides these, there are some other studies analysing the social media presence of CSR communication (Lee et al., 2013; Adi & Grigore, 2015; Fraustino & Connolly-Ahern, 2015; Cho, Furey & Mohr, 2016; Stohl, Etter, Banghart & Woo, 2017; Araujo & Kollat, 2018; Chae & Park, 2018; Okazaki, Plangger, West & Menendez, 2019) and web publication/presence/availability of CSR activities (Maignan & Ralston, 2002; Chaudri & Wang, 2007; Rosca et al., 2015; Illia et al., 2017; Maier & Ravazzani (2019). Studies also reveal that using digitally co-created CSR campaigns strengthen the relationship between consumer and brand (Kull & Heath, 2016), though not in the short run (Elden et al., 2016).

Yet, though it is considered as an important and trustworthy tool to communicate CSR practices (Jahdi & Acikdilli, 2009; Ali et al., 2015), the presence of corporations on social media are found to be limited (Esrock & Leichty, 1998; Chaudri & Wang, 2007; Rybalko & Seltzer, 2010; Fraustino & Connolly-Ahern, 2015). The study of Cho et al. (2016) revealed that corporations have the inclination to publish their CSR practices through their web sites, and they do not use social media actively. The results indicate that social media tools are not used to their full potential. Instead, they are used as complementary to traditional media. However, Lee et al. (2013) concluded that digital age provided more opportunities and competitiveness for socially responsible firms.

RESEARCH AIMS

Research Purpose

In line with the aim of the book, the purpose of this chapter is to unite an understanding of business world practices with an academic perspective, and thus to inform the reader on the developments in CSR practices in the digital age. It is considered essential to see if the CSR practices also have kept up with the digital transformations. There is ample literature on the definition and characterization of CSR, yet development and implementation of this topic is still in its infancy (Moan, Lindgreen & Swaen, 2010). In line with this, academic research on this issue has lagged. Literature in Turkey is also in a similar situation with limited studies on digitalisation of CSR, analysing the companies (Aktan, Sumer-Inci & Ozgoren, 2009; Pelenk Ozel & Yılmaz Sert, 2014), a specific industry or a project (Polat, 2018) in Turkey. Thus, this research is expected to contribute current knowledge base by comprising leading companies from different industries and analysing their CSR practices.

Research Methodology

In order to reveal a picture of the CSR projects of corporations in Turkey, a descriptive research is planned, which will include a content analysis of their web pages. Content analysis is "a research technique for the systematic classification and description of communication content according to certain usually predetermined categories" (Wright, 1986). It will help the researcher to attain his purpose of getting preliminary information, which will later on turn into hypothesised relationships analysed. It allows systematic and objective collection of data. In order learn about the current situation among the top companies operating in Turkey with regards to their CSR practices and digitalisation of those projects, a frequency analysis method of content analysis was employed, which consists of enumerating message content using a previously settled criteria. The frequency analysis method explains the analysis indicators in the form of frequency. This approach enables an understanding of the importance of the analysed issue, which can be a basis for further analysis. With regards to the current study, having an overall picture of the situation in Turkey as a preliminary understanding of CSR practices and their digitalisation, this approach would provide the expected results.

Using web page content analysis has been a prevalently employed approach in previous studies, on CSR (Chaudhri and Wang, 2007; Campopiano & De Massis, 2015; Parker, Bellucci, Zutshi, Torlina & Fraunholz, 2015; McDaniel, Cadman & Malone, 2016) or other topics (Kim & Kuljis, 2010; Llopis, Gonzales & Gasco, 2010; Metaxas & Tsavdaridou, 2013).

Using content analysis, it is expected to find answers to four questions. The first one asks if the analysed company publishes its annual report online. Web published annual reports provide numerous benefits such as access ease, information consistency, low cost, unlimited usage, etc. It includes all activities of the company throughout the year and relates to all stakeholders. Although the companies prepare an annual report, it is wondered if all of them publish these reports online. So, the companies were first evaluated from this perspective. The second issue was whether the annual report consisted of CSR practices/projects. The public adjustments which were published in 2003 by Capital Markets Boards required companies to publish their Corporate Governance Compliance Report. This fact forced the companies to take CSR campaigns more seriously. Therefore, it became the second question of the study to see if the companies publish their CSR practices within their annual report or do they only web publish them?

The purpose of the third question that was tried to be answered in the study was to list and classify the CSR practices/projects. Providing a list of the projects will enable an understanding if there is a general tendency towards certain fields in CSR projects. And the final question is related to the digitalisation of CSR. It is expected to reveal the digital CSR projects and the details about them. By this way, it would be possible to see if the companies in Turkey are able to keep up with global trends in digitalisation of CSR. It is expected that answering all these questions would provide a clear picture of the current situation in Turkey.

As the unit of analysis, top 100 companies from the Fortune 500 list of Turkey were selected. In this list, the largest firms of Turkey are presented according to their net sales, the change in net sales, earnings before interest and tax, change in earnings before interest and tax, total assets, resources or import. For this study, ordering based on net sales of companies was used. In order to find annual reports of the companies, first their web pages were used, and if it could not be found, it was googled.

Important Findings of this Study and Impact of Digital Transformations on Corporate Social Responsibility (CSR) Practices in Turkey

The analysis of top 100 company web pages on Fortune 500 list indicated that only 59 of them have an annual report published online, whereas two companies have old-dated reports, one company does not have a local website and the reports of 38 companies could not be accessed. So, with regards to the first inquiry of the study, it could be seen that publishing online annual reports is not a much widely adopted practice. However, it has been already mentioned that publishing annual reports online provides many advantages both for the firm and its stakeholders. Moreover, it is part of the digitalisation era, so the results display that nearly half of the companies have not yet kept up with the trends of the age.

With regards to the second question of whether the online published reports include the CSR practices of the companies, the findings show that only 39 (66%) of those companies reported their CSR practices, and in total, nearly 60% of the analysed companies (57 in total) carry out CSR projects, either published in the annual report or on the web. This finding reveals that while some companies account their CSR practices in their annual reports, 18% still only use web publishing. This fact denotes that CSR has still not been acknowledged by some of the largest companies as a major part of the annual report. They only do with publishing their projects on their web site.

The third inquiry of the study was to analyse the kind of CSR projects that the companies carry out and the results bear a variety on this issue. Yet, CSR practices on education by far lead the list. Of the 124 projects in total, 44 projects (33%) are on education. This result is also found in a research carried out by a research company in Turkey with the firms within their database in order to understand the main fields that the companies support in their CSR projects, and education was found as the main area that the companies make projects in. This is followed by health projects (17, 13%), environment projects (11, 8%) and culture and arts (11, 8%) projects. Besides these prominent subjects, there are CSR projects on handicapped, sports, women employment, agriculture, animal rights, social solidarity, volunteering, foods, gender, tourism, etc. Of the companies analysed, one of them mentioned in kind aids as CSR practice and two companies listed responsible business practices under this title.

The final question about the CSR practices of the top 100 companies on the existence of digital CSR practice indicated that there is only one company with a CSR campaign which is carried out in digital platforms. The project is developed by a major appliance company on awareness of responsible food consumption. The campaign is not linked to a charity contribution, but it tries to raise awareness on food waste and how to reduce it. This finding indicates that the largest companies operating in Turkey are far behind the digital revolution with regards to adopting CSR practices.

CONCLUSION

With the technological developments, conceptualisation and awareness of corporate social responsibility increases. This is followed by carrying the projects to the digital world. It has become a significant issue not only to include CSR in annual reports or corporate web pages (Rosca et al., 2015) but also initiate digital campaigns as all stakeholders expect a mutual communication with the company, which is easily attained through digital tools. Therefore, it is considered essential to understand the current situation with regards to digitalisation of large companies.

The results of the study, which consists of web site content analysis with the purpose of revealing digitalisation of CSR practices of the top 100 companies of Fortune 500 Turkey, draw a picture of the situation. The findings indicate that none of the companies in Turkey has a digital CSR campaign, except for one company. This shows that they are lagging behind global companies with regards to digitalisation of CSR practices. Although digitalisation has turned into a widespread phenomenon in every part of business practices, CSR has not taken its share from it yet. Considering that carrying out social responsibility projects is not very common among the companies, not having any digital responsibility projects can be considered as a normal result. Corporations have not yet realised the role of digital tools in making CSR campaigns more useful and effective, both for the brand and the society. Moreover, companies do not pay necessary attention to publicising their projects through their web sites, as some CSR links of the web pages were very difficult to locate. However, it should be foregrounded as web sites provides the relationship between company and its stakeholders and modern day business requires a company to be a responsible citizen also, informing about all its good practices. This finding indicates a rather wide field for companies to improve their competitiveness. They should consider increasing their communication with their stakeholders while performing their deeds as responsible citizens.

The results also indicate that businesses have not institutionalised their CSR practices when compared to the corporations in developed countries as most companies did not list their CSR projects in their annual reports. And only the some of the ones who have listed did follow a certain approach or standard in reporting it. In other words, there are differences in the approaches of corporations in communicating their CSR campaigns. Although there is a determined standard by Corporate Governance Compliance Report, not all of the largest companies are seen to comply with it, which is another issue that would contribute to the competitiveness of businesses.

Due to practical constraints, the paper cannot provide a comprehensive review of all Fortune 500 companies operating in Turkey, which is the major limitation of this study. Also, the data was taken only from the web sites of the relevant companies, excluding social media tools. Therefore, future studies extending the analysed group will present a clearer picture of the digitalisation of CSR in Turkey. Moreover, including social media practices would also enhance our understanding about the practices.

REFERENCES

Adi, A., & Grigore, G. (2015). Communicating CSR on social media: the case of Pfizer's social media communications in Europe. Corporate Social Responsibility in the Digital Age. doi:10.1108/S2043-052320150000007009

Aguinis, H., & Glavas, A. (2012). What we know and don't know about corporate social responsibility: A review and research agenda. *Journal of Management*, *38*(4), 932–968. doi:10.1177/0149206311436079

Aktan, C., Sumer-Inci, B., & Ozgoren, F. (2009). Kurumsal sosyal sorumluluk faaliyetlerinde glokal yaklaşımlar: 100 değerli global markanın Türkiye'deki web sitelerinin içerik analizi. Ulusal Pazarlama Kongresi, 14.

Ali, I., Jimenez-Zarco, A. I., & Bicho, M. (2015). Using social media for CSR communication and engaging stakeholders. Corporate Social Responsibility in the Digital Age. doi:10.1108/S2043-052320150000007010

Antal, A. B., Dierkies, M., MacMillan, K., & Marz, L. (2002). Corporate social reporting revisited. *Journal of General Management*, *28*(2), 22–42. doi:10.1177/030630700202800202

Araujo, T., & Kollat, J. (2018). Communicating effectively about CSR on Twitter: The power of engaging strategies and storytelling elements. *Internet Research*, *28*(2), 419–431. doi:10.1108/IntR-04-2017-0172

Basil, D. Z., & Erlandson, J. (2008). Corporate social responsibility website representations: A longitudinal study of internal and external self-presentations. *Journal of Marketing Communications*, *14*(2), 125–137. doi:10.1080/13527260701858497

Bowen, H. R. (1953). *Social responsibilities of the businessman*. New York: Harper and Row.

Buyukkupcu, A., Atilgan, E., & Akinci, S. (2007). *Corporate social responsibility: Cases in Turkey*. In *Strategic Management Conference*, Antalya, Turkey.

Campopiano, G., & De Massis, A. (2015). Corporate social responsibility reporting: A content analysis in family and non-family firms. *Journal of Business Ethics*, *129*(3), 511–534. doi:10.100710551-014-2174-z

Carroll, A. B. (1979). A three-dimensional conceptual model of corporate performance. *Academy of Management Review*, *4*(4), 497–505. doi:10.5465/amr.1979.4498296

Castello, I., Morsing, M., & Schultz, F. (2013). Communicative dynamics and the polyphony of corporate social responsibility in the network society. *Journal of Business Ethics*, *118*(4), 683–694. doi:10.100710551-013-1954-1

Castro-Gonzales, S., Bande, B., Fernandez-Ferrin, P., & Kimura, T. (2019). Corporate social responsibility and consumer advocacy behaviors: The importance of emotions and moral virtues. *Journal of Cleaner Production*, *231*, 846–855. doi:10.1016/j.jclepro.2019.05.238

Chae, B. & Park, E. (2018). Corporate social responsibility (CSR): A survey of topics and trends using Twitter data and topic modelling. *Sustainability*, *10*(7), 22-31.

Chaudhri, V., & Wang, J. (2007). Communicating corporate social responsibility on the internet: A case study of the top 100 information technology companies in India. *Management Communication Quarterly*, *21*(2), 232–247. doi:10.1177/0893318907308746

Cho, M., Furey, L. D., & Mohr, T. (2016). Communicating corporate social responsibility on social media: Strategies, stakeholders, and public engagement on corporate Facebook. *Business and Professional Communication Quarterly*, *80*(1), 52–69. doi:10.1177/2329490616663708

Coluccia, D., Fontana, S., & Solimene, S. (2016). Disclosure of corporate social responsibility: A comparison between traditional and digital reporting: an empirical analysis on Italian listed companies. *International Journal of Managerial and Financial Accounting, 8*(3-4), 230-246.

Crisan, C., & Zbuchea, A. (2015). CSR and social media: Could online repositories become regulatory tools for CSR related activities reporting? In A. Adi, G. Grigore, & D. Crowther (Eds.), *Corporate Social Responsibility in the Digital Age* (pp. 197–220). Bingley: Emerald Publishing Group. doi:10.1108/S2043-052320150000007011

Doane, D. (2005). Beyond corporate social responsibility: Minnows, mammoths and markets. *Futures*, *37*(2-3), 215–229. doi:10.1016/j.futures.2004.03.028

Du, S., Bhattacharya, C. B., & Sen, S. (2010). Maximising business returns to corporate social responsibility (CSR): The role of CSR communication. *International Journal of Management Reviews*, *12*(1), 1, 8–19. doi:10.1111/j.1468-2370.2009.00276.x

Elden, M., Yeygel Cakir, S., & Bakir, U. (2011). Corporate social responsibility campaigns in the digital age: The case of Vodafone "Red light application/Between us". In *Conference on e-Business, e-Services and e-Society* (120-127). Springer.

Esrock, S. L., & Leichty, G. B. (1998). Social responsibility and corporate web pages: Self presentation or agenda-setting? *Public Relations Review*, *24*(3), 305–319. doi:10.1016/S0363-8111(99)80142-8

Fraustino, J. D., & Connolly-Ahern, C. (2015). Corporate associations written on the wall: Publics' responses to Fortune 500 ability and social responsibility Facebook posts. *Journal of Public Relations Research*, *27*(5), 452–474. doi:10.1080/1062726X.2015.1098543

Friedman, M. (1962). *Capitalism and Freedom*. Chicago: University of Chicago Press.

Galbreath, J., & Shum, P. (2012). Do customer satisfaction and reputation mediate the CSR-FP link? Evidence from Australia. *Australian Journal of Management*, *37*(2), 211–229. doi:10.1177/0312896211432941

Garriga, E., & Mele, D. (2004). Corporate social responsibility theories: Mapping the territory. *Journal of Business Ethics*, *53*(1/2), 51–71. doi:10.1023/B:BUSI.0000039399.90587.34

Grigore, G., Molesworth, M., & Watkins, R. (2016). New corporate responsibilities in the digital economy. In Corporate Social Responsibility in the Post-Financial Crisis Era. Palgrave Macmillan.

Idowu, S. O. (2017). Current issues in corporate social responsibility: An introduction. In S. O. Idowu, C. Sitnikov, D. Simion & C. G. Bocean (Eds.), Current issues in corporate social responsibility: An international consideration (pp. 1-7). Springer.

Idowu, S. O. (2018). Current issues in corporate social responsibility: An introduction. In S. O. Idowu & R. Schmidpeter (Eds.), *Current Issues in Corporate Social Responsibility: An International Consideration*. Springer. doi:10.1007/978-3-319-70449-4_1

Illia, L., Romenti, S., Rodriguez-Canavas, B., Murtarelli, G., & Carroll, C. E. (2017). Exploring corporations' dialogue about CSR in the digital era. *Journal of Business Ethics*, *146*(1), 39–58. doi:10.100710551-015-2924-6

Jahdi, K. S., & Acikdilli, G. (2009). Marketing communications and corporate social responsibility (CSR): Marriage of convenience or short gun wedding? *Journal of Business Ethics*, *88*(1), 103–113. doi:10.100710551-009-0113-1

Kang, J., & Namkung, Y. (2018). The effect of corporate social responsibility on brand equity and the moderating role of ethical consumerism: The case of starbucks. *Journal of Hospitality & Tourism Research (Washington, D.C.)*, *42*(7), 1130–1151. doi:10.1177/1096348017727057

Kaplan, A. M., & Haenlein, M. (2010). Users of the world, unite! The challenges and opportunities of social media. *Business Horizons*, *53*(1), 59–68. doi:10.1016/j.bushor.2009.09.003

Kim, H., Youn, S., & Lee, D. (2019). The effect of corporate social responsibility on consumer support for cause-related marketing. *Total Quality Management*, *30*(6), 682–707. doi:10.1080/14783363.2017.1332482

Kim, I., & Kuljis, J. (2010). Applying content analysis to web based content. *CIT. Journal of Computing and Information Technology*, *18*(4), 369–375. doi:10.2498/cit.1001924

Klein, J., & Dawar, N. (2004). Corporate social responsibility and consumers' attributions and brand evaluations in a product-harm crisis. *International Journal of Research in Marketing*, *21*(3), 203–217. doi:10.1016/j.ijresmar.2003.12.003

Knaut, A. (2017). How CSR should understand digitalization. In S. O. Idowu & R. Schmidpeter (Eds.), *Sustainability in a Digital World.* Springer. doi:10.1007/978-3-319-54603-2_21

Kull, A. J., & Heath, T. B. (2016). You decide, we donate: Strengthening consumer-brand relationships through digitally co-created social responsibility. *International Journal of Research in Marketing*, *33*(1), 78–92. doi:10.1016/j.ijresmar.2015.04.005

Lee, K., Oh, W., & Kim, N. (2013). Social media for socially responsible firms: Analysis of Fortune 500's Twitter profiles and their CSR/CSIR ratings. *Journal of Business Ethics*, *118*(4), 791–806. doi:10.100710551-013-1961-2

Lee, K., & Shin, D. (2010). Consumers' responses to CSR activities: The linkage between increased awareness and purchase intention. *Public Relations Review*, *36*(2), 193–195. doi:10.1016/j.pubrev.2009.10.014

Lee, M. P. (2008). A review of the theories of corporate social responsibility: Its evolutionary path and the road ahead. *International Journal of Management Reviews*, *10*(1), 53–73. doi:10.1111/j.1468-2370.2007.00226.x

Leeflang, P. S. H., Verhoef, P. C., Dahlström, P., & Freundt, T. (2014). Challenges and solutions for marketing in the digital era. *European Management Journal*, *32*(1), 1–12. doi:10.1016/j.emj.2013.12.001

Llopis, J., Gonzales, R., & Gasco, J. (2010). Web pages as a tool for a strategic description of the Spanish largest firms. *Information Processing & Management*, *46*(3), 320–330. doi:10.1016/j.ipm.2009.06.004

Luo, X., & Bhattacharya, C. B. (2006). Corporate social responsibility, customer satisfaction and market value. *Journal of Marketing*, *70*(4), 1–18. doi:10.1509/jmkg.70.4.001

Maier, C. D., & Ravazzani, S. (2019). Bridging diversity management and CSR in online external communication. *Corporate Communications*, *24*(2), 269–286. doi:10.1108/CCIJ-01-2018-0015

Maignan, I., & Ralston, D. A. (2002). Corporate social responsibility in Europe and the U.S.: Insights from businesses' self-presentations. *Journal of International Business Studies*, *33*(3), 497–514. doi:10.1057/palgrave.jibs.8491028

Maon, F., Lindgreen, A., & Swaen, V. (2010). Organisational stage and cultural phases: A critical review and a consolidative model of corporate social responsibility development. *International Journal of Management Reviews*, *12*(1), 20–38. doi:10.1111/j.1468-2370.2009.00278.x

Martinez, P., & Nishiyama, N. (2017). Enhancing customer-based brand equity through CSR in the hospitality sector. *International Journal of Hospitality & Tourism Administration*, *20*(3), 329–353. doi:10.1080/15256480.2017.1397581

McDaniel, P. A., Cadman, B., & Malone, R. E. (2016). Shared vision, shared vulnerability: A content analysis of corporate social responsibility information on tobacco industry websites. *Preventive Medicine*, *89*, 337–344. doi:10.1016/j.ypmed.2016.05.033 PMID:27261411

McGuire, J. B., Sundgren, A., & Schneeweis, T. (1988). Corporate social responsibility and firm financial performance. *Academy of Management Journal*, *31*(4), 854–872.

Metaxas, T., & Tsavdaridou, M. (2013). CSR in metallurgy sector in Greece: A content analysis. *Resources Policy*, *38*(3), 295–309. doi:10.1016/j.resourpol.2013.03.010

Mishra, S., & Suar, D. (2010). Does corporate social responsibility influence firm performance of Indian companies? *Journal of Business Ethics*, *95*(4), 571–601. doi:10.100710551-010-0441-1

Moan, F., Lindgreen, A., & Swaen, V. (2010). Organizational stages and cultural phases: A critical review and a consolidative model of corporate social responsibility development. *International Journal of Management Reviews*, *12*(1), 20–38. doi:10.1111/j.1468-2370.2009.00278.x

Mohr, L. A., & Webb, D. J. (2005). The effects of corporate social responsibility and price on consumer responses. *The Journal of Consumer Affairs*, *39*(1), 121–147. doi:10.1111/j.1745-6606.2005.00006.x

Okazaki, S., Plangger, K., West, D., & Menendez, H. D. (2019). Exploring digital corporate social responsibility communications on Twitter. *Journal of Business Research*. doi:10.1016/j.jbusres.2019.09.006

Orbik, Z., & Zozul'akova, V. (2019). Corporate social and digital responsibility. *Management Systems in Production Engineering*, *27*(2), 79–83. doi:10.1515/mspe-2019-0013

Parker, C. M., Bellucci, E., Zutshi, A., Torlina, L., & Fraunholz, B. (2015). SME stakeholder relationship descriptions in website CSR communications. *Social Responsibility Journal*, *11*(2), 364–386. doi:10.1108/SRJ-09-2013-0114

Pelenk Ozel, A., & Yılmaz Sert, N. (2014). Corporate blogs as a tool of digital public relations: A research on Turkey's first 100 companies. *Global Media Journal: TR Edition*, *5*(9), 303–321.

Polat, A. F. (2018). *Social media reflections and consequences of corporate social responsibility projects: Samsung sample of hearing hands project* (Unpublished Master of Arts Thesis). The University of Fırat, Elazığ, Turkey.

Roşca, M. I., Sarău, A. C., & Vonţea, A. A. (2015). Classifying social causes derived from the communication of CSR initiatives online: A theoretical and practical approach. Corporate Social Responsibility in the Digital Age.

Rybalko, S., & Seltzer, T. (2010). Dialogic communication in 140 characters or less: How Fortune 500 companies engage stakeholders using Twitter. *Public Relations Review*, *36*(4), 336–341. doi:10.1016/j.pubrev.2010.08.004

Sheikh, S., & Beise-Zee, R. (2011). Corporate social responsibility or cause-related marketing? The role of cause specificity of CSR. *Journal of Consumer Marketing*, *28*(1), 27–39. doi:10.1108/07363761111101921

Sheldon, O. (1923). *The Philosophy of Management*. Sir Isaac Pitman & Sons.

Stohl, C., Etter, M., Banghart, S., & Woo, D. (2017). Social media policies: Implications for contemporary notions of corporate social responsibility. *Journal of Business Ethics*, *142*(3), 413–436. doi:10.100710551-015-2743-9

Sun, W., & Price, J. M. (2016). The impact of environmental uncertainty on increasing customer satisfaction through corporate social responsibility. *European Journal of Marketing*, *50*(7/8), 1209–1238. doi:10.1108/EJM-02-2015-0077

UNIDO (United Nations International Development Organization). (2019). https://www.unido.org/our-focus/advancing-economic-competitiveness/competitive-trade-capacities-and-corporate-responsibility/corporate-social-responsibility-market-integration/what-csr

Visser, W. (2014). *CSR 2.0 Transforming Corporate Sustainability and Responsibility*. Springer.

Wang, D. H., Chen, P., Yu, T. H., & Hsiao, C. (2015). The effects of corporate social responsibility on brand equity and firm performance. *Journal of Business Research*, *68*(11), 2232–2236. doi:10.1016/j.jbusres.2015.06.003

Wright, C. R. (1986). *Mass communication: A sociological perspective* (3rd ed.). New York: Random House.

Zadek, S. (2004). The path to corporate responsibility. *Harvard Business Review*, *82*(12), 125–132. PMID:15605571

ADDITIONAL READING

Adi, A., Grigore, G., & Crowther, D. (2015). Corporate Social Responsibility in the Digital Age. (Developments in Corporate Governance and Responsibility, Vol. 7). Emerald Group Publishing Limited, p. iv.

Crowther, D., & Aras, G. (2008). *Corporate Social Responsibility*. Bookboon.

Drisko, J. W., & Maschi, T. (2015). *Content Analysis*. New York: Oxford University Press. doi:10.1093/acprof:oso/9780190215491.001.0001

Grigore, G., Molesworth, M., & Watkins, R. (2017). New corporate responsibilities in the digital economy. In *Corporate Social Responsibility in the Post-Financial Crisis Era* (pp. 41–62). Cham: Palgrave Macmillan. doi:10.1007/978-3-319-40096-9_3

Idowu, S. O., & Filho, W. L. (2008). *Global Practices of Corporate Social Responsibility*. Berlin: Springer.

Kotler, P., Kartajaya, H., & Setiawan, I. (2017). *Marketing 4.0 Moving From Traditional to Digital*. New Jersey: John Wiley and Sons, Inc.

Kotler, P., & Lee, N. (2004). *Corporate Social Responsibility. Doing the Most Good for Your Company and Your Cause*. New Jersey: John Wiley and Sons, Inc.

Lidgreen, A., Vanhamme, J., Maon, F., & Mardon, R. (Eds.). (2017). *Communicating Corporate Social Responsibility in the Digital Era*. Routledge. doi:10.4324/9781315577234

KEY TERMS AND DEFINITIONS

Annual Report: It is a comprehensive report of company about all the operations and activities performed in the previous year.

Content Analysis: It is a research method that studies documents, texts, pictures, etc. is a predetermined and systematic way to examine the patterns.

Corporate Social Responsibility: It is a term describing obligations of a company towards all its stakeholders in all its activities to behave ethically and contributing their welfare. Companies are required to consider their need to profit together with their societal influence.

Digital CSR: A corporate social responsibility campaign that is a carried out only through digital tools such as web site or social media accounts of the company. It can aim raising awareness or participating in any social activity which would result in philanthropy.

Digital Transformation: It is the process of using advanced digital technologies to develop or change business processes in order to meet the requirements of the modern-day business approach and the market.

Fortune 500: It is a list published annually by the *Fortune* magazine that ranks companies according to certain criteria.

Web Publishing: It is publishing a content on the internet.

Chapter 7
A Study of Factors Influencing Digital Accounting Software Selection in Thailand

Supawadee Moss
University of New England, Australia

Kamaljeet Sandhu
https://orcid.org/0000-0003-4624-6834
University of New England, Australia

ABSTRACT

Accounting software selection, implementation, and use have received close interest for business efficiency purposes in a fast-changing global digital environment. This study reports the results of a survey for small-medium accounting firms in Thailand that have focused on the factors used to select the accounting software. The researchers have examined whether different firms have different factors in selecting the accounting software and which factor is most influential for accounting and auditing firms for their decision to select accounting software. A structured questionnaire survey instrument was used to collect data from 49 accounting firms. New findings from this study suggest that, firstly, there are no significant differences between accounting and auditing firms in the factors used to select accounting software. Secondly, it was found that the accuracy of data processing, calculation, and reports is the most influential factor that accounting and auditing firms will consider for using the accounting software.

INTRODUCTION

Accounting firms are businesses that provide professional services including accounting and auditing services such as production of financial statements, provision of consulting on business or tax planning, and the provision of auditing or assurance services to corporations on a digital platform. Presently, modern accounting practice is focused on automated data processing and companies around the world are increasingly using information technology (IT) to deal with large amounts of digital financial data

DOI: 10.4018/978-1-7998-5175-2.ch007

(Sandhu & Terdpaopong 2019). This change has seen a move from paper-based transaction recording to electronic-based transaction recording on a digital platform (Sandhu & Corbitt 2007). Along with these changes, a number of accounting software are developed to simplify the digital accounting preparation process (Syafrudin, 2012). When technology allows corporations to record, analyze and report the large amount of digital financial data, suitable accounting software choice becomes an important factor for professional service firms such as accounting firms and hence to innovate. Identical to manual accounting systems, accounting software used by accounting firms and auditing firms still need to evaluate a company's past performance, present condition and future prospects (Ghasemi, Shafeiepour, Aslani, & Barvayeh, 2011). Accounting and auditing software are crucial components of the professional service. For example, in auditing firms, apart from auditor's judgment and auditor's experience, the use of computer analyses to identify audit risk and for audit sampling has become a very important part of auditing work. Accounting software can also help accountants, auditors and business owners improve the accuracy of financial reports as it has internal and automated check and balance system built in to ensure that all transactions are properly balanced and correct. It also allows fast processing for large amounts of financial information.

Furthermore, the variety of accounting practices, accounting systems and accounting policy have changed the decision in selecting accounting software for both accounting and auditing firms. For example, if companies have to deal with multiple currencies and different accounting and tax rules, new and more sophisticated accounting software packages for handling these issues will be required (Adhikari, Lebow, & Zhang, 2004).

Similar to the other countries around the world, small and medium business enterprises (SMEs) in Thailand comprise the majority of corporations. The performance of the SMEs sector is very important for the overall economic growth of any nation. However, poor financial management and accounting knowledge are found to be one of the main problem among SMEs (Ismail & Mat Zin, 2009). Also, SMEs are reported to have poor internal control, lack of training and insufficient planning due to the lack of internal expertise and internal professional advice (Alasadi & Abdelrahim, 2008; Berry, Sweeting, & Goto, 2006). It is also reported that usage of computerized accounting information system (AIS) is minimal among SMEs in Malaysia (Ismail & Mat Zin, 2009) which has a similar business environment to Thailand.

Hence, due to the accounting and auditing standards and tax compliance, these businesses may seek for financial/accounting/auditing advice from accounting firms. According to Bressler and Bressler (2006), the small-medium entrepreneurs cannot afford to hire big accounting firms to give consulting advice, audit their financial statements, or for processing of their accounting books. Since small-medium accounting firms play an important professional role in Thailand, this study aims to explore the factors that small-medium accounting and auditing firms use in selecting accounting software for their professional work. The results of this study could help accounting software developers to improve their product offerings and enable them to offer products which match with the needs of their users.

BACKGROUND AND LITERATURE REVIEW

Among the accounting profession, it is not only the change of the accounting or auditing standards but also the digital accounting tools such as accounting software that has been changing dramatically. Zarowin (1998) states that the accounting software products get more powerful each year and taking on more financial chores and doing them better and faster with each upgrade. Adamyk, Adamyk, and Khorunzhak (2018) reason that the driver of the changes for accounting software are from the significant changes in standards and accounting environment for both accounting and auditing. Therefore, software developer cannot only follow the new trends in IT knowledge but also need to follow the changes in accounting and auditing standards, other accounting rules and the accounting environment to be able to improve the product to match the user's needs. Adhikari et al. (2004) mentions that companies around the world are becoming more international in their outlook. This is why new and more sophisticated accounting software packages that are able to deal with the complexity of international accounting issues are required by users.

While technology is changing the way businesses conduct its operations, managers need to rethink what kind of digital accounting software is appropriate for their businesses (Collins, 1999). In general, Collins (1999) states that accounting software should be able to publish real-time information on inventory where we can see prices and quantities on hand, retrieve other data directly from their websites, print all reports directly from their websites, and allow users to access reports and financial data across the network. For SMEs, Collins (1999) suggest that even small businesses still need software capable of handling complex accounting transactions such as foreign currency and its fluctuations.

In SMEs, Bressler and Bressler (2006) find that it is not solely purchase and maintenance costs that SMEs consider when obtaining new accounting software. Often, their choice relies on the recommendations from professional advisers from accounting firms or salespeople from the various software companies. This is because the management of SMEs usually do not have the time and expertise required to research all available options to select the most appropriate software. The result of the study of Bressler and Bressler (2006) evidenced that the most common factor used in selecting accounting software in SMEs is the recommendation by business counsel of consultants, the second most common is the recommendation by another business owner, the third factor used is the recommendation by accountants or CPAs, cost of the software was the fourth factor used in the decision making process of obtaining new accounting software and the ease of use of the accounting software rounded out the top five factors. Ghaffar, Mokhtar, Ismail, and Othman (2019) investigate the influence of decision maker, technological, organizational and the environment on the E-accounting adoption of SMEs in Malaysia. They find that only the organization (proxy for business industry) has influence on the E-accounting adoption (Rogers 1995). Their results suggest that different business industries such as oil and gas are facing increased complexity in digital accounting transactions. Professional support from the software developer becomes more important for the business. Ismail and Mat Zin (2009) investigated the usage of accounting information and computerized accounting information systems among non-manufacturing SMEs firms in Malaysia. However, they found that more than sixty-six per cent of non-manufacturing SMEs firms do not use accounting software because they believe that their existing manual system is already sufficient to prepare financial reports. The other reason for not using IT systems is that the lack of IT knowledge, uncertainty of the costs and benefits and an inability to obtain an appropriate accounting software package. In the cost accounting area, Hyvönen, Järvinen, and Pellinen (2006) found evidence that activity-based costing (ABC) can be effectively achieved by using standard software packages.

In New Zealand, Pulakanam and Suraweera (2010) investigated the implementation of digital accounting software among SMEs in New Zealand. They found that the lack of external guidance and support, and the lack of accounting skills were the main challenges faced by SMEs in New Zealand. Their result also suggests that SMEs have often been frustrated with the digital accounting software because they are difficult to use and expensive. Rushinek and Rushinek (1995) state that the digital accounting software selection process is difficult because there are many choices available and each software has different strengths and weaknesses making the decision a complex process. In terms of the cost of the software, Rushinek and Rushinek (1995) found this to be one of the most important factors in selecting an accounting software. However, the cost of software itself was not generally prohibitively expensive but rather if firms purchased the wrong software, they found it is likely to cost much more. They also provided the criteria that should always be considered when evaluating the accounting software such as trouble-free installation, ease of use, comprehensive documentation, vendor support and upgradability. For SMEs businesses, Rushinek and Rushinek (1995) recommend that low-cost software are better-suited to the needs of small clients and firms because sometimes small firms do not need a complex features. Furthermore, Rushinek and Rushinek (1995) conclude that regardless of whether expensive or low-cost software, human accounting knowledge is still an important factor because accounting software cannot fully replace human as accounting transactions still requires skilled and specialized operator knowledge.

MAIN FOCUS

The main focus of this study is to find the important factors that can have an impact on the selection of the digital accounting software in Thailand. In term of accounting education, Lai (2008) examined the level of information and communication technology (ICT) readiness of 500 professional accounting students. Lai (2008) finds that professional accounting students were neither highly techno-ready nor highly techno-resistant towards new technologies. It was also found that e-mail and the internet has widespread use among professional accounting students. However, digital accounting software knowledge among these student is significantly lower when compared to other information and communication technology components. Lee, Kerler, and Ivancevich (2018) argue that the ability to use various software and tools is important for accounting students. After investigating 197 participants in south-east United States, they found that Excel was the most frequently utilized and recommended software used in university accounting degrees. They also find that data analytic skills and data visualization skills are important among accounting students. Furthermore, Syafrudin (2012) analyses the acceptance of the digital accounting software by 162 accounting students using the Technology Acceptance Model (Davis 1989, TAM). Syafrudin (2012) finds that the perceived ease of use is significantly positively associated with the perceived usefulness of the accounting software. This result also suggests that if students can easily operate the accounting software, this would increase adoption.

In the area of agricultural accounting, Taragola, Van Lierde, and Van Huylenbroeck (2001) identify factors influencing the adoption of farm accounting software of 148 glasshouse holdings in Belgium. Their study results reveal that 43% of holdings own a personal computer for management purposes only. The most frequently used software was word processing, Excel spreadsheet and bank electronic transactions. As well, the result also reveals that the adoption of farm accounting software was strongly influenced by personal characteristic of the farm managers. Price was also a factor with farmers willing to adopt farm accounting software if it was offered for free.

In research of Indonesian firm characteristics of accounting software selection, Putra (2019) found that personal characteristics such as employees education level and accounting knowledge were not influential factors in accounting software selection. However, the key decision-making characteristics include cost, software stability, ability to customize and useful help from the vendors. Business characteristics such as company size and the age of the business were also found to not be determining factors in Indonesia.

A study of US based firms by Elikai, Ivancevich, and Ivancevich (2007) found that functionality, cost of software, compatibility with other digital systems, vendor stability and vendor support were the most important factors firms consider when selecting their digital accounting software.

There has been a considerable rise in firms' use of professional service firms such as account firms (Berry et al., 2006). Ghasemi et al. (2011) state that up-to date professional accountants should be able to use and be familiar with the available software tools to help them prepare accounting information more effectively and efficiently. They also state that nowadays, information technology enables companies to significantly improve their business operation through cost and time savings. Pulakanam and Suraweera (2010) also mention that the external consultants or accounting firms are likely to recommend the digital accounting software that they are familiar with to their clients. Since different firms use different accounting systems or accounting rules, digital accounting software used by accounting firms needs to be able to deal with all accounting issues.

Hence this study examined the factors used by accounting firms in selecting accounting software. Given the unique, complex and often politically and culturally entangled factors influencing decision making in Thailand, this research focuses on the decision making in the Thai context. The specific research question which was used to guide this research was: what are the factors SMEs in Thailand consider most important when deciding which digital accounting software to purchase?

RESEARCH METHODOLOGY

A survey design is adopted in the form of a structured questionnaire with Likert five-point scale to collect data from the owners or managers of 49 randomly selected small and medium size accounting firms in Thailand. The questionnaire was divided into three sections. The first section collected demographic data including number of employees, number of clients and firm's capital. Section two examined the factors used by accounting firms in the selection of their accounting software, while section three included open-ended questions for participants to provide additional information. Accounting firms were selected randomly from the list of accounting firms provided by Thailand's Department of Business Development in the Ministry of Commerce.

DATA ANALYSIS AND IMPORTANT FINDINGS

The mean and standard deviation scores of each individual factor used in the selection of digital accounting software by accounting firms are shown in Table 1. Table 1 reports that factors ranked in terms of identified importance in the selection of digital accounting software by accounting firms. From Table 1, it can be seen that the accuracy of calculations and reports, customer care and their problem solving skills, security of software and access, processing speed and cost vs benefits are the five most important factors in selecting software by accounting firms in Thailand, with mean value of 4.62, 4.60, 4.58, 4.52 and 4.50, respectively. From this result, it could be argued that the cost of digital accounting software is not primarily nor sole decision factor for accounting firms where the accuracy of their service such as the financial information and financial statements is the most important factors to be considered when selecting digital accounting software in their firms. On the other hand, this study finds that contemporary

Table 1. Ranking of factors used to select accounting software

Factors Used in Selecting Digital Accounting Software by Accounting Firms	$\bar{X}$	S.D.	Rank
Accuracy of calculations and reports	4.62	0.567	1
Customer care and their problem-solving skills	4.60	0.606	2
Security of software and access	4.58	0.499	3
Processing speed	4.52	0.505	4
Cost vs benefits	4.50	0.580	5
Real-time processing	4.42	0.673	6
Useful help functions	4.40	0.699	7
Quick accessing	4.38	0.635	8
Cloud storage database	4.36	0.663	9
Ease of use	4.28	0.573	10
Font and formatting	4.28	0.730	11
Useful user manual	4.26	0.664	12
Software developer's advice	4.18	0.661	13
Information distribution and communication channels	4.12	0.627	14
Contemporary designed user-interface	4.06	0.652	15

designed user-interface is the least important feature that accounting firms will consider when making purchasing decisions.

While the majority of respondents provided limited useful or additional information in response to the open-ended questions asked in the questionnaire, one of respondents provided a valuable insight into an important factor influencing accounting software selection by Thai firms. This respondent stated that one of the greatest factors influencing accounting software selection is the software that their staff were trained in when they attended university. This highlights that Thai accounting firms would rather adopt software that their staff are already proficient in rather than retraining them in new software.

Our findings show that the decision-making process for Thailand places emphasis on different characteristics compared to other regions across the world. For example, in a study of SMEs in Indonesia, Putra (2019) found factors including price, stability of software, adaptability and customization of software and vendor support all influence the decision to adopt digital accounting software. While these factors were also found to be important in Thailand, this Indonesian research found that ease of use was the most important factor for SMEs in their selection of accounting software. This contrasts our findings from Thailand which places ease of use at only the tenth most important characteristic in the decision-making process for accounting software. In a similar fashion, the ability to customize accounting software has been found to be the most important factor for firms in the United States of America when deciding on accounting software (Elikai et al., 2007). However, the ability to format the software in a personalized way did not even factor in the top ten reason Thai firms selected their software. Cost was the second most important characteristic in US firms selection but this only ranked fifth in the current study of Thailand. Thai's are prevalent users of social media and are very aware of the speed any negative service will travel around social media and the consequential impact on their businesses.

This might help explain why culturally, Thai firms place a higher emphasis on the accuracy of digital accounting software compared to other countries.

SOLUTIONS AND RECOMMENDATIONS

The data in this study clearly supports important elements that are required for providing valuable solutions and recommendations to the accounting firms in Thailand when making an important decision on the selection of the accounting software. Often the selection process for choosing a suitable digital accounting software is not clearly understood due to various complexities and other criteria's that an accounting firm is influenced to follow, such as influential advertisements by local and international digital accounting software firm that a particular software is well catered and will meet the requirements. Another solution adopted by accounting firms to make a selection of the software is based on hiring/ or inviting a specialist software consultant to first make an assessment from a pool of important digital accounting software (shelf products) that are available in the local market that would cater to their particular needs of the accounting firm.

A specialist can be one person, or a team of expert accounting professionals, or an accounting firm specialising in making an assessment, detailed analysis, and recommendation of a particular accounting software. Such a criteria is also based on carefully analysing home-developed software products that are widely adopted and used by the businesses and customers and suppliers and that meets the accounting regulations criteria for the government. For example, some digital accounting software will have inbuilt tools for GAAP principles whereas others will have inbuilt tools for IFRS principles. The standards that govern financial reporting and accounting vary from country to country and the digital accounting software needs to meet those requirements in that particular country of use. If the accounting firm is a trading partner with another country the digital accounting software are required to meet those regulations.

In another example, in the United States, financial reporting practices software are set forth by the Financial Accounting Standards Board (FASB) and organized within the framework of the generally accepted accounting principles (GAAP). Whereas in Asia many countries have either one or both the systems (GAAP & IFRS) implemented into their digital accounting software to meet the requirements of local as well as international trading partners. Generally accepted accounting principles refer to a common set of accepted accounting principles, standards, and procedures that companies and their accountants and the software firms must follow when they compile their financial statements and filing of those reports to the government and professional bodies for examination.

The aspect of familiarity with software, which a respondent raised in their open-ended response to the questionnaire, highlights the important role that Academic Institutions play in accounting firms selection of software. Universities and other academic educational facilities need to closely consider the relevance, practicality and all the relevant factors that our research find as important decision making criteria as their choices will in turn have some influence on the accounting firms decisions. From the accounting software developers point of view, they could look at adopting partnership agreements or adjust their licensing agreements to provide free or low-cost academic licences to encourage universities and other educational providers to adopt their software in accounting courses as a long-term strategy that will ultimately increase their potential adoption and client bases in accounting firms.

FUTURE RESEARCH DIRECTIONS

The future research needs to take the findings of this study forward to understand the complex nature of tasks that the digital accounting software is required to perform. This study has demonstrated important findings such as the accuracy of calculations and reports, customer care and their problem-solving skills, security of software and access, processing speed and cost vs benefits are the five most important factors in software selection by accounting firms in Thailand. Future research needs to unravel more data on how the complexities of the software are linked to particular accounting work processes and how those issues impact on people doing their task. Training accounting staff members on how to use the digital accounting software is also an important element that needs to be studies in future research to understand the impact of learning on the selection of the accounting software. Even though the use of digital accounting software have become reasonably easy to use and provides usefulness to the user, nevertheless these important elements are not to be underestimated in future studies to guide the researcher how the impact by users is mitigated on a positive perception to use such software in a regular basis that adds value to the task being performed.

From the result of this study, it could be argued that the cost of digital accounting software is not primarily nor sole decision factor for accounting firms where the accuracy of their service such as the financial information and financial statements is the most important factors to be considered when selecting digital accounting software in their firms. Future research need to unravel more information based on cost-benefit analysis of the digital accounting software and the value provided by different software products e.g. integration of third party software for exchange of data, new plugin, inbuilt capability to monitor data redundancy and data cleaning, inbuilt analytical and modelling tools, cybersecurity, reports and statement generations, accounting data on the cloud, and ethical accounting practices amongst others. On the other hand, this study finds that contemporary designed user-interface is the least important feature that accounting firms will consider when making purchasing decisions which needs to be explored further why such an important aspect of human computer interface (HCI) have been reported low. Also, other important aspects of user interface for local people understanding local languages (e.g. Thai) needs to be built-in to the digital accounting software systems so that local user with little or no understanding of English language can still use and interact with the digital accounting software for their tasks. Often the local user characteristics for the use of the software are either not clearly understood or not built into the software by the international vendors of accounting software, which is a very important element for successful acceptance of the software (Sandhu and Corbitt 2007; Davis 1989).

CONCLUSION

This study presents the results of a survey of accounting firms in Thailand to determine the factors used in the selection of accounting software. The result of this study indicates that the accounting firms consider the accuracy of calculations and reports the most important features in the selection of accounting software. This highlights that the decision for accounting firms is not primarily centred on the cost to the firm. This reaffirms that Thailand accounting firms believe the core business of accounting firms is to provide accurate accounting information to the users. The customer care and problem-solving skills provided with the purchase of a digital accounting software package was also identified as an important feature when accounting firms select an appropriate software. Since cybercrime is becoming an increasingly important issue for businesses, the security of software and access rounds out the top three most important factors accounting firms consider when selecting their software. While a contemporary designed user-interface is classified of the least used factor to determine the digital accounting software feature considered by accounting firms. These findings can be used to inform software developers, software vendors and businesses, along with providing in depth analysis on the features, characteristics, and tools for digital accounting software that require consideration in the selection process.

REFERENCES

Adamyk, O., Adamyk, B., & Khorunzhak, N. (2018). *Auditing of the Software of Computer Accounting System*. Academic Press.

Adhikari, A., Lebow, M. I., & Zhang, H. (2004). Firm characteristics and selection of international accounting software. *Journal of International Accounting, Auditing & Taxation*, *13*(1), 53–69. doi:10.1016/j.intaccaudtax.2004.02.001

Alasadi, R., & Abdelrahim, A. (2008). Analysis of small business performance in Syria. *Education, Business and Society*, *1*(1), 50–62. doi:10.1108/17537980810861510

Bazhair, A., & Sandhu, K. (2015). Factors influencing the acceptance of Enterprise Resource Planning System (ERP) and financial performance of Saudi Arabia listed companies: Multivariate data analysis using Structural Equation Modeling (SEM). *International Journal of Business and Management Review*, *3*(4), 93–118.

Berry, A. J., Sweeting, R., & Goto, J. (2006). The effect of business advisers on the performance of SMEs. *Journal of Small Business and Enterprise Development*, *13*(1), 33–47. doi:10.1108/14626000610645298

Bressler, L. A., & Bressler, M. S. (2006). How entrepreneurs choose and use accounting information systems. *Strategic Finance*, *87*(12), 56.

Collins, J. C. (1999). How to select the right accounting software. *Journal of Accountancy*, *188*(4), 67.

Davis, F. D. (1989). Perceived usefulness, perceived ease of use, and user acceptance of information technology. *Management Information Systems Quarterly*, *13*(3), 319–340. doi:10.2307/249008

Elikai, F., Ivancevich, D. M., & Ivancevich, S. H. (2007). Accounting software selection and user satisfaction. *The CPA Journal*, *77*(5), 26–31.

Ghaffar, A. M., Mokhtar, M. Z., Ismail, W. N. S. W., & Othman, M. R. (2019). Determinant of e-accounting (EA) adoption among Malaysian maritime SMES. *International Journal of Engineering & Technology*, *8*(1.8), 102-105.

Ghasemi, M., Shafeiepour, V., Aslani, M., & Barvayeh, E. (2011). The impact of Information Technology (IT) on modern accounting systems. *Procedia: Social and Behavioral Sciences*, *28*, 112–116. doi:10.1016/j.sbspro.2011.11.023

Hyvönen, T., Järvinen, J., & Pellinen, J. (2006). The role of standard software packages in mediating management accounting knowledge. *Qualitative Research in Accounting & Management*, *3*(2), 145–160. doi:10.1108/11766090610670677

Ismail, N. A., & Mat Zin, R. (2009). Usage of accounting information among Malaysian Bumiputra small and medium non-manufacturing firms. *Journal of Enterprise Resource Planning Studies*.

Lai, M.-L. (2008). Technology readiness, internet self-efficacy and computing experience of professional accounting students. *Campus-Wide Information Systems*, *25*(1), 18–29. doi:10.1108/10650740810849061

Lee, L., Kerler, W., & Ivancevich, D. (2018). Beyond Excel: Software Tools and the Accounting Curriculum. *AIS Educator Journal*, *13*(1), 44–61. doi:10.3194/1935-8156-13.1.44

Pulakanam, V., & Suraweera, T. (2010). Implementing accounting software in small business in New Zealand: An exploratory investigation. *Accountancy Business and the Public Interest*, *9*(64), 98–124.

Putra, Y. M. (2019). Analysis of factors affecting the interests of SMEs using accounting applications. *Journal of Economics and Business*, *2*(3), 818–826. doi:10.31014/aior.1992.02.03.129

Rogers, E. (1995). *Diffusion of Innovations* (4th ed.). The Free Press.

Rushinek, A., & Rushinek, S. F. (1995). Accounting software evaluation: Hardware, audit trails, backup, error recovery and security. *Managerial Auditing Journal*, *10*(9), 29–37. doi:10.1108/02686909510100887

Sandhu, K. (2008). *Information quality for a university accounting information system*. Elsevier. doi:10.2139srn.1289508

Sandhu, K., & Corbitt, B. (2007). Framework for Electronic Services System. In *The Fifth International Conference on Supply Chain Management and Information Systems (SCMIS)*. Monash University.

Sandhu, K., & Terdpaopong, K. (2018). *New research findings from a university web-based information systems*. Asia-Pacific Management Accounting Association. (14th) Annual Conf., Waseda Uni, Tokyo, Japan.

Sandhu, K., & Terdpaopong, K. (2019). *Digital Transformation of Accounting Systems*. Asia-Pacific Management Accounting Association (APMAA) 15th Annual Conference, at Qatar University, Doha, Qatar.

Syafrudin, V. (2012). An empirical study of Accounting software Acceptance among Bengkulu City students. *Asian Journal of Accounting and Governance, 3*, 99-112.

Taragola, N., Van Lierde, D., & Van Huylenbroeck, G. (2001). *Adoption of computers, internet and accounting software at the glasshouse holdings of the Belgian farm accountancy data network*. Paper presented at the Proc. 3rd EFITA Conference, Montpellier, France.

Terdpaopong, K., Visedsun, N., Nitirojntanad, K., & Sandhu, K. (2018). Advancement of the Management Accounting Practices of Large Thai Manufacturing Companies. In *Asia-Pacific Management Accounting Association (14th) Annual Conference*. Waseda University.

Zarowin, S. (1998). Accounting software: The road ahead. *Journal of Accountancy*, *185*(1), 67.

Chapter 8
Blockchain Architecture Stack to Smart Education

Palanivel Kuppusamy
Pondicherry University, India

ABSTRACT

Blockchain is an emerging technology that serves as an immutable ledger and publicly available infrastructure for building decentralized applications. Blockchain-based applications ensure transparency and trust between all parties involved in the interaction. Nowadays, educational organizations focus on online education and propose to create a system based on educational smart contracts in a public ledger. This public ledger shall be shared between major online and offline educational institutes around the world. From a software architecture perspective, blockchain enables new forms of distributed software architectures across a large network of untrusted participants. The objective of this chapter is to propose a blockchain architecture stack to smart education. The proposed architecture exploits the benefits of the blockchain and global ecosystem simplification to create a globally trusted higher education credit system.

INTRODUCTION

Blockchain is an emerging technology (Evris, 2018), which provide significant opportunities to disrupt traditional products and services due to the distributed and decentralized in nature. The features such as the permanence of the blockchain record and the ability to run smart contracts make blockchain technology-based products or services significantly different from previous internet-based commercial developments and of particular interest to the education sector. Besides, currently, stakeholders within education are largely unaware of the social advantages and potential of blockchain technology.

The increased interest and the variety of blockchain technologies lead to the growth of their application domains. The idea of storing educational records in the blockchain has been circulating in the press and academic papers for several years. Nowadays, most of the educational organizations focus on online education. These educational organizations propose to create a system based on the educational smart contracts in a public ledger. This public ledger can be shared between major offline educational institutes.

DOI: 10.4018/978-1-7998-5175-2.ch008

Context

Blockchain technology is forecast to disrupt any field of activity that is founded on time-stamped record-keeping of titles of ownership. Within education, activities likely to be disrupted by blockchain technology include the award of qualifications, licensing and accreditation, management of student records, intellectual property management and payments.

In education systems (St. Laurent, Andrew M. 2008) student records are endless, and with blockchain technology, assets like attendance, courses, payments toward tuition if they attend a private school, grades, coursework, and even their diploma can become part of their blockchain record. Since these records cannot be deleted, this helps with data security in that it is immutable. It also belongs to the student, rather than to the school. With blockchain, no participant can tamper with a record after it has been saved. If a record has an error, a new record must be added to correct it, and both the incorrect and correct records will remain visible.

Challenges in Present Education System

As of today, the standard process of education sector examinations has become very slow which causes uneven delays in the grading process (Anirudh Bhardwaj, 2018, Guang Chen, Bing Xu, Manli Lu and Nian-Shing Chen, 2018). When everything from sending copies to finalizing results is handled manually, it is not just expensive and time-consuming, but also causes a discrepancy in results, which is just not fair. At some places where still paperwork is involved, things get even worse. Some of the challenges in the present education systems are discussed below.

Student identity verification is a perennial problem for educational institutions, requiring manual intervention and presenting many opportunities for data tampering. Within larger institutions, students need to regularly identify themselves to different parts of the organization. In such cases, either each part of the institution collects the student data for itself, or the organization uses single sign-on, whereby one shared copy of the student data is used by all parties within the organization. Under both of these models, tens if not hundreds of people might have access to a student's personal information. Keeping that data safe requires managing access rights for all those people, and ensuring their devices are also secured – a mammoth, if not impossible, undertaking.

Intellectual property protection. Teachers regularly publish research articles, reports and papers as part of their teaching and research work. Under the traditional system, there is little way to know if a similar academic study is underway when a teacher begins his or her research. Also, there is much piracy of the research itself.

Transfer of credits has been another perennial challenge for institutions, often leaving students at a disadvantage when they find, for example, that they must repeat courses to fulfil a new institution's requirements. Students also experience difficulties transferring to another higher education institution, while still preserving and proving courses completed at a previous institution. This problem is even more vivid in cases when a student wants to transfer to an institution in another country, where language and disparate processes are likely to pose additional barriers. Moreover, standards for record storage vary, which can make inter-institutional record exchange difficult.

Formative Assessment. Evaluation is also a problematic issue in the education system. Formative assessment has been advocated for a long time, and yet it is still not ripe because it is not easy to track every detail of teaching and learning. From the perspective of teachers, the instruction is sophisticated and artistic so that it is difficult to evaluate. The traditional method based on students' feedback tends to be one-sidedness, lacking subjectivity and is hardly helpful for teachers' improvement. A new assessment system can be constructed with the latest technology.

Applying blockchain and smart contract can cope up with this challenge. Blockchain can be used to construct a balance to measure the learning process and outcomes. It is a reliable and equal proof of value for everyone.

Motivation Example

Employees in the education sector misplace essential papers now and then, and they include students who lose their diplomas at the most inopportune time. Then, there are students from war-torn areas intending to continue their education elsewhere, and students of a school whose server breaks down or the data completely wiped out, for some reason. The research question for this study is critical to the shaping of a qualitative study:

- How to keep a reliable repository of academic records in a decentralized manner?
- How does a recruiter seamlessly verify certificates from educational institutes in a good amount of time?
- What is the best technology available that the learners can constantly upgrade their skills for professional and personal growth in the world today?

These and others who have trouble getting a copy of their school records can benefit from blockchain-encrypted credentials. Due to the nature of the platform, it has to operate on sensitive data, such as courses, assignments, solutions, payment, grades, certificates, etc.

The blockchain in education (Arodek) sector can help schools, colleges, universities to function in a streamlined manner by accessing candidate details from a shared database for verification purpose. Students can benefit from an easy certificate issuance process driven by smart contracts on completion of their course and establish self-sovereignty of their degrees and diplomas. Additionally, a student's stored e-portfolio on the blockchain can help accelerate processes in banks to verify candidature for an educational loan; and an employer to scrutinize the candidate's suitability for a position in his organization can access the very same e-portfolio.

The blockchain technology in the education sector can very well do wonders for the students and examination cell alike. Blockchain cannot only help in keeping the educational data safe and readily available but also cuts down the costs and saves time. With the use of blockchain, it aims to eradicate all the issues related to degree printing, verification and storage. Using advanced smart contracts, academic records will be transferred on the blockchain. It will enable educational institutes and e-learning platforms to issue certificates on the blockchain. Blockchain offers several benefits in streamlining the examination process. Some of the key benefits of Blockchain in the education sector are the elimination of bias, elimination of intermediaries and reduced costs and paperwork.

Blockchain is an emerging technology enables new forms of distributed software architectures, where agreement on shared states can be established without trusting a central integration point. This circumvents the need to rely on a central, trusted integration point, which has the power to control and manipulate the system and is a single point of failure. Educational applications built on blockchains can take advantage of properties such as data immutability, integrity, fair access, transparency, and non-

Figure 1. Motivation example

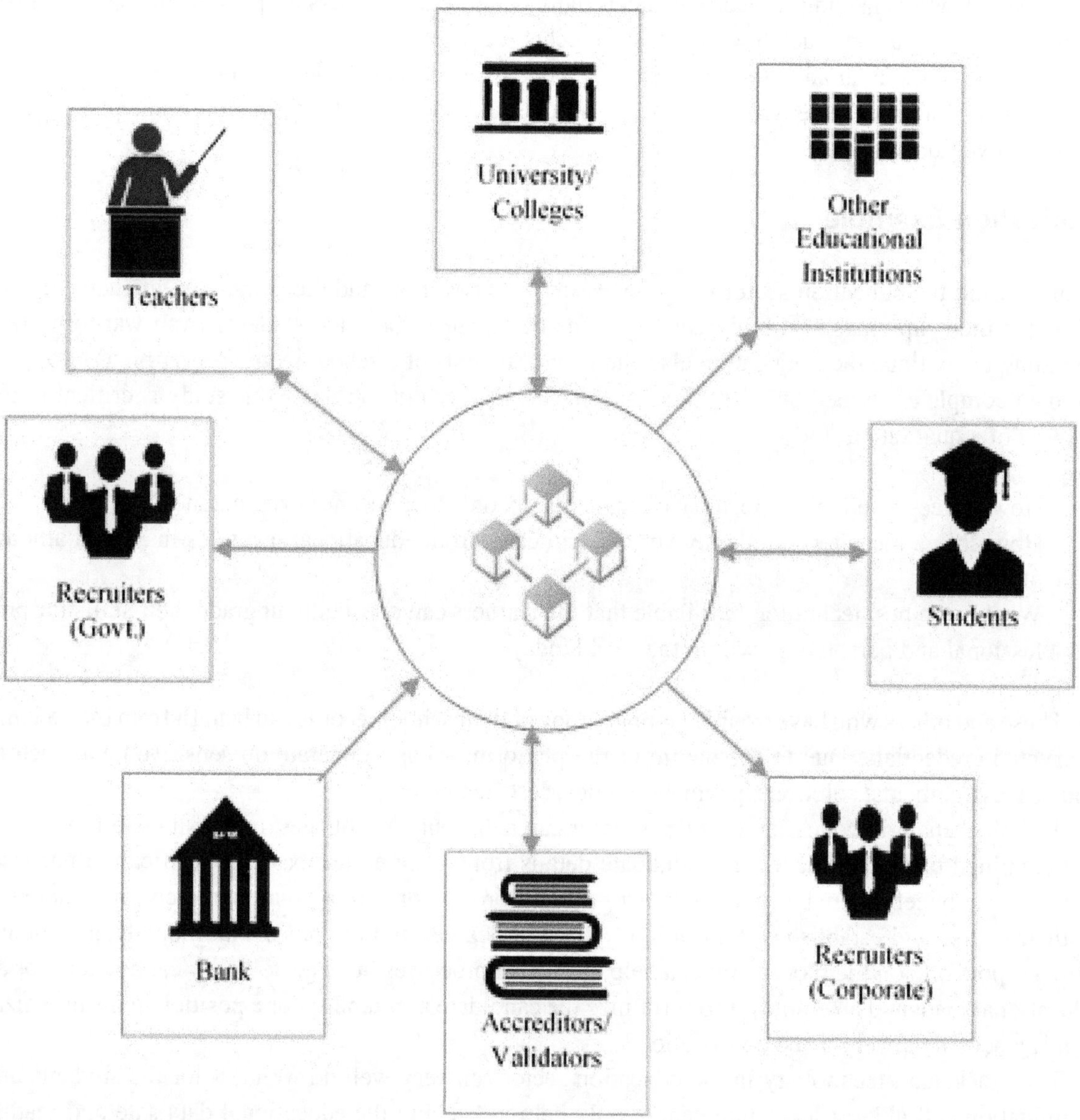

repudiation of transactions. A major difficulty for architects designing applications based on blockchain is that technology has many configurations and variants.

The design of Blockchain architectures requires many different architectural design decisions to be taken, each of which with a strong impact on the quality of the resulting system. As of now, however, only little is known about the impact of decisions in the design of Blockchain architectures on the quality of the resulting system.

Proposed Solution

It is proposed a blockchain-based decentralized architecture for higher education learning solutions. This architecture is built on the distributed P2P network system. The proposed architecture called proof of educational transcript system (or PETS) is flexible, secure and resilient because of their storage capacity and resource sharing on a global scale. The PETS architecture transfers the higher education grading system from the analogue and physical world into a globally efficient, simplified, ubiquitous version, based on the blockchain technology.

This paper is organized as follow: In the *technical background section*, terminology and recent taxonomies for blockchain systems are discussed. A Blockchain architecture stack to smart education is presented in *Solutions and Results section*. Finally, in *conclusion, section* a conclusion is drawn and an outlook presented.

Technical Background: State-of-Art

This section presents on blockchain technology and the impact of blockchain technology in higher education institutions. It starts by formulating a definition for the basic concept, which is followed by a presentation of the technology's inherent characteristics.

In a centralized system, it clear that all the personal data on the Internet is stored in a Server with huge storage. Private organizations own all of the data. Therefore, this poses a serious threat to the privacy of data. This centralized system had caused quite the fuss over the last few years. For example, the data breach of Facebook and Apple's i-Cloud hack. Too many sensitive data were leaked to the public. On the other hand, a decentralized network is free from the threat of data breaching. All the data will be distributed over the whole network. This the true beauty of Blockchain Technology - a decentralized, secured and private network that focuses on being humane.

Introduction to Blockchain

Blockchain technology is lauded as having the potential to transform the global economy due to its ability to increase transparency and trust. A blockchain is a distributed digital ledger of transactions, the contents of which are verified and agreed upon by a network of independent actors. Transactions are recorded in a series of blocks that gives a clear timeline of who did what and when. Blocks of information (time stamping of life events) are secured by complex algorithms that are hard to hack and cannot be manipulated. Therefore, it has a huge role to play in validating identity management, without the use of an independent third party.

A more wordy definition (Audrey Watters, 2016):

The blockchain is a distributed database that provides an unalterable, (semi-) public record of digital transactions. Each block aggregates a timestamped batch of transactions to be included in the ledger. A cryptographic signature identifies each block. These blocks are all back-linked; that is, they refer to the signature of the previous block in the chain, and that chain can be traced back to the very first block created. As such, the blockchain contains an un-editable record of all the transactions made.

Since each block of transactions is cryptographically linked to the previous block, it is extraordinarily difficult to change data stored in a blockchain thus making it immutable. For a new piece of data to be added to the blockchain, the independent verifiers must come to a consensus about its validity. Therefore, blockchain has multiple layers of verification, which makes the platform tamper-proof and robust against any fraudulent activity. Nodes or computers connected to the blockchain network get updated version of the ledger as and when new transactions are made.

The benefits of blockchain are now going beyond the world of finance into other industries, including education, where trust is essential.

Characteristics of Blockchain

The blockchain technology can provide a secure chain of custody for both digital and physical assets through its functional characteristics that facilitate transactions through trust, consensus, security, and smart contracts. The blockchain technology generally has key characteristics of decentralization, persistence, anonymity and auditability. According to Karim Sultan, Umar Ruhi1, Rubina Lakhani, 2018, the afore-noted features of the blockchain are immutable, decentralization, transparency and consensus-driven – (trust verification). Also, Paolo Tasca, Claudio J. Tessone, 2019 took a bird's-eye view and described blockchains by looking at their key driving principles, such as data decentralization, transparency, security, immutability, and privacy:

- **Decentralization:** In conventional centralized transaction systems, each transaction needs to be validated through the central trusted agency (e.g., the central bank), inevitably resulting in the cost and the performance bottlenecks at the central servers. Contrast to the centralized model, third-party is no longer needed in the blockchain;
- **Persistency:** Transactions can be validated quickly and honest miners would not admit invalid transactions. It is nearly impossible to delete or rollback transactions once they are included in the blockchain. Blocks that contain invalid transactions could be discovered immediately;
- **Anonymity:** Each user can interact with the blockchain with a generated address, which does not reveal the real identity of the user;
- **Auditability:** Bitcoin blockchain stores data about user balances based on the unspent transaction output (UTXO) model. Once the current transaction is recorded into the blockchain, the state of those referred unspent transactions switches from unspent to spent. Therefore, transactions could be easily verified and tracked;
- **Transparency:** Records are auditable by a predefined set of participants, although the set can be more or less open. For example, in public blockchains, everyone with an Internet connection to the network holds equal rights and ability to access the ledger. The records are thus transparent and traceable. Participants have also the option to pool together their weighted rights;
- **Security:** Blockchains are shared, tamper-proof, replicated ledgers where records are irreversible and cannot be forged thanks to one-way cryptographic hash functions. Although security is a relative concept, it can say that blockchains are relatively secure because users can transfer data only if they possess a private key. Private keys are used to generate a signature for each blockchain transaction a user sends out. This signature is used to confirm that the transaction has come from the user, and to prevent the transaction from being altered by anyone once it has been issued.

With the above traits, blockchain can greatly save cost and improve efficiency.

Types of Blockchain

Blockchain networks can be categorized based on their permission model, which determines who can maintain them (e.g., publish blocks). It can be permissionless and permissioned. If anyone can publish a new block, it is *permissionless*. If only particular users can publish blocks, it is *permissioned*. A permissioned blockchain network is like a corporate intranet that is controlled, while a permissionless blockchain network is like the public internet, where anyone can participate:

- **Permissionless Blockchain:** Permissionless blockchain networks are decentralized ledger platforms open to anyone publishing blocks, without needing permission from any authority. Any blockchain network user within a permissionless blockchain network can read and write to the ledger. Permissioned blockchain networks are often deployed for a group of organizations and individuals, typically referred to as a consortium;
- **Permissioned Blockchain:** Permissioned blockchain networks are ones where users publishing blocks must be authorized by some authority (centralized or decentralized). Permissioned blockchain may thus allow anyone to read the blockchain or they may restrict read access to authorized individuals. They also may allow anyone to submit transactions to be included in the blockchain or, again, they may restrict this access only to authorized individuals.

The blockchain systems can also be categorized into three types: *public blockchain, private blockchain* and *consortium blockchain*. In public blockchain, all records are visible to the public and everyone could take part in the consensus process. Differently, only a group of pre-selected nodes would participate in the consensus process of a consortium blockchain. As for private blockchain, only those nodes that come from one specific organization would be allowed to join the consensus process. A private blockchain is regarded as a centralized network since it is fully controlled by one organization. The consortium blockchain constructed by several organizations is partially decentralized since only a small portion of nodes would be selected to determine the consensus.

Components of Blockchain

Blockchain technology can seem complex. However, it can be simplified by examining each component individually. The main components (Dylan Yaga, 2018) of blockchain are *cryptographic hash functions, transactions, asymmetric-key cryptography, addresses, ledgers and blocks.*

Cryptographic Hash Functions: An important component of blockchain technology is the use of cryptographic hash functions for many operations. This component calculates a relatively unique output for an input of nearly any size (e.g., a file, text, or image). It allows individuals to independently take input data, hash that data, and derive the same result – proving that there was no change in the data.

Transactions: A transaction represents a transfer of the cryptocurrency between blockchain network users. Each block in a blockchain can contain zero or more transactions. A blockchain network user sends information to the blockchain network. The information sent may include the sender's address, sender's public key, a digital signature, transaction inputs and transaction outputs.

Asymmetric-Key Cryptography: Asymmetric-key cryptography uses a pair of keys: a public key and a private key. Asymmetric-key cryptography enables a trust relationship between users who do not know to each other, by providing a mechanism to verify the integrity and authenticity of transactions while at the same time allowing transactions to remain public. In contrast, symmetric-key cryptography in which a single secret key is used to both encrypts and decrypt. The data is encrypted with symmetric key cryptography and then the symmetric key is encrypted using asymmetric-key cryptography.

Addresses and Address Derivation: Blockchain networks make use of an address along with some additional data (e.g., version number and checksums). The blockchain implementations make use of addresses in a transaction. To generate an address, it creates a public key, applying a cryptographic hash function to it, and converting the hash to text. Addresses may act as the public-facing identifier and oftentimes an address will be converted into a QR code for easier use with mobile devices.

Ledgers: A ledger is a collection of transactions. In modern times, ledgers have been stored digitally, often in large databases owned and operated by a centralized trusted third party (i.e., the owner of the ledger) on behalf of a community of users. These ledgers can be implemented in a centralized or distributed fashion. There is a growing interest in exploring having distributed ownership of the ledger. The growing interest in distributed ownership of ledgers is due to possible trust, security, and reliability concerns related to ledgers with centralized ownership.

Blocks: Blockchain network users submit candidate transactions to the blockchain network via software. The software sends these transactions to nodes (non-publishing full nodes as well as publishing nodes) within the blockchain network. The submitted transactions are then propagated to the other nodes in the network. Transactions are added to the blockchain when a publishing node publishes a block. A block contains a block header and block data. The block header contains metadata for this block. The block data contains a list of validated and authentic transactions, which have been submitted to the blockchain network. The other full nodes will check the validity and authenticity of all transactions in a published block.

Chaining Blocks: Blocks are chained together through each block containing the hash digest of the previous block's header. If a previously published block were changed, it would have a different hash. This, in turn, would cause all subsequent blocks to also have different hashes since they include the hash of the previous block. This makes it possible to easily detect and reject altered blocks.

WORKING PRINCIPLE OF BLOCKCHAIN

The working principle of Blockchain is shown Figure2. A blockchain is a tamper-proof, shared digital ledger, which records transactions in either a public or a private network. As it is distributed to all participants in the network, the ledger makes a permanent record as *blocks*. Each computer on the network is known as a "node". Instead of relying on a third party, such as a financial institution, to mediate transactions, participants in a blockchain network use a consensus protocol to agree on ledger content, and cryptographic hashes and digital signatures to ensure the integrity of transactions (Blog, 2017).

The peer-to-peer blockchain network prevents any single participant or group of participants from controlling the underlying infrastructure or system. Participants in the network are all equal, adhering to the same protocols. At its core, the system records the chronological order of transactions with all agreeing to the validity of transactions using the chosen consensus model. The result is transactions that are irreversible and agreed to by all participants in the network.

Figure 2. Working principle of Blockchain

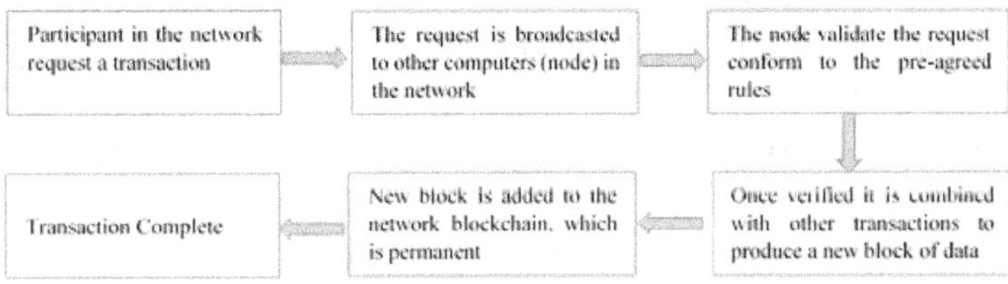

Consensus Models of Blockchain

A key aspect of blockchain technology is determining which user publishes the next block. This is solved through implementing one of many possible consensus models. Blockchain technologies use consensus models to enable a group of mutually distrusting users to work together. There are several consensus models (Arati Baliga, 2017, Dylan Yaga, 2018) as well as the most common conflict resolution approach are discussed.

Proof of Work (PoW) Model: In this model, a user publishes the next block by being the first to solve a computationally intensive puzzle. The solution to this puzzle is the "proof" they have performed work. The puzzle is designed such that solving the puzzle is difficult but checking that a solution is valid is easy. This enables all other full nodes to easily validate any proposed next blocks, and any proposed block that did not satisfy the puzzle would be rejected. For example, Bitcoin, which uses the proof of work model, adjusts the puzzle difficulty every 2016 blocks to influence the block publication rate to be around once every ten minutes. This adjustment is to maintain the computational difficulty of the puzzle, and therefore maintain the core security mechanism of the Bitcoin network:

- **Proof of Stake (PoS) Model:** This PoS model is based on the idea that the more stake a user has invested into the system, the more likely they will want the system to succeed, and the less likely they will want to subvert it. Proof of stake blockchain networks uses the amount of stake a user has as a determining factor for publishing new blocks. With this consensus model, there is no need to perform resource-intensive computations (involving time, electricity, and processing power) as found in proof of work. The methods for how the blockchain network uses the stake can vary are *a random selection of staked users*, *multi-round voting*, *coin ageing systems* and *delegate systems*. Regardless of the exact approach, users with more stake are more likely to publish new blocks;
- **Round Robin Model:** This consensus model is used by some permissioned blockchain networks. Within this model of consensus, nodes take turns in creating blocks. This model ensures no one node creates the majority of the blocks. It benefits from a straightforward approach, lacks cryptographic puzzles, and has low power requirements. Since there is a need for trust amongst nodes, round-robin does not work well in the permissionless blockchain networks used by most cryptocurrencies. This is because malicious nodes could continuously add additional nodes to increase their odds of publishing new blocks;
- **Proof of Authority (Proof of Identity) Model:** This consensus model relies on the partial trust of publishing nodes through their known link to real-world identities. The idea is that the publishing node is staking its identity/reputation to publish new blocks. Blockchain network users directly

affect a publishing node's reputation based on the publishing node's behaviour. Publishing nodes can lose reputation by acting in a way that the blockchain network users disagree with, just as they can gain reputation by acting in a manner that the blockchain network users agree with. The lower the reputation, the less the likelihood of being able to publish a block. Therefore, it is in the interest of a publishing node to maintain a high reputation. This algorithm only applies to permissioned blockchain networks with high levels of trust;

- **Proof of Elapsed Time Model:** In this (PoET) consensus model, each publishing node requests a wait time from a secure hardware time source within their computer system. Once a publishing node wakes up from the idle state, it creates and publishes a block to the blockchain network, alerting the other nodes of the new block; any publishing node that is still idle will stop waiting, and the entire process starts over. After waiting the assigned time, the publishing node could request a signed certificate that the publishing node waited the randomly assigned time. The publishing node then publishes the certificate along with the block.

From a social perspective, blockchain technology offers significant possibilities beyond those currently available. In particular, moving records to the blockchain can allow for self-sovereignty, trust, transparency & provenance, immutability, disintermediation, and collaboration. Blockchain mechanism brings everyone to the highest degree of accountability. Therefore, solves the problem of manipulation. The data that belongs to us we can own it that is online identity and reputation will be decentralized. It provides durability, reliability, and longevity with the decentralized network. The data that are entered in blockchain-based systems are immutable which prevent against fraud through manipulating transactions and the history of data. Therefore, all the transactions can be investigated and audited easily.

Blockchain Applications

Since the fundamental use-case for blockchain technology is to drive greater transparency and substantiate the accuracy of transaction data across the digital information ecosystem, potential applications of such technology are practically endless. Since blockchain technology is still new, many organizations are looking at ways to incorporate it into their businesses. The nature of the blockchain network has the potential to enable the development of a wide range of different applications (Dylan Yaga, 2018)) that are decentralized. Decentralized applications are becoming more and more important in recent years. Blockchain-based applications cannot be stopped censored or controlled and they ensure transparency and trust between all parties involved in the interaction. The use of decentralized application often depends on the context of the usage. Blockchain shows potential to be used in many different fields and some of them are domain registration, trading assets, cloud storage, voting, crowdfunding, car sharing, gambling and prediction markets, Internet of Things (IoT) and education.

According to Michael Crosby, et al. 2015, classified a different kind of interesting applications and they were financial and non-financial. Mougayar (2016) classifies the role of blockchains as spanning four aspects: development platform, smart contract utility, marketplace and finally, trusted service application:

- **As a Development Platform:** At present, the development of Blockchain applications and services requires a highly specialized skillset, and the state of the blockchain developer toolkits is immature. The *Blockchain as a Service* (BaaS) platforms such as those by Microsoft (Azure) and IBM (Cloud) provide an inexpensive environment for developers to rapidly prototype on test blockchains before deploying to live ones. These BaaS solutions form the basis for programmable trust, ownership and identity, and facilitate the operation and governance of enterprise blockchain applications and services;

- **As a Smart Contract Utility:** Smart contracts provide a programmatic interface to blockchains. The smart contract, when triggered, transacts value based on digital assets. Activities often managed by third party central authorities are mitigated to the blockchain instead, disintermediating transactions. Examples include escrow, multi-party transactions, digital notarization, and time stamping;
- **As a Marketplace:** Any robust ecosystem requires a market for generating value. In the crypto-economics marketplace, blockchain provides a payment infrastructure (via cryptocurrencies) and a proof-of-ownership structure (via digital asset tracking). This has enabled peer-to-peer marketplaces with no governing authority, such as OpenBazaar6 and Soma7 providing accessible, disintermediated trade. In such instances, blockchain platforms can ensure that service providers are not constrained by any central authority – hence, allowing them to extend flexible offerings, and payment interactions and service transactions can function in a transparent environment. Overall, as a marketplace enabler, blockchains can be used to operationalize programmable assets, ownership and money;
- **As a Trusted-Service Application:** In trusted service application, blockchain technology comprises end-to-end functionality by facilitating highly specialized applications for any purpose imaginable. The trusted service applications built on the Blockchain using smart contracts can provide disintermediated, secure services to end-users.

This more generalized use of blockchains to enable all types of applications through a combination of programmable assets, trust, ownership, money, identity, and contracts.

Software Architecture for Blockchain Applications

The software architecture refers to the high-level structures of the blockchain system. Each structure is composed of software elements, the relations between them, and the properties that emerge from those elements and relations. According to Paolo Tasca, Claudio J. Tessone, 2019, there are two possible layouts for software architecture and they are monolithic design and polylithic design:

- **Monolithic Design:** In this case, all the aspects of a decentralized ledger are handled by a blockchain built as a single-tier software application without modularity. Examples of blockchains with monolithic design include Bitcoin and Ethereum. These architectures suffer from a lack of extensibility in the long run;
- **Polylithic Design:** The Polylithic approach decouples the consensus engine and P2P layers from the details of the blockchain application state. For example, Hyperledger Fabric follows a polylithic design as it is composed of interchangeable modules representing different components of blockchain technologies. Also, in Tendermint the blockchain design is "decomposed." Between the application process and its application-agnostic "consensus engine", it offers a very simple API, which enables it to run Byzantine fault-tolerant applications.

The choice of software architecture is very important to better manage changes once implemented. Software architecture choices include specific structural options among the possibilities that are available for software design.

BlockChain in Smart Education

According to Rachael Hartley, 2018, Education is a multifaceted sector where different systems need to adapt to prepare students for the jobs of tomorrow. Having a foolproof system that records a student's academic history before and during a working life can not only help in battling dishonesty but can also help to tackle the issues of bespoke learning. This will ultimately give people the best chance of determining their education path and successful future career.

It can allow workers to build up a secure, verifiable digital record of formal qualifications, experience and soft skills gained over their lifetime. Also, by using a smart contract, blockchain applications could provide students with the ability to gain greater control over their education through offering flexible access to content and courses suggested based on previous successes or failures and attainment.

Blockchain technology provides a simple and encrypted way of ensuring that a person is qualified and educated enough to fulfil the requirements for a position. They provide a plausible means of security for employers and employees to prove their credentials in certain areas. It would be easy for employers to authenticate this information. This can provide a more secure solution to teacher-readiness accountability in educational institutions. It can also ensure that teachers have taken appropriate classwork for the job they are taking on, or help teacher show they are qualified in various areas (Alexander Grech, Anthony F, 2017):

- The Blockchain technology will accelerate the end of a paper-based system for certificates. Any kinds of certificates issued by educational organizations can be permanently and reliably secured using blockchain technology;
- The Blockchain technology allows users to be able to automatically verify the validity of certificates directly against the blockchain, without the need to contact the educational organization that originally issued them;
- The Blockchain technology can also be applied to intellectual property management, for the tracking of first publication and citations, without the need for a central authority to manage these databases;
- The Blockchain technology is applied to create data management structures where users have increased ownership and control over their data could significantly reduce educational organizations' data management costs, as well as their exposure to liability resulting from data management issues;
- Blockchain technology is also found that blockchain-based cryptocurrencies are likely to be used to facilitate payments within educational institutions.

From the above, blockchain technology is considered for creating and promoting a label for 'open' educational records and only supports or adopts technologies in compliance with such a label. The main beneficiaries of the adoption of blockchain-based technologies in education are likely to be networks of educational organizations and learners. It suggests outreach to the educational networks to help them understand the benefits of technology, the incorporation of the principles behind the technology into digital competency education for learners.

Blockchain in the Higher Education Sector

Education is the exchange of knowledge and skills through several channels. The process is more efficient if there is trust between all parties involved. This trust can play a crucial role in transforming higher education in the future. Most educational institutions keep students' completed course records in proprietary formats. These databases are structured for exclusive access by an institution's staff and in dedicated online systems, with little or no interoperability. Further, the majority of institutions have their specialized system for keeping students' completed course records, which preserves the proprietary data structure of the database. Also, in the traditional education () system are *recordkeeping, badges, on the job training, continuous professional training, etc.*:

- *For recordkeeping,* blockchain technology provides a secure repository of such records, time-stamped can be a big help for all stakeholders;
- Using blockchain, *badges* would be recorded and time-stamped. Badges could subsequently be used for up-skilling and used as learning currency for progression;
- *Badges* can be used to keep a record of all *credentials* earned during a lifetime. Such credentials would be more valuable than the current practice of issuing certificates;
- For on the *job training*, blockchain technology could help centralize humongous data and validate the process and certification for such learners;
- For *continuous professional education*, the blockchain technology is used to seamlessly record fragmented data such as continuous learning's from multiple sources and stack this up in a repository.

Some of the challenges that affect the Higher Education Sector (HES) are fraud detection, universal academic credentials, smart contracts, decentralized classrooms and transparency of scholarships. The solution to the above challenges is the use of Blockchain technology in the education system. The blockchain technology has the potential to change the HES (Blockchain News, 2018) for the better, through decentralization and immutability.

In HES, Blockchain records are stored permanently, so documents such as degrees and course certificates can be secured and verified, regardless of whether or not a user has access to an institution's record-keeping system as shown in Figure 3. Even if the institution that issued the certificates were to close, or if the entire education system collapsed, those certificates would still be verifiable against the records stored in a Blockchain. Also, once institutions issue a certificate, no further efforts are required to confirm the validity of that certificate to third parties, since the certificate can verify itself directly on the blockchain.

Blockchain provides a more durable and flexible system for storing student credentials as they move from course to course throughout their professional careers, as well as their secondary education. Via blockchain, credentials cannot be modified, providing a more reliable system of storing credentials for a lifetime of learning. Blockchain allows personal data to stay personal to the learner. Students gain control and ownership of all their education data, including accreditation and portfolios of work, in a secure place that is accessible to anyone who needs to verify it. With blockchain, learners could store their evidence

Figure 3. Educational institution's record-keeping system

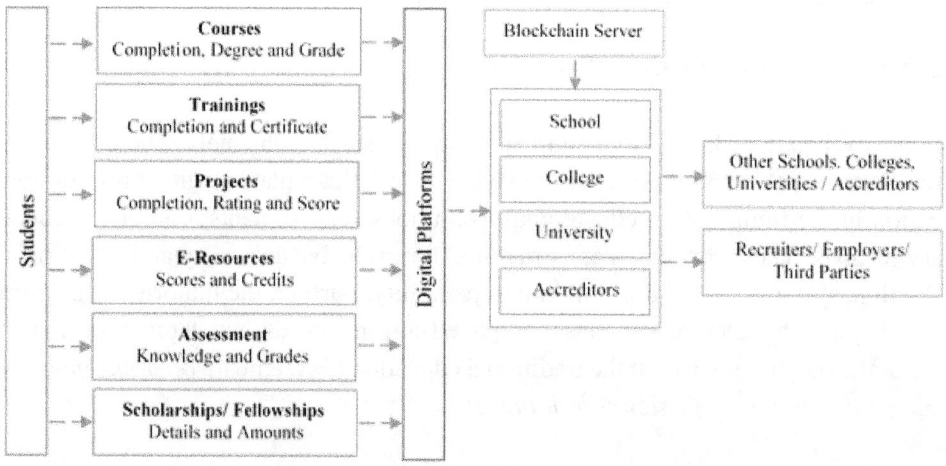

of formal or informal learning, share it with the desired audience, and ensure instant verification. This means students can have self-updating curriculum vitae that can easily be shared with employers. Employers, meanwhile, could reduce their workload since they would not have to verify curriculum vitae and could simply search to see whether candidates have the skills required.

Blockchain by design is non-editable. With technology, learners are finding newer ways to do so without any fuss. The learners are realizing that smaller chunks of learning, acquired over some time works much better than a conventional credential driven certificate from the educational institutions. Also, a blockchain is an immutable ledger of records. Once the information has been entered and verified, it cannot be changed. Additionally, no one can append information on the blockchain without the approval of the network users.

Blockchain mechanism brings everyone to the highest degree of accountability. Therefore, solves the problem of manipulation. It provides durability, reliability, and longevity with the decentralized network. The data that are entered in blockchain-based systems are immutable. Therefore, all the transactions can be investigated and audited easily.

As a nascent technology, blockchain adoption presents numerous challenges. Blockchain requires wide-ranging business process change, with the technological component being only a small part of its implementation. For blockchain to make a significant impact on the education space, grassroots-level change is required, as well as collaboration from all the stakeholders across borders.

Methodology

With an emerging technology such as blockchain, with almost daily industry announcements and posts on specialist media, the use of qualitative methods currently represents a pragmatic approach in engaging with the subject at a time when research on the subject is at an embryonic stage, and where case studies involving the blockchain and education are exploratory and / or pilot initiatives. This study is based on qualitative research methods, using desk research, literature review and case studies to generate evidence.

The research approach involves literature review and desk review (Stefan Seebacher, Ronny Schüritz, 2017). The *literature review* of any published literature on applications of blockchain technology to education, non-financial applications of blockchain technology more generally and digital methods for storing, securing, sharing and verifying academic credentials. The *desk review* utilizing primary sources covering technical specifications of major blockchain implementations, in particular, Bitcoin, Ethereum, and technical specifications of products released by vendors offering products built on top of blockchain technology, as well as of their governing structure, operations and intellectual property arrangements.

Architectural Design

With the emergence and increasing popularity of decentralized cryptocurrencies, blockchain architectures have become more and more important. The design of Blockchain architectures requires many different architectural design decisions to be taken, each of which with a strong impact on the quality of the resulting system. As of now, however, only little is known about the impact of decisions in the design of Blockchain architectures on the quality of the resulting system.

The design taxonomy (Xiwei Xu, 2017) is intended to help software architects evaluate and compare blockchains, and to enable research into architectural decision-making frameworks for blockchain-based systems. The discussion of architectural design issues for blockchain-based systems has structured the level of decentralization, support for client storage and computation, blockchain infrastructural configuration, and other issues.

Decentralization

It devolves responsibility and capability from a central location or authority. In a centralized system, all users rely on a central authority to mediate transactions. In contrast, a fully decentralized system allows people to reach agreement on who owns what without having to trust each other or a separate third party. Such a system is highly available since every full node downloads every block and transaction, checks them against core consensus rules and provides the required functionality to process transactions. It partly guards against this using its proof-of-work mechanism. A decentralized system can be defeated unless there is a majority of authority (nodes, computational power, or stakeholding).

Verification

The execution environment of a blockchain is self-contained. It can only access information present in a transaction or the transaction history of the blockchain, and the states of external systems are not directly accessible. To address this limitation, a *verifier* role can be introduced to evaluate conditions that cannot be expressed in a smart contract running within the blockchain network. A verifier can be implemented as a Server outside the blockchain and inside a blockchain network. To decentralize the verifier, a *distributed verifier* can be introduced. The whole network trusts all the verifiers.

Storage and Computation

In Blockchain network, due to some unique properties, the amount of computational power and data storage space available on a blockchain network remains limited. Computation in a blockchain-based system can be performed on-chain (*e.g.*, through smart contracts) or off-chain. Different blockchains offer different levels of expressiveness for on-chain computation. In regards to cost efficiency, performance, and flexibility, major design decisions in using a blockchain include choosing what data & computation should be placed on-chain and what should be kept off-chain.

Configuration

When using a blockchain, one design decision is the *scope*, *i.e.* whether to use a public blockchain, consortium/community blockchain or private blockchain. Most digital currencies use public blockchains, which can be accessed by anyone on the Internet. Whether using a consortium blockchain, private blockchain or permissioned public blockchain, a permission management component will be required to authorize participants within the network.

The other design choices concern anonymity, incentives and deployment.

Anonymity

The blockchain is perceived to be anonymous. The research has shown that transactions can be linked to compromise the anonymity of users. Different techniques have been proposed to preserve anonymity on the blockchain. A zero-knowledge proof construction is used to allow the blockchain network to maintain a secure ledger and enable private payment without disclosing the parties or amounts involved. Anonymity is preserved because it is hard to track which output address is paid by which input address.

Incentive

Blockchains and their applications introduce financial incentives for miners to join the network, validate transactions and generate blocks correctly. In Blockchain, miners have two incentives: the reward for generating new blocks and the fees associated with transactions. Miners also charge a fee to execute smart contracts. They have a fixed price for storage, data retrieval, and computation within the network. Reputation and rating mechanisms are generally used in peer-to-peer systems as a sign of trustworthiness of the peer as judged by others.

Deployment

Deployment of blockchain also has an impact on the quality attributes of the system. For example, deploying a blockchain on a cloud provided by third-party, or using a blockchain-as-a-service model directly introduces the uncertainty of cloud infrastructure into the system. Also, deploying a public blockchain system on a virtual private network can make it a private blockchain, with permissioned access controls provided at the network level.

Literature Survey

By looking at the main concepts, it finds that innovation, decentralization and digital innovation is amongst the most common concepts found in the literature. However, by categorizing the concepts, it discovers the – technological features, innovation, decentralization and ecosystems themes mentioned in the literature about the blockchain technology. It should be noted that some of the concepts are present within one or more categories as these present ideas that fall outside one category. Hence, these will establish a foundation for further analysis of the topic:

- Stefan K. Johansen, 2018 provided comprehensive and detailed documentation of the current technological and literary state of the Blockchain technology within Information Systems research. He outlined in detail what is required for the Blockchain technology to function as a technological enabler for innovation and the required factors for success;
- According to Stefan Seebacher and Ronny Schüritz, 2017, blockchain technology was expected to revolutionize the way transactions are performed, thereby affecting a vast variety of potential areas of application. They identified a set of characteristics that enable trust and decentralization, facilitating the formation and coordination of a service system;
- Karim Sultan, 2018 presented the overview of blockchain technology, key functional characteristics, and classification of current and emerging blockchain applications;
- BitRice, 2018, aimed to create a future-oriented data storage and content sharing ecosystem. It will enable users to commercialize their spare storage space and digitalize the value of their original contents (photos, videos and files) by sharing, and therefore become a mature project with real-life applications seamlessly integrating smart hardware with blockchain technology;
- Zhaoyang 2018 gave a perspective on using Blockchain as a secure, distributed cyberinfrastructure for the future grid. Some promising application domains of Blockchain in future grids are presented. Following this, some potential challenges are discussed;
- Leonardo, 2019, developed an ontology that helps to identify and clarify in detail what are the concepts and structures revolving around this technology and built a continuum of blockchain architectural solutions, ranging from a classic centralized IT architecture to one completely distributed within a public ecosystem.

Blockchain technology shall also apply to higher education institutions. Several HEIs have employed Blockchain technology to design different solutions and approaches related to higher education:

- The National University of La Plata (UNLP) has started developing a framework (Media Lab) for a blockchain-based verification of academic achievement. It has proposed a platform for creating, sharing, and verifying blockchain-based educational certificates within the scope of the digital certificates project. This approach addressed the issues of digitizing academic certificates and does not investigate the possibility of the blockchain to be used in a global higher education credit and grading platform;
- The Argentinian College CESYT (Amati, F. 2015) also adopted the same approach. Both solutions use blockchain technology and cryptography (i.e. digital signature, time stamps, etc.) to issue diplomas for students. The approach is focused only on issuing diplomas (degrees) using the bitcoin blockchain;
- Das, S. 2016 stated that the Parisian Leonardo da Vinci Engineering School (ESILV) announced it would certify diplomas on a bitcoin blockchain. A prototype has been published so far. There are also other higher education institutions, which have or intend to use the blockchain technology;
- L. Coleman, 2015 announced using the technology to help employers verify academic credentials;

- Muhamed Turkanović, et al. 2018, aimed to incorporate global stakeholders into the EduCTX initiative and inclusion of any HEI through a publicly available platform and web presence. The proposed EduCTX blockchain platform is thus the basis of the EduCTX initiative, opened globally to all HEIs for building an efficient, simplified, ubiquitous solution for student's credit assignment, while eliminating language and administrative obstacles;
- Alok Kumar Jain, 2018, the education industry is changing before our eyes. No longer solely the province of a centralized learning environment in either the physical or virtual worlds, education now occurs via peer-to-peer interactions, online and from anywhere on the planet. Educational providers, particularly in higher education, are struggling to harness digital technology as a tool for transformation.

Most of the aforementioned projects in the higher education domain rely on closed concepts or ideas and often do not discuss details or even remain on an idea level. Some of the related projects are offered exclusively to a closed circle of entities.

Purpose, Scope and Objectives

This above study investigates the feasibility, challenges, and benefits of blockchain technology architecture in education, with a focus on the application of the blockchain to formal and non-formal credentials. It needs to overcome challenges on many fronts where educational credentials are concerned.

This paper focuses on identifying all relevant literature, due to the novelty of the technology. With the identification of relevant literature, it will analyze and synthesize the results found in the literature to identify gaps and propose model and architecture for future research. A conclusion will be established to provide researchers with the main contributions of the paper. The primary objectives of the study are to:

1. Provide an introduction to blockchain technology in education and the use of blockchain technology in education landscape;
2. Determine if the technology is fit-for-purpose for the recording of academic achievements and HESs should it be deployed as an open standard;
3. Identify opportunities and challenges for the take-up of blockchain technology in higher education institutions;
4. Provide a generic architecture to academic institutions.

This study is primarily aimed at policy-makers in HES, educators and researchers. It may also be of interest to a more general readership with an interest in emerging technology, and its deployment within a wider socio-economic context. The design analysis performed here may not be valid, relevant or rigorous enough since they are yet to be widely identified, used and studied for blockchain-based systems. However, it believes that the high-level qualitative approaches to support the indicative qualitative findings in our study.

Solutions and Results: Blockchain Architecture to Smart Education

This section outlines the proposed architecture called PETS, a blockchain-based higher education learning solutions. Blockchain technology is a growing area of interest for educational institutions. The exploratory study addresses the value-decentralized ledgers; in particular, those based on blockchain technology may bring to stakeholders within the educational sector, with a particular focus on its potential for digital accreditation of personal and academic learning.

Blockchain Design Taxonomy

The Taxonomy can be used during the process of architecting blockchain systems to guide the system design. The following illustrates how the taxonomy can be used to guide the Blockchain system design at different stages of the design process:

1. The process starts with the decision to decentralize trust (authority) – or not. A blockchain is used in scenarios where no single trusted authority is required and the trusted authority can be decentralized or partially decentralized;
2. Given the limitations of blockchains, the next major decision is splitting computation and data storage between on-chain and off-chain components;
3. After that, a collection of design decisions around blockchain configuration need to be made, like the type of blockchain, consensus protocol, block size and frequency;
4. Other design decisions are also may be considered. Some decisions mainly affect scalability (like block size and frequency), security (like consensus protocol), cost efficiency (like a type of blockchain) and performance (like data structure);
5. There are also trade-offs between the fundamental properties of the blockchain;
6. Finally, where to deploy the modules of the blockchain-based system is also important.

Blockchain Considerations in Smart Education

When deciding whether to utilize a blockchain, the designer must take into consideration of factors and determine if these factors limit one's ability to use a blockchain in smart education: educational data visibility, full transactional history, fake certificate or data input, tamper-evident and tamper-resistant, transactions per second, compliance, recruiters permissions, node diversity, etc.

The proposed solution makes use of blockchain technologies to authenticate consumers at digital identity providers. The contribution is to provide a distributed and interoperable architecture model for the smart education for the higher education credit system, which addresses a globally unified viewpoint for students and educational institutions. Potential employers and recruiters can benefit from the proposed system. The proposed or PETS architecture is envisioned for processing, managing and controlling the academic credits and resting on a globally distributed P2P network, where peers of the blockchain network are HEI and users of the platform are students and organizations (e.g. companies as potential employers).

Features of PETS

The most important features of Blockchain architecture to smart education are decentralized, P2P, immutable and tamper-proof and they discussed below:

- **Decentralized:** The proposed system includes nodes of educational institutions (primary, middle, higher secondary, diploma, undergraduate, postgraduate, research, trainers, etc.), recruiters, payment, Hyperledger, etc. In the proposed system, no single person or group holds the authority of the overall network. While everybody in the network has the copy of the distributed ledger with him or her, no one can modify it on his or her own. This unique feature of blockchain allows transparency and security while giving power to users;

- **Peer-to-Peer (P2P) Network:** Blockchain uses P2P protocol, which allows all the network participants to hold an identical copy of transactions, enabling approval through a machine consensus. For example, if a Recruiter wishes to make any transaction from one part of the world to another, it can do that with blockchain all by the Recruiter within a few seconds. Moreover, any interruptions or extra charges will not be deducted in the transfer;
- **Immutable:** The immutability refers to the fact that any data once written on the educational blockchain network cannot be changed. Once the data has been processed, it cannot be altered or changed. In case, any educational organization tries to change the data of one block, it will have to change the entire blockchain following it as each block stores the hash of its preceding block. Hence, the data stored in a blockchain is non-susceptible to alterations or hacker attacks due to immutability;
- **Tamper-Proof:** With the immutability, it becomes easier to detect tampering of any data in the Blockchain network. There are two key ways of detecting tampering namely, hashes and blocks. Each hash function associated with a block is unique. Any change in the data will lead to a change in the hash function. Since the hash function of one block is linked to next block, for a hacker to make any changes, he/she will have to change hashes of all the blocks after that block which is quite difficult to do.

PETS Design Factors

Several considerations need to be evaluated when providing a blockchain solution in the education section. They are security, scalability, data sovereignty, resilience, etc.:

- **Scalability:** In the proposed blockchain architecture, the number of transactions can be very large. Transformation and connectivity need to provide scalable messaging and scalable transformation of data in the cloud for the data flows;
- **Data Sovereignty:** The physical location in which data is stored may be regulated, with the regulations varying from place to place. As a result, any blockchain system must take into account data sovereignty rules and store and process data only in those locations permitted by the regulations;
- **Resilience:** Educational Blockchain systems should not depend on one single component at any point and should tolerate the failure of a single component. Components in the blockchain provider should be made resilient with multiple instances of programs and cloud services allied with data replication and redundancy on multiple storage systems;
- **Security:** As more data about students, teachers, trainers, recruiters, transactions, certificates and operational decisions are collected, refined, and stored, the challenges related to information governance and security increase. A secure community process validates the security of the execution of transactions, enabling a foundation of trust and the robust processing of transactions.

PETS Properties

The fundamental functional properties supported in proposed architecture are immutability, non-repudiation, integrity, transparency, and equal rights. If any educational data is contained in a committed transaction, it will eventually become in practice *immutable*. The immutable chain of cryptographically signed historical transactions provides *non-repudiation* of the stored data. Cryptographic tools also support data *integrity*, the public access provides data *transparency*, and *equal rights* allow every participant the same ability to access and manipulate the blockchain.

A distributed consensus mechanism consists of the rules for validating and broadcasting transactions and blocks, resolving conflicts, and the incentive scheme. The consensus ensures all stored transactions are valid, and that each valid transaction is added only once. *Trust* in the blockchain is achieved from the interactions between nodes within the educational Blockchain network. The participants of the blockchain network rely on the blockchain network itself rather than relying on trusted third-party organizations to facilitate transactions.

Data privacy and *scalability* are non-functional properties of public blockchains. The setting of privacy is limited. There are no privileged users, and every participant can join the network to access all the information on blockchain and validate new transactions. There are scalability limits on the size of the data on the blockchain, the transaction-processing rate, and the latency of data transmission.

PETS Architectural View

A decentralized blockchain smart education is designed just the same as any other normal software product. Functional specification, user interface designs, and an architecture plan are required for its development. It is crucial to identify the app's functionality, user roles, and think over the system flow and the interaction between users and information. Designing the Blockchain architecture to smart education comes with a large number of degrees of freedom. There is no standard architecture and depending on the concrete requirements and the blockchain technology chosen, an architect has to come up with many individual decisions. Blockchain architecture to smart education possesses many benefits for businesses. Here are several embedded characteristics – cryptography, immutability, provenance, decentralization, anonymity and transparency. The education process from the platform's perspective is as follows:

1. A student chooses an educational organization and a course that she wants to enroll in;
2. If the course is offered on a paid basis, the student uses the education app to pay the fee;
3. The educational organizations then verify the payment in the public ledger;
4. During the course, the educational organizations provide assignments and conduct exams that the student has to complete to get the score;
5. The student acquires the assignment, completes it and sends the signed solution back to the educational organizations;
6. The educational organizations then store the solution locally, grades, certificate, and transfers the score with the hash of the solution to the blockchain;
7. Upon the completion of the course, the student acquires a final score and this final score is added to the educational organization's chain;
8. The Recruiters can verify the score and certificate added in the public ledger.

Blockchain Model to Smart Education

It is proposed to introduce proof of educational transcript system (PETS). In this model, the PETS application model will connect educational institutions into a single educational blockchain network of credits earned by learners/students. They will be able to choose courses and instructors from a pool of institutions, collecting the credits over a lifetime, and 'cashing them in' when they are degree-ready and the issuing institution agrees. PETS is an educational blockchain actual tool to ensure it. Figure 4 shows the various actors in the proposed proof of educational transcript system model.

Figure 4. Actors in the PETS model

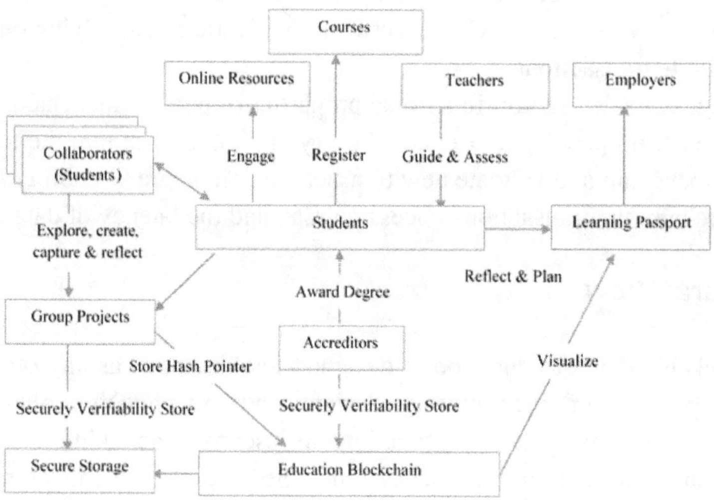

The proposed model is based on the PoW consensus algorithm. Its architecture consists of a network of nodes, each of which stores a private copy of the Blockchain. Nodes may receive copies of other nodes' Blockchains at every point in time, while they are also able to broadcast copies of their Blockchain versions themselves. Moreover, a node can try to mine a new block, in which case it generates random numbers until it obtains one, which is below a certain target value. To simulate DSAs, we distinguish between trusted and untrusted (or attacking) nodes.

Blockchain Model to Smart Education: Workflow

The proposed model is ideal for a smart education powered by Blockchain. It may start changing as Blockchain itself evolves as a technology. The data privacy and compliance regulations will largely dictate the adoption or inhibition of such a model. To understand how blockchain can contribute to the education sector (Chaitali Acharya), let us have a look at Figure 5.

A student/candidate uploads degree certificates and work experience letters from past educational organization/ employers on a server. The educational institutions and previous employers could verify the documents. These verified documents get stored on an interplanetary file system (IPFS). It is a versioned

Figure 5. The workflow of the PETS model

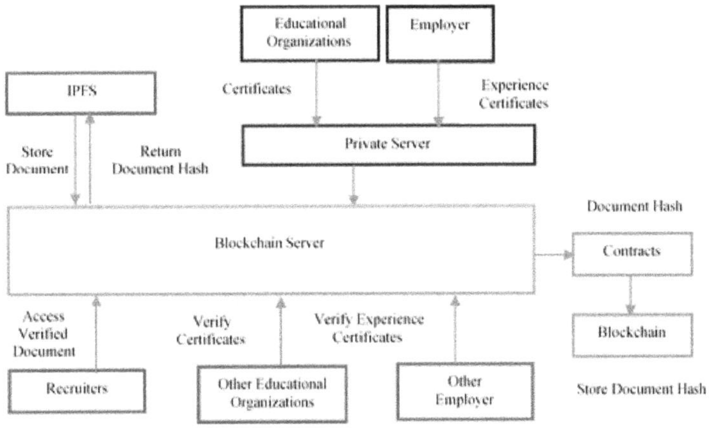

file system, which stores files and tracks versions over time. After the documents are stored on IPFS, the IPFS then returns the document hash. The hash values of these documents can be stored into blockchain ledger by using smart contracts. When a recruiter accesses the documents verified by past employers and educational institutions, the recruiter is assured about their authenticity. Such blockchain-based verification platforms would require that the hiring employers pay a fee to get the verified candidate details.

The blockchain-based educational applications can provide students with the ability to gain greater control over their education by offering flexible access to content and courses suggested based on previous successes or failures and attainment.

Blockchain Architecture to Smart Education

The proposed architecture is derived from PETS model. The PETS contains private chain which consists of sensitive data and public chain which, the information necessary to validate the integrity and authenticity of the private blocks. The key entities of the proposed blockchain architecture are presented in Figure 6.

Educational organizations can be either large educational institutes or some trusted party that runs the chain for the self-employed teachers and small institutions. This private chain is maintained by each educational organizations or independently of others. This private chain contains personalized information on the interactions between the students and the educational organizations. All the interactions, such as receiving an assignment, submitting solutions, or being graded, are treated as transactions in the private chain. Students get access to the platform through a Web browser and mobile applications. Using the applications, they choose educational organizations, enroll in courses, get assignments and submit solutions. The scores and the criteria of whether the student has finished the course successfully are determined by the educational organizations.

Making the educational organization' chains private opens the possibility for Educators to tamper with the data in their chains. To overcome this issue and make the private transactions publicly verifiable, it introduces a public chain. The public chain consists of Witnesses. They do so by writing the authentication information of a private block into the public chain, which is used in the future by an arbitrary Verifier to substantiate a proof of transaction inclusion given to it by a Student or an educational organization.

Figure 6. Key entities of the PETS model

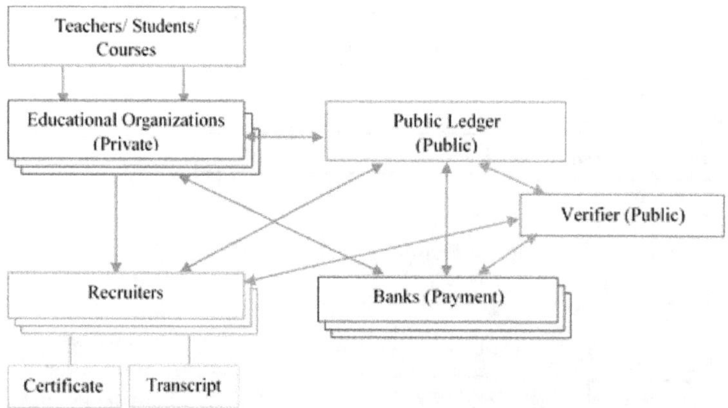

The Recruiters are the entities interested in gathering data about students from educational institutions. They buy this data from the educational organization using a secure data disclosure protocol. Witnesses also ensure validity and security of every data trade, because corresponding transactions and actions of each party are also stored in public blockchain.

The entries in "blockchain" can significantly reduce the workload of both students who would end the inconvenience of making paper copies of certificates or procedures to request a course in educational institutions and they can instantly verify an individual or organizational credentials.

Blockchain Architecture

The proposed blockchain architecture for higher education institutions is shown in Figure 7. This architecture included various components and they are *data consumer, data provider, data portal, a blockchain platform, data storage, data engine*, *blockchain access, etc.*

The key components of a proposed PETS architecture are as follows:

- **Data Consumer:** A user interface, system or tool that uses data. Users who use data for a specific purpose and can be affected by its quality. The users shall be HEIs, recruiters, research centre, etc.;
- **Data Provider:** A user interface, system or device that collects data that is relevant to educational organizations;
- **Data Portal:** This is the data portal that the educational data providers, gateway service provides and the data consumers will use to either put up data for sale or checkout data for purchase. Given that the user experience is going to be the most critical thing for this portal to succeed, this can be assumed a custom website or a third-party portal customized with the right set of security and access built into it;
- **Blockchain Access APIs:** There are multiple protocols or mechanisms through which a blockchain platform can be accessed. Standardizing on a common access layer that leverages something as common as *application programming interfaces* (APIs) makes it easy for the developer community around this initiative to work together easily. APIs allow for abstraction that enables a fair amount of future-proofing;

Figure 7. Blockchain architecture to smart education

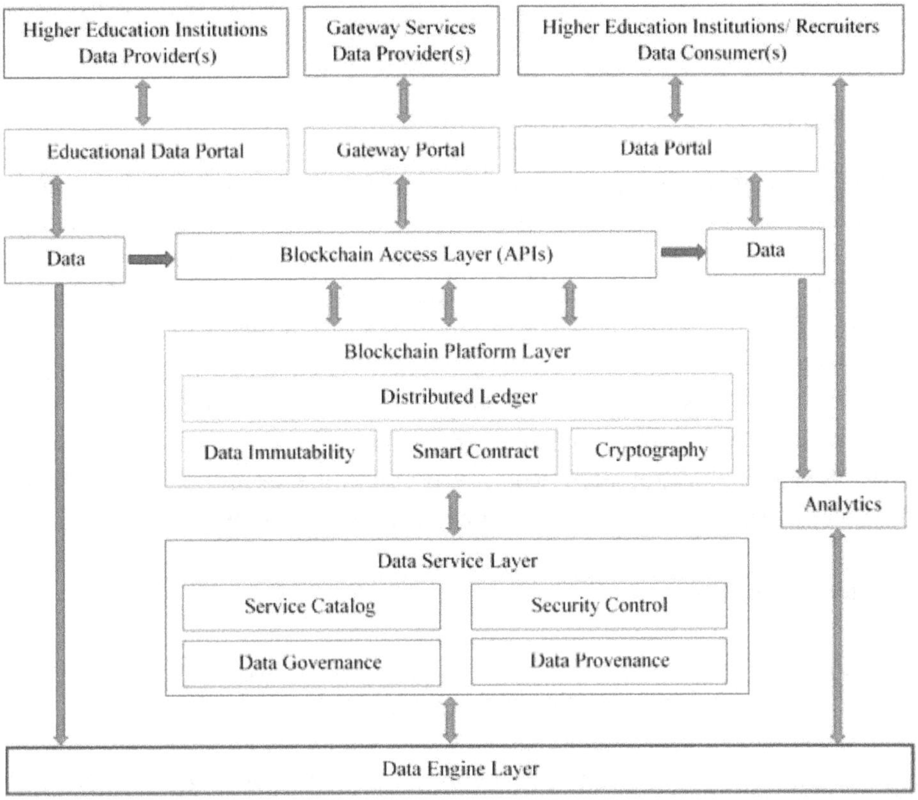

- **Blockchain Platform:** It is an appropriate platform that supports some of the key capabilities – distributed ledger, support for cryptography, immutability assurance, smart contracts, oracles etc. Based on the ecosystem, the players within that and the sensitivity of the data, you may end up choosing a permissioned or permissionless blockchain;
- **Data Service:** A high volume of information is being exchanged here, it needs to consider storage in terms volume, variety, location of data and maybe sensitivity. It stores all of the actual data on-chain or off-chain. Big data storage options should be leveraged to handle such massive volumes. The "variety" factor can also determine which storage option may be structured or unstructured data;
- **Data Engine:** To function effectively, the connecting between the on-chain data and the off-chain data will be a set of services that offer unified security, governance, management and visibility across all data sets. This brings forth a seamless and unified data plane that both data providers and consumers can leverage easily. The services will include a data catalogue that can make data discoverability and searchability a breeze across multiple data sources.

The proposed architecture may also be included in ideal technologies for data ingestion and advanced analytics. The *data logistics platform* automates the movement of data between disparate systems. It provides real-time control that makes it easy to manage the movement of data between any source and any destination. This is perfect for the proposed architecture where different providers have different types of data to offer.

RESULTS

The proposed blockchain architecture provides a rich, secure, and transparent platform on which to create a global network for higher education learning. The blockchain architecture applies to recapture the real-time records of learning. It believes that higher education works best when it works for all types of teaching and learning. Also, it transforms the architecture of higher education for the future generation of lifelong learners.

Education is a multifaceted sector where different systems need to adapt to prepare students for the jobs of tomorrow. Having a foolproof system that records a student's academic history before and during a working life can not only help in battling dishonesty but can also help to tackle the issues of bespoke learning. The PETS architecture can allow workers to build up a secure, verifiable digital record of formal qualifications, experience and soft skills gained over their lifetime.

Benefits and Drawbacks

There are some benefits to applying blockchain technology in education. The *increased transparency, accountability through smart contracts* and *incentivization of learning*:

- **Increased Transparency:** Blockchains technology creates a chronological list of events that have transpired in real-time education. This is useful for verifying transcripts, showing a complete report card and keeping the students honest about their progress. Having a student submit their homework via blockchain ensures that they cannot "lose" their homework or claim the teacher lost it;
- **Accountability Through Smart Contracts:** Teachers, educational institutions administrators and students will soon be able to engage in smart contracts. For example, students and teachers could enter into a digital agreement that stipulates an assignment's parameters, due date and grading deadline. Smart contracts can also be deployed for student loan payments;
- **Incentivization of Learning:** Tokenization has become a mainstay of blockchain. Before long, academic institutions will be able to incentivize students to pay student loans on time and teachers to motivate students by awarding cryptocurrency to those who perform highly or complete a certain major. The gamification aspect of education created by tokenization has been tremendously beneficial.

It is undeniable that there are potential drawbacks of applying blockchain technology (Guang 2018) in education:

- As a complex system, some learning behaviours and learning outcomes need to be reviewed by the instructors subjectively such as essays and classroom presentations. It is quite hard to evaluate this kind of learning activities by the pre-programmed smart contract without human intervention;

- If an educational blockchain system were put into use in schools, all students' educational data would be integrated into blockchain ledgers. The immutability feature of blockchain technology would act as a double-edged sword. It removes the possibility of modifying educational record for legitimate reasons for some students;
- The classic Proof of Work consensus model wastes energy and has a poor performance in terms of many transactions per second (Vukolić 2015), which would cost an extra expense, and hinder its application in schools.

According to Zhaoyang Dong, Fengji Luo, Gaoqi Liang, 2018, the Blockchain shows huge potential to be a secure, distributed cyberinfrastructure solution for future learning systems, there still are potential limitations and practical challenges existed. They are information redundancy, coordination of blockchain with other parties, integration of blockchain and energy physical infrastructure, the security of smart contract and performance scalability. Therefore, corresponding solutions need to be developed to coordinate the smart education infrastructures and ensure the secure, reliable, and efficient operation of educational blockchains.

Use Cases

According to Donald Clark, 2016 reports, the Blockchain could be implemented within individual educational institutions, groups of educational institutions, and both national and international educational bodies. Anyone wanting to securely store badges, credits, and qualifications could consider using blockchain technology.

Some of the use cases or examples of how blockchain is being implemented in education (Sam Daley, 2018) are Blockcerts, APPII, Gilgamesh Platform, ODEM, Sony Global Education, Blockchain Education Network, Disciplina, Parchment, BitDegree.

CONCLUSION

Blockchain is an emerging technology for decentralized and transactional data sharing across a large network of a participant who does not need to trust each other. It enables new forms of distributed software architectures, where components can find agreement on their shared states without trusting a central integration point or any particular participating components. Blockchain, as a software connector with a complex internal structure, has various configurations and different variants. Using blockchain in different scenarios requires the comparison of blockchain options and products with different implementations and configurations. Blockchain is essentially a distributed ledger technology, which uses the cryptography techniques and distributed consensus algorithms to create the features of decentralization, traceability, immutability, and currency properties.

Blockchain has shown its potential in industry and academia. Its currency properties have the potential to trigger many innovative applications for education. It can store a complete, trustworthy set of record of educational activities including the processes and results informal as well as informal learning environments. As proof of concept, it is proposed to design a blockchain architecture to learning solutions. This proposed PETs architecture is a global blockchain-based architecture for the higher education learning system. The proposed architecture addresses a globally unified viewpoint for learners and educational organizations. The beneficiaries of the proposed architecture are potential employers, who can directly validate the information provided by students, the learners benefit from a single and transparent view of their completed courses and the HEIs have access to up-to-date data regardless of a student's educational origins. The proposed solution is based on the distributed P2P network system.

As for data management, blockchain could be used to store important data, as it is distributed and secure. Blockchain could also ensure the data is original. When it comes to data analytics, transactions on the blockchain could be used for big data analytics. In future, it is planned to introduce the architecture based on big data analytics and an appropriate version of the blockchain technology.

REFERENCES

Acharya. (2018). *How can Blockchain help in Background Check?* Harbinger Systems.

Baliga. (2017). *Understanding Blockchain Consensus Models*. Corporate CTO Office Persistent Systems Ltd.

Bhardwaj, A. (2018). *Using Blockchain Can Do Wonders In Education Sector*. https://www.oodlestechnologies.com/blogs/Using-Blockchain-Can-Do-Wonders-In-Education-Sector

BitRice. (2018). *Create the optimum data storage and content sharing eco-chain*. White Paper of Bit Rice (BTR), BitRice Foundation Singapore.

Blockchain News. (2018). How will blockchain technology affect higher education in the future? *Blog, 2017. Introduction to Blockchain Technology*. https://netsend.com/blog/introduction-to-blockchain-technology/

Chen, G., Xu, B., Lu, M., & Chen, N.-S. (2018). Exploring blockchain technology and its potential applications for education. *Smart Learning Environments*, *5*(1), 1. doi:10.118640561-017-0050-x

Clark, D. (2016). *10 ways Blockchain could be used in education*. https://oeb.global/oeb-insights/10-ways-blockchain-could-be-used-in-education

Crosby, M., Nachiappan, P. P., Verma, S., & Kalyanaraman, V. (2015). Blockchain Technology, Beyond Bitcoin. Sutardja Center for Entrepreneurship & Technology Technical Report.

Daley, S. (2018). *Blockchain education companies earning straight A's*. https://builtin.com/blockchain/blockchain-in-education

De Rossi, L. M., Salviotti, G., & Abbatemarco, N. (2019). Towards a Comprehensive Blockchain Architecture Continuum. *Proc. of the 52nd Hawaii Intel. Conference on System Sciences*. 10.24251/HICSS.2019.557

Dong, Z., Luo, F., & Liang, G. (2018). Blockchain: A secure, decentralized, trusted cyberinfrastructure solution for future energy systems. *Journal of Mod. Power Syst. Clean Energy*, *6*(5), 958–967. doi:10.100740565-018-0418-0

Grech, A., & Camilleri, A. F. (2017). Blockchain in Education. Joint Research Centre, the European Commission's Science and Knowledge Service.

Hartley, R. (2018). *What is the role of blockchain in education?* Cognizant Education Technology.

Jain. (2018). *Blockchain Goes to School, Digital Solutions, Innovation & Domain Consulting*. Cognizant's Education Practice, Cognizant 20-20 Insights.

Johansen, S. K. (2018). *A comprehensive literature review on the Blockchain as a technological enabler for innovation*. Dept. of Information Systems, Mannheim University.

Karamitsos, I., Papadaki, M., & Al Barghuthi, N. B. (2018). Design of the Blockchain Smart Contract: A Use Case for Real Estate. *Journal of Information Security*, *9*(03), 177–190. doi:10.4236/jis.2018.93013

Laurent, St., & Andrew, M. (2008). *Understanding Open Source and Free Software Licensing*. O'Reilly Media.

Mougayar, W. (2016). *The business blockchain: promise, practise, and application of the next Internet technology*. Wiley.

Seebacher, S., & Schüritz, R. (2017). Blockchain Technology as an Enabler of Service Systems: A Structured Literature Review. *Springer International Publishing AG, 2017*, 12–23. doi:10.1007/978-3-319-56925-3_2

Sultan, K., Ruhi, U., & Lakhani, R. (2018). Conceptualizing Blockchains: Characteristics & Applications. *11th IADIS Intel. Conference Information Systems*.

Tasca, P., & Tessone, C. J. (2019). A Taxonomy of Blockchain Technologies: Principles of Identification and Classification. *Ledger*, *4*, 1–39. doi:10.5195/ledger.2019.140

Tien, T. A. D., Wang, J., Chen, G., Liu, R., Ooi, B. C., & Tan, K.-L. (2017). *Blockbench: A Framework for Analyzing Private Blockchains*. SIGMOD.

Turkanović, M., Hölbl, M., Košič, K., Heričko, M., & Kamišalić, A. (2018). EduCTX: A Blockchain-Based Higher Education Credit Platform. *IEEE Access : Practical Innovations, Open Solutions*, *6*, 2018. doi:10.1109/ACCESS.2018.2789929

Watters, A. (2016). *The Blockchain for Education: An Introduction, 2016*. http://hackeducation.com/2016/04/07/blockchain-education-guide

Xu, X., Weber, I., Staples, M., Zhu, L., Bosch, J., Bass, L., ... Rimba, P. (2017). A Taxonomy of Blockchain-Based Systems for Architecture Design. *IEEE International Conference on Software Architecture (ICSA)*, 243-252. 10.1109/ICSA.2017.33

Yaga, Mell, Roby, & Scarfone. (2018). *Blockchain Technology Overview*. National Institute of Standards and Technology, Internal Report 8202.

ADDITIONAL READING

Arodek. (n.d.). https://arodek.com/innovation/blockchain

Blockchain is it the future to education. (n.d.). Retrieved from https://education.siliconindiamagazine.com/viewpoint/blockchain-is-it-the-future-to-education-nwid-8576.html

Blockchain: The future emerging technology for building trust in the labour market. (2019). Retrieved from https://www.everis.com/belgium/en/page/blockchain-labour-market

Eccleston, S. (2018, November 15). How will blockchain technology affect higher education in the future? Retrieved from https://www.openaccessgovernment.org/how-blockchain-technology-affects-higher-education/54512/

Chapter 9
Traffic Signal Control for a Single Intersection-Based Intelligent Transportation System

Nouha Rida
Mohammadia School of Engineers, Morocco

Mohammed Ouadoud
https://orcid.org/0000-0003-0715-0573
Abdelmalek Essaâdi University, Morocco

Abderrahim Hasbi
Mohammadia School of Engineers, Morocco

ABSTRACT

Traffic optimization at an intersection, using real-time traffic information, presents an important focus of research into intelligent transportation systems. Several studies have proposed adaptive traffic lights control, which concentrates on determining green light length and sequence of the phases for each cycle in accordance with the real-time traffic detected. In order to minimize the waiting time at the intersection, the authors propose an intelligent traffic light using the information collected by a wireless sensors network installed in the road. The proposed algorithm is essentially based on two parameters: the waiting time in each lane and the length of its queue. The simulations show that the algorithm applied at a network of intersections improves significantly the average waiting time, queue length, fuel consumption, and CO_2 *emissions.*

DOI: 10.4018/978-1-7998-5175-2.ch009

INTRODUCTION

Road congestion has become one of the main issues in urban cities due to the growth of vehicles numbers and the limitation of road infrastructure.

The results of this congestion could be seen through a difficult vehicles displacement, an increasing environmental pollution by higher CO_2 emission, an increasing energy consumption, stressed drivers and the dismantling of the road safety. This is why traffic control has become an important area of research with one main objective being the reduction of traffic congestion.

Traffic regulation is an important component of the intelligent transportation system, which is defined as the integration of communication and information technologies in vehicles and road infrastructure to improve road traffic and safety. This regulation plays an important role in managing the flow of vehicles when controlling traffic lights. So, in this paper we choose to integrate a wireless sensor network into the road infrastructure to know the traffic status in real time, to design smart traffic signal control that dynamically and intelligently on the change of the traffic at the road intersection.

In this paper, we present an adaptive traffic management algorithm that allows to specify the sequence of phases and the green light time according to the waiting time and the number of vehicles in each lane.

The document is organized as follows: after a presenting the traffic light regulation context, its operation, and its main approaches.We expose later the wireless sensors network characteristics for traffic monitoring. Then, in the next section we present the shortest Job First method for phases scheduling and its effectiveness in reducing wait times, and we propose also in this section our ALCA algorithm based in SFP concept. Finally, we evaluate our solutions via the SUMO simulator and we demonstrate their effectiveness by comparing the results to other methods.

TRAFFIC LIGHT REGULATION

In cities, most traffic lights control systems are of two types: fixed lights control plan and adaptive control. The first type of regulation is older and less expensive, while the second is more complex and efficient. We present in this part the specifications of each of those types of regulation. But first, we will give a number of definitions for the intersection and its operation.

Definitions

Our intersection illustrated in Figure 1 consists mainly of four directions (N, S, E and W) each of which contains two lanes (go straight and turn left).

- **Movement:** A "movement" is defined by its origin and destination, in Figure 1 and 2 each arrow presents a movement. A movement is represented by a symbol consisting of a combination of two characters. The two characters represent the cardinal directions (S for the south, N for the north, E for the east, and W for the west) for the source lane with the first character and the destination lane with the second character.

Figure 1. Intersection model

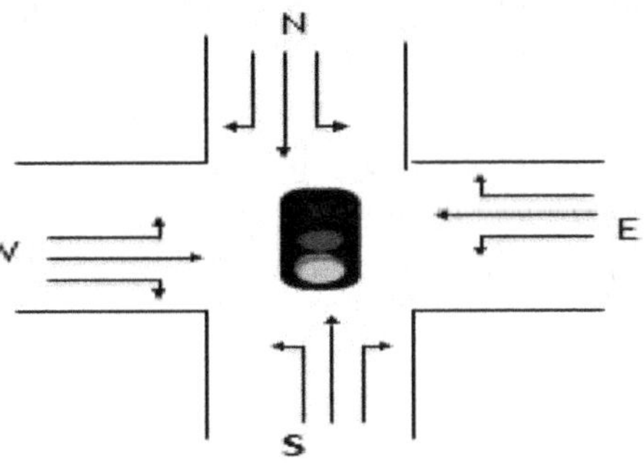

Figure 2. The possible movements for the studied intersection model

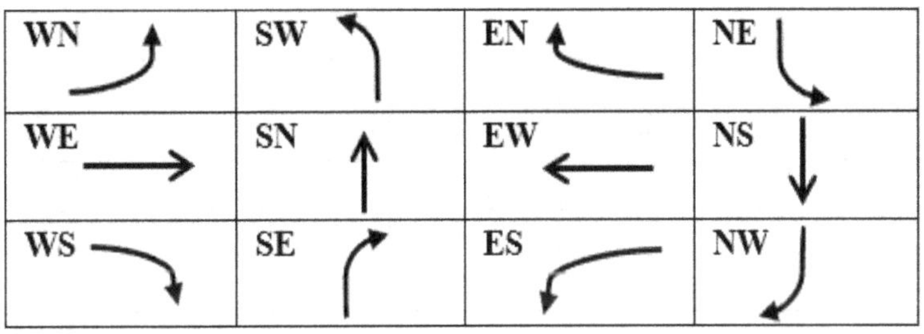

In our intersection model used, the directions to go to the right are always allowed for the vehicles. hence the management of the sequence of signal lights is only interested for the set P of the movements presented below:

P = {WE, WN, SN, SW, NS, NE, EW, ES}

One lane is allocated to each type of movement, some movements can be grouped in "phase" to have access at the same time to the intersection without producing a conflict in the conflict zone of the intersection:

- **A Phase:** Thus, a group of movement or flux of vehicles coming from the same road or the different roads of access to a crossroads and which are admitted simultaneously by means of the same signals group without causing a conflict in the intersection. Table 1 is a matrix that shows the types of possible combinations between two different movements: the number 0 indicates that access simultaneous of the vehicles of the two movements of corresponding line and the column generates a conflict in the intersection. And the number 1 indicates that the vehicles of the column movements and the corresponding line may have access to the intersection at the same time without causing a blockage or a conflict in the intersection. The main principle of the traffic lights control being to ensure a certain security between the flows of users;

- **A Cycle:** The indications of the lights - green, orange, red - succeed each other within a "cycle", defined as the time separating two successive passes of all the signals by the same state. The cycle is divided into "phases";
- **A Traffic Lights Plan:** Corresponds to the description of a given cycle, and defines the different phases to be unfolded as well as their duration. Generally, a traffic lights plan is designed for a specific time slot, depending on the average level of traffic to be absorbed (eg, a shorter traffic lights plan for the night, a longer one in rush hour).

Table 1. The conflict directions matrix

	WN	WE	SN	SW	EW	ES	NS	NE
WN		1	0	0	0	1	0	0
WE	1		0	0	1	0	0	0
SN	0	0		1	0	0	1	0
SW	0	0	1		0	0	0	1
EW	0	1	0	0		1	0	0
ES	1	0	0	0	1		0	0
NS	0	0	1	0	0	0		1
NE	0	0	0	1	0	0	1	

Static Traffic Lights Control

The construction of the traffic lights plans, phase sequences and green times - are the foundation of the traffic control system.

The means of calculating a traffic lights plan best suited to a given traffic situation are various. The simplest traffic lights plan is to repeat indefinitely the same sequence of phases with fixed durations, always arranged in the same order, so as to constitute a fixed cycle.

The fixed traffic lights plan is the simplest, but there is also a well-known method. The duration of the phases and their sequences are defined by the function of the historical states.

The intersection studied model includes 8 different movements (the set P) which require the authorization of traffic light so that the vehicles can cross the intersection.

Table 2 shows an example of a static traffic light plan. In this example, the flows that compose the phases as well as the phase time will always be identical from one cycle to another. At the beginning of the cycle and for the first phase, the WE and EW movements go green for 30 seconds. For the next phase, the WN and ES movements are entitled to the green light for 20 seconds while the other movements have the red light. For the third phase, the movements NS and SN have the green light for 30 seconds. For the last phase of the cycle, the movements NE and SW are entitled to the green light for 20 seconds. It is clear that the second cycle is identical to the first cycle.

Although, the regulation of road traffic in junctions with the fixed cycle is less expensive, the disadvantage of this type of strategy is clear: the fact that the traffic management quality at the intersection (safety and efficiency) depends only on a traffic lights fixed plan. As the traffic situation can change (the peak hours, accident ...), the fixed cycle may be totally unsuited to traffic at these times, more traffic

Table 2. Example of a static traffic lights plan

Movements	1st Cycle				2nd Cycle			
	WE	WN	NS	NE	WE	WN	NS	NE
	EW	ES	SN	SW	EW	ES	SN	SW
Duration	30	20	30	20	30	20	30	20
Time	30	50	80	100	130	150	180	200

jams and vehicle delays will also be increased. For this reason, researchers are trying to find the most advanced strategies, which can automatically adapt to changes in traffic through intelligent traffic light control systems (ITL).

In this context, a new method: adaptive regulation (also called reactive or intelligent regulation) has attracted more and more attention since the 80s of the last centuries. This control strategy can change the cycle time and is based on the real-time measurement of traffic by a traffic monitoring system.

INTELLIGENT TRAFFIC LIGHTS (ITL)

Operating mode

An Intelligent Traffic Light (ITL) system or adaptative traffic lights control is an intelligent traffic light controller that allows to build traffic lights plans and cycles, determine the sequence of phases and the duration of each phase in real time according to the traffic conditions. the intersection concerned (Isolated Strategy) or in a network of intersections (distributed strategy), in normal cases and in cases of presence of emergency vehicles or accidents.

These systems build their traffic lights plans according to the actual traffic state in order to maximize road safety and speed of traffic flows, with minimizing wait times, energy consumption and the number of stops that the vehicles must perform while traveling on the network.

State of the Art

Some intelligent traffic light management models have been commercialized. They use either sensors that determine the position of vehicles in real time, or a method that simulates the vehicles movement or both.

Some intelligent traffic light management models have been commercialized, such as:

- **TRANSYST:** Traffic Network Study Tool: is the first model commercialized (Robertson, 1969). TRANSYST is a fixed-time model that works with historical data and assumes that flow rates are constant. It allows the optimization of offsets and the distribution of green light durations for a multi- intersection. The cycle is, in this case, a data that is common to all intersections in the network. The optimization module, tries to minimize a performance index. This index is a function of the sum of all the vehicles stopped on all the intersections considered as well as the sum of the average number of vehicles in the queues for each flow at each intersection. The method consists in determining the optimal offset for an intersection while considering that the other offsets of the other intersections are fixed. Once an intersection is optimized, we move to the next crossroads again considering that the offset of other crossroads is fixed for this "iteration" and so on. The same method is used for the duration of the green light. The optimal solution is found using the descent method. This method consists of going from one solution to another by checking if the new solution is better than the previous one. If so, we adopt it, otherwise we move on to the next iteration;

- **SCOOT:** Split Cycle and Offset Optimization technique - it is an adaptive system (Hunt et al, 1981; Robertson& Bretherton, 1991; Robertson & Hunt, 1982) that allows the optimization in real time of the distribution of green times, cycle times and offsets of traffic lights. The intersection is an element from intersections network. The sensors used in this case are magnetic loops located upstream of the junction:
    - SCOOT is based on a network division into several disjoint areas. However, the total number of intersections that can be processed is limited and the cycle of intersections within each zone is identical. SCOOT predicts vehicle delays and stops using sensor information. It makes it possible to optimize the change of the state of the lights of several intersections within an area on a short-term horizon. The cycle for each of its intersections is identical which allows less flexibility. Small variations in green light time, cycles, and phases decrease the efficiency of the model. This model has yielded interesting improvements in tests but it does not seem to be able to handle large problems and the articles consulted do not mention the efficiency of the model when saturation of the traffic conditions;
- **SCATS:** Sydney Coordinated Adaptive Traffic System (Luk, 1984;) another commercialized system has been developed in Australia. It also varies the distribution of the green light of a network of intersections, offsets and cycle times to minimize delays and stops. This model has three different modes of operation: the dynamic mode that uses the real data to optimize each subsystem, the isolated dynamic mode or the actual data used, but each intersection makes its own optimization and the delayed mode or the plans are predetermined according to the day and the time of day.

The sensors used are magnetic loops located at each junction which serve to determine the flow at a given junction as well as the vacancy time of junctions during the green light.

SCOOT and SCATS (Selinger & Schmidt, 2009) are systems that allow changes to certain parameters to minimize a compound goal of delays and number of stops. Their weakness is that they operate to make changes to the traffic lights with the data being measured and do not try to predict the entry of new vehicles into the intersection. SCOOT however predicts the behavior of vehicles already inside the intersection using its flow histogram. This one is updated regularly with the new data comes from the sensors. SCATS consists rather in calculating the degree of saturation with the information coming from the sensors and thus adjusting the traffic conditions using the various plans contained in the libraries. They react to the current state of the system, that is to say, the situation presents at the intersections but do not anticipate the evolution of this situation.

According to (Mimbela & Klein, 2000), the installation of one of these solutions would take an average of 365 hours (630h for SCOOT), would cost in total an average of $ 55,000 per intersection, and would require an average training time of 41 hours (of which 60h for SCATS). Considerable figures explained primarily by the equipment used (Dey et al, 2002). The authors of (Gartner, Pooran & Andrews, 2001) estimate that compared to a fixed system, SCATS globally reduces travel time by 8%, waiting time by

28% and stops by 42%. SCOOT, for its part, globally reduces travel time by 8%, waiting time by 22% and stops by 17%.

While SCATS and SCOOT are designed to make only one decision per cycle (semi-adaptive control), other models such as OPAC (Gartner, Pooran & Andrews, 2001), (Head, Mirchandani & Sheppard, 1992), CLAIRE-SITI (Cemama & Laffont, 2013) or InSync (Chandra & Gregory, 2010) have been designed to improvc traffic conditions by analyzing rcal-timc traffic and making sccond-to-second decisions to dynamically adapt a cycle. Unfortunately, the cost and installation time of these systems is a hindrance to their development.

Obviously, adaptive regulation can improve the quality of the circulation by the cycle change. However, although some cities are benefiting from the evolution of modern traffic control tools, congestion, security and nuisance issues remain. An important reason is that microscopic and macroscopic approaches in the classical sense have indeed been developed to exploit sensors such as electromagnetic loops, which have a limited information capacity.

As part of ITS, many new methods are being developed to detect and control vehicle flows and infrastructure. It is common for dynamic models of traffic control existing in the literature that they use theoretical tools, sometimes making a connection to reality, sometimes without any physical concept (technology used). Here are studied several tools, widespread in the literature and serving as a basis for some models studied.

In the literature, we find several theoretical models: fuzzy logic (Zou, & Cao, 2009), fluid mechanics, ant colony optimization, neural networks (Wei & Zhang, 2002), and queues theory (Yousef, Al-Karaki & Shatnawi, 2010).

In (Zou, & Cao, 2009), a method based on fuzzy logic is employed. In this method, the authors present a table which defines the green light time according to the numbers of waiting vehicles. For example, for an intermediate flow with a number of vehicles between 5/min and 10/min, we allow duration of 20s for green light.

The research work (Zhou, Zeng & Wu, 2010) proposes a light plan based on movement combinations can make simultaneously without any conflict. The authors use the same model of intersection presented in Figure 4 with a topology of two sensors in such movement, which are separated by a variable distance that depends on the maximum green time. In this model of intersection, there are 4 lanes and 8 distinct combinations of non-conflict movements. This algorithm then selects the sequence of phases composing a cycle, according to several criteria: the presence of priority vehicles, the duration of the periods when there is no detection of new arrival, the cases of famine, the total waiting time and the length of the queues wait.

The model proposed in (Zhou, Zeng & Wu, 2010), however, is based on unrealistic assumptions, requiring vehicles to be of the same type and run at the same speed.

In (Yousef, Al-Karaki & Shatnawi, 2010), each lane equipped by two sensors is separated by a distance of 10 m. The authors presented each lane as an M/M/1 queue model and they use the Little law $W = \frac{Q_L}{\lambda}$ to give Equation 1 to calculate the queue length in each direction:

$$Q_{L_j} = Q_{L_{(j\text{-}1)}} + \lambda G_G - \mu G_G + \lambda G_R$$

Table 3.

W	The waiting time
Q_L	The queue length
λ	The vehicles arrival rate
j	Traffic cycle number
Q_{L_j}	The expected queue length for this cycle
$Q_{L_{(j-1)}}$	The queue length from the previous cycle
λG_G	The arrival vehicles number in green light
λG_R	The arrival vehicles number in red light
μ	departure rate
G	The green light period for the phase
R	The red-light period for the phase

The algorithm proposed in (Yousef, Al-Karaki & Shatnawi, 2010) selects for each phase a combination of non-conflicting movements with the largest number of vehicles, in order to minimize the average queue length in the intersection.

Rida (2018) proposes a study based on the GLD simulator to know the impact of the change of the wireless sensors network on the vehicles waiting time.

Firstly, the authors make a comparison between two topologies of the wireless sensors network, the first topology with one sensor per movement and the other with two sensors per movement. From the results of simulations with GLD simulator, the authors find that a topology with two sensors per direction gives a reduced waiting time compared to that with a sensor. After having arrived at this result, they studied the influence of the distance between the two sensors on the management of road traffic as well as on the variation of vehicles waiting time at the level of the intersection and they found that the distance between the two sensors does not have a big impact on the waiting time.

In (Faye, Chaudet & Demeure, 2012), the authors propose a topology of two sensors per movement. The first is just after the intersection and the other is placed before the intersection at a given distance. The data collected by these sensors are used to determine the sequence of phases for an intersection. To determine this sequence, the authors defined for each movement a score that classifies the movements according to the local score of the intersection and the state of the two neighboring intersections to this movement. The local score of a movement is defined as a weighted sum of the waiting time and the number of vehicles waiting at the level of this movement.

A cooperative algorithm for traffic lights synchronization based in real time traffic conditions in adjacent intersections was presented in (Faye, Chaudet & Demeure, 2012).

Rida and Hasbi (2018, pp. 1036-1044) and (2018, p. 14) were inspired by the "Smallest job first" method of scheduling tasks to run them by a computer processor. We proposed the "Smallest phase first" algorithm which gives priority to phases with the smallest queues. Subsequently in (Rida, Ouadoud & Hasbi, 2018), they proposed a new approach based in the waiting time.

In (Kumaran et al, 2019), to solve the problem of traffic lights synchronization, the authors use a centralized approach. The main objective of the optimization method proposed in the first work is to minimize the total delay time of the network in a given finite horizon, while in the second, is to optimize the vehicles flow in a fixed lapse of time. Similarly, the signaling control method proposed in [Gao et al, 2016).] aims to minimize queue lengths and maximize throughput. In (Ahmad, F., Mahmud, S. A., & Yousaf, F. Z., 2016) Relative backlog rate-based signaling has been proposed. The algorithm proposed in [Younes, Boukerche & Mammeri, 2016)] is based on the delay to optimize the flow of vehicles crossing the intersection during the green light. In (Younes & Boukerche, 2018), the authors proposed two methods, the Minimum Destination Distance First (MDDF) and the First Minimum Average Destination Distance (MADDF) to maximize the flow of traffic.

Ge et al (2019) proposes a traffic light management algorithm according to the real-time distribution of vehicle flows around the intersection. The proposed algorithm also allows the management of the emergency vehicle passage by defining the sequence of phases in such a lane as to allow the emergency vehicles approaching the intersection to go green without stopping.

In (Gardner & Stohrer (2018, March). How intelligent transportation systems are changing the industry. Retrieved from URL), the authors explain how intelligent transportation systems are changing the industry, by an interconnected transport network using adoption techniques for innovation in digital services to enhance personal travel opportunities and the efficient movement of goods.

For intersections control, the main difference between the proposed multi-agent systems models in the literature exists in their agent design approaches. They choose to classify different entities as agents, such as an intersection, the traffic light controller, or a vehicle.

In order to adapt traffic lights to traffic changes, researchers used reinforcement learning (RL) methods (Scemama, 2013; Chandra, 2010; Kumaran et al, 2019; Gao et al, 2016; Shi et al, 2016; Yen et al, 2018; Ahmad, 2016; Ge, 2019; Van & Oliehoek, 2016; Liang, 2019; Zhou et al, 2019; Aslani,, Seipel & Wiering, 2018; Mannion et al, 2019 ; Van & Oliehoek, 2016). Traditional reinforcement learning is difficult to use and implement, due to two main challenges: the presentation models of the environment, and the modeling of the link between the decision and the environment. In order to meet these challenges, researchers use deep reinforcement learning techniques, such as Q-Learning and Deep Q-Learning (Van & Oliehoek, 2016; Liang et al, 2019; Li, Lv & Wang, 2016; Wei et al, 2018; Van Hasselt & H, 2012; Khorov et al, 2015).

WIRELESS SENSORS NETWORK FOR TRAFFIC MONITORING

The addition of a wireless transceiver to magnetic sensors makes it possible to build a conventional wireless sensor network. Wireless sensor networks typically rely on short-range, low-cost communications, speed and power. Among the multiple appropriate communication standards, IEEE 802.15.4, Zigbee technology, provides coverage of around 50-100 meters at 2.4GHz for a maximum data rate of 250 Kbps and low power consumption. IEEE 802.11p (Jeong & Jaehoon, 2009) is also a very reliable candidate, as it is intended to be deployed in vehicles and infrastructure equipment, it would allow the creation of a coordinated system.

433 MHz technologies are also attractive because they provide low-bandwidth and high-speed communication interfaces.

All of these technologies share some common features in terms of performance and give similar network modeling: the formed communication network has all the characteristics of a wireless LAN and can be used as a multi-hop network, or interconnected by WAN interfaces.

The technology is therefore ready to support a distributed application.

Wireless sensor networks are a special case of ad-hoc networks and consist of a large set of generally limited capacitance and energy sensors, making them massively accessible and low cost. In many cases, the sensors consist of the following units (Knaian, 2000):

- An acquisition unit, which collects environmental data and is in charge of analogue to digital conversion. In our case, this unit is a magnetometer;
- A computing unit, allowing the launching of procedures and protocols. A communication unit, making it possible to connect to a wireless network (radio links, transmission and reception). This type of communication is done step by step and makes it possible to overcome wired constraints (installation time and ease of access);
- Energy unit, which allows the distribution of the power supply between the different components. In many cases, the sensors are scattered in energy-poor areas, and have a non-rechargeable and non-renewable battery (Warrier & Kumar, 2016). In the case of road traffic, the batteries can last for several years and it is possible to abstain from energy constraints (eg by connecting the sensors to the urban electricity grid).

The low cost, size and ease of installation of these devices, compared to electromagnetic loops, allow the creation of a dense and more responsive network (Corredor et al, 2008).

Knaian (2000) mentions a manufacturing cost of less than $ 30 per unit with a 16-bit microcontroller and a size comparable to a room. Once deployed, these devices can exchange information with all relevant nterings and quickly resolve a situation without the intervention of a central server. The set of relevant intersections can be dynamically adapted to the situation and the wireless communication that can support the dissemination of data.

Cameras are also a low-cost solution because they require little work to install, and they can perform good detections with image processing techniques unless their angle or vision is limited. In [Liu & Liu, 2011), the authors propose to combine magnetic sensors with cameras.

The development of a transportation system involves communication technologies that already exist, or that will develop in the near future (eg, coordinated networks). In addition, the intersection models studied allow us to understand the behavior of a traffic control system. It is thus possible to control the lights one by one, and to apply a distributed algorithm that adapts, in each case, queues. However, this distributed management policy will be detailed in the rest of this paper.

DIGITAL TRAFFIC SIGNALS CONTROL BASED WSN

WSN Topology for Traffic Monitoring

For traffic monitoring in a road intersection, each lane was equipped with two magnetic sensors, presented in Figure 3: one is located near the traffic light to count the number of departures of vehicles and the other is installed at a variable distance from the first sensor to detect the arrival of vehicles. This distance

Figure 3. The WSN topology for traffic monitoring

depends on the maximum time allowed for the green light. Each controller of the traffic lights defines a time called cycle which is a sequence of the phases, a phase presents a time of green light necessary for two movements (for example ES, EW, SN ...) that can cross the intersection in the same time.

All sensors communicate and transfer traffic information to base station, the base station summarize the received date to calculate the queues' lengths for each direction and its average waiting time. These parameters will be used in the control traffic flow strategy.

Shortest Job First and, Shortest Remaining Time First

In computer science, SJF stands for Shortest Job First. It designates a method of scheduling processes. It is a scheduling algorithm, that is, an algorithm for choosing which of several processes will be processed first by the processor. The choice is made according to the estimated execution time of the process. This way, the scheduler will let the shortest process in the queue go first.

There are two versions of this algorithm: a preemptive version, and a non-preemptive version. In the latter, a process that has taken control of the CPU does not leave it until the burst is over.

The preemptive version, also called SRTF, Shortest Remaining Time First, is more flexible. If a process whose execution time is shorter than the rest of the processing time of the process being processed enters the queue, then it will take its place. Then there is a context switch, and the processing of the interrupted process will resume later where it was left.

SJF is one of the most cost-effective algorithms for reducing the time spent in the process queue. However, it is rarely used outside of specialized environments, because it requires an accurate evaluation of the execution time of all processes waiting for processing.

Algorithm

1. Sort all the processes in increasing order according to burst time;
2. Then simply, choose the first task or process.

In the following section, we show that the application of the SPF and specifically the SRTF method to the road traffic control problem in an isolated intersection reduces the waiting time of the vehicles compared to the method that prioritizes the important flows of vehicles.

SJF Efficiency for Road Traffic in Reducing Waiting Time

The adaptive traffic lights control exploits the traffic information (waiting time, the lengths of the queues ...) collected in real to react instantly to these variations. The main objective is finding the phases sequence that optimize traffic and enhance traffic throughput of intersections.

The existing methods in the literature give priority to the phase with the greatest number of vehicles. In the opposite of these methods, we study a solution based on the choice of the phase with smallest queue length or that needs the shortest duration of green light. The solution consists to give the green light to phase with the smallest number of vehicles.

To study the effectiveness of this method for the traffic regulation problem, we compare the overall waiting time for a cycle obtained by this method with that obtained with the method that prioritizes the phases with the highest queue's length.

In Table 4 we calculate the total waiting time at each change of traffic light and for one cycle at isolated intersection. After, we show that the waiting time will be reduced with the shortest phase first method then the longest phase first method, which choses the phases with longest queue length:

$$GWT(t = t_3) = WT_i + 6GT_1 + 4GT_2 + 2GT_3 \tag{1}$$

Table 4. The waiting time variation during a cycle

Time	The Remaining Phases	GWT	The Current Phase	Green Time Duration
	8		Phase1	
	6		Phase2	
	4		Phase3	
	2		Phase4	GT_4

Equation 1 presents the global waiting time at the end of the cycle, which shows that the waiting time of a cycle is proportional to the green light duration. While the green light T_G duration is relative to the vehicles number according to the following equation:

$$T_G = T_S + T_h * Q_l \tag{2}$$

With $Q_l = \max(Q_u, Q_v)$ and (u,v) are the two flows component the phase, and T_S is the average starting time of a queue, T_h is the mean time of light traversal for a vehicle, and Q_l is the vehicle size of the largest queue for the chosen phase.

Then, the equation 5 becomes:

$$\begin{aligned} GWT &= WT_i + 6(T_s + T_h * Q_1) + 4(T_s + T_h * Q_2) + 2(T_s + T_h * Q_3) \\ &= WT_i + 12 * T_s + T_h * (6 * Q_1 + 4 * Q_2 + 2 * Q_3) \end{aligned} \tag{3}$$

where Q_i, with i∈ {1,2,3}, is the maximum queue of the two lanes for the phase i.

Equation 1 shows that the total waiting time is propositional to the queues of the first three phases.

Then, the total waiting time will be minimal when

$$WT_i + 12 * T_s + T_h * \left(6 * Q_1 + 4 * Q_2 + 2 * Q_3\right)$$

is minimal and it is obvious that the latter will be minimal only when $Q_1 < Q_2 < Q_3 < Q_4$, and maximum if $Q_1 > Q_2 > Q_3 > Q_4$.

It is therefore possible to obtain a minimum waiting time if we choose the shortest phase first. Consequently, the scheduling of the phases with this method is optimal that allows giving a minimum of waiting time.

Traffic Light Control Algorithm (ALCA)

Previously, we have demonstrated the effectiveness of the application of SPF method in traffic light control problem.

According to simulations the method decreases the overall waiting time in an intersection and during a cycle, but on the other hand, it has increased congestion which is contradictory to the main objective of the road traffic management. To solve this problem, we added above another criterion (the waiting time) for the choice of the next phase.

In order to select the next phase that will have the green light according to the reel traffic flow, we have defined a score S bases in two criteria: the vehicles number Q_u, Q_v and the waiting times W_u and W_v for two movements u and v of a phase that are able to cross at the same time the intersection without causing conflict. The movements are chosen respecting the conflict matrix presented in Table 1.

The score is defined as follows:

$$If Q_u + Q_v \text{ then S=0}$$

$$Else\ S = \frac{(W_u + W_v)^{\alpha}}{(Q_u + Q_v)^{\beta}} \tag{4}$$

The values of α and β are chosen so that one objective is privileged to another, u and v are two lanes that can get the green light at the same time without conflict.

The queues' length for an instant t and for the lane k is given by (5). The first step is to collect the information received by the wireless sensors and analyze it in order to determine the lengths of the queues and their waiting times:

$$Q_j\left(t\right) = AR_j + AG_j + Q_j(t-1) - DP_j \tag{5}$$

where:

- $Q_j(t)$: The queue length for lane j and at time t;
- AR_j: The vehicles number was arriving during the red light and for the lane j;
- AG_j: The vehicles number was arriving during green light and for the lane j;
- $Q_j(t\text{–}1)$: The vehicles number was remaining from the last green light;
- DP_j: The departures number during current green light.

AR, AG and DP are calculated from the information received by the two sensors.

To calculate the waiting time W, there are two cases:

- If there are no vehicles waiting from the last green light, the waiting time is the time of the first vehicle arrived during this red time;
- If there are still vehicles from the last green light, the waiting time is the current red-light time.

Equation 6 gives the waiting time value for each lane as a function of FA the time of the first vehicle arrived, RT the time of the current red light, and K which is an index equal to 1 if there are vehicles waiting from the last selection of the green light and 0 otherwise:

$$W = \begin{cases} FA \quad if \quad K = 0 \\ \\ RT \quad if \quad K = 1 \end{cases} \tag{6}$$

Algorithm 1: Adaptive Traffic Light Control Algorithm (ALCA)

Input: ARj, AGj, FA, DPj.

1. if there exists a lane with green light priority, then Assign green light to this phase next.
2. S= {ES, EW, SW, SN, NS, NE, WE, WS}
3. Calculate W and Q for each element in S:

$$W = FA + K * RT; \; Q_j\left(t\right) = AR_j + AG_j + Q_j\left(t-1\right) - DP_j$$

4. Calculate the Score S:

$$S = \frac{(W_u + W_v)^\alpha}{(Q_u + Q_v)^\beta}$$

(u,v)ϵ S and they can get the green light in same time

If $Q_u + Q_v = 0$ then S(u,v)=0

5. Calculate max(S(i,j)) and select the lanes (u, v) wich composes the phase with max(S(i,j))
6. Assign the next green light to this phase (u, v)
7. Calculate the green time T_G for phase (u,v)

$$T_G = T_S + T_h * Q_l$$

If $T_G > T_{max}$ then $T_G = T_{max}$

8. S=S - {u,v}
9. If S={ } go to step 2, else go to step 3.

SIMULATION AND EVALUATION

In order to test ours approaches, we use the SUMO (Behrisch, Michael et al, 2011) traffic simulator. We test our algorithm and other approaches to different traffic conditions. These tests were then analyzed using different criteria to measure the potential benefits of the proposed approach.

We used the intersection model shown in Figure 1. Several types of traffic have been created in order to better evaluate the solution according to the variations of traffic during the day. These are summarized in Table 5.

Table 5. The traffic intensities used in the simulation

Scenario	Traffic Intensity	Number of Vehicles
S1	Low	300
S2	intermediate	700
S3	high	1500

In order to properly analyze the results, we compared our algorithm ASTL to three other methods:

- Static plan with four phases of duration of 25 or 20 seconds and which is illustrated below:

```
<tlLogic id="0" type="static" programID="0" offset="0">
        <phase duration="20" state="GrrGrrGrrGGG"/>
        <phase duration="25" state="GrrGGGGrrGrr"/>
        <phase duration="25" state="GrrGrrGGGGrr"/>
         <phase duration="25" state="GGGGrrGrrGrr"/>
</tlLogic>
```

- TSTMA dynamic method presented in (Yousef, Al-Karaki & Shatnawi, 2010), which based on the choice of the phase with the largest queue;
- And the last method is the controller that implements our algorithm in this work ALCA.

The simulation duration is about 1000 seconds. The computer program was coded in python and the tests were done on a PC equipped with Intel® Core ™ i7-4702MQ @ 2.20GHz processor.

Table 1 shows the average queues lengths the intersection for the four approaches to traffic control and for the three traffic intensity scenarios. The results obtained indicate that:

- For the S1 scenario, when we use low intensity traffic, the simulations show that the results of the ALCA and TSTMA methods are better than the other approaches. Specifically, for TSTMA the average queue is 2 vehicles, for SJF is 2.5, and 3 vehicles for the static plane;
- For the S2 scenario, we can notice that the adaptive methods give the best results with a small difference between them of 0.1 and that our ALCA approach is the best in terms of reducing the queue length;
- For the S3 scenario, which has high intensity traffic, our SJF method gives the best result in terms of queue reduction with 14.35 on average compared to 15.36 for TSTMA and 23.5 with a static plan.

Table 7 presents the total waiting time of the vehicles in the intersection and during the simulation, for the four approaches tested by the three scenarios. The results obtained confirm the results of the average queue length: the SJF method gives the best results for S2 and S3. It allows a reduction of almost half the waiting time compared to the waiting time obtained by the static plan and it gives a reduction of the waiting time of 30% compared to TSTMA with the S3 traffic type.

Table 6. The average queues lengths

Approaches	S1	S2	S3
Predetermined	3	8	23.5
TSTMA	2	5,59	15.36
SJF	2,5	5,49	14.35
ALCA	2	5.3	14.4

Table 7. The total waiting time of vehicles in the intersection for each scenario

Approaches	S1	S2	S3
Predetermined	3455,25	8094,01	51325,15
TSTMA	1890,08	7849,91	37686,88
SJF	2072,85	6041,75	25988,45
ALCA	1820	6101,41	2616,88

For reduced traffic S1 the TSTMA method gives a wait time less than 8% compared to SJF and 45% compared to the static plan.

Tables 8 and 9 show the volume of fuel consumption and the amount of CO2 emitted by the vehicles in the simulation, respectively. The results show that the adaptive control methods ALCA and TSTMA provide the lowest fuel consumption and CO2 emissions and that TSTMA offers the highest reduction rate with:

Table 8. The volume in ml of fuel consumption by all vehicles in the simulation and for each test

	S1	S2	S3
Predetermined	321,8	44658	2452,5
TSTMA	275,1	674,1	212,4
SJF	290,8	694,4	1739,6
ALCA	260,4	654,4	1991,2

Table 9. The quantity in mg of the CO2 emission by the vehicles of the simulation and for each test

	S1	S2	S3
Predetermined	748771.2	1731470	5705179
TSTMA	640148.4	1568179.8	3867310
SJF	676635	1615600.7	4029232
ALCA	6451.2	1578974	3974313

- For S1, a reduction rate of 14% compared to a static plan and 5% compared to SJF for both criteria; CO2 emission and fuel consumption;
- For S2, a reduction rate of 9% compared to a static plan and 2% compared to SJF;
- For S3, a reduction rate of 30% compared to a static plan and 4% compared to SJF for both criteria; CO2 emission and fuel consumption.

We can say that the TSTMA method is the best to reduce CO2 emissions and fuel consumption.

From the results, it can be seen that the TSTMA method is the best suited for traffic with a low intensity such as traffic intensity at night. As we move from S1 to S2 and then to S3, and each time the traffic intensity increases, our ALCA approach provides better results by reducing the lengths of the average queues and the waiting time of vehicles in the intersection. So, we can say that ALCA is able to adapt to the change in traffic and improve the flow of traffic.

FUTURE RESEARCH DIRECTIONS

First of all, all of our results were simulated, not experimentally or in the field. A real deployment could introduce new issues that we have not addressed. In addition, taking pedestrians into account is also a possible prospect. One could for example want to minimize a pedestrian waiting time. Assuming sensors are available to detect the number of pedestrians at a given location. Another direction for future research is to equip the system with the ability to detect emergencies (such as the presence of ambulances in the queue, trucks, public transportation, etc.) through inexpensive sensors and implement appropriate emergency measures to prioritize.

Our approach also aims to add more advanced applications. In fact, the sensor nodes used for real-time monitoring of traffic conditions are not necessarily limited to this application. For example, a multifunctional wireless traffic monitoring system can be developed by adding other detection modalities to existing sensor node platforms, such as cameras to keep track of certain events such as accidents, temperature or humidity sensors to detect ice, snow, rain or fog. This multifunctional feature of WSN offers great potential for the development of even more advanced ITS applications.

CONCLUSION

In this chapter, we have adopted a new strategy for digital traffic management at a road intersection. These new strategies are based on wireless sensor network technologies (IEEE 802.15.4). With the information collected from the vehicles thanks to these digital technologies, we can know the precise state of the traffic flows in each lane of the junction. Using this information received from the wireless sensor network, we were able to formulate our problem of dynamic traffic lights control and propose efficient algorithms to optimize the traffic in an isolated intersection. The proposed algorithm aims to minimize the waiting time and the queues lengths in the intersection.

In our solution, we have mathematically modeled the problem of signal lights management at a single intersection with the queue's theory type M / M / 1. A solution for minimizing the waiting time was proposed based in Shortest Job First (SJF) scheduling method applied on the system. Then, we showed theoretically the effectiveness of our algorithm in reducing the waiting time and queues length of vehicles. Simulations with continuous flows of vehicles and with different intensities of traffic were also performed on a single intersection. Our algorithm performances better than the fixed control in all traffic density scenarios, particularly in the medium and high traffic density scenarios. The results demonstrate the efficiency and practicability of our algorithm in reducing traffic load and the waiting time for vehicles, thus enhancing traffic throughput of intersections.

REFERENCES

Ahmad, F., Mahmud, S. A., & Yousaf, F. Z. (2016). Shortest processing time scheduling to reduce traffic congestion in dense urban areas. *IEEE Transactions on Systems, Man, and Cybernetics. Systems*, *47*(5), 838–855. doi:10.1109/TSMC.2016.2521838

Aslani, M., Seipel, S., & Wiering, M. (2018). Continuous residual reinforcement learning for traffic signal control optimization. *Canadian Journal of Civil Engineering*, *45*(8), 690–702. doi:10.1139/cjce-2017-0408

Behrisch, M. (2011). SUMO–simulation of urban mobility: an overview. In *Proceedings of SIMUL 2011, The Third International Conference on Advances in System Simulation*. ThinkMind.

Chandra, R., & Gregory, C. (2010). *Insync adaptive traffic signal technology: Real-time artificial intelligence delivering real-world results*. Academic Press.

Corredor, I., García, A., Martínez, J. F., & López, P. (2008). Wireless sensor network-based system for measuring and monitoring road traffic. 6th Collaborative Electronic Communications and eCommerce Technology and Research (CollECTeR 2008), Madrid, Spain.

Dey, D. W., Fitzsimons, S., Morris, A., & Ng, D. (2002). *Adaptive Traffic Signal Interconnect in Menlo Park and Sunnyvale*. Academic Press.

Faye, S., Chaudet, C., & Demeure, I. (2012a, October). *Un algorithme distribué de contrôle des feux de circulation sur plusieurs intersections par un réseau de capteurs sans fil*. Academic Press.

Faye, S., Chaudet, C., & Demeure, I. (2012b). *Contrôle du trafic routier urbain par un réseau fixe de capteurs sans fil*. Academic Press.

Gao, K., Zhang, Y., Sadollah, A., & Su, R. (2016). Optimizing urban traffic light scheduling problem using harmony search with ensemble of local search. *Applied Soft Computing*, *48*, 359–372. doi:10.1016/j.asoc.2016.07.029

Gardner, S., & Stohrer, H. (2018, March). *How intelligent transportation systems are changing the industry*. Retrieved from https://www.dxc.technology/digital_transformation/insights/141104-how_intelligent_transportation_systems_are_changing_the_industry.

Gartner, N. H., Pooran, F. J., & Andrews, C. M. (2001, August). Implementation of the OPAC adaptive control strategy in a traffic signal network. In ITSC 2001. 2001 IEEE Intelligent Transportation Systems. Proceedings (Cat. No. 01TH8585) (pp. 195-200). IEEE. doi:10.1109/ITSC.2001.948655

Ge, H., Song, Y., Wu, C., Ren, J., & Tan, G. (2019). Cooperative Deep Q-Learning With Q-Value Transfer for Multi-Intersection Signal Control. *IEEE Access : Practical Innovations, Open Solutions*, *7*, 40797–40809. doi:10.1109/ACCESS.2019.2907618

Head, K. L., Mirchandani, P. B., & Sheppard, D. (1992). *Hierarchical framework for real-time traffic control* (No. 1360). Academic Press.

Hunt, P. B., Robertson, D. I., Bretherton, R. D., & Winton, R. I. (1981). *SCOOT-a traffic responsive method of coordinating signals* (No. LR 1014 Monograph). Academic Press.

Jeong, J. (2009). *Wireless sensor networking for intelligent transportation systems*. Academic Press.

Khorov, E., Lyakhov, A., Krotov, A., & Guschin, A. (2015). A survey on IEEE 802.11 ah: An enabling networking technology for smart cities. *Computer Communications*, *58*, 53–69. doi:10.1016/j.comcom.2014.08.008

Knaian, A. N. (2000). *A wireless sensor network for smart roadbeds and intelligent transportation systems* (Dissertation). Massachusetts Institute of Technology.

Kumaran, S. K., Mohapatra, S., Dogra, D. P., Roy, P. P., & Kim, B. G. (2019). Computer Vision-guided Intelligent Traffic Signaling for Isolated Intersections. *Expert Systems with Applications*, *134*, 267–278. doi:10.1016/j.eswa.2019.05.049

Li, L., Lv, Y., & Wang, F. Y. (2016). Traffic signal timing via deep reinforcement learning. *IEEE/CAA Journal of Automatica Sinica, 3*(3), 247-254.

Liang, X., Du, X., Wang, G., & Han, Z. (2019). A Deep Reinforcement Learning Network for Traffic Light Cycle Control. *IEEE Transactions on Vehicular Technology*, *68*(2), 1243–1253. doi:10.1109/TVT.2018.2890726

Liu, B., & Liu, W. (2011, May). Evaluation of traffic control methods at traffic circles. In *2011 Chinese Control and Decision Conference (CCDC)* (pp. 3371-3377). IEEE. 10.1109/CCDC.2011.5968698

Luk, J. Y. K. (1984). Two traffic-responsive area traffic control methods: SCAT and SCOOT. *Traffic Engineering & Control*, *25*(1).

Mannion, P., Talpaert, V., Sobh, I., Kiran, B. R., Yogamani, S., El-Sallab, A., & Perez, P. (2019). *Exploring applications of deep reinforcement learning for real-world autonomous driving systems*. Academic Press.

Mimbela, L. E. Y., & Klein, L. A. (2000). *Summary of vehicle detection and surveillance technologies used in intelligent transportation systems*. Academic Press.

Rida, N., & Hasbi, A. (2018, October). Dynamic Traffic Lights Control for Isolated Intersection Based Wireless Sensor Network. In *The Proceedings of the Third International Conference on Smart City Applications* (pp. 1036-1044). Springer.

Rida, N., & Hasbi, A. (2018, October). Traffic Lights Control using Wireless Sensors Networks. In *Proceedings of the 3rd International Conference on Smart City Applications* (p. 14). ACM. 10.1145/3286606.3286791

Rida, N., Ouadoud, M., Hasbi, A., & Chebli, S. (2018, October). Adaptive Traffic Light Control System Using Wireless Sensors Networks. In *2018 IEEE 5th International Congress on Information Science and Technology (CiSt)* (pp. 552-556). IEEE. 10.1109/CIST.2018.8596620

Robertson, D. I. (1969). 'Tansyt' method for area traffic control. *Traffic Engineering & Control*, *8*(8).

Robertson, D. I., & Bretherton, R. D. (1991). Optimizing networks of traffic signals in real time-the SCOOT method. *IEEE Transactions on Vehicular Technology*, *40*(1), 11–15. doi:10.1109/25.69966

Robertson, D. I., & Hunt, P. B. (1982). Method of estimating the benefits of co-ordinating signals by TRANSYT and SCOOT. *Traffic Engineering & Control*, *23*, 527–531.

Scemama, G., & Laffont, P. (2013). CLAIRE-SITI Système pour la supervision intelligente, intermodale, intégrée des réseaux de transport de surface. *TEC Transport environnement circulation*, (219), 11.

Selinger, M., & Schmidt, L. (2009). *A review of the cost, maintenance and reliability of popular adaptive traffic control technologies*. Adaptive Traffic Control Systems in the United States.

Shi, M. K., Jiang, H., & Li, S. H. (2016, November). An intelligent traffic-flow-based real-time vehicles scheduling algorithm at intersection. In *2016 14th International Conference on Control, Automation, Robotics and Vision (ICARCV)* (pp. 1-5). IEEE. 10.1109/ICARCV.2016.7838779

Van der Pol, E., & Oliehoek, F. A. (2016). Coordinated deep reinforcement learners for traffic light control. *Proceedings of Learning, Inference and Control of Multi-Agent Systems (at NIPS 2016).*

Van der Pol, E., & Oliehoek, F. A. (2016). Coordinated deep reinforcement learners for traffic light control. *Proceedings of Learning, Inference and Control of Multi-Agent Systems (at NIPS 2016).*

Van Hasselt, H. (2012). Reinforcement learning in continuous state and action spaces. In *Reinforcement learning* (pp. 207–251). Berlin: Springer. doi:10.1007/978-3-642-27645-3_7

Warrier, M. M., & Kumar, A. (2016). An energy efficient approach for routing in wireless sensor networks. *Procedia Technology*, *25*, 520–527. doi:10.1016/j.protcy.2016.08.140

Wei, H., Zheng, G., Yao, H., & Li, Z. (2018, July). Intellilight: A reinforcement learning approach for intelligent traffic light control. In *Proceedings of the 24th ACM SIGKDD International Conference on Knowledge Discovery & Data Mining* (pp. 2496-2505). ACM. 10.1145/3219819.3220096

Wei, W., & Zhang, Y. (2002, May). FL-FN based traffic signal control. In *2002 IEEE World Congress on Computational Intelligence. 2002 IEEE International Conference on Fuzzy Systems. FUZZ-IEEE'02. Proceedings* (Cat. No. 02CH37291) (Vol. 1, pp. 296-300). IEEE. 10.1109/FUZZ.2002.1005004

Yen, C. C., Ghosal, D., Zhang, M., Chuah, C. N., & Chen, H. (2018, December). Falsified Data Attack on Backpressure-based Traffic Signal Control Algorithms. In *2018 IEEE Vehicular Networking Conference (VNC)* (pp. 1-8). IEEE. 10.1109/VNC.2018.8628334

Younes, M. B., & Boukerche, A. (2018). An efficient dynamic traffic light scheduling algorithm considering emergency vehicles for intelligent transportation systems. *Wireless Networks, 24*(7), 2451–2463. doi:10.100711276-017-1482-5

Younes, M. B., Boukerche, A., & Mammeri, A. (2016, April). Context-aware traffic light self-scheduling algorithm for intelligent transportation systems. In *2016 IEEE Wireless Communications and Networking Conference* (pp. 1-6). IEEE. 10.1109/WCNC.2016.7564924

Yousef, K. M., Al-Karaki, M. N., & Shatnawi, A. M. (2010). Intelligent traffic light flow control system using wireless sensors networks. *Journal of Information Science and Engineering, 26*(3), 753–768.

Zhou, B., Cao, J., Zeng, X., & Wu, H. (2010, September). Adaptive traffic light control in wireless sensor network-based intelligent transportation system. In *2010 IEEE 72nd Vehicular Technology Conference-Fall* (pp. 1-5). IEEE.

Zhou, P., Braud, T., Alhilal, A., Hui, P., & Kangasharju, J. (2019, March). ERL: Edge based Reinforcement Learning for optimized urban Traffic light control. In *2019 IEEE International Conference on Pervasive Computing and Communications Workshops (PerCom Workshops)* (pp. 849-854). IEEE.

Zou, F., Yang, B., & Cao, Y. (2009, August). Traffic light control for a single intersection based on wireless sensor network. In *2009 9th International Conference on Electronic Measurement & Instruments* (pp. 1-1040). IEEE. 10.1109/ICEMI.2009.5273994

KEY TERMS AND DEFINITIONS

Detector: Is a technology that collects and transmits environmental information to a processing node.

Green Light Time: Is a time interval during which several movements are allowed in the intersection. A cycle is divided into several phases, each of which has a duration of green light that it is essential to properly regulate. Indeed, a phase too short may not allow enough time for a queue to discharge. Conversely, a phase that is too long increases the waiting time for drivers present on the other phases, without being useful.

Intelligent Transportation Systems (ITS): Have attracted considerable attention in recent years especially with the significant progress made in the field of computer and telecommunication technologies. ITS intervenes in a global context of traffic congestion on the one hand and development of new information technologies on the other, particularly in the areas of simulation, real-time traffic control. telecommunication networks.

Junction or Road Intersection: Is located at the intersection of several streets defining entrance and exit lanes. It can take many forms, both in infrastructure and in crossing rules. The directions of vehicles are either go straight, turn left, or flow to turn right. Vehicles are always allowed to turn right without restricting traffic.

SUMO Simulator (Simulation of Urban Mobility): Is a road traffic simulator that models the behavior of vehicles at the different flows of an intersection or a network of intersections. This simulator allows us to reproduce user behavior by generating the observations that would normally come from the detectors. This makes it possible to replace the ITS information and to evaluate the performance of the traffic control approach as a whole. They are called "Intelligent" because their development is based on functions generally associated with intelligence: sensory capabilities, memory, communication, information processing and adaptive behavior.

Traffic Lights Plan: Corresponds to the description of a given cycle, and defines the different phases to be unfolded as well as their duration. Generally, a traffic lights plan is designed for a specific time slot, depending on the average level of traffic to be absorbed (eg, a shorter traffic lights plan for the night, a longer one in rush hour).

Wireless Sensor Network (WSN): A wireless sensor network is a set of sensor nodes communicating wirelessly. These sensor nodes are able to self-organize into distributed subnets to collect information from the physical world on which they are deployed.

Chapter 10
Various Models to Evaluate Quality in the Service Industry

Jeganathan Gomathi Sankar
Saveetha School of Management, India

Peter Valan
Saveetha School of Management, India

M. S. Siranjeevi
Saveetha School of Management, India

ABSTRACT

Service quality has turned out to be the most important topic of consideration to academicians and practitioners. It has been proven that the influence of service quality on business performance, cost leadership, customer satisfaction, customer loyalty, and profitability. The accomplishment of quality in services has turned out to be a vital concern of all services organisations. Quality in services is mainly undefined and becomes the crucial issue. Increased competition and knowledge of customer satisfaction made the service organisations use new service parameters and implement quality management tools as competitive advantage. Service quality is hard to evaluate, as it is subjective in nature. Many researchers did explore and confirm the dimensions of service quality. This study focuses on various studies of service quality conducted by earlier researchers in an array of industries. The chapter details the development of service quality theory and different models hypothesised to measure service quality.

INTRODUCTION

A prevailing Japanese philosophy quote is quality is "zero defects-doing it right the first time". Quality is defined as "conformance to requirements" Crosby (1979). Garvin (1983) assesses quality by counting the incidence of "internal" failures and "external" failures. Quality is an elusive and indistinct factor. Often mistaken for inaccurate adjectives like "goodness, or luxury, or shininess, or weight" (Crosby 1979), quality and its requirements are not easily articulated by consumers (Takeuchi and Quelch 1983).

DOI: 10.4018/978-1-7998-5175-2.ch010

Explication and measurement of quality also present problems for researchers (Monroe and Krishnan 1983), who often bypass definitions and use unidimensional self-report instrument to capture the concept (McConnell 1968; Shapiro 1972). While the factors that determine the quality may be undefined, its significance to organisations and consumers is unequivocal. The search for quality is arguably the imperative consumer trend of all time (Rabin 1983) as consumers started expecting and demanding greater quality in products and services than ever before (Leonard and Sasser 1982, Takeuchi and Quelch 1983).

Services quality is entirely different from goods quality, thus knowledge about goods quality, is not enough to understand service quality. The unique characterises of services such as intangibility, heterogeneity, and inseparability ought to be included for a full understanding of service quality. Services are intangible in nature (Lovelock 1981) because services are performances rather than objects so it cannot be measured and verified the quality in advance. Because of heterogeneity, their performance often varies from time to time, provider to provider, and customer to customer. Production and consumption of many services are inseparable, so quality of service is not engineered at the plant rather delivered at moment of truth.

SERVICE QUALITY MODELS

Technical and Functional Quality Model

The understanding of service quality influence and perception of the customer is essential in the competitive market scenario. The service always extends its hands towards customers. The company meeting the expectation of customers at service quality has more success stories. The Service never comprised only at addressing customer issues. Modern industries look service in various forms. Technical quality is given in their product or service, the quality enhanced at the functionality of usage of product and service and unique image of the firm exhibited through its work.

GAP Model of Service Quality

The novelty of service quality well visualized through implementing a GAP model. The name GAP itself suggests this model identifies halo areas at service quality.

The five GAP addressed in GAP model is:

Gap 1: Failing to understand what are the customer expectations.
Gap 2: Failing to provide better quality at service.
Gap 3: The gap identified between at assured service and delivered service.
Gap 4: The evaluation of service delivered.
Gap 5: The gap majorly depends on the above four variables and identifies customer expectation and perception at service facilitation.

Figure 1.
Source: Gronroos, 1984

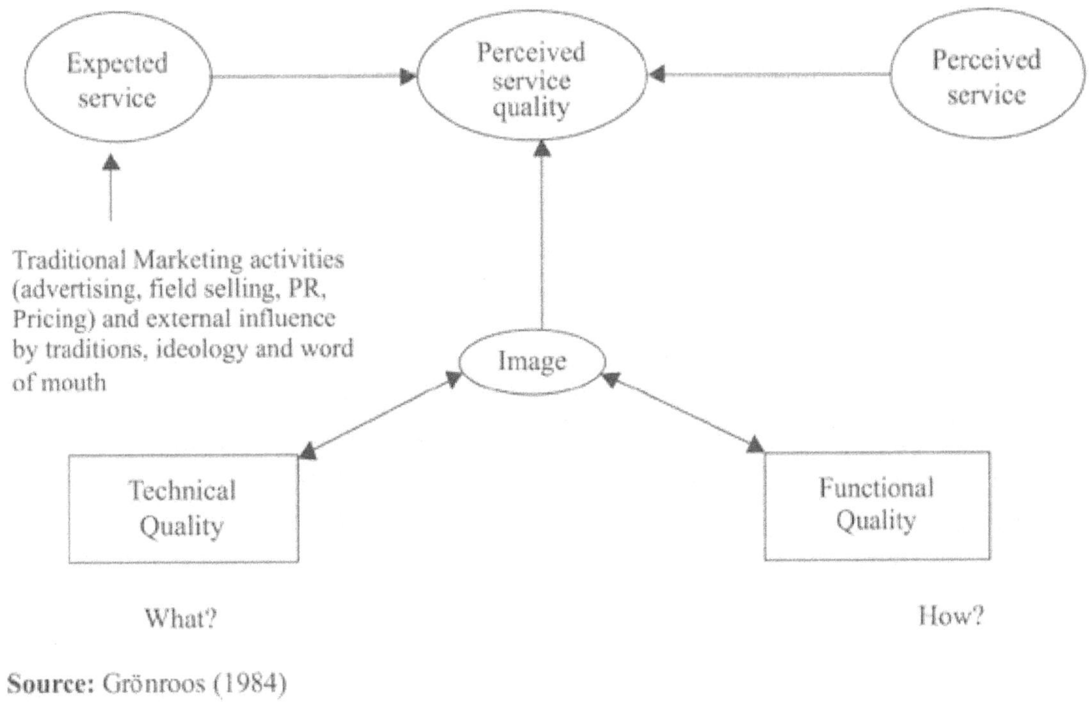

Attribute Service Quality Model

The firm wins more customer preferences if it has high standard of service quality along with meeting expectations of the customer. Service is a cluster of many participants. Haywood and Farmer divided all those participants into three different categories. Physical facilities were available at the service and process of it, Consumer behaviour trait, and the professional judgment are three dividends of this model. Each has its influence over the other. The firm cannot neglect one attribute or give importance to one particular attribute.

Synthesised Model of Service Quality

The customer learns about the firm through word of mouth, marketing campaign and by media communication. But the customer may not be experienced with the actual service provided by the firm. The model identifies the actual service provided and experienced service quality. The firm has to consider this service gap by integrating service design, service operation, marketing activities, and traditional framework. This model was developed by Brogowicz, Delene, and Lyth (1990).

Figure 2. GAP model of service quality
Source: Parasuraman et al., 1985

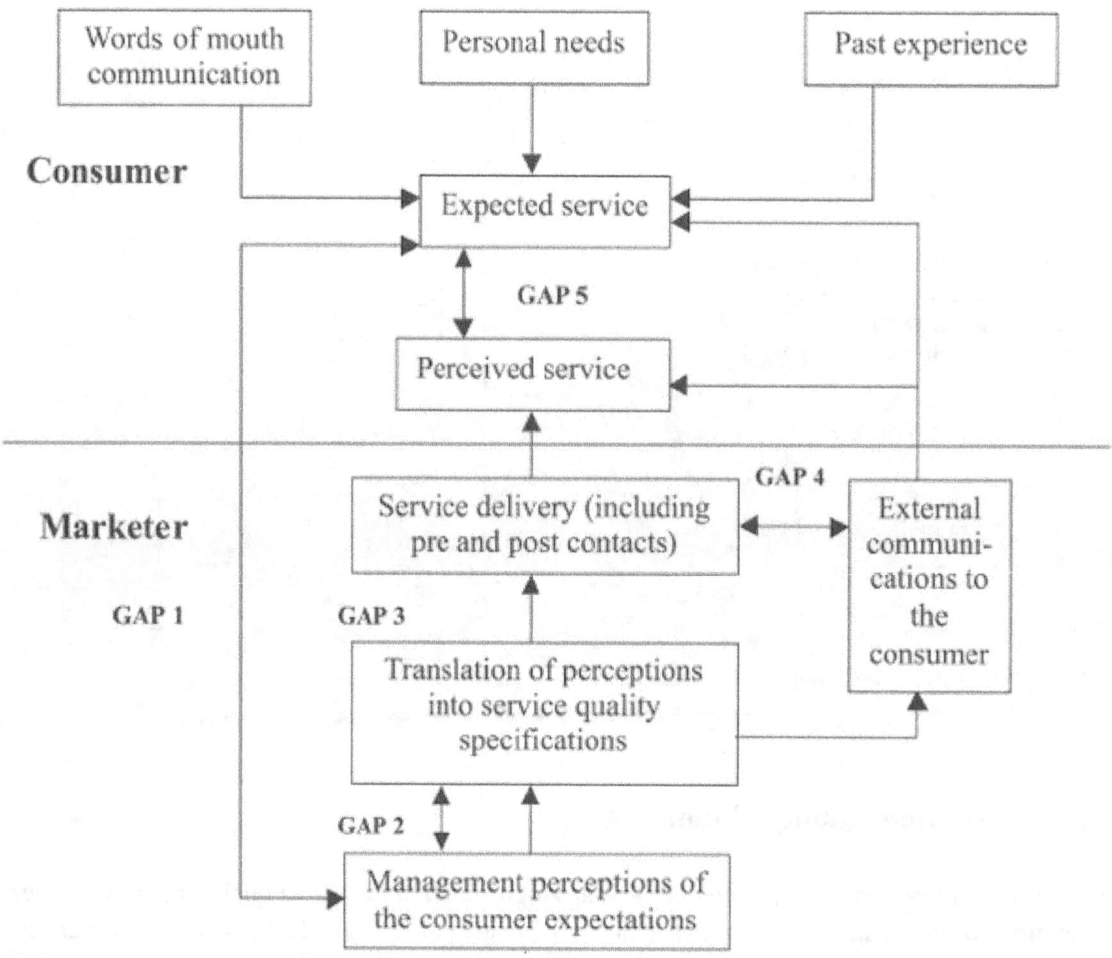

Performance Only Model

Cronin and Taylor developed a performance only model in 1992. The authors showed the importance of conceptualizing the Parasuraman et al (1985) work. This model formally addressed as SERVPERF. They discussed SERVQUAL is a blend of satisfaction and attitude. Their argument is that the attitude of the consumer determines the service quality. Thus, the model fully focused on satisfaction and purchase intention with defined conceptualization and measurement of service quality.

Figure 3. Attribute service quality model
Source: Haywood-Farmer, 1988

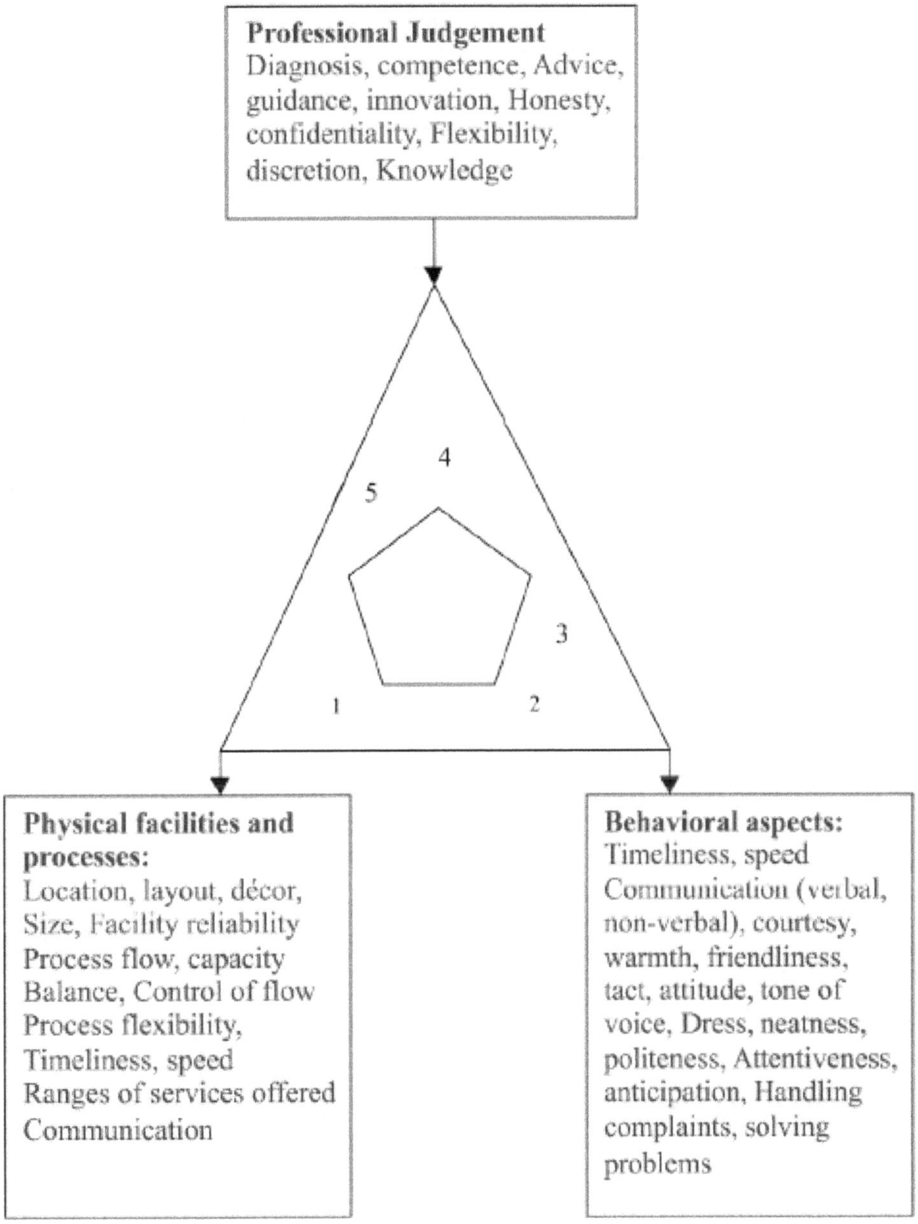

Figure 4. Model of service quality
Source: Brogowicz et al., 1990

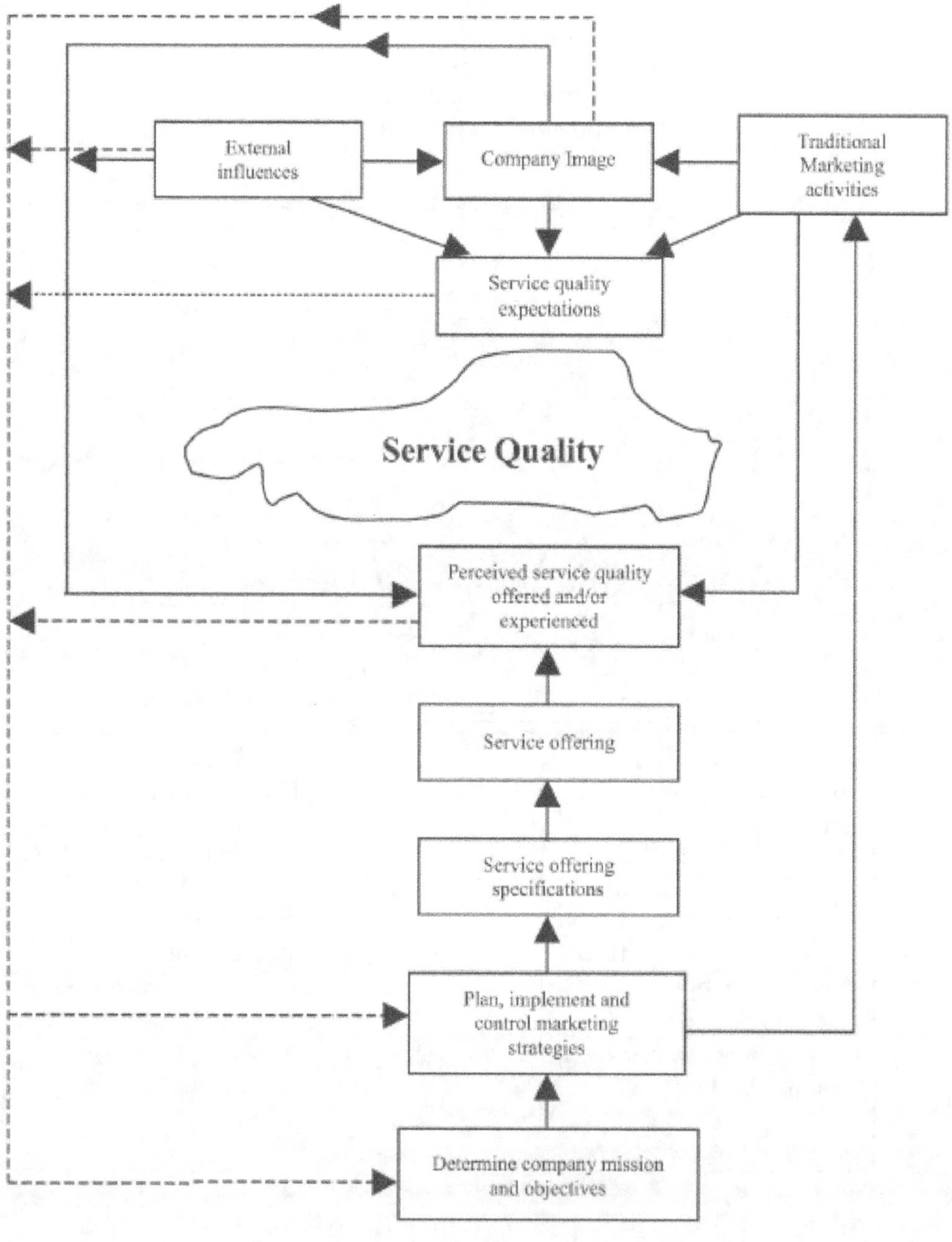

Ideal Value Model of Service Quality

How standard for measuring Service quality can be defined is a major argument at most of the studies. Ideal value model was constructed by Mattsson (1992). The need for experience-oriented, ideal and good endurance level of standards needed as determinants of service quality. This model gives a value-based measurement of service quality.

Figure 5. Ideal model of service quality
Source: Mattsson, 1992

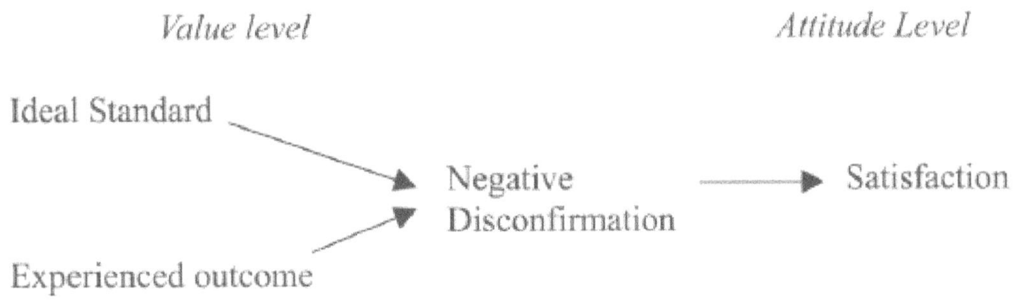

Information Technology Alignment Model

The Information technology adoption has significant impact at firms and organisations. The acceptance of technology has greater influence at every industry. Thus, technology has its own influence at service facility availed by consumers. The IT alignment model with the assistant of various case studies from the different sectors describes the use of information technology towards improved service quality. The focal point of the model urges firms to align and coordinate service quality and information system. This gives new scope of service quality through aligning service and aligning strategies.

Attribute and Overall Affect Model

Dabholkar work on service quality focused on self-service options. The self-service majorly accepted by customers due to its instant nature. This instantaneous brings certain engagement between customer and firm. This model deals self service quality in two different models. Attribute model postulated by Dabholkar (1996) details what could be the expectation of customer using information technology for availing service. The overall affect model describes sympathy shown towards technology by the user.

Model of Perceived Service Quality and Satisfaction

This model was developed by Spreng and Mackoy (1996). This model brings an update on Oliver's (1993) model. The service quality perception and satisfaction of the consumer understood with the context of performance desire, effect of expectation, harmony of service, and overall service quality.

Figure 6. Information technology alignment model
Source: Berkley and Gupta, 1994

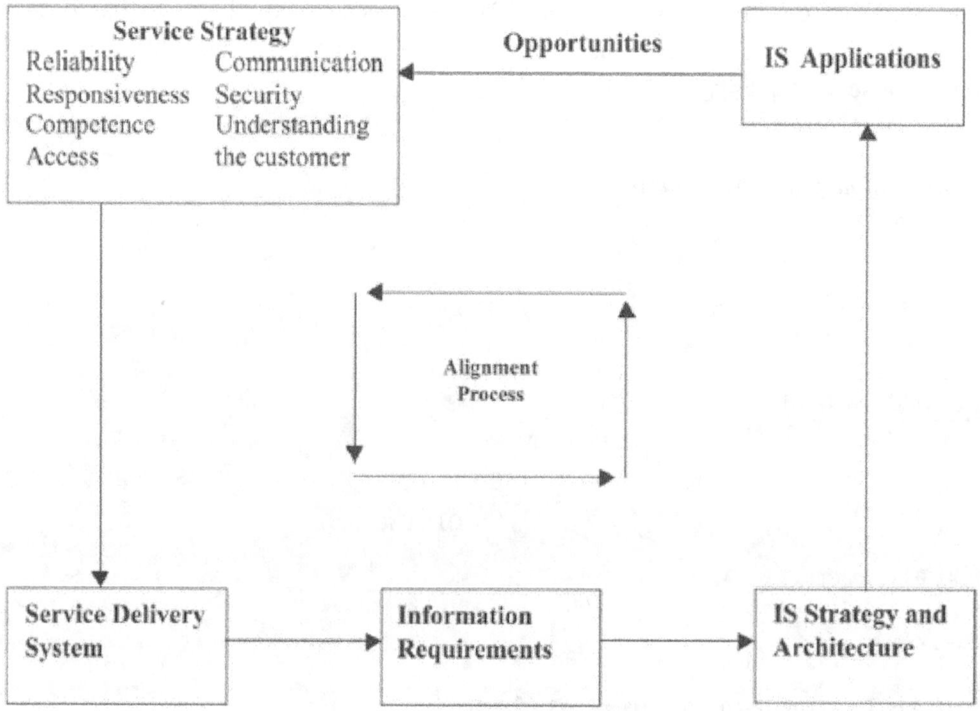

Figure 7. Attribute and overall affect model
Source: Dabholkar, 1996

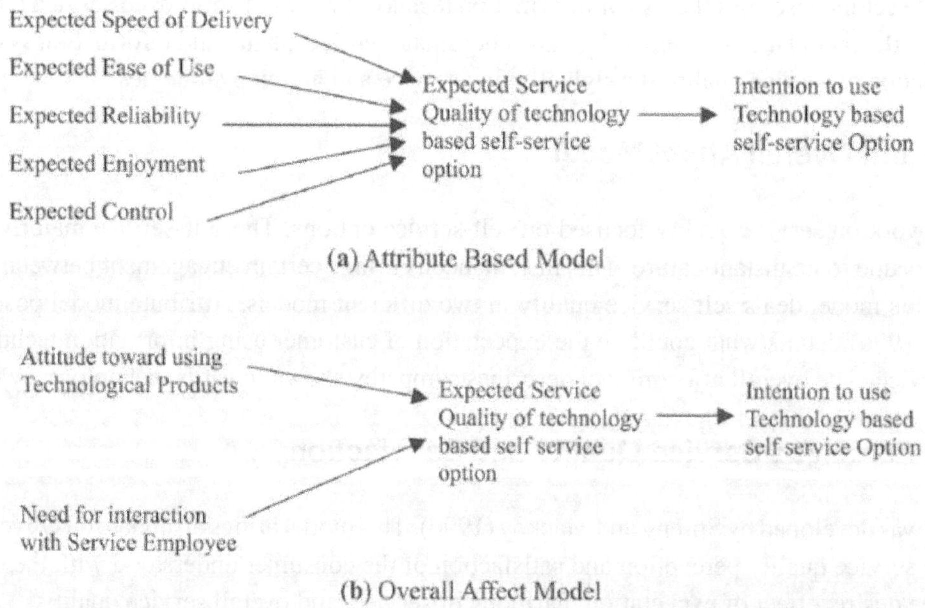

Figure 8. Model of perceived service quality and satisfaction
Source: Spreng and Mackoy, 1996

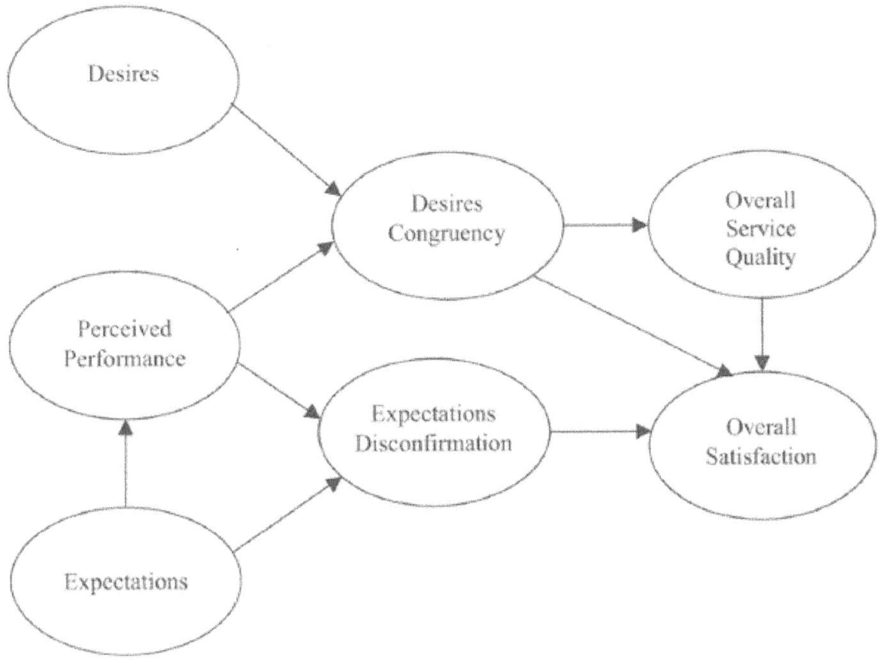

Retail Service Quality and Perceived Value Model

Consumer always evaluates value and benefit of the service. The argument between benefits and sacrifices (Zeithaml et al., 1988) at availing service determines the value of the service. This model considers value of money in its two phases. The first phase states value perception influenced by perceptions of price, functional service quality and technical service quality. The second phase states above discussed perception influences the willingness of the consumer to buy a service.

Service Quality, Customer Value and Customer Satisfaction Model

This model was developed by Oh (1999). The author argued that the post purchase behaviour very important at valuing the service quality. The fusion showed in this model combines perception of customer, quality of service provided, satisfaction level of customer, value given to consumer and also intentions to repurchase or avail the service from the firm organisation. This model emphasises the importance of the word of mouth and its influence.

Internal Service Quality Model

The model by Frost and Kumar (2000), evaluates internal customers and internal suppliers or front-line staff and support staff perception on service quality. The model clearly states three GAPs i.e. internal customers' and internal suppliers' perception contradicts one other, there is significant difference found

Figure 9. Retail service quality and perceived value model
Source: Sweeney et al. 1997

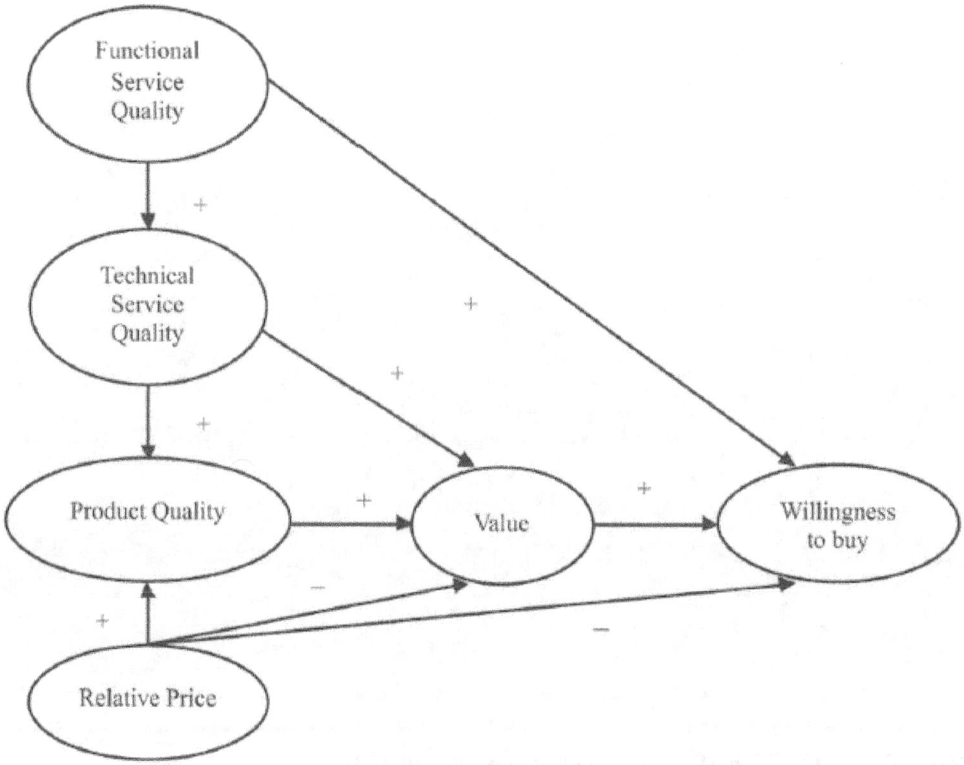

at specifications of service quality and the actual service delivered. Final and third GAP is dedicated towards front line staff.

Internet Banking Model

The authors Broderick and Vachirapornpuk (2002) conceptualised this model. The internet revolutionised service delivery point. Internet brings remote service stations even at our home. The interaction and behaviour pattern of the customer differed through implementing internet-based service facilitation. Internet based service quality analysed in this model through five key points which are expectation of service, the organisation's social image, how service provided, how consumer encounters they system and participation.

Model of E-Service Quality

Electronic commerce platforms are well accepted by the consumers. This service eco system defined Cyberspace Service points (Rust and Lemon, 2001). Addressing the quality of these service methods conceptualised as e-service quality. Here the quality measured in terms of hit rates, stickiness, and customer retention.

Figure 10. Internal service quality model
Source: Frost and Kumar, 2000

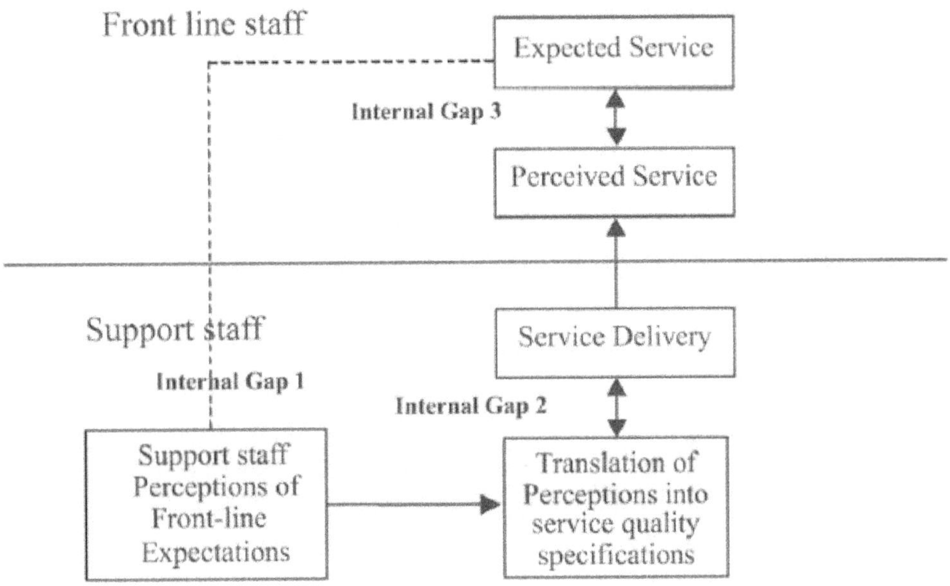

Figure 11. Internet banking model
Source: Broderick and Vachirapornpuk, 2002

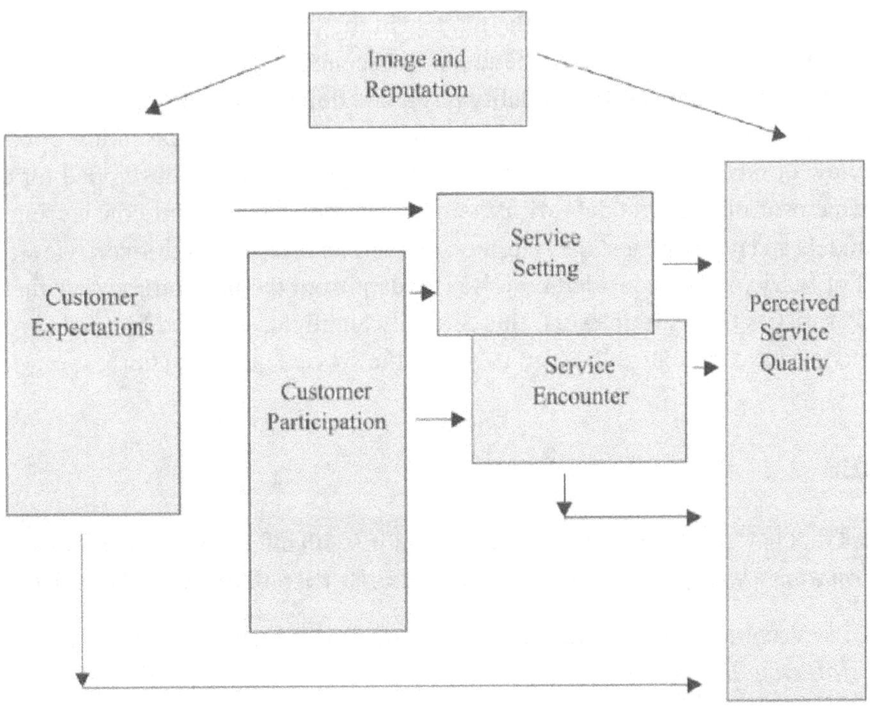

Figure 12. Model of e-service quality
Source: Santos, 2003

CONCLUSION

It is interesting to trace the development of the models in the literature. This is an attempt to evaluate various service quality models published in literature. These models give a useful framework for quality of service. It is ascertained that the service quality result and dimension is dependent on service setting, time, and need of the customer. Furthermore, it is based on customers' expectation upon a particular service. The review of models detailed the various service quality models developed for different service setting, refinement of these models with the new service settings, and considering new factors with existing models and remodel/ test the findings. Academicians and practitioners view the subject in the background of service under consideration. It is evident from the literature review that none of the models currently satisfies the set framework, this certainly highlights the need for further research. New variables and models have to be hypothesised to assess the service quality in current service setting.

REFERENCES

Berkley, B. J., & Gupta, A. (1994). Improving service quality with information technology. *International Journal of Information Management*, *14*(2), 109–121. doi:10.1016/0268-4012(94)90030-2

Broderick, A. J., & Vachirapornpuk, S. (2002). Service quality in internet banking: The importance of customer role. *Marketing Intelligence & Planning*, *20*(6), 327–335. doi:10.1108/02634500210445383

Brogowicz, A. A., Delene, L. M., & Lyth, D. M. (1990). A synthesised service quality model with managerial implications. *International Journal of Service Industry Management*, *1*(1), 27–44. doi:10.1108/09564239010001640

Cronin, J. J. Jr, & Taylor, S. A. (1992). Measuring service quality: A reexamination and extension. *Journal of Marketing*, *6*(July), 55 68. doi:10.1177/002224299205600304

Cronin, J. J. Jr, & Taylor, S. A. (1994). SERVPERF versus SERVQUAL: Reconciling performance-based and perception minus-expectations measurement of service quality. *Journal of Marketing*, *58*(1), 125–131. doi:10.1177/002224299405800110

Crosby, P. B. (1979). *Quality is free: The art of making quality certain* (Vol. 94). New York: McGraw-hill.

Dabholkar, P. A. (1996). Consumer evaluations of new technology-based self-service operations: An investigation of alternative models. *International Journal of Research in Marketing*, *13*(1), 29–51. doi:10.1016/0167-8116(95)00027-5

Frost, F. A., & Kumar, M. (2000). INTSERVQUAL: An internal adaptation of the GAP model in a large service organization. *Journal of Services Marketing*, *14*(5), 358–377. doi:10.1108/08876040010340991

Garvin, D. A. (1986). Quality problems, policies, and attitudes in the United States and Japan: An exploratory study. *Academy of Management Journal*, *29*(4), 653–673.

Gronroos, C. (1984). A service quality model and its marketing implications. *European Journal of Marketing*, *18*(4), 36–44. doi:10.1108/EUM0000000004784

Haywood-Farmer, J. (1988). A conceptual model of service quality. *International Journal of Operations & Production Management*, *8*(6), 19–29. doi:10.1108/eb054839

Lovelock, C. H. (1981). *Why marketing management needs to be different for services.*

Mattsson, J. (1992). A service quality model based on ideal value standard. *International Journal of Service Industry Management*, *3*(3), 18–33. doi:10.1108/09564239210015148

McConnell, J. D. (1968). The price-quality relationship in an experimental setting. *JMR, Journal of Marketing Research*, *5*(3), 300–303. doi:10.1177/002224376800500309

Monroe, K. B., & Krishnan, R. (1983). *A procedure for integrating outcomes across studies.* ACR North American Advances.

Oh, H. (1999). Service quality, customer satisfaction and customer value: A holistic perspective. *International Journal of Hospitality Management*, *18*(1), 67–82. doi:10.1016/S0278-4319(98)00047-4

Parasuraman, A., Berry, L. L., & Zeithaml, V. A. (1991). Refinement and reassessment of the SERVQUAL scale. *Journal of Retailing*, *67*(4), 420–450.

Parasuraman, A., Zeithaml, V. A., & Berry, L. L. (1985). A conceptual model of service quality and its implications for future research. *Journal of Marketing*, *49*(3), 41–50. doi:10.1177/002224298504900403

Parasuraman, A., Zeithaml, V. A., & Berry, L. L. (1988). SERVQUAL: A multiple item scale for measuring consumer perception of service quality. *Journal of Retailing*, *64*(1), 12–37.

Parasuraman, A., Zeithaml, V. A., & Berry, L. L. (1994). Reassessment of expectations as a comparison standard in measuring service quality: Implications for further research. *Journal of Marketing*, *58*(1), 111–124. doi:10.1177/002224299405800109

Rabin, J. H. (1983). Accent is on quality in consumer services this decade. *Marketing News*, *17*(4), 12.

Santos, J. (2003). E-service quality: A model of virtual service quality dimensions. *Managing Service Quality*, *13*(3), 233–246. doi:10.1108/09604520310476490

Shapiro, S. S., & Francia, R. S. (1972). An approximate analysis of variance test for normality. *Journal of the American Statistical Association*, *67*(337), 215–216. doi:10.1080/01621459.1972.10481232

Spreng, R. A., & Mackoy, R. D. (1996). An empirical examination of a model of perceived service quality and satisfaction. *Journal of Retailing*, *722*(2), 201–214. doi:10.1016/S0022-4359(96)90014-7

Sweeney, J. C., Soutar, G. N., & Johnson, L. W. (1997). Retail service quality and perceived value. *Journal of Consumer Services*, *4*(1), 39–48. doi:10.1016/S0969-6989(96)00017-3

Takeuchi, H., & Quelch, J. (1983). *Quality is more than making a good product*. Academic Press.

Chapter 11
Evaluation of Customer Satisfaction in the Digital Environment:
Development of a Survey Instrument

Hamed Taherdoost
https://orcid.org/0000-0002-6503-6739
Research Club, Hamta Group, Canada

ABSTRACT

Internet has become an important tool to deliver products, information, and services. Thus, customer satisfaction is increasingly recognized as a significant aspect of online business activities and is considered as a key determinant for successful digital services. Furthermore, since keeping current customers is more profitable than acquiring new clients, it is vital to gain customer satisfaction to achieve organizational goals. This introduces a new requirement to measure customer satisfaction as a factor for continuous business improvement. Therefore, there is a clear need for a theoretical survey instrument that integrates all aspects of customer satisfaction in the digital environment. The chapter responds to this need by its exploratory nature. In the first step, exploratory analysis is used to extract all customer satisfaction dimensions. Then, the exploratory factor analysis is used to cluster the factors effectively; thereby, further analysis including content validity, discriminate, and constructive testing is used to test the proposed survey instrument.

INTRODUCTION

In today's advanced development in ICT, Internet has become an important tool to deliver the products, information, and services of organizations, governments and also individuals (Alawneh et al., 2013). The Internet is one of the major means for communication between companies and clients. Its main feature is the ability to exchange complex information in a friendly environment (NIST-Special-Publication-800-16). Generally, businesses and organizations use the Internet for customer service (IS07498-2). Most companies

DOI: 10.4018/978-1-7998-5175-2.ch011

place great emphasis on customer satisfaction (Taherdoost, 2018a). This introduces a new requirement to measure customer satisfaction as a factor for continuous business improvement (Thomas et al., 2013).

Customer satisfaction as a baseline standard of performance will help organizations to achieve their goals and objectives (Hussain et al., 2014). Chen (2012) articulated that customer satisfaction is one of the factors that influence on clients' intention to use e-service and also repeating the usage. On the other hand, according to Boulter (2014), keeping current customers is more profitable than acquiring new clients. Thus, it can be realized that customer satisfaction is a key factor for e-service usage and will lead to loyalty (Gummerus et al., 2004).

Consumer's satisfaction is not a new concept and many studies try to find its antecedents and consequences, because it is considered as a significant measure of an organization's success (Ramasubbu et al., 2008) especially in Information System (Montesdioca and Maçada, 2014, DeLone and McLean., 1992), however, customer satisfaction is multi-dimensional factor including marketing, behavioural and technical aspects (Alawneh et al., 2013).

In order to explain the system use, it is essential to develop tools to measure and analysing customers' satisfaction (Legris et al., 2003) although there are some scholars that developed instruments to evaluate user satisfaction based on the information and system characteristics (Bailey and Pearson, 1983, Baroudi and Orlikowski., 1988, Doll and Torkzadeh., 1988, Ives et al., 1983). Furthermore, although there are some developed tools to assess web-based services (Cho and Park, 2001, Huang et al., 2004, Muylle et al., 2004) still certain modifications are needed to provide more accurate instrument relevant to web-based service (Tojib et al., 2006). However, there is still not widely accepted the consensus on the satisfaction constructs thus it is significant to provide a set of dimensions which influence customer satisfaction (Al-Kasasbeh et al., 2011).

Information technology researchers evaluated the processes and factors influencing on information technology success and value from the perspective of user perceptions about information technology and how it impacts their work (Wixom and Todd, 2005, Taherdoost, 2019), however, this examinations have been done in various studies (such as general computing by (Doll and Torkzadeh., 1988), data warehouse (Chen et al., 2000) and decision support system (McHaney and Cronan, 1998) in different ways (DeLone and McLean., 1992). Hoffman and Bateson (2010) articulated that every client shares his/her usage experience with nine people, so if they are unsatisfied with the provided service, others may not intend to use the service and the system may fail.

Although measuring the satisfaction of e-services is more complex than good/product, there is no specific method to evaluate the e-service satisfaction (Taherdoost, 2018b). In order to achieve customer satisfaction, managers of companies with Web presences must first understand how customers perceive and evaluate electronic service. This involves defining what e-service satoisfaction is, identifying its underlying dimensions, and determining how it can be conceptualized and measured.

In this research, the theoretical foundation of e-service satisfaction is reviewed and examine through comprehensive exploratory analysis in order to gather all motioned characteristic in a comprehensive pattern. This chapter has the following structure. First, it examines and discusses the concept, special characteristics and definitions of service satisfaction. Then, it extracted the e-service satisfaction dimensions based on literature review analysis. Third, the survey distributed among e-service users to categorize the satisfaction dimensions and highlights the related factors based on exploratory factor analysis. Formerly, after introducing the e-service satisfaction factors, related measurement items are extracted via previous studies then content validity survey is conducted among experts in the field of e-service satisfaction. Finally, exploratory factor analysis is conducted to approach validity testing via discriminate and convergent validity in order to introduce a reliable and valid instrument.

The contribution of this chapter relates to the fact that the proposed theoretical survey instrument integrates in a holistic way various relevant factors affecting e-service satisfaction into a single template. These factors are characteristics common to both traditional and e-service, distinctive characteristics of e-services, relevant e-service satisfaction dimensions.

User Satisfaction Definitions

As Al-Kasasbeh et al. (2011) stated, if customers are satisfied with the services which they received via electronic channel, they will come back to use the system again and if not satisfied so they would not keep utilizing the e-service. Customer satisfaction is conceptualized as an outcome of exceeding expectations (Oliver, 1997, Oliver, 1980). Also, since satisfaction is the emotional reaction to a service/product experience (Cristobal et al., 2007) and the difference between actual received service/product and clients' expectation (Geng and Chu, 2012). Table 1 presents the definitions of satisfaction in previous studies although for this study satisfaction is defined as the extent to which users believe that the provided electronic service meets their needs and expectation.

Table 1. Satisfaction's definitions as articulated in previous studies

Study	Satisfaction Definition
(Oliver, 1980)	"… customers' evaluations of a product or service with regard to their needs and expectations"
(Bailey and Pearson, 1983)	"… in a given situation, is the sum of one's feelings or attitudes towards a variety of factors affecting that situation"
(Ives et al., 1983)	"… the extent to which users believe that the information system available to them meets their information requirement"
(Doll and Torkzadeh., 1988)	"… an affective attitude towards a specific computer application by someone who interacts with the application directly"
(Bitner, 1990)	"… as a transactional comparison of perceived performance against expectations"
(Johnson et al., 1995)	"… a cumulative evaluation of a consumer's total experience with a product or service"
(Oliver, 1997)	"… a judgment that a product or service feature, or the product or service itself, provided (or is providing) a pleasurable level of consumption- related fulfillment, including levels of under or over fulfillment"
(Szymanski and Hise, 2000)	"… consumers' judgment of their internet retail experience as compared to their experiences with traditional retail stores"
(Legris et al., 2003)	"… the sum of one's feelings or attitudes toward a variety of factors affecting the situation"
(Chang and Chen, 2008)	"… the contentment of the consumer with respect to his or her prior purchasing experience with a given electronic firm"
(Anderson and Srinivasan, 2003, Chen, 2012)	"… the contentment of the consumer with deference to his/her previous purchase experiences with an e-commerce firm"
(Manasra et al., 2013)	"… the evaluations of a product or service with regard to their consumers' needs and expectations"

Satisfaction Dimensions

Since the main difference between traditional services and e-service is the channel of communication and the replacement of the human to human interaction with human to machine interaction so new measurement method is required to measure customer satisfaction of the e-service (Evanschitzky et al., 2004). According to the comprehensive literature review, thirty-six dimensions have been extracted from previous studies in the field of information system namely; Accessibility, Accuracy, Adequacy, Assistance, Assurance, Attentiveness, Availability, Communication, Commitment, Completeness, Convenience, Credibility, Currency, Delivery, Ease of Use, Efficiency, Expectation, Flexibility, Format, Friendliness, Fulfillment, Integration, Precision, Price, Product Information, Product Offerings, Quality, Relevancy, Reliability, Responsiveness, Security, Speed, Timeliness, Training, Usefulness, and Website Design. The source of each of these dimensions can be found in Table 2.

FACTORS INFLUENCE ON E-SERVICE SATISFACTION

As mentioned earlier, by conducting a comprehensive literature review in the field of information system, thirty-six dimensions have been extracted. In the next step and in order to categorize and reduce the number of dimensions, Exploratory Factor Analysis (EFA) as a theory generating procedure (Stevens, 2001), is applied. The reason for applying exploratory factor analysis to this study is to determine factors that are affecting e-service satisfaction and to identify the constructs that characterize the user satisfaction of e-service. Thus, it is used to identify the number of key factors (known as principal factors) that explain the majority of variance (Kline, 1997) among defined satisfaction dimensions.

A structured questionnaire was used as data collection instrument, because questionnaire is very flexible to use (Moore, 2006). An online survey was conducted and the subjects of the study were a group of students who had relevant knowledge to respond regarding the context of the study. Using student subjects is highly acceptable for e-service research since, (a) e-services are technology-based and students are much more into technology than the old generation, and (b) the most frequent users of Internet and e-services are students and this has become part of their daily routine, and consequently, they are considered better candidates to assess the issues related to e-services (Alawadhi and Morris, 2008, Zhang et al., 2006).

Hair et al. (1995a) suggested that the sample size for EFA should be 100 or greater. For the current study, the researcher obtained 193 questionnaires after data filtering to eliminate invalid responses. Almost the same sample size has been chosen by other researchers (Lean et al., 2009, Lai and Lai, 2013, Semeijn et al., 2005, Taherdoost, 2020). Each item of the survey was evaluated using a 5-point Likert scale with strongly agree, agree, neutral, disagree and strongly disagree. Table 3 presents the frequency analysis of satisfactions dimensions.

It is very important to evaluate the reliability of a measuring instrument to make sure it is consistent across the parts (Huck, 2007). Cronbach Alpha Coefficient is known as the most appropriate for measuring reliability while Likert Scales is used. Following recommendations by Nunnally (1978) values for Cronbach's alpha α ranging from 0.80 to 0.95 are considered as representing very good reliability, Cronbach's alpha α ranging from 0.70 to 0.80 are considered as representing good reliability, Cronbach's alpha α ranging from 0.60 to 0.70 are considered as representing fair reliability. As it is shown in Table 3, the Cronbach Alphas range from 0.931 to 0.941, so the dimensions are deemed to have adequate reliability.

Table 2. Dimensions of satisfaction with their related references

Dimension	(DEBONS, 1978)	(Bailey and Pearson, 1983)	(Ives et al., 1983)	(Baroudi and Orlikowski., 1988)	(Doll and Torkzadeh., 1988)	(Saraph et al., 1989)	(Oliver, 1997)	(Johnston, 1997)	(Szymanski and Hise, 2000)	(Verhoef and Langerak, 2001)	(Cho and Park, 2001)	(Yang and Jun, 2002)	(Srinivasan et al., 2002)	(Yang et al., 2003)	(Yen and Gwinner 2003	(Shih, 2004)	(Jun et al., 2004)	(Huang et al., 2004)	(Semeijn et al., 2005)	(Wixom and Todd, 2005)	(Dritsas et al., 2006)	(Tojib et al., 2006)	(Verdegem and Verleye, 2009)	(Yoon, 2010)	(Al-Kasasbeh et al., 2011)	(Zavareh et al., 2012)	(Alawneh et al., 2013)	(Thomas et al., 2013)	(Ariff et al., 2013)	(Bressolles et al., 2014)	(Chakraborty and Sengupta, 2014)	(Montesdioca and Maçada, 2014)
Accessibility	✓	✓	✓																		✓		✓				✓	✓	✓			✓
Accuracy	✓	✓	✓	✓	✓													✓												✓		✓
Adequacy	✓																															
Assistance	✓																															
Assurance																			✓													
Attentiveness								✓									✓															
Availability																					✓		✓									✓
Communication	✓	✓	✓	✓																								✓	✓			
Commitment								✓																								
Completeness		✓	✓	✓	✓																											✓
Convenience									✓	✓		✓	✓	✓				✓														
Credibility												✓		✓																		
Currency		✓	✓		✓																											
Delivery										✓								✓														
Ease Of Use		✓	✓	✓	✓	✓				✓		✓		✓			✓				✓			✓		✓				✓		✓
Efficiency					✓											✓					✓								✓			
Expectation		✓	✓				✓																									
Flexibility		✓	✓																												✓	✓
Format		✓			✓																							✓				
Friendliness					✓			✓															✓									✓
Fulfillment						✓	✓																						✓			
Integration		✓	✓																													
Precision		✓	✓	✓	✓																											
Price	✓									✓								✓					✓								✓	
Product Information									✓	✓														✓						✓		
Product Offerings									✓	✓																						
Quality											✓									✓						✓	✓			✓	✓	✓
Relevancy		✓	✓	✓	✓																											✓
Reliability	✓	✓	✓	✓	✓	✓						✓		✓			✓															✓
Responsiveness		✓	✓									✓		✓			✓															✓
Security		✓				✓			✓									✓			✓		✓	✓		✓	✓		✓	✓		
Speed																					✓			✓								
Timeliness	✓	✓	✓		✓												✓															✓
Training		✓	✓	✓																												✓
Usefulness		✓	✓		✓																		✓								✓	
Website Design									✓	✓								✓						✓		✓		✓		✓		

Table 3. Descriptive results of satisfaction dimensions in exploratory factor analysis

Dimension	Mean	Median	Std. Deviation	Variance	Corrected Item-Total Correlation	Cronbach's Alpha if Item Deleted
Accessibility	4.32	4	0.729	0.532	.656	.931
Accuracy	4.25	4	0.81	0.657	.535	.932
Adequacy	4.23	4	0.779	0.607	.625	.931
Assistance	3.98	4	0.866	0.75	.602	.931
Assurance	3.9	4	0.884	0.781	.544	.932
Attentiveness	3.63	4	1.034	1.068	.522	.932
Availability	4.35	4	0.713	0.509	.492	.932
Communication	4.47	5	0.771	0.594	.626	.931
Commitment	4.03	4	0.841	0.707	.591	.931
Completeness	4.45	5	0.699	0.488	.388	.933
Convenience	3.82	4	0.965	0.93	.539	.932
Credibility	4.1	4	0.764	0.583	.575	.931
Currency	3.94	4	0.942	0.887	.554	.932
Delivery	4.59	5	0.773	0.598	.475	.932
Ease of Use	3.88	4	0.958	0.918	.434	.933
Efficiency	4.11	4	0.819	0.67	.528	.932
Expectation	4.01	4	0.893	0.797	.435	.933
Flexibility	4.37	4	0.719	0.516	.624	.931
Format	4.55	5	0.645	0.416	.554	.932
Friendliness	3.92	4	0.92	0.847	.537	.932
Fulfillment	4.28	4	0.801	0.642	.615	.931
Integration	4.35	4	0.749	0.561	.575	.932
Precision	3.91	4	0.882	0.779	.605	.931
Price	4.48	5	0.744	0.553	.587	.931
Product Information	3.63	4	0.95	0.902	.392	.933
Product Offering	4.09	4	0.972	0.944	.566	.931
Quality	4.28	4	1.488	2.215	.051	.941
Relevancy	4.37	5	0.76	0.578	.509	.932
Reliability	4.2	4	0.837	0.701	.603	.931
Responsiveness	3.74	4	0.951	0.904	.583	.931
Security	4.21	4	0.853	0.728	.425	.933
Speed	4.25	4	0.812	0.659	.611	.931
Timeliness	4.36	4	0.718	0.516	.620	.931
Training	4.28	4	0.846	0.715	.498	.932
Usefulness	4.05	4	0.799	0.638	.594	.931
Web Design	4.56	5	0.734	0.539	.485	.932

On the other hand, the KMO (Kaiser-Meyer-Olkin) index is a measure of sampling adequacy and the Sphericity statistic tests whether the correlations among variables are too low for the factor model to be appropriate. Kaiser-Meyer-OIkin (KMO) measure should be greater than .70 (Leech et al., 2005). As it is shown in Table 4, the KMO = 0.883. This shows that the degree of common variance among the variables is quite high.

Table 4. KMO and Bartlett's test for satisfaction explortory analysis

Kaiser-Meyer-Olkin Measure of Sampling Adequacy.		.883
Bartlett's Test of Sphericity	Approx. Chi-Square	3792.133
	df	630
	Sig.	.000

In the next step, it should be decided that how many factors must be retained for rotation. In order to make this decision, the Kaiser criterion (Kraiser, 1958) was applied and factors with eigenvalues greater than 1.0 are selected. the Kaiser criterion is the most used approach since it is easy to use (Gorsuch, 1983, Fabrigar et al., 1999). Table 5 shows the initial eigenvalues and proportions of variance explained by each factor. The eigenvalue criterion tells us that eight constructs should be retained. Varimax rotation which was developed by Thompson (2004) and is the most common form of rotational methods for exploratory factor analysis is utilized in this study. Table 6 presents the rotated component matrix and the components loaded on their corresponding construct. The items with loading factor less than 0.4 are the minimum value suggested for Information System studies (Straub et al., 2004) and cross-loading greater than 0.4 are eliminated (Straub et al., 2004, Dwivedi et al., 2006). Therefore, a total of eleven items are deleted.

In next step, the interpretation process is carried out for allocating a name for each of eight remained constructs. Interpretation is the process of examination to select variables which are attributable to a construct and allocating a name for that construct. The labelling of constructs is a theoretical, subjective and inductive process (Pett et al., 2003). It is significant that labels of constructs reflect the theoretical and conceptual intent. Eight generated factors are labelled as; (1) Performance, (2) Trust, (3) User Friendly, (4) Usability, (5) Design, (6) Security, (7) Training and (8) Quality. Table 7 presents the satisfaction factor classifications and their factor loadings.

SATISFACTION MEASUREMENT DEVELOPMENT

Figure 1 shows the instrument development steps. In order to develop the survey, a comprehensive literature review has been done to extract the existing items for each of the constructs of e-service satisfaction. Although some of the items were specifically composed for the purpose of this research, since measures suitable for this study were not available. Table 8 presents the number of survey items with their references for content validity survey.

Table 5. Total variance explained for satisfaction factors

Component	Initial Eigenvalues			Extraction Sums of Squared Loadings			Rotation Sums of Squared Loadings		
	Total	% of Var	Cum %	Total	% of Var	Cum %	Total	% of Var	Cum %
1	12.044	33.454	33.454	12.044	33.454	33.454	5.567	15.463	15.463
2	2.879	7.998	41.453	2.879	7.998	41.453	4.266	11.850	27.313
3	1.986	5.516	46.968	1.986	5.516	46.968	3.562	9.896	37.209
4	1.590	4.416	51.384	1.590	4.416	51.384	2.763	7.676	44.885
5	1.435	3.985	55.369	1.435	3.985	55.369	2.517	6.992	51.876
6	1.296	3.601	58.970	1.296	3.601	58.970	2.051	5.696	57.573
7	1.212	3.367	62.337	1.212	3.367	62.337	1.650	4.583	62.156
8	1.129	3.137	65.475	1.129	3.137	65.475	1.195	3.319	65.475
9	1.009	2.803	68.278						
10	.872	2.422	70.700						
11	.820	2.278	72.978						
12	.759	2.109	75.087						
13	.702	1.951	77.038						
14	.663	1.841	78.879						
15	.620	1.723	80.603						
16	.596	1.657	82.259						
17	.541	1.503	83.763						
18	.532	1.478	85.241						
19	.486	1.350	86.591						
20	.481	1.335	87.926						
21	.427	1.186	89.113						
22	.426	1.183	90.296						
23	.401	1.113	91.410						
24	.369	1.024	92.434						
25	.343	.953	93.387						
26	.325	.901	94.288						
27	.302	.840	95.129						
28	.267	.742	95.871						
29	.251	.697	96.568						
30	.234	.650	97.218						
31	.202	.561	97.779						
32	.188	.522	98.300						
33	.175	.487	98.788						
34	.164	.457	99.245						
35	.146	.406	99.650						
36	.126	.350	100.000						

Extraction Method: Principal Component Analysis.

a. When components are correlated, sums of squared loadings cannot be added to obtain a total variance.

Table 6. Rotated component matrix fsor satisfaction factors

Dimension	Component							
	1	2	3	4	5	6	7	8
Accessibility	.606	.257	.116	.314	.049	.104	.300	.051
Accuracy	.408	.154	.128	.108	.049	.686	.046	-.125
Adequacy	.261	.640	.032	.106	.218	.325	.165	-.080
Assistance	.564	.349	.268	.155	.007	.096	-.231	-.151
Assurance	.180	.611	.176	.248	.017	.033	.070	-.062
Attentiveness	.204	.306	.466	.298	-.090	.179	-.190	.073
Availability	.323	.084	.032	.550	-.027	.177	.439	.193
Communication	.687	.118	.181	.027	.408	.179	-.047	-.144
Commitment	.208	.703	.324	.003	.045	-.009	.120	.101
Completeness	.039	.190	-.060	.071	.516	.564	.114	.115
Convenience	-.028	.213	.705	.104	.249	.199	.115	.091
Credibility	.010	.781	.166	.108	.205	.102	.207	.043
Currency	.433	.026	.639	.136	.012	.012	.103	-.008
Delivery	.635	.013	.138	-.100	.280	.171	.253	-.280
Ease of Use	-.103	.292	.650	.098	-.084	.343	.039	.013
Efficiency	.385	.152	.148	.710	-.063	-.064	.081	-.110
Expectation	-.054	.076	.204	.751	.206	.269	-.034	-.048
Flexibility	.608	.375	.020	.077	.089	.338	-.014	.104
Format	.387	.153	.114	.031	.598	.140	.295	-.031
Friendliness	.203	.243	.676	.238	.064	-.192	-.001	-.117
Fulfillment	.767	.153	.103	.157	.203	-.011	-.021	.068
Integration	.210	.675	-.050	.128	.445	.105	-.030	.032
Precision	.175	.450	.438	.006	.030	.359	.294	-.020
Price	.764	.132	.014	.132	.128	.125	.164	.150
Product Information	-.122	.303	.224	.328	.376	-.053	.344	-.071
Product Offering	.409	.058	.534	.216	.255	-.073	-.098	.076
Quality	.022	.012	.059	-.016	.068	-.039	.007	.910
Relevancy	.414	.073	.231	.002	.594	.041	-.012	.184
Reliability	.204	.614	.360	.134	-.047	.212	-.113	-.001
Responsiveness	.206	.453	.303	.466	.101	.039	-.348	-.053
Security	.330	.235	.064	.107	.062	-.035	.699	-.023
Speed	.616	.150	.164	.096	.179	.209	.238	-.022
Timeliness	.424	.116	.385	.360	.098	.103	.149	.117
Training	.355	.177	.213	.142	.000	.571	-.151	-.032
Usefulness	.125	.315	.341	.569	.148	.001	.107	.083
Web Design	.378	.167	-.001	.155	.717	-.026	-.097	-.014

Extraction Method: Principal Component Analysis. Rotation Method: Varimax with Kaiser Normalization.

Table 7. Satisfaction factor classifications

Factor	Dimension	Loading							
Performance	Accessibility	.606							
	Assistance	.564							
	Delivery	.635							
	Flexibility	.608							
	Fulfillment	.767							
	Price	.764							
	Speed	.616							
	Timeliness	.424							
Trust	Adequacy		.640						
	Assurance		.611						
	Commitment		.703						
	Credibility		.781						
	Reliability		.614						
User Friendly	Attentiveness			.466					
	Convenience			.705					
	Ease of Use			.650					
	Friendliness			.676					
Usability	Efficiency				.710				
	Expectation				.751				
	Usefulness				.569				
Design	Format					.598			
	Web Design					.717			
Security							.699		
Training								.571	
Quality									.910

Figure 1. Instrument development steps

Content Validity of Final Survey

Engaging a comprehensive review of the literature helps to identify a sample of items for each construct. A total of 325 items for eight constructs related to the e-service satisfaction and its own were identified. Then, a content validity questionnaire was generated that comprised definitions of the constructs and associated items on a three-point scale (not necessary, useful but not essential and essential). A total of twelve experts (Dwivedi et al., 2006, Taherdoost, 2017) were identified on the basis of their experience in the field of e-services. Then, a survey was sent to them and responses have been collected. In next step, the content validity ratio (CVR) for each of the items was calculated and was estimated and items that were not significant at the 0.05 level were eliminated (Lawshe 1975). The finding illustrates that among the 325 items, 33 items remained for the final survey instrument. Table 9 shows the items included in

Table 8. Number of initial items for final survey with their related sources

Construct	Research	Number of Items
Satisfaction	(Wu et al., 2008, Wixom and Todd, 2005, Hernandez et al., 2011, Spreng et al., 1996, Bhattacherjee, 2001, Winsted, 1997, Dwivedi et al., 2006, Pavlou, 2003, Zhang and Prybutok, 2005, Janda et al., 2002, Colwell et al., 2008)	19
Quality	(Wu et al., 2008, McKnight et al., 2002b, Wixom and Todd, 2005, Ruyter et al., 2001, Zhang and Prybutok, 2005, Riel et al., 2003)	20
User Friendly	(Luo et al., 2011, Dwivedi et al., 2006, Vijayasarathy, 2004, Taylor and Todd, 1995a, Dickerson and Gentry, 1983, Pedersen, 2005, Pavlou, 2003, Venkatesh et al., 2003, Davis et al., 1989, Al-Gahtani and King, 1999, Tan et al., 2003, Loonam and O'Loughlin, 2008, Wixom and Todd, 2005, Carter and Bélanger, 2005, Davis, 1989, Yu et al., 2005)	20
Training	(R. Ryan Nelson et al., 1991, Lu et al., 2003, Shareef et al., 2011, Anthopoulos et al., 2007, Shareef et al., 2009)	7
Usability	(Mahinda and Whitworth, 2006, Ok and Shon, 2006, Loonam and O'Loughlin, 2008, Jiang et al., 2000a, Parasuraman et al., 1991a, Riel et al., 2003, Wixom and Todd, 2005, Venkatesh et al., 2003, Mao and Palvia, 2006, Gwebu and Wang, 2011, Davis, 1989, Davis et al., 1989, Yu et al., 2005, Luo et al., 2011, Taylor and Todd, 1995a, Carter and Bélanger, 2005, Pavlou, 2003, Sheikhshoaei and Oloumi, 2011, Anandarajan et al., 2000, Wu et al., 2008, Vijayasarathy, 2004, Tan et al., 2003)	47
Design	(Semeijn et al., 2005, Smith, 2001, Riel et al., 2003, Wixom and Todd, 2005, Mahinda and Whitworth, 2006, Loonam and O'Loughlin, 2008, Li et al., 2006, Mittal and Tsiros, 2007, Tsai et al., 2006, Tan et al., 2003)	45
Trust	(McKnight et al., 2002b, Li et al., 2006, Carter and Bélanger, 2005, Bélanger and Carter, 2008, Semeijn et al., 2005, Zhang and Prybutok, 2005, Tan et al., 2003, Parasuraman et al., 1991a, Jiang et al., 2000a, Ruyter et al., 2001, Shachaf and Oltmann, 2007, Parasuraman et al., 1988, Riel et al., 2003, Mahinda and Whitworth, 2006, Lu et al., 2003, Vijayasarathy, 2004, Torkzadeh and Dhillon, 2002, Salisbury et al., 2001, Pikkarainen et al., 2004, Janda et al., 2002, Wolfinbarger and Gilly, 2003, Collier and Bienstock, 2006, Anthopoulos et al., 2007, Shareef et al., 2009, Yoo and Donthu, 2001, Yenisey et al., 2005, Shin, 2010)	57
Performance	(Wixom and Todd, 2005, Lu et al., 2003, Loonam and O'Loughlin, 2008, Venkatesh et al., 2003, Li et al., 2006, Al-Gahtani and King, 1999, Mosbeh and Soliman, 2008, Semeijn et al., 2005, Janda et al., 2002, Torkzadeh and Dhillon, 2002, Mahinda and Whitworth, 2006, Riel et al., 2003, Ruyter et al., 2001, Ko, 1990, Leong, 1997, Stephanie et al., 2008, Premkumar and Bhattacherjee, 2008, Luo et al., 2011, Lu, 2001, Lu and Zhang, 2003, Dwivedi et al., 2006, Tan et al., 2003, Taylor and Todd, 1995a, Dickerson and Gentry, 1983, Pedersen, 2005, Pavlou, 2003, Davis, 1989, Davis et al., 1989)	73
Security	(Torkzadeh and Dhillon, 2002, Zhang and Prybutok, 2005, McKnight et al., 2002b, Li et al., 2006, Mahinda and Whitworth, 2006, Smith, 2001, Vijayasarathy, 2004, Lu et al., 2003, Janda et al., 2002, Wolfinbarger and Gilly, 2003, Collier and Bienstock, 2006, Anthopoulos et al., 2007, Shareef et al., 2009, Yoo and Donthu, 2001, Buchanan et al., 2007, Metzger, 2004, Shin, 2010, Pikkarainen et al., 2004)	37

the survey with their abbreviations used for further analysis. The experts also suggested using 7-point scale to test the validity of the proposed instrument because its values are widely spread in comparison to 5 points scale and respondents would have more choices to select.

Pilot Study

A pilot study was conducted before distribution of the final questionnaire to determine the response rate and any disharmony within the questions such as questionnaire format and questions' understandability. Survey was sent to thirty (Luo et al., 2006) postgraduate students in Malaysia by email. The majority of

Table 9. E-service satisfaction survey items

	Construct	Abbreviation	Item
1	Design	DESIGN1	I am satisfied with design of e-service.
2		DESIGN2	Websites are organized logically and by anticipated user need.
3		DESIGN3	I believe that e-service would be employed in my best interest.
4		DESIGN4	E-service attractively displays Information.
5	User Friendliness	FRIEND1	Learning to use e-service is easy to me.
6		FRIEND2	E-service is easy to use.
7		FRIEND3	It is easy to get to do what I want it to do.
8	Performance	PERF1	E-service delivers product/ service in a way that I like.
9		PERF2	It is fast to use e-service.
10		PERF3	I successfully use e-service to perform my job.
11		PERF4	It is not too costly to use e-services.
12		PERF5	E-service provides service in a timely fashion.
13		PERF6	E-service makes information very accessible.
14		PERF7	E-service can be adapted to meet a variety of needs.
15	Usability	USAB1	I accomplish my tasks easier and quicker with e-service.
16		USAB2	Using e-service improves the quality of the work I do.
17		USAB3	Using e-service is helpful and influential.
18		USAB4	The advantages of e-service are important to me.
19	Trust	TRUST1	I feel assured that legal and technological structures adequately protect me from problems on the e-service.
20		TRUST2	E-service has the ability to perform the promised service dependably and accurately.
21		TRUST3	In general, e-services are robust and safe.
22	Security	SEC1	I believe that my confidential information is kept secure.
23		SEC2	There is an appropriate procedure in e-services to prevent accidental loss of data.
24		SEC3	When using e-service, I am sure that certain managerial and technical procedures exist to protect my personal information.
25		SEC4	In e-service, if a certain transaction is performed, it never could be denied by party.
26	Training	TRAIN1	I have received training from my college/company/self/other to use e-service.
27		TRAIN2	I would use e-service if I received training about how to use it.
28	Quality	QUAL1	Overall, e-service works very well technically.
29		QUAL2	The overall quality of e-service appears to me as being good.
30		QUAL3	The quality of e-service is very good.
31	Satisfaction	SAT1	All things considered, I am very satisfied with e-service.
32		SAT2	I am satisfied with my previous using e-service experience.
33		SAT3	Overall speaking, the effect of using e-service makes me feel satisfied,

the respondents reported that the questionnaire was easily understandable and required 15-20 minutes for completion.

Data Collection

Data were collected from e-service users in Malaysia using online survey. The survey website has been introduced to 2450 e-service users and 426 responses have been received (response rate of 17%). The response rate is close to the study done by Wixom and Todd (2005) as 21%. The collected data was filtered and improper responses were removed. The remaining data was 403 valid responses which were taken as the sample of the study.

The first part of the survey was about the demographic information of participants such as age, gender and education. There were more female respondents than male with almost 60% than 40%. Moreover, the majority of respondents were young generation aging 20-29 with almost half participants and then 30-39 with almost one-third of respondents. Almost half of the e-service users are using e-service for more than five years and the interesting point is that all respondents have experience using e-services. Besides, more than two-third of respondents are using e-service once or more than once a day. Table 10 presents the descriptive analysis of the items related to all constructs included in the research.

Reliability of Final Survey

In the case, Likert Scales are utilized for a study; Cronbach Alphas are considered the most appropriate measures of reliability (Robinson, 2009). As it is shown in Table 10, the Cronbach's Alphas range from 0.907 to .912, thus, the constructs are deemed to have adequate reliability. Furthermore, to measure the sampling adequacy, a KMO and Bartlett test was conducted. The KMO overall (0.883) is higher than the conventional cut-off point (0.60) and the Bartlett has a significant value (p = .000). This indicates that the correlations observed in the variables are likely to contain common variance and the data are likely to factor well (Wu 2009).

Instrument Validation

Factor analysis using PCA was applied with SPSS software to verify the construct validity (discriminant and convergent validity). Table 11 presents the eigenvalues and explained total variance for the extracted factors. According to Straub, et al. (2004), only factors with eigenvalues greater than one are considered for further analysis. Results indicate that all nine factors possess eigenvalues greater than one. Results from the analysis also suggest that no extracted new factor consisted of an eigenvalue greater than 1.

Table 12 presents the factor loadings for all nine factors. Results clearly suggest that all nine components loaded on their corresponding factor. Items loaded above 0.40 are considered to be remained in the survey instrument. Also, items cross loading above 0.40 are deleted, thus items DESGN3, FRND1, TRUST3, SAT2 and TRAIN2 are removed. Therefore, both convergent and discriminant validity met the baseline criteria in information system research.

In this chapter, concepts and special characteristics of e-service satisfaction based on the existing literature has discussed. It discussed the concept of e-service satisfaction considering its features and dimensions. In order to develop a survey instrument to assess customer satisfaction of e-services, it examined various research findings on e-service satisfaction dimensions in which they categorized through

Table 10. Cronbach's Alpha statistics and descriptive analysis for final satisfaction survey

	Scale Mean if Item Deleted	Scale Variance if Item Deleted	Corrected Item-Total Correlation	Cronbach's Alpha if Item Deleted	Mean	Std. Deviation	Variance
DESIGN1	166.01	448.413	.352	.910	4.62	1.396	1.948
DESIGN2	164.67	443.902	.506	.908	5.96	1.210	1.463
DESIGN3	165.58	444.533	.499	.908	5.05	1.198	1.435
DESIGN4	165.69	438.105	.541	.907	4.94	1.377	1.897
FRIEND1	165.49	443.012	.493	.908	5.14	1.277	1.631
FRIEND2	165.72	441.771	.544	.908	4.91	1.220	1.487
FRIEND3	165.07	439.542	.580	.907	5.56	1.237	1.531
PERF1	166.36	460.668	.107	.916	4.27	1.672	2.796
PERF2	165.69	442.638	.520	.908	4.94	1.234	1.522
PERF3	165.56	442.894	.515	.908	5.07	1.234	1.522
PERF4	165.86	440.447	.469	.909	4.77	1.454	2.116
PERF5	165.84	442.965	.435	.909	4.79	1.427	2.037
PERF6	165.57	444.634	.457	.909	5.06	1.290	1.663
PERF7	165.64	443.733	.545	.908	4.99	1.138	1.296
USAB1	165.00	443.876	.451	.909	5.63	1.341	1.797
USAB2	165.07	441.188	.520	.908	5.56	1.296	1.680
USAB3	165.27	444.122	.470	.909	5.36	1.282	1.645
USAB4	166.00	447.408	.393	.910	4.63	1.323	1.751
TRUST1	165.79	442.716	.469	.909	4.84	1.351	1.824
TRUST2	165.18	445.439	.509	.908	5.45	1.137	1.293
TRUST3	165.98	449.788	.300	.912	4.65	1.503	2.259
SEC1	165.67	442.441	.521	.908	4.96	1.241	1.541
SEC2	165.34	445.791	.464	.909	5.29	1.219	1.486
SEC3	165.18	442.021	.545	.908	5.45	1.207	1.457
SEC4	164.83	443.018	.582	.907	5.80	1.100	1.209
TRAIN1	164.96	445.130	.513	.908	5.67	1.143	1.307
TRAIN2	164.72	444.068	.547	.908	5.91	1.121	1.256
QUAL1	164.83	447.915	.402	.910	5.80	1.271	1.616
QUAL2	165.05	441.761	.531	.908	5.58	1.248	1.558
QUAL3	164.89	441.346	.532	.908	5.74	1.263	1.596
SAT1	165.46	447.463	.446	.909	5.17	1.182	1.396
SAT2	166.36	444.141	.403	.910	4.27	1.464	2.144
SAT3	165.83	444.200	.461	.909	4.80	1.301	1.693

Table 11. Total variance explained for final survey

Component	Initial Eigenvalues			Extraction Sums of Squared Loadings			Rotation Sums of Squared Loadings		
	Total	% of Vari	Cum %	Total	% of Var	Cum %	Total	% of Var	Cum %
1	9.162	27.764	27.764	9.162	27.764	27.764	3.725	11.289	11.289
2	2.862	8.672	36.435	2.862	8.672	36.435	2.826	8.565	19.854
3	1.671	5.064	41.500	1.671	5.064	41.500	2.702	8.188	28.042
4	1.395	4.226	45.726	1.395	4.226	45.726	2.571	7.791	35.834
5	1.293	3.917	49.643	1.293	3.917	49.643	2.090	6.334	42.167
6	1.188	3.599	53.242	1.188	3.599	53.242	2.037	6.174	48.341
7	1.122	3.400	56.642	1.122	3.400	56.642	1.967	5.960	54.302
8	1.092	3.310	59.952	1.092	3.310	59.952	1.643	4.978	59.279
9	1.021	3.094	63.046	1.021	3.094	63.046	1.243	3.767	63.046
10	.984	2.983	66.029						
11	.907	2.748	68.776						
12	.803	2.434	71.210						
13	.740	2.241	73.452						
14	.695	2.106	75.558						
15	.636	1.927	77.485						
16	.616	1.866	79.350						
17	.597	1.810	81.161						
18	.580	1.757	82.917						
19	.546	1.655	84.573						
20	.514	1.556	86.129						
21	.489	1.483	87.612						
22	.466	1.414	89.026						
23	.460	1.393	90.418						
24	.420	1.273	91.691						
25	.406	1.230	92.921						
26	.381	1.155	94.076						
27	.372	1.127	95.203						
28	.316	.959	96.162						
29	.293	.889	97.051						
30	.273	.826	97.877						
31	.251	.760	98.637						
32	.236	.716	99.353						
33	.214	.647	100.000						

Extraction Method: Principal Component Analysis.

Table 12. Rotated Component Matrix for final survey

	Component								
	1	**2**	**3**	**4**	**5**	**6**	**7**	**8**	**9**
PERF1	.738	-.123	.079	.196	.149	.044	.105	.040	-.092
PERF2	.677	.030	-.029	.291	.158	-.053	.145	.265	-.086
PERF3	.620	.312	-.008	-.068	.138	-.020	.186	.086	.113
PERF4	.684	.156	.185	.359	.037	.140	-.017	-.036	.053
PERF5	.654	.174	.163	-.051	.027	.325	.023	-.001	.296
PERF6	.489	.157	.166	.386	.020	.264	-.090	.126	-.118
PERF7	.446	.203	.307	.164	-.038	.391	.140	-.129	-.039
DESGN1	.080	.771	.221	.132	.144	.117	.101	.049	-.133
DESGN2	.069	.740	.179	.064	.124	-.006	.152	.123	.116
DESGN3	.163	.622	-.035	.276	.048	.457	.195	.016	.020
DESGN4	.112	.479	.086	-.066	.198	.171	.379	.283	.123
USAB1	.081	.269	.587	.056	.145	.112	.021	.311	.112
USAB2	.145	.004	.768	.002	.157	.222	.058	.068	-.012
USAB3	-.078	.190	.495	.344	-.045	.168	.395	-.045	.090
USAB4	.068	.142	.729	.015	.185	.083	.116	.096	-.083
SEC1	.340	.089	.180	.595	.202	-.042	.039	.106	-.032
SEC2	.118	.132	.015	.756	.194	.075	.159	-.046	.180
SEC3	.371	.075	.029	.464	.011	.355	.154	.221	-.020
SEC4	.397	-.016	.014	.646	-.007	.170	-.204	.225	-.124
FRND1	.183	.445	.201	-.150	.567	-.078	.095	.002	.080
FRND2	.036	.168	.145	.312	.595	.177	.227	.134	-.026
FRND3	.173	.029	.113	.183	.806	.180	.037	-.017	-.012
TRUST1	.074	.170	.281	.003	.256	.561	.176	.221	-.131
TRUST2	.232	.026	.296	.183	.233	.641	.001	.081	.079
TRUST3	.465	-.048	-.090	.236	.141	.415	.201	.291	-.050
QUAL1	.031	.251	.119	-.036	-.019	.164	.628	.020	.250
QUAL2	.231	.235	-.029	.056	.121	.179	.619	.193	.032
QUAL3	.192	-.061	.232	.091	.243	-.162	.569	-.058	-.253
SAT1	.192	.092	.239	.050	.024	.240	-.019	.719	.092
SAT2	.116	.248	.222	.090	.487	.149	.022	.427	.044
SAT3	.032	.166	.112	.243	.062	-.113	.386	.541	-.010
TRAIN1	.021	.039	.011	.054	.021	-.044	.083	.068	.899
TRAIN2	.093	.442	.493	.160	-.025	-.160	.005	.100	.078

exploratory factor analysis. It is also provided a concluding big data table on them. Thus, thirty-six dimensions of satisfaction have been extracted from previous studies in the field of information system (accessibility, aesthetic design, appearance of website, assurance, credibility, currency, communication, content quality, customer service, customer support, customization, delivery, empathy, ease of use, efficiency, enjoyment, flexibility, fulfillment, functionality, information accuracy, information quality, navigation, processing speed, recovery, relevancy, responsiveness, reliability, security, site attraction, site presentation, structure and layout, tangibility, timeliness, user control, and web usability). Then exploratory factor analysis has been carried out to reduce and categorized the satisfaction dimensions. Therefore, eight factors namely (1) Performance, (2) Trust, (3) User Friendly, (4) Usability, (5) Design, (6) Security, (7) Training and (8) Quality proposed as the main constructs to measure customer satisfaction of e-service. In the final step, in order to develop the final e–service satisfaction survey below steps were followed:

- A literature review has been done to extract the related items for each factor and new questions were designed;
- Content Validity Survey was conducted to develop the final survey. A total of 12 experts were identified and the content validity questionnaire was then sent to them. For each item, the CVR was evaluated and estimated for a statistical significance level of 0.05;
- Factor analysis as a statistical technique was employed to confirm the construct validity utilizing principal component analysis with varimax rotation method. Both the discriminant validity (loading of at least 0.40, no cross-loading of items above 0.40) and convergent validity (eigenvalues of 1, loading of at least 0.40, items that load on posited constructs) were calculated;
- Reliability which refers to the consistency across the parts of a measurement tool, applied using Cronbach Alpha coefficient that is known as the most proper internal consistency measure while using Likert scales. All items have the minimum internal consistency coefficient of .70.

After conducting above mentioned steps, the final survey instrument to assess customer satisfaction of e-services includes 28 items.

FUTURE RESEARCH DIRECTIONS

This research surveyed in Malaysia, and they may not be representative of the entire population so further quantitative studies on e-service satisfaction are needed. Besides, e-service satisfaction could be investigated in other countries. Besides, the sample size for this study was 403 e-service users and this may affect the statistical power of the findings. However, the results seem to suggest that the sampling method used has a good exploratory power. Nevertheless, future studies may be conducted with a larger sample size to gain a higher statistical power of the findings.

CONCLUSION

Findings indicated that performance (including; accessibility, delivery, ease of use, flexibility, fulfillment, functionality, and processing), trust (including; assurance, credibility and reliability), usability (including; efficiency and web usability), user friendliness (including; ease of use and convenience), design (including; aesthetic design, appearance of website, customization, navigation, site presentation, site attraction, and structure and layout), training, security and quality are most important characteristics of e-service satisfaction in which should be taken into consideration in order to have high customer satisfaction of provided e-service.

Measuring the customer satisfaction of e-service is the concern of both researchers and practitioners. Thus, some tools have been developed to assess customer satisfaction but there is no specific theoretical framework that defines the e-service satisfaction construct and its dimensions consistently.

Service-centred firms may give more attention to their customer satisfaction in eight e-service canon of performance, trust, design, usability, user friendliness, training, security and quality. However, for more specific gauging of service maturity, users, IT experts, and other audiences can refer to sub-clusters of each canon. Therefore, it will be valuable to find out the customer expectation and fill gaps to investigate customer satisfaction. The findings will help e-service policy makers in which they can increase their customers' satisfaction.

On the other hand, the knowledge generated from this research can be used as a platform for e-service providers on how to increase the customer satisfaction of their e-service. With careful strategy implementation by policy makers, agencies, and system developers, high quality and secure e-services could be successfully implemented to increase customer satisfaction. However, additional steps need to be taken to encourage users to use e-service more frequently.

ACKNOWLEDGMENT

This research was supported by Research Club & Hamta Academy at Hamta Group | Hamta Business Solution Sdn Bhd; and Tablokar Co | Switchgear Manufacturer.

REFERENCES

Al-Gahtani, S., & King, M. (1999). Attitudes. Satisfaction and usage: Factors contributing to each in the acceptance of information technology. *Behaviour and Information Technology Studies: Special Issue on Research Methodology*, *18*(4), 277–297. doi:10.1080/014492999119020

Al-Kasasbeh, M. M., Dasgupta, S., & Al-Faouri, A. H. (2011). Factors Affecting E-Service Satisfaction. *Communications of the IBIMA*, *2011*, 12.

Alawadhi, S., & Morris, A. (2008). The Use of the UTAUT Model in the Adoption of E-government Services in Kuwait. *Proceedings of the 41st Hawaii International Conference on System Sciences*, 219 - 230. 10.1109/HICSS.2008.452

Alawneh, A., Al-Refai, H., & Batiha, K. (2013). Measuring user satisfaction from e-Government services: Lessons from Jordan. *Government Information Quarterly*, *30*(3), 277–288. doi:10.1016/j.giq.2013.03.001

Anandarajan, M., Igbaria, M., & Anakwe, U. P. (2000). Technology Acceptance in the Banking Industry: A prospective from a less developed country. *Information Technology & People*, *13*(4), 298–312. doi:10.1108/09593840010359491

Anderson, R. E., & Srinivasan, S. S. (2003). E-satisfaction and eloyalty: A contingency framework. *Psychology and Marketing*, *§§§*, 20.

Anthopoulos, L. G., Siozos, P., & Tsoukalas, L. A. (2007). pplying Participatory Design and Collaboration in Digital Public Services for Discovering and Re-designing E-government Services. *Government Information Quarterly*, *24*(2), 353–376. doi:10.1016/j.giq.2006.07.018

Ariff, M. S. M., Yun, L. O., Zakuan, N., & Ismail, K. (2013). The Impacts of Service Quality and Customer Satisfaction on Customer Loyalty in Internet Banking. *Procedia: Social and Behavioral Sciences*, *81*, 469–473. doi:10.1016/j.sbspro.2013.06.462

Bailey, J. E., & Pearson, S. W. (1983). Development of a tool for measuring and analyzing computer user satisfaction. *Management Science*, *29*(5), 530–544. doi:10.1287/mnsc.29.5.530

Baroudi, J., & Orlikowski, W. J. (1988). A short-form measure of user information satisfaction: A psychometric evaluation and notes on use. *Journal of Management Information Systems*, *4*(4), 44–59. doi: 10.1080/07421222.1988.11517807

Bélanger, F., & Carter, L. (2008). Trust and risk in e-government adoption. *The Journal of Strategic Information Systems*, *17*(2), 165–176. doi:10.1016/j.jsis.2007.12.002

Bhattacherjee, A. (2001). An empirical analysis of the antecedents of electronic commerce service continuance. *Decision Support Systems*, *32*(2), 201–214. doi:10.1016/S0167-9236(01)00111-7

Bitner, M. J. (1990). Evaluating Service Encounters: The Effects of Physical Sur-roundings and Employee Responses. *Journal of Marketing*, *54*(2), 69–82. doi:10.1177/002224299005400206

Boulter, J. (2014). *How to build profitable customer relationships*. Academic Press.

Brensinger, R. P., & Lambert, D. M. (1990). Can the SERVQUAL Scale be Generalized to Business-to-Business Services? *Knowledge Development in Marketing1990 AMA's Summer Educators' Conference Proceedings*, 289.

Bressolles, G., Durrieu, F. & Senecal, S. (2014). A consumer typology base done-service quality and e-satisfaction. *Journal of Retailing and Consumer Services, 21*, 889-896.

Buchanan, T., Paine, C., Joinson, A. N., & Reips, U.-D. (2007). Development of measures of online privacy concern and protection for use on the internet. *Journal of the American Society for Information Science and Technology*, *58*(2), 157–165. doi:10.1002/asi.20459

Carter, L., & Bélanger, F. (2005). The utilization of e-government services: Citizen trust, innovation and acceptance factors. *Information Systems Journal*, *15*(1), 5–26. doi:10.1111/j.1365-2575.2005.00183.x

Chakraborty, S., & Sengupta, K. (2014). Structural equation modelling of determinants of customer satisfaction of mobile network providers: Case of Kolkata, India. *IIMB Management Review*, *§§§*, 1–15.

Chang, H. H., & Chen, S. W. (2008). The impact of customer interface quality, satisfaction and switching costs on e-loyalty: Internet experience as a moderator. *Computers in Human Behavior*, *24*(6), 2927–2944. doi:10.1016/j.chb.2008.04.014

Chen, L. D., Soliman, K. S., Mao, E., & Frolick, M. N. (2000). Measuring user satisfaction with data warehouses: An exploratory study. *Information & Management, 37*(3), 103–110. doi:10.1016/S0378-7206(99)00042-7

Chen, S.-C. (2012). The customersatisfaction–loyaltyrelationinaninteractivee-servicesetting: The mediators. *Journal of Retailing and Consumer Services, 19*, 202-210.

Cho, N., & Park, S. (2001). Development of Electronic Commerce User-Consumer Satisfaction Index (ECUSI) for Internet Shopping. *Industrial Management & Data Systems, 101*(8), 400–405. doi:10.1108/EUM0000000006170

Churchill, G. A. Jr. (1979). A paradigm for developing better measures of marketing constructs. *JMR, Journal of Marketing Research, 16*(1), 64–73. doi:10.1177/002224377901600110

Collier, J. E., & Bienstock, C. C. (2006). Measuring Service Quality in E-Retailing. *Journal of Service Research, 8*(3), 260–275. doi:10.1177/1094670505278867

Colwell, S. R., Aung, M., Kanetkar, V., & Holden, A. L. (2008). Toward a measure of service convenience: Multiple-item scale development and empirical test. *Journal of Services Marketing, 22*(2), 160–169. doi:10.1108/08876040810862895

Cristobal, E., & Flavian, C. & GUINALIU, M. (2007). Perceived E-Service Quality: Measurement Validation and Effects on Consumer Satisfaction and Website Loyalty. *Managing Service Quality, 17*, 317–340. doi:10.1108/09604520710744326

Davis, F. D. (1989). Perceived usefulness, perceived ease of use and user acceptance of information technology. *Management Information Systems Quarterly, 13*(3), 319–340. doi:10.2307/249008

Davis, F. D., Bagozzi, R. P., & Warshaw, P. R. (1989). User Acceptance of Computer Technology: A Comparison of two Theoretical models. *Management Science, 35*(8), 982–1003. doi:10.1287/mnsc.35.8.982

Debons, A., Ramage, W., & Orien, J. (1978). Effectiveness Model of Productivity. Research on Productivity Measurement Systems for Administrative Services: Computing and Information Services. NSF Grant APR-20546.

Delone, W. H., & McLean, E. R. (1992). Information systems success: The quest for the dependent variable. *Information Systems Research, 3*(1), 60–95. doi:10.1287/isre.3.1.60

Dickerson, M. D., & Gentry, J. W. (1983). Characteristics of adopters and non-adopters of home computers. *The Journal of Consumer Research, 10*(2), 225–235. doi:10.1086/208961

Doll, W. J., & Torkzadeh, G. (1988). The measure of end-user computing satisfaction. *Management Information Systems Quarterly, 12*(2), 259–274. doi:10.2307/248851

Dritsas, S., Gymnopoulos, L., Karyda, M., Balopoulos, T., Kokolakis, S., Lambrinoudakis, C. & Katsikas, S. (2006). A knowledge-based approach to security requirements for e-health applications. *The electronic Journal on Emerging Tools and Applications, In the Special Issue: Emerging Security Paradigms in the Knowledge Era, 2*.

Dwivedi, Y. K., Choudrie, J., & Brinkman, W.-P. (2006). Development of a survey instrument to examine consumer adoption of broadband. *Industrial Management & Data Systems*, *106*(5), 700–718. doi:10.1108/02635570610666458

Evanschitzky, H., Iyer, G. R., Hesse, R. J., & Ahlert, D. (2004). E-satisfaction: A Re-Examination. *Journal of Retailing*, *80*(3), 239–247. doi:10.1016/j.jretai.2004.08.002

Fabrigar, L. R., Wegener, D. T., Maccallum, R. C., & Strahan, E. J. (1999). Evaluating the use of exploratory factor analysis in psychological research. *Psychological Methods*, *4*(3), 272–299. doi:10.1037/1082-989X.4.3.272

Geng, X., & Chu, X. (2012). A new importance–performance analysis approach for customer satisfaction evaluation supporting PSS design. *Expert Systems with Applications*, *39*(1), 1492–1502. doi:10.1016/j.eswa.2011.08.038

George, D., & Mallery, P. (2003). *SPSS for Windows step by step: A simple guide and reference*. Boston: Allyn & Bacon.

Gorsuch, R. (1983). *Factor Analysis*. Hillsdale, NJ: Erlbaum.

Gummerus, J., Liljander, V., Pura, M., & Riel, A. V. (2004). Customer loyalty to content-basedWeb sites: The case of an online healthcare service. *Journal of Services Marketing*, *18*(3), 175–186. doi:10.1108/08876040410536486

Gwebu, K. L., & Wang, J. (2011). Adoption of Open Source Software: The role of social identification. *Decision Support Systems*, *51*(1), 220–229. doi:10.1016/j.dss.2010.12.010

Hair, J., Anderson, R., Tatham, R., & Black, W. (1995a). *Multivariate data analysis*. New Jersey: Prentice-Hall Inc.

Hair, J. F., Anderson, R. E., Tatham, R. L., & Black, W. C. (1998). *Multivariate Data Analysis*. Englewood Cliffs, NJ: Prentice Hall.

Hernandez, B., Jimenez, J., & Martin, M. J. (2011). Age, gender and income: Do they really moderate online shopping behaviour? *Online Information Review*, *35*(1), 113–133. doi:10.1108/14684521111113614

Hoffman, K. D., & Bateson, J. E. G. (2010). *Services Marketing: Concepts, Strategies*. Cengage Learning.

Huang, J. H., Yang, C., Jin, B. H., & Chiu, H. (2004). Measuring satisfaction with business-to-employee systems. *Computers in Human Behavior*, *20*(1), 17–35. doi:10.1016/S0747-5632(03)00047-5

Huck, S. W. (2007). *Reading Statistics and Research*. Allyn & Bacon.

Hussain, R., Nasser, A. A., & Hussain, Y. K. (2014). (in press). Service quality and customer satisfaction of a UAE-based airline: An empirical investigation. *Journal of Air Transport Management*, 1–9.

IS07498-2 (2004). Information Processing Systems – Open Systems Interconnection – Basic Reference Model – Part 2: Security Architecture. International Organization for Standardization.

Ives, B., Olson, M. H., & Baroudi, J. J. (1983). The measurement of user information satisfaction. *Communications of the ACM*, *26*(10), 785–793. doi:10.1145/358413.358430

Janda, S., Trocchia, P. J., & Gwinner, K. P. (2002). Consumer perceptions of Internet retail service quality. *International Journal of Service Industry Management*, *13*(5), 412–431. doi:10.1108/09564230210447913

Jiang, J. J., Klein, G., & Crampton, S. M. (2000a). A Note on SERVQUAL Reliability and Validity in Information System Service Quality Measurement. *Decision Sciences*, *31*(3), 725–744. doi:10.1111/j.1540-5915.2000.tb00940.x

Johnson, M. D., Anderson, E. W., & Fornell, C. (1995). Rational and adaptive performance expectations in a customer satisfaction framework. *The Journal of Consumer Research*, *21*(4), 128–140. doi:10.1086/209428

Johnston, R. (1997). Identifying the critical determinants of service quality in retail banking: Importance and effect. *International Journal of Bank Marketing*, *15*(4), 111–116. doi:10.1108/02652329710189366

Jun, M., Yang, Z., & Kim, D. (2004). Customers' perceptions of online retailing service quality and their satisfaction. *International Journal of Quality & Reliability Management*, *21*(8), 817–840. doi:10.1108/02656710410551728

Kline, P. (1997). *An Easy Guide to Factor Analysis*. London: Routledge.

Ko, K. H. (1990). Promotion of IT Applications in Singapore: Policy Issues and Strategic Thrusts. In Information Technology and Singapore Society: Trends, Policies and Applications. Singapore: Singapore University Press.

Kraiser, H. (1958). The varimax criterion for analytic rotation in factor analysis. *Psychometrika*, *23*(3), 187–200. doi:10.1007/BF02289233

Lai, I. K. W., & Lai, D. C. F. (2013). User acceptance of mobile commerce: An empirical study in Macau. *International Journal of Systems Science*, *45*(6), 1321–1331. doi:10.1080/00207721.2012.761471

Lean, O. K., Zailani, S., Ramayah, T., & Fernando, Y. (2009). Factors influencing intention to use e-government services among citizens in Malaysia. *International Journal of Information Management*, *29*(6), 458–475. doi:10.1016/j.ijinfomgt.2009.03.012

Lederer, A. L., Maupin, D. J., Sena, M. P., & Zhuang, Y. (2000). The technology acceptance model and the World Wide Web. *Decision Support Systems*, *29*(3), 269–282. doi:10.1016/S0167-9236(00)00076-2

Leech, N., Barrett, K., & Morgan, G. A. (2005). SPSS for intermediate statistics: Use and interpretation. London: Lawrence Erlbaum Associates.

Legris, P., Ingham, J., & Collerette, P. (2003). Why do people use information technology? A critical review of the technology acceptance model. *Information & Management*, *40*(3), 191–204. doi:10.1016/S0378-7206(01)00143-4

Leong, Y. L. (1997). ECH Programme Hits Its Stride. *Computerworld*, *§§§*, 3.

Li, X., Hess, T. J., & Valacich, J. S. (2006). Using Attitude and Social Influence to Develop an Extended Trust Model for Information Systems. *The Data Base for Advances in Information Systems*, *37*(2-3), 108–124. doi:10.1145/1161345.1161359

Loonam, M., & O'Loughlin, D. (2008). Exploring e-service quality: A study of Irish online banking. *Marketing Intelligence & Planning*, *26*(7), 759–780. doi:10.1108/02634500810916708

Lu, J. (2001). Measuring cost/benefits of e-business applications and customer satisfaction. *Proceedings of the 2nd International Web Conference*, 139-147.

Lu, J., Yu, C. S., Liu, C., & Yao, J. E. (2003). Technology acceptance model for wireless Internet. *Internet Research*, *13*(3), 206–222. doi:10.1108/10662240310478222

Lu, J., & Zhang, G. (2003). Cost benefit factor analysis in e-services. *International Journal of Service Industry Management*, *14*(5), 570–595. doi:10.1108/09564230310500237

Luo, M. M., Chea, S., & Chen, J.-S. (2011). Web-based information service adoption: A comparison of the motivational model and the uses and gratifications theory. *Decision Support Systems*, *51*(1), 21–30. doi:10.1016/j.dss.2010.11.015

Luo, M. M.-L., Remus, W., & Chea, S. (2006). Technology Acceptance of Internet-based Information Services: An Integrated Model of TAM and U&G Theory. *Proceedings of the Twelfth Americas Conference on Information Systems*, 1139-1150.

Mahinda, E., & Whitworth, B. (2006). *Using The WOSP Model To Improve End-User Productivity Of Information Systems*. International Conference on Business IT (BIZIT 2006): Collaborating with ICT Innovations for Business Survival, Kuala Lumpur, Malaysia.

Manasra, E. A. A., Zaid, M. K. S. A., & Taherqutaishat, F. (2013). Investigating the Impact of Website Quality on Consumers' Satisfaction in Jordanian Telecommunication Sector. *Arab Economic and Business Journal, 8*, 31-37.

Mao, E., & Palvia, P. (2006). Testing an Extended Model of IT Acceptance in the Chinese Cultural Context. *The Data Base for Advances in Information Systems*, *37*(2-3), 20–32. doi:10.1145/1161345.1161351

Mchaney, R., & Cronan, T. P. (1998). Computer simulation success: on the use of the end-user computing satisfaction instrument: a comment. *Decision Sciences*, *29*(2), 525–534. doi:10.1111/j.1540-5915.1998.tb01589.x

Mcknight, D. H., Choudhury, V., & Kacmar, C. (2002b). Developing and Validating Trust Measures for e-Commerce: An Integrative Typology. *Information Systems Research*, *13*(3), 334–359. doi:10.1287/isre.13.3.334.81

Metzger, M. (2004). Privacy, trust, and disclosure: Exploring barriers to electronic commerce. *Journal of Computer-Mediated Communication*, *9*(4), 9. doi:10.1111/j.1083-6101.2004.tb00292.x

Mittal, V., & Tsiros, M. (2007). Customer Loyalty in Electronically Mediated Environments. *Journal of Value Chain Management*, *1*, 80–109.

Montesdioca, G. P. Z., & Maçada, A. C. G. (2014). Measuring User Satisfaction with Information Security Practices. *Computers & Security*.

Moore, N. (2006). *How to do research: a practical guide to designing and managing research projects*. London: Facet Publishing.

Mosbeh, R., & Soliman, K. S. (2008). An exploratory analysis of factors affecting users' adoption of corporate intranet; A Tunisian study. *Management Research News*, *31*(5), 375–385. doi:10.1108/01409170810865172

Muylle, S., Moenert, R., & Despontin, M. (2004). The conceptualization and empirical validation of website user satisfaction. *Information & Management*, *41*(5), 543–560. doi:10.1016/S0378-7206(03)00089-2

NIST-SPECIAL-PUBLICATION-800-16. (1998). *Information Technology Security Training Requirements: A Role-and Performance-Based Model*. Gaithersburg: National Institute of Standards and Technology.

Nunnally, J. (1978). *Psychometric Theory*. New York, NY: McGraw-Hill.

Ok, S.-J. & Shon, J.-H. (2006). The Determinant of Internet Banking Usage Behavior in Korea: A Comparison of Two Theoretical Models. *CollECTeR '06*.

Oliver, R. L. (1980). A cognitive model of the antecedents and consequences of satisfaction decisions. *JMR, Journal of Marketing Research*, *17*(4), 460–469. doi:10.1177/002224378001700405

Oliver, R. L. (1997). *Satisfaction: A Behavioral Perspective on the Consumer*. New York: McGraw-Hill.

Parasuraman, A., Berry, L. L., & Zeithaml, V. A. (1991a). Refinement and Reassessment of the SERVQUAL Scale. *Journal of Retailing*, *67*, 420–450.

Parasuraman, A., Zeithaml, V. A., & Berry, L. L. (1988). SERVQUAL: A multi-item scale for measuring consumer perceptions of service quality. *Journal of Retailing*, *64*, 2–40.

Pavlou, P. (2003). Consumer acceptance of electronic commerce: Integrating trust and risk with the technology acceptance model. *International Journal of Electronic Commerce*, *7*, 69–103.

Pedersen, P. E. (2005). Adoption of mobile Internet services: An exploratory study of mobile commerce early adopters. *Journal of Organizational Computing and Electronic Commerce*, *15*(3), 203–222. doi:10.120715327744joce1503_2

Pett, M. A., Lackey, N. R., & Sullivan, J. J. (2003). *Making Sense of Factor Analysis: The use of factor analysis for instrument development in health care research*. Sage Publications Inc. doi:10.4135/9781412984898

Pikkarainen, T., Pikkarainen, K., Karjaluoto, H., & Pahnila, S. (2004). Consumer acceptance of online banking: An extension of the technology acceptance model. *Internet Research*, *14*(3), 224–235. doi:10.1108/10662240410542652

Premkumar, G., & Bhattacherjee, A. (2008). Explaining information technology usage: A test of competing models. *Omega*, *36*(1), 64–75. doi:10.1016/j.omega.2005.12.002

Ramasubbu, N., Mithas, S., & Krishnan, M. (2008). High tech, high touch: The effect of employee skills and customer heterogeneity on customer satisfaction with enterprise system support services. *Decision Support Systems*, *44*(2), 509–523. doi:10.1016/j.dss.2007.06.005

Riel, A. C. R. V., Semeijn, J., & Pauwels, P. (2003). Online Travel Service Quality: The Importance of Pre-transaction Services. METEOR, Maastricht research school of Economics of Technology and Organizations.

Robinson, J. (2009). Triandis theory of interpersonal behaviour in understanding software privace behaviour in the South African context (Masters degree). University of the Witwatersrand.

Ruyter, K. D., Wetzels, M., & Kleijnen, M. (2001). Customer adoption of e-service: An experimental study. *International Journal of Service Industry Management, 12*(2), 184–207. doi:10.1108/09564230110387542

Ryan Nelson, R., Michael, W. K., & Cheney, P. H. (1991). An Empirical Re-Examination of the Relationship among Training, Ability, and the Acceptance of Information Technology. *SIGCPR '91 Proceedings of the 1991 conference on SIGCPR*, 177-186.

Salisbury, W. D., Pearson, R. A., Pearson, A. W., & Miller, D. W. (2001). Perceived security and World Wide Web purchase intention. *Industrial Management & Data Systems, 101*(4), 165–176. doi:10.1108/02635570110390071

Saraph, J. V., Benson, P. G., & Schroeder, R. G. (1989). An instrument for measuring the critical factors of quality management. *Decision Sciences, 20*(4), 810–829. doi:10.1111/j.1540-5915.1989.tb01421.x

Saxe, R., & Weitx, B. A. (1982). The SOCO Scale: A Measure of the Customer Orientation of Sales people. *Journal of Marketing, 19*(3), 343–351. doi:10.1177/002224378201900307

Semeijn, J., Riel, A. C. R. V., Birgelen, M. J. H. V., & Streukens, S. (2005). E-services and offline fulfilment: How e-loyalty is created. *Managing Service Quality, 15*(2), 182–194. doi:10.1108/09604520510585361

Shachaf, P., & Oltmann, S. M. (2007). E-quality and e-service equality. *Proceedings of the 40th Hawaii International Conference on System Sciences.*

Shareef, M. A., Kumar, U., Kumar, V., & Dwivedi, Y. K. (2009). Identifying critical factors for adoption of e-government. *Electronic Government: An International Journal, 6*(1), 70–96. doi:10.1504/EG.2009.022594

Shareef, M. A., Kumar, V., Kumar, U., & Dwivedi, Y. K. (2011). e-Government Adoption Model (GAM): Differing service maturity levels. *Government Information Quarterly, 28*(1), 17–35. doi:10.1016/j.giq.2010.05.006

Sheikhshoaei, F., & Oloumi, T. (2011). Applying the technology acceptance model to Iranian engineering faculty libraries. *The Electronic Library, 29*(3), 367–378. doi:10.1108/02640471111141106

Shih, H.-P. (2004). Extended technology acceptance model of Internet utilization behavior. *Information & Management, 41*(6), 719–729. doi:10.1016/j.im.2003.08.009

Shin, D.-H. (2010). The effects of trust, security and privacy in social networking: A security-based approach to understand the pattern of adoption. *Interacting with Computers, 22*(5), 428–438. doi:10.1016/j.intcom.2010.05.001

Smith, A. G. (2001). Applying evaluation criteria to New Zealand government Web sites. *International Journal of Information Management, 21*(2), 137–149. doi:10.1016/S0268-4012(01)00006-8

Spreng, R. A., Mackenzie, S. B., & Olshavsky, R. W. (1996). A re-examination of the determinants of consumer research. *Journal of Marketing, 60*(3), 15–32. doi:10.2307/1251839

Srinivasan, S. S., Anderson, R., & Ponnavolu, K. (2002). Customer loyalty in e-commerce: An exploration of its antecedents and consequences. *Journal of Retailing*, *78*(1), 41–50. doi:10.1016/S0022-4359(01)00065-3

Stephanie, A. J., Abdul Nasir, Z., & Nur Fadziana, F. M. (2008). A Study on the Acceptance of E-Ticketing in Universiti Utara *Malaysia Bus Service*. *Knowledge Management International Conference*. Langkawi, Malaysia.

Stevens, J. (2001). *Applied multivariate statistics for the social sciences*. Mahwah, NJ: Lawrence Erlbaum.

Straub, D., Boudreau, M.-C., & Gefen, D. (2004). Validation guidelines for IS positivist research. *Communications of the Association for Information Systems*, *13*, 380–427. doi:10.17705/1CAIS.01324

Szymanski, D. M., & Hise, R. T. (2000). E-satisfaction: An initial examination. *Journal of Retailing*, *76*(3), 309–322. doi:10.1016/S0022-4359(00)00035-X

Taherdoost, H. (2017). Understanding of E-service Security Dimensions and its effect of Quality and Intention to Use. *Information and Computer Security, 25*(5), 535–559. doi:10.1108/ICS-09-2016-0074

Taherdoost, H. (2018a). Development of an adoption model to assess user acceptance of e-service technology: E-Service Technology Acceptance Model. *Behaviour & Information Technology*, *37*(2), 173–197. doi:10.1080/0144929X.2018.1427793

Taherdoost, H. (2018b). A Review of Technology Acceptance and Adoption Models and Theories. *Procedia Manufacturing Journal, 22*, 960–967. doi:10.1016/j.promfg.2018.03.137

Taherdoost, H. (2019). Electronic Service Quality Measurement (eSQM); Development of a Survey Instrument to Measure the Quality of E-Service. *International Journal of Intelligent Engineering Informatics*.

Taherdoost, H., & Hassan, A. (2020). Development of An E-Service Quality Model (eSQM) to Assess the Quality of E-Service. In Strategies and Tools for Managing Connected Customers. IGI Global. Doi:10.4018/978-1-5225-9697-4.ch011

Tan, K. C., Xie, M., & Li, Y. N. (2003). A service quality framework for Web-based information systems. *The TQM Magazine*, *15*(3), 164–172. doi:10.1108/09544780310469262

Taylor, S., & Todd, P. (1995a). Understanding information technology usage: A Test of Competing Models. *Information Systems Research*, *6*(2), 144–176. doi:10.1287/isre.6.2.144

Thomas, B., Basil, M., Christina, M., Fedra, K., & Manuela, T. (2013). Measuring Users Satisfaction of an e-Government portal. *Procedia Technology*, *8*, 371–377. doi:10.1016/j.protcy.2013.11.049

Thompson, B. (2004). *Exploratory and confirmatory factor analysis: understanding concepts and applications*. Washington, DC: American Psychological Association. doi:10.1037/10694-000

Tojib, D. R., Sugianto, L.-F., & Sendjaya, S. (2006). A Conceptual Model for B2E Portal User Satisfaction. *Proceedings of the International Conference on Business and Information.*

Torkzadeh, G., & Dhillon, G. (2002). Measuring factors that influence the success of Internet commerce. *Information Systems Research*, *13*(2), 187–204. doi:10.1287/isre.13.2.187.87

Tsai, H.-T., Huang, H.-C., Jaw, Y.-L., & Chen, W.-K. (2006). Why on-line customers remain with a particular e-retailer: An integrative model and empirical evidence. *Psychology and Marketing*, *23*(5), 447–464. doi:10.1002/mar.20121

Venkatesh, V., Morris, M. G., Davis, G. B., & Davis, E. D. (2003). User acceptance of information technology: Towards a unified view. *Management Information Systems Quarterly*, *27*(3), 425–478. doi:10.2307/30036540

Verdegem, P., & Verleye, G. (2009). User-centered e-Government in practice: A comprehensive model for measuring user satisfaction. *Government Information Quarterly*, *26*(3), 487–497. doi:10.1016/j.giq.2009.03.005

Verhoef, P., & Langerak, J. (2001). Possible determinants of consumers' adoption of electronic grocery shopping in the Netherlands. *Journal of Retailing and Consumer Services*, *8*(5), 275–285. doi:10.1016/S0969-6989(00)00033-3

Vijayasarathy, L. R. (2004). Predicting consumer intentions to use on-line shopping: The case for an augmented technology acceptance model. *Information & Management*, *41*(6), 747–762. doi:10.1016/j.im.2003.08.011

Whitley, B. E. (2002). *Principals of Research and Behavioural Science*. Boston: McGraw-Hill.

Winsted, K. F. (1997). The service experience in two cultures: A behavioral perspective. *Journal of Retailing*, *73*(3), 337–360. doi:10.1016/S0022-4359(97)90022-1

Wixom, B. H., & Todd, P. A. (2005). A theoretical integration of user satisfaction and technology acceptance. *Information Systems Research*, *16*(1), 85–102. doi:10.1287/isre.1050.0042

Wolfinbarger, M., & Gilly, M. C. (2003). Etailq: Dimensionalizing, Measuring and Predicting Etail Quality. *Journal of Retailing*, *79*(3), 183 198. doi:10.1016/S0022-4359(03)00034-4

Wu, Y.-L., Tao, Y.-H., & Yang, P.-C. (2008). The use of unified theory of acceptance and use of technology to confer the behavioral model of 3G mobile telecommunication users. *Journal of Statistics & Management Systems*, *11*(5), 919–949. doi:10.1080/09720510.2008.10701351

Yang, Z., & Jun, M. (2002). Consumer perception of e-service quality: From Internet purchaser and non-purchaser perspectives. *Journal of Business Strategies Huntsville*, *19*, 19–41.

Yang, Z., Peterson, R. T., & Cai, S. (2003). Services quality dimension of Internet retailing: An exploratory analysis. *Journal of Services Marketing Science*, *17*(7), 685–690. doi:10.1108/08876040310501241

Yenisey, M. M., Ozok, A. A., & Salvendy, G. (2005). Perceived security determinants in ecommerce among Turkish University students. *Behaviour & Information Technology*, *24*(4), 259–274. doi:10.1080/0144929042000320992

Yoo, B., & Donthu, N. (2001). Developing a scale to measure perceived quality of an Internet shopping site (SITEQUAL). *Quarterly Journal of Electronic Commerce*, *2*, 31–46.

Yoon, C. (2010). Antecedents of customer satisfaction with online banking in China: The effects of experience. *Computers in Human Behavior*, *26*(6), 1296–1304. doi:10.1016/j.chb.2010.04.001

Yu, J., Ha, I., Choi, M., & Rho, J. (2005). Extending the TAM for a t-commerce. *Information & Management*, *42*(7), 965–976. doi:10.1016/j.im.2004.11.001

Zavareh, F. B., Ariff, M. S. M., Jusoh, A., Zakuan, N., Bahari, A. Z., & Ashourian, M. (2012). e-Service quality dimensions and their effects on e-Customer satisfaction in internet banking services. *Procedia: Social and Behavioral Sciences*, *40*, 441–445. doi:10.1016/j.sbspro.2012.03.213

Zhang, X., & Prybutok, V. (2005). A consumer perspective of e-service quality. *IEEE Transactions on Engineering Management*, *52*(4), 461–477. doi:10.1109/TEM.2005.856568

Zhang, X., Prybutok, V., & Huang, A. (2006). An empirical study of factors affecting e-service satisfaction. *Human Systems Management*, *25*, 279–291.

Chapter 12
Business Communication, Digital Innovation, and Decoding Possibilities for the Student Receiver

Andrea S. Wallace
https://orcid.org/0000-0002-4684-5039
University of New England, Australia

ABSTRACT

Research conducted within the business communication milieu frequently reports that university graduates do not possess sufficient business communication skills. In this chapter, the author explores what communication skills the graduate of today may require for the business world of tomorrow. Klaus Schwab refers to tomorrow's business world as the Fourth Industrial Revolution, where digital innovation will amalgamate nearly every aspect of human lives, and where demographic change, coupled with industrial transitions and changing consumer requirements, necessitates the need for today's business communication student to learn how to be a creative problem solver, have emotional intelligence, be able to communicate across borders, and be able to persuasively communicate in a variety of written mediums. In light of Schwab's observations, this chapter explores why creativity, social skills, intercultural and written communication skills are so essential for today's business graduate.

INTRODUCTION

Communication skills are largely a neglected topic in studies of business education. This state of affairs requires explanation. Good communication are critical to the success of any enterprise and critical for their continued growth (Drucker, 1974). Well-honed communication can assist organisations to build positive workplace relationships, create effective teams, facilitate innovation and increase profits. Open and clear channels of information and instruction are critical to every aspect of the routine functioning of the modern enterprise. The effectiveness of internal communication plays has a major impact on

DOI: 10.4018/978-1-7998-5175-2.ch012

how well managers and employees within an organisation work together to reach organisational goals (Dwyer, 2016). Effective coordination of the modern enterprise depends on the use of multiple communication channels. These include written communication through memos or emails, oral communication through presentations or business pitches, and the management of non-verbal communication such as body language. In recent years, businesses began to make use of new forms of communication: social media for communication and Web-based project tools to get things done. In essence, good business communication is crucial process of effective human interchange (Bryer, 2011), coupled with the ability to combine discipline-specific knowledge to create the desired impact on a relevant professional community (Bhatia & Bhatia, 2011).

There is a growing body of empirical and theoretic research examining the importance of business communication. Accounting students' communication skills have been the subject of numerous studies over the years. Academic research in the topic dates back to at least 1947 (see, for example, Owen & Gerfen, 1951; O'Connell, et al., 2015). Professional bodies echo the sentiment that this is an important field. The ability to communicate well, both orally and in writing, is widely recognised an essential, non-negotiable attribute to a good accountant (American Accounting Association, 1968). This insight is supported by a significant body of research. Despite this realisation, there is growing evidence that effective communication skills are lacking among a significant proportion of accounting students and the profession as a whole (Maupin & May, 1993; Zaid & Abraham, 1994; Albrecht & Sack, 2000; Jones, 2011; O'Connell, et al., 2015; Riley & Simons, 2016).

Much of the previously cited research examines what may be referred to be as traditional communication skills. This research has focused largely on written expression, for example correct grammar, spelling and sentence construction. Other avenues of research have explored communication within the new media context. The ability for enterprises to communicate effectively using online social media is now regarded as a critical area. Businesses must master these new media if they are to remain competitive in an increasingly global marketplace (see for further, Crossman & Bordia, 2012; Hooker, 2012; Sharp & Brumberger, 2013). During the last two decades, there has been increasing awareness of the important role of creativity in designing the effective communication strategies which foster problem –solving and innovation (Howieson, 2003; Bruce, 2009). Social skills (now often referred to as Emotional Intelligence) have been a particularly fruitful area of enquiry since Daniel Goleman's 1995 seminal work (Goleman, 2005).

The critical importance of so-called 'soft skills' (including empathy with others, the ability to network, and practice emotional self-regulation) been the focus of extensive research in recent years (Ballantine & McCourt Larres, 2009; Daff, de Lange, & Jackling, 2012; Evans, Gbolahan, Wells, & Scott, 2012; Stretcher Sigmar, Hynes, & Hill, 2012). Researchers have concluded that the possession of superior skills in these areas is at least as important as professional and technical mastery to career success in business. This body of research has examined business communication from a variety of perspectives. Unfortunately, this research has often raised more problems and unanswered questions than it has proffered solutions (Parker, Guthrie, & Linacre, 2011). One overarching question remains for the academic in the field of business studies: what communication skills should be taught to today's university student?

This chapter will provide on an exploratory overview of the developments which necessitate a new conceptual perspective regarding academic business communication. It will look at how business communication must evolve to suit the ever-changing commercial environment. The chapter will also present some of the more significant problem areas in business communication. These are the topics which are most likely to provide fruitful areas for future academic research.

The present chapter is divided into five sections. The first will provide a brief conceptual overview of the background drivers which have shaped recent changes in the business environment. Building on the insights in the first section, section two will look at the implications of each of these driving factors. This second is split into three subsections. Each subsection will examine specific topics. These include creativity; emotional intelligence; and written communication. Solutions and recommendations to the questions raised in this section will be explored in the next section. Future research directions will be covered in section four. Section five will form a conclusion.

BACKGROUND

The preceding pages have outlined some of the more significant issues raised by recent business communication research, including the importance of 'soft skills' (Stone & Lightbody, 2012). These skills include effective listening, teamwork, emotional intelligence and intercultural communication. This section will outline the factors which have prompted the need for a renewed emphasis on the teaching of communication in tertiary-level business courses. In particular, it will look at the global drivers of change which compel these new requirements.

The twenty-first century has entered a new era, one often referred to as The Fourth Industrial revolution see (Schwab, 2016). The Fourth Industrial revolution is driven by rapid technological, political and socio-economic change, which has disrupted existing business models (Forum, 2016). The business sphere has undergone a metamorphosis from the familiar to uncharted territory. Business is now conducted in a world-market dominated by unprecedented capital and trade flows. Businesses must rise to the challenges posed by data-driven complexity and global rise in the mobility of labour, capital and ideas.

These changes have transformed the range of skills required by employees. Once a non-transferable professional speciality would be sufficient for individuals to remain current in a labour market. This is no longer the case. The skills required by today's business employees have fundamentally changed due to the globalisation of business and the impact of rapid digital innovation. The world of work has been transformed as rapid change forces enterprises to explore new and different ways of achieving organisational goals or risk being left behind in the marketplace. Even the most fundamental assumptions of commercial life have been challenged by new business models and ideas (O'Connell, et al., 2015; Forum, 2020).

The World Economic Forum identifies a number of drivers for change. These are propelling the global business world into uncharted territory. Some of these trends have attracted a good deal of recent media attention. They include more sophisticated forms of Artificial Intelligence (AI) and an increased use of robots to perform manual or routine work, big data and the changing geography of supply, production and distribution. Other drivers of change include demographic shifts, increased generational diversity and developments in the market for labour (Forum, 2018). These shifting sands of business, employment and technological change have displaced some employment types. There are claims that as many as half the employees in some industries will need to reskill (Forum, 2018, p. 13). Changes in the demand for labour will mean increasing demands for higher productivity. To remain relevant in the labour market, will need to commit to lifelong learning. Individuals will also need to be more flexible in their career choices. Employees are increasingly unlikely to remain in one profession throughout their working life (Forum, 2016). These are new demands that have the potential to perplex, but for an astute graduate equipped with a sufficiently wide range of skills, these changes could create new opportunities (Forum, 2018).

Globalisation, propelled by technical advances in transport and telecommunications, has altered how business is conducted world-wide. Cheaper telecommunications and lower transport costs have resulted in an increased flow of labour, capital and trade (Baldwin, 2016) A new "knowledge-based economy" has emerged. This increased flow of capital, goods, people and ideas has altered the ways that organisations achieve their goals and has reshaped their work practices. For example, global collaboration between teams in different countries has necessitated an increased awareness of how intercultural communication can facilitate business projects (Cox, 2009). The same factor has raised important questions as to how employees can best adapt to working across countries and cultures. The current emphasis on global business outsourcing and international collaboration has highlighted the particular importance of equipping individuals to deal with workplace diversity (Forum, 2016). Associated with the rapid change in the structure of the labour force and the new skills demanded by employers, future employees need to be adaptable and develop transferable skill sets (Forum, 2016). The importance of this mission has been highlighted by predictions of a future wave of automation, driven by improvements in fields such as robotics and AI (Forum, 2020). There are fears that an increasingly number of routine tasks will become automated, leading to the massive shifts in the demand for labour across the economy (Autor, 2015; Balliester & Elsheikhi, 2018; Berg, Buffie, & Zanna, 2018; Frey & Osborne, 2013; Susskind & Susskind, 2015).

These challenges are likely to impact on enterprises as well as individual workers. It is now crucial for enterprises to properly manage recruitment in terms of gender, age, culture or sexuality (Bujaki, Durocher, Brouard, Neilson, & Pyper, 2018). They must also develop policies to conform to new community expectations regarding the way diversities are presented by corporate communicators across an ever-widening media spectrum (Arai, Wanca-Thibault, & Shockley-Zalabak, 2001; Hooker, 2012; Okoro & Washington, 2012). Advertising strategies, internal communications, recruitment and relations with external stakeholders must all conform to new standards. In order to conform to these requirements, business professionals will need a wider range of communication skills.

Against this background of rapid change, educators must forecast what is required to prepare students to meet the demands in the coming years. What role does business communication play in preparing today's tertiary students to become tomorrow's business leaders and professionals? The future of work in the financial services sphere is changing as a result both of changes in technology and power shifts in politics and economics (see, for example, PwC, 2014; Dawson, 2015; Forum, 2018; Forum, 2020). Many observers foresee changes in the roles of the business and financial professional. It is argued that new technologies and increasing economies of scale will lead to automated compliance and regulation. The expectation is that, for example, future accountants will be far more involved in advocacy and ideas (Howieson, 2003; PwC, 2014; O'Connell, et al., 2015; Forum, 2018; Forum, 2020). As today's students confront a changing business environment, they will require a larger, transferable skill set. These wider attributes will equip them for highly skilled positions which involve them in the creation of new business strategies and forms of value (Roos, 2014). How can academics meet these demands and create salient teaching content to equip students to meet tomorrow's workplace challenges?

Universities generally fail to equip students with the communication skills they require to flourish in professional roles (Buzarna-Tihenea, 2019; Schartel Dunn & Lane, 2019). Business communication is often regarded as a necessary (Swanson & Swanson, 1990), yet un favoured secondary skill (McPherson, 1998).There is a perception on the part of many students and faculty that good communication skills are unnecessary or simply something an individual is born with (O'Connell, et al., 2015; Yong, Ryan, Yap, & Goela, 2011). Research has noted that the written communication skills of recent graduates seem to lack the necessary elements of good sentence construction, spelling and grammar required for clear, professional communication. Many business graduates simply do not possess the ability to construct sound, written professional communication (Maupin & May, 1993; Wardrope, 2002).

Australian research has analysed the communication skills taught to accounting students at universities. This research emphasises that communication skills within the business realm can add value and substance to professional transactions in a world constantly disrupted by change and technological growth (Jackson, Watty, Yu, & Lowe, 2006; Kavanagh & Drennan, 2008; Hancock, et al., 2009). Accounting educators, including academics teaching business communication (along with employers seeking to foster graduate talent), must be cognisant of the challenges faced by their students. An effective response will require relevant course content and learning opportunities tailored to future demands.

Future-oriented analyses conducted by professional bodies have looked at trends in the employment landscape in light of the Fourth Industrial Revolution. An example is the Price Waterhouse Cooper's report *The Future of work: A journey to 2022* (PwC, 2014). This report reviews the trends and innovation shaping the future professional employment landscape. These include digital innovation, political and economic power shifts and climate concerns. The authors state that:

Overall, social skills—such as persuasion, emotional intelligence and teaching others—will be in higher demand across industries than narrow technical skills such as programming or equipment operation and control. Content skills (which include ICT literacy and active learning), cognitive abilities (such as creativity and mathematical reasoning) and process skills (such as active listening and critical thinking) will be a growing part of the core skills requirements for many industries...Overall, our respondents anticipate that a wide range of occupations will require a higher degree of cognitive abilities—such as creativity, logical reasoning and problem sensitivity—as part of their core skill set. (PwC, 2014, pp. 22-24)

What aspects of these future trends can be actioned into teachable concepts beneficial for business students? Much of the previously cited literature in this chapter maintains that business communication should respond to a range of pressures. These challenges include: the demands from professional bodies; the new global labour market; the increasingly complex business world of the post-global financial crisis era; and businesses requirements to become more innovative and entrepreneurial. Another factor is the growing need for employees to work closely together in a world where the division between professional and personal life is expected to shrink or disappear altogether (PwC, 2014; Forum, 2016). Social skills, combined with emotional intelligence and active listening, are likely to be in higher demand than narrowly defined technical skills (PwC, 2014). What remains is to consider how tomorrow's demands translate into educational content teachable now.

The next section provides an exploratory overview of some of the most significant teaching content areas. It will explain the crucial importance of a range of critical skills. These include the ability to foster workplace creativity, apply emotional intelligence, and master art and skill of sound written communication. The section will explore the benefits of equipping today's students with a wider range of communication skills. These benefits include facilitating the application of other professional skills and cultivating an attitude of life-long learning.

ISSUES, PROBLEMS AND CONTROVERSIES

Creativity in the Marketplace

This subsection explores the role of creativity within the milieu of business communication. It seeks to outline why creativity is such a significant content area for university tuition in business communication. The subsection will outline the rise of creativity within the enterprise, and examine the relationship between creativity, innovation and entrepreneurship. Finally, it will look at how creativity, coupled with good communication skills, can equip today's business communication student to meet tomorrow's demands.

Researchers have noted that there is a trend toward the automation of routine compliance and regulatory work (Howieson, 2003; Forum, 2016). In this context, it is often argued that fostering workplace creativity will become an increasingly important aspect of university teaching. Creativity was once seen as the exclusive domain of the arts. It is now recognised as a valued attribute that can assist the business professional to generate better work practices and solve problems. In this manner, creativity is increasingly regarded as conferring a competitive edge upon individuals and organisations in terms of their long-term strategies and goals.

This approach has gained in cogency as corporations face the challenges of the post-global financial crisis era. Creativity has emerged as an ever-more essential component of revolutionary approaches to business communication. New forms of communication, particularly online social media, have emerged as critical tools as businesses seek to make themselves heard (Chen, Davison, & Qu, 2016). Many business thinkers have embraced the idea that new media channels will be critical to the efforts of enterprises to offset the limitations imposed by the prevailing climate of austerity and caution.

Creativity is the use of imagination and ingenuity to solve problems. In the business context, it is the positive impact of creativity on the design of goods or services that leads to innovation. Only creativity ("the systematic transformation of ideas in reality") allows entrepreneurs and other business leaders to capture the value that arises from new technologies and ways of doing business (Bruce & Bessant, 2002). Creativity is now seen as part of a critical creativity, innovation and entrepreneurship matrix.

How, then does communication fit into this matrix? The answer is simple. Communication is the essential skill and basic technique that holds together the creativity, innovation and entrepreneurship matrix. Good ideas must be articulated effectively if they are to be brought to fruition. In the current day, creativity has equipped businesses to leverage universal human facilities such as curiosity and care for others in the pursuit of new value propositions (Achtenhagen & Johannisson, 2018, p. 64). Creativity is critical to business success in the modern Web-centric world. By teaching creativity, university courses in business can help equip students to compete in an ever-changing job market.

Strategic use of creativity within the business organisation depends on sound communication practices. Effective communication is essential to the process of adding value through the creation of products that consumers will want to purchase (Bruce, 2009) or through the development of revolutionary, thoughtful solutions to new consumer problems (Brown & Wyatt, 2010). Communication is critical to the effective consultation processes which facilitate a 'customer active paradigm' (von Hippel, 2005). Without good two-way communication — the process where clear messages are sent and their meaning is accurately decoded — it will be difficult for businesses to streamline the production and distribution processes that enhance value and sell goods and services in an ever-more crowded marketplace (Freeman, 1982).

Teaching creativity as a component of business communication will be essential to equip students for the business world of the future. The world continues to change. It evolves toward a digital world where automation and artificial intelligence replace many of the business functions once performed by people. In this context, there will be new demands for genuine meaning in business relationships, occupations and products. In this context, it is expected that so-called "soft skills" will becomes increasingly important (Fletcher, 2018). Faced with a future in which human interaction and the human itself are at a premium, it becomes even more important to consider how business students can be taught to communicate in ways that emphasise the authentic and the personal.

Social Skills and Emotional Intelligence

The previous subsection outlined the role of creativity within business communication. It looked at the importance of creativity in producing new forms of value. If future enterprises are to innovate effectively, they will need to employ intellectual and emotional intelligence when framing their internal and external communications. When conversations are framed in the absence of such knowledge, it is difficult to retain a genuine and authentic human touch. This authenticity is likely to become and ever more highly valued commodity as digital innovation continues at its current break-neck pace (Achtenhagen & Johannisson, 2018).

This subsection explores the role of social skills and emotional intelligence within professional business communication. It will endeavour to outline how social and emotional intelligence concepts have evolved. The subsection explains why social skills and emotional intelligence should be an essential component of university education. Further, it explains why fostering these softer skills in today's students will create lasting value and enduring success for both individuals and organisations in the future.

Emotional intelligence and social skills, as psychological concepts, have been the subject of research for nearly a century. Academic interest began with Thorndike and Stein's theory of social intelligence. Thorndike and Stein identified social intelligence as a distinctive kind of human intelligence in the 1930s (Thorndike, 1936; Thorndike & Stein, 1937). Despite the future importance of this insight, the dominance of the behaviourist paradigm in the early part of the century meant that researchers were slow to build on their work. The topic of social intelligence did not attract serious research again until the work of Howard Gardner in the 1980s (Gardner, 1985).

Gardner's achievement in resurrecting the concept of social intelligence as a focus of research led to an explosion of new research. Emotional intelligence, now a field of investigation within its own right, emerged as a fully formed research area in the 1990s (Salovey & Mayer, 1990). This concept gained broad, popular recognition with Goleman's famous 1995 work, which also exposed the concept to the wider reading public (Goleman, 2005). Emotional intelligence has succeeded largely because of its explanatory power. The concept explains why some individuals, despite their high intelligence, are not as successful as their intellectual peers in the same field of employment.

This insight lies at the heart of the concept of emotional intelligence. Goleman posits the question: is emotional intelligence a better predictor of success than intelligence? (Goleman, 2001; Goleman, 2005). Goleman has provided examples where this does indeed seem to be the case. Goleman's taxonomy of emotional intelligence also reveals a range of competencies. These include crucial skills such as self-regulation, self-motivation and self-awareness. These are often-overlooked, but fundamental, attributes that assist individuals to regulate themselves and their social interactions. Goleman also looked at other social competencies: empathy, relationship building and the ability to communicate clearly and convincingly (Goleman, 2005). These are the essential attributes that allow some individuals to go further than peers with equal or greater technical skills.

Goleman's research has critical implications for the future of work. Emotional intelligence is likely to become increasingly valuable in the future. As everyday life becomes more intertwined with technology, there are dangers of growing isolation and the progressive dissolution of the bonds between individuals and communities. In particular, there are acute concerns that the kindness, cooperation and compassion that are essential to human happiness will be lost (Schwab, 2016). Inevitably, many individuals will seek out and cling most fiercely to signs of authenticity and humanity. Those professionals best able to frame future conversations which meet these needs will be in high demand. Emotional intelligence is likely to become an ever-more desirable attribute as a direct result of digital transformation, not in spite of this process. Technological change dictates that the education of today's student must change too (Meall, 2018).

Integrating emotional intelligence into the academic curricula does not, however, come without challenges from both academics and students. Both groups often perceive that emotional intelligence, often grouped under the misnomer of 'soft skills', is not directly applicable to business education. There is a widespread myth that the acquisition of technical skills is far more valuable (Henderson, 2001). Despite this myth, employers want and continue to select graduates who possess fewer technical skills, but are more emotionally intelligent and have higher interpersonal skills (Badenoch and Clark, 2009).

This reality has become increasingly apparent in the post-global financial crisis era. When employers are able to pick and choose due to a swollen labour market, it is clear that they prefer to select graduates with higher emotional intelligence (Bui & Porter, 2010). Such new hires are better able to communicate and translate complex information to non-specialists, such as customers and co-workers (Evans, Gbolahan, Wells, & Scott, 2012). These individuals are also more likely to make better managers. The reason is that they are better able to transmit organisational information and instruction clearly, to build upon existing relationships, and to establish new networks (Nguyen, White, Hall, Bell, & Ballentine, 2019).

The simple fact that employers want and continue to demand emotional intelligence from graduates (along with other relationship building and creative skills) testifies to their value, both to businesses and potential employees. Not only are such skills expected to directly add value from the perspective of employers (see, for further, PwC, 2014; Schwab, 2016; Forum, 2016; Forum, 2018; Forum, 2020), they are equally advantageous to job-seekers. Equipped with these skills, graduates are more likely to gain employment in their chosen field. In addition, their greater emotional intelligence will assist graduates in their search for promotion, additional skills and professional satisfaction.

Written Skills

The preceding subsection looked at the concept of emotional intelligence. It explained why emotional intelligence is such an essential skill for today's tertiary students. The present subsection centres on the longstanding problem of teaching writing skills to business students. In particular, it looks at why written skills have emerged as a particularly wicked problem.

Written communication skills include a range of sub-skills. These include sentence construction, good grammar, spelling and correct word choice. Ensuring that students acquire these skills is a longstanding problem for academics, graduates and employers (Hancock et al., 2009; Jones, 2011). The most frequent topic of research and comment is the written skills of accountants. In part, this is perhaps because in no other profession is the art and skill of written communication so vital to the clear and transparent transmission of information to clients (Gray, Hamilton, & Wilson, 2015). Although accountants deal in numbers, their clients almost inevitably require written advice which explain what these numbers mean.

There has been continued criticism of accounting graduates' writing skills over the years. This is despite the fact that clear written communication is one of the most important skills employers in the financial services industry demand from graduates (Pennington & Stanford, 2019). There is widespread agreement that the ability to be able to communicate clearly in a multitude of channels and with different audiences is an essential attribute for the profession. In simple terms, these skills are necessary for the successful practice of accountancy in the twenty-first century (Dale-Jones, Hancock, & Willey, 2015). The conclusion of much recent research is that 'knowing what to say and how to say it makes a profound difference' (Hummer, 2018).

The necessity to communicate transparently and clearly has become even more urgent in recent years. In the decade since the global financial crisis, negative public perceptions regarding the financial services industry have reached new heights (Carnegie & Napier, 2010). Good communication is critical if professionals in the industry are to regain the trust of clients. Knowing how to articulate thoughts or complex facts into actionable or understandable messages is a non-negotiable attribute that every accounting, and business student, should acquire by the end of their degree.

Despite this reality, employers continue to lament that graduates' written communication skills are, at best, woeful. Researchers have agreed with this conclusion. This appears to be a global problem. Complaints appear in the latest academic literature, from Pakistan (see (Abbasi, Ali, & Bibi, 2018) to Scotland (McMurray, Dutton, McQuaid, & Richard, 2016) and in both Australia and the United States (Jackson, 2010). The existence of a global problem should perhaps not be too surprising. The financial services profession is now a global one. Financial and business professionals, including accountants in every part of the world seek to compete in a marketplace shaped by a globalised flow of ideas, technology, people and capital. The possession of the ability to write clear, precise and purposeful prose is now not only a question of success in the local job market. Increasingly, this ability is recognised as a vital transferable skill that enables favoured individuals to compete effectively in a global profession (Jackson & Chapman, 2012).

SOLUTIONS AND RECOMMENDATIONS

Business communication skills have been, as demonstrated through research (see Owen & Gerfen, 1951), a longstanding wicked problem. In light of this fact it may appear that providing solutions and recommendations to improve, *inter alia*, the creativity, emotional intelligence and written skills of business students and graduates could potentially be a fraught exercise.

This chapter has demonstrated how important the so-called soft skills of creativity, social (emotional) intelligence and written skills are to the new business environment of the Fourth Industrial Revolution. The human-scale of genuine, authentic human interaction will likely be transformed into a valued commodity, particularly with the increasingly amount of technological and digital innovation that have the potential to engulf, if left unfettered, the very essence of humanity.

Research conducted by the World Economic Forum (see (Forum, 2018; Forum, 2020) reiterate the importance of human interaction for both emerging and existing professions. This research also states that communication skills, including the ability to creatively solve problems, regulate one's own emotion and recognise the emotions of others', will be demanding far more than what it is currently realised. How then, can the academic provide teachable content to tertiary students embarking on their future career?

This subsection will provide three potential solutions and recommendations which may prove useful for those academics who want to integrate more communication skills into their curricula.

Closer Professional and Academic Alignment

University business graduates require sufficient business communication skills to be able to perform at a satisfactory level within a professional organisation. Employers often state that communication and social skills are more valuable attributes for a potential candidate and university education does not provide graduates' with these skills, there has been very little action from either professional regulating bodies, for example CAANZ (Charted Accountants of Australia and New Zealand), to create a constructive alignment between themselves and academic. This lack of constructive industry and research alignment has often created gaps in knowledge required of university graduates (see, for example, Zaid & Abraham, 1994; O'Connell, et al., 2015).

The accounting profession has attempted to remedy this deficit in graduate skills by creating learning standards (see, for an Australian example, Hancock, Watty, Birt, & Tyler, 2016) which outline what standards of knowledge are professionally expected from Australian university graduates. Whilst this is essential information, the practicalities of how to action the standards into teachable content and curricula for the professional academic may prove vexing. Business communication courses, as taught at universities, are often very large, are not specific to one particular business discipline and academic processes are often not nimble enough to respond quickly to change or alteration (see Maupin & May, 1993; Zaid & Abraham, 1994). One suggestion to remedy this is, for both the teaching and research business communication academic, is to integrate more 'real life' examples of business communication into teaching content. For example, business newsletters, company reports and professional industry speakers (see O'Connell, et al., 2015) may prove to be useful adjunct content due to the fact these examples are an easy entrée into Problem Based Learning (PBL). This approach can also go some way to equipping students for the real-life workplace (Dauletova, 2016), and can also assist students' to appreciate how their studies align to career outcomes and practice.

Communication Integration

The ability to communicate well is an essential attribute for any profession and should be emphasised throughout every step of a university student's degree. Business communication courses at most universities are large and do not specifically cater to an individual discipline (Sharp & Brumberger, 2013). This approach, whilst financially advantageous to university faculty, has result in students graduating and entering their chosen profession with several gaps in their required professional knowledge (Maupin & May, 1993). To remedy this problem could be to integrate communication skills throughout the degree as to provide discipline-specific communication skills.

Work Integrated Learning

Preparing today's students to become tomorrow's business leaders is a significant responsibility. Universities have been criticised for their inability to achieve this (Daymon & Durkin, 2013). One solution to assist students to better learn business communication skills, within a suitable context, is to recommend that students undertake some form of Work Integrated Learning (WIL) that would both allow students to experience authentic professional work and gain much needed experience, but would also encourage greater networks to develop between business and professional bodies. The caveat for WIL is, however, the experience can be stressful and financially detrimental for students (Lu, Scholz, & Nguyen, 2018).

FUTURE RESEARCH DIRECTIONS

This chapter has introduced some background regarding some future directions for business communication and how these could potentially be integrated into academic curricula. However, this chapter is limited in so far as business communication is a vast discipline and not every potential possibility could be explored. The role of teamwork and intercultural communication within the sphere of business communication and its pedagogy are two salient examples of future research directions. The rapid rate of globalisation and anticipated changes during the age of the Fourth Industrial Revolution these are two research directions that require a great more research.

CONCLUSION

The Fourth Industrial Revolution is driving rapid change in the way that business is conducted and communicated. Globalisation is being driven by digital innovation where complex data, information and ideas can cross boundaries instantly. Existing business models are being disrupted and new methods and opportunities are emerging from the once-familiar. The future of employment and business is now unchartered territory where technology is predicted to blur the lines between human and machine, but one salient aspect of this disruption is that communication skills, including creativity, emotional intelligence and the ability to write is now more valued than ever.

The present chapter has provided an overview of why, now more than ever, business communication skills are required. Inculcating sound business communication skills to tertiary students, in tandem with technical, discipline specific mastery, will prepare today's students' to become tomorrow's business leaders and professionals. Possessing the capacity to communicate, with clarity, empathy and kindness, will become an ever increasingly valued skill in an era of digital innovation: we must decode these possibilities for the student receiver if we are to prepare them well.

REFERENCES

Abbasi, F. K., Ali, A., & Bibi, N. (2018). Analysis of skill gap for business graduates: Managerial perspective from banking industry. *Education + Training*, *60*(4), 354–367. doi:10.1108/ET-08-2017-0120

Achtenhagen, L., & Johannisson, B. (2018). Exploring conscientization in entrepreneurship education. In K. Berglund & K. Verdujin (Eds.), *Revitalizing Entrepreneurship Education: Adopting a Critical Approach in the Classroom* (p. 64). London: Routledge.

Albrecht, W. S., & Sack, R. J. (2000). *Accounting education: Charting the course through a perilous future*. Sarasota: American Accounting Association.

American Accounting Association. (1968). *A Guide to Accounting Instruction: Concepts & Practices*. Cincinnati: South-Western Publishing.

Arai, M., Wanca-Thibault, M., & Shockley-Zalabak, P. (2001). Communication theory and training approaches for multiculturally diverse organizations: Have Academics and Practitioners Missed the Connection? *Public Personnel*, *30*(4), 445–455. doi:10.1177/009102600103000402

Autor, D. (2015). Why are there still so many jobs? The history and future of workplace automation. *The Journal of Economic Perspectives*, *29*(3), 3–30. doi:10.1257/jep.29.3.3

Badenoch and Clark. (2009). *Balancing act: is the accounting and finance profession ready to step up?* Retrieved from Badenoch and Clark: https://www.badenochandclark.com/

Baldwin, R. (2016). *The Great Convergence: Information Technology and the New Globalization*. Cambridge, MA: Harvard University Press.

Ballantine, J., & McCourt Larres, P. (2009). Accounting undergraduates' perceptions of cooperative learning as a model for Enhancing their interpersonal and communication skills to interface successfully with professional accountancy education and training. *Accounting Education*, *18*(4-5), 387–402. doi:10.1080/09639280902719366

Balliester, T., & Elsheikhi, A. (2018). *The Future of Work: A Literature Review ILO Research Department* Working Paper No. 29. Geneva: International Labour Organisation.

Berg, A., Buffie, E., & Zanna, L. (2018). *Should We Fear the Robot Revolution? (The Correct Answer is Yes)*. IMF Working Paper No. 18/116. Washington, DC: International Monetary Fund.

Bhatia, V., & Bhatia, A. (2011). Business communication. In J. Simpson (Ed.), *The routledge handbook of applied linguistics* (pp. 24–35). Oxfordshire: Routledge.

Brown, T., & Wyatt, J. (2010). Design thinking for social innovation. *Stanford Social Innovation Review*, (Winter): 31–35.

Bruce, M. (2009). Unleashing the creative potential of design in business. In T. Rickards, M. A. Runco, & S. Moger (Eds.), *The Routledge Companion to creativity*. Oxfordshire: Routledge.

Bruce, M., & Bessant, J. (2002). *Design in Business: Strategic Innovation through Design*. Englewood Cliffs: Prentice Hall.

Bryer, A. R. (2011). Accounting as learnt social practice: The case of the empresas recuperades in Argentina. *Accounting, Organizations and Society*, *36*(8), 478–495. doi:10.1016/j.aos.2011.09.002

Bui, B., & Porter, B. (2010). The expectation-performance gap in accounting education: An exploratory study. *Accounting Education*, *19*(1-2), 23–50. doi:10.1080/09639280902875556

Bujaki, M., Durocher, S., Brouard, F., Neilson, L., & Pyper, R. (2018). Protect, profit, profess, promote: Establishing legitimacy through logics of diversity in Canadian accounting firm recruitment documents. *Canadian Journal of Administrative Sciences*, *35*(1), 162–178. doi:10.1002/cjas.1392

Buzarna-Tihenea, A. (2019). Written business communication. Case study: Auditor's Report. *"Ovidus" University Annals, Economic Sciences Series, 19*(1).

Carnegie, G., & Napier, C. (2010). Traditional accountants and business professionals: Portraying the accounting profession after Enron. *Accounting, Organizations and Society*, *35*(3), 360–376. doi:10.1016/j.aos.2009.09.002

Chen, R. R., Davison, R. M., & Qu, C. X. (2016). Using social media for business communication: A symbolic interaction perspective. In *Australasian Conference on Information Systems*, (pp. 1-11). Wollongong: Academic Press.

Cox, A. (2009). Creating or destroying business value: understanding the opportunities and the limits of a win-win collaboration. In T. Rickards, M. A. Runco, & S. Moger (Eds.), *The Routledge companion to creativity*. Oxfordshire: Routledge.

Crossman, J., & Bordia, S. (2012). Piecing the puzzle. *Journal of International Education in Business*, *5*(1), 71–88. doi:10.1108/18363261211261773

Daff, L., de Lange, P., & Jackling, B. (2012). A comparison of generic skills and emotional intelligence in accounting education. *Issues in Accounting Education*, *27*(3), 627–645. doi:10.2308/iace-50145

Dale-Jones, G., Hancock, P., & Willey, K. (2015). Accounting Students in an Australian University Improve their Writing: But How did it Happen? In R. M. Wilson, F. E. Gray, & L. Hamilton (Eds.), *Communication in Accounting Education* (pp. 160–178). Oxfordshire: Routledge.

Dauletova, V. (2016). Innovating business communication courses in Oman: From design to implementation. *Innovations in Education and Teaching International*, *53*(5), 545–554. doi:10.1080/14703297.2015.1015594

Dawson, R. (2015). What is the future of work? In E. Evans, R. Burritt, & J. Guthrie (Eds.), *Future proofing the profession: preparing business leaders and finance professional for 2025*. Sydney: Chartered Accountants Australia and New Zealand.

Daymon, C., & Durkin, K. (2013). The impact of marketisation on postgraduate career prepardness in a high skills economy. *Studies in Higher Education*, *38*(4), 595–612. doi:10.1080/03075079.2011.590896

Drucker, P. F. (1974). *Management: Tasks, Responsibilities, Practices*. New York: Haper & Row.

Dwyer, J. (2016). *Communication for Business and the Professions*. Melbourne: Pearson Australia.

Evans, C., Gbolahan, G., Wells, J., & Scott, I. (2012). Balancing the yin and yang: The role of universities in developing softer skills in accounting. *Industry and Higher Education*, *26*(1), 36–70. doi:10.5367/ihe.2012.0081

Fletcher, D. (2018). Prologue Looking to the Future: How can we further develop critical pedagogies in entrepreneurship education? In K. Berglund & K. Verduijn (Eds.), *Revitalizing Entrepreneurship Education: Adopting a Critical Approach in the Classroom* (pp. xvii–xviii). London: Routledge.

Forum, W. E. (2016). *The Future of Jobs Employment, Skills and Workforce Strategy for the Fourth Industrial Revolution*. Retrieved from World Economic Forum: http://www3.weforum.org/docs/WEF_Future_of_Jobs.pdf

Forum, W. E. (2018). *The Future of Jobs Report.* Retrieved from World Economic Forum: http://www3.weforum.org/docs/WEF_Future_of_Jobs_2018.pdf

Forum, W. E. (2020). *Jobs of Tomorrow Mapping Opportunity in the new economy.* Retrieved from World Economic Forum: http://www3.weforum.org/docs/WEF_Jobs_of_Tomorrow_2020.pdf

Freeman, C. (1982). *The Economics of Industrial Innovation.* London: Frances Pinter.

Frey, C., & Osborne, M. (2013). *The Future of Employment: How susceptible Are Jobs to Computerisation.* Oxford: Oxford University Press.

Gardner, H. (1985). *The mind's new science: a history of the cognitive revolution.* New York: Basic Books.

Goleman, D. (2001). Issues in Paradigm Building. In C. Chermiss & D. Goleman (Eds.), *The emotionally intelligent workpalce: How to select for, measure, and improve emotional intelligence in individuals, groups, and organizations* (pp. 13–26). San Francisco: Jossey-Bass.

Goleman, D. (2005). *Emotional Intelligence.* New York: Bantam Dell.

Gray, F. E., Hamilton, L., & Wilson, R. M. (2015). Introduction: Communication in Accounting Education. In R. M. Wilson, F. E. Gray, & L. Hamilton (Eds.), *Communication in Accounting Education* (pp. 1–3). Oxfordshire: Routledge.

Hancock, P., Howieson, B. A., Kavanagh, M., Kent, J., Tempone, I., & Segal, N. (2009). *Accounting for the future: more than numbers: volume 1, Final Report.* Canberra: Australian Learning and Teaching Council.

Hancock, P., Watty, K., Birt, J., & Tyler, J. (2016). *Accounting learning standards.* Australian Business Deans Council (ABDC). Retrieved from https://abdc.edu.au/data/Accounting_LS/New_TLS_Final_2016.pdf

Henderson, S. (2001). The education of accountants- a comment. *Accounting Forum, 25*(4), 398–400. doi:10.1111/1467-6303.00074

Hooker, J. (2012). Cultural Differences in Business Communication. In C. B. Paulston, S. F. Kiesling, & E. S. Rangel (Eds.), *Handbook of intercultural discourse and communication.* Malden: John Wiley & Sons. doi:10.1002/9781118247273.ch19

Howieson, B. (2003). Accounting practice in the new millennium: Is accounting education ready to meet the challenge? *The British Accounting Review, 35*(2), 69–103. doi:10.1016/S0890-8389(03)00004-0

Hummer, R. L. (2018). Do You Want to Work in Tall Buildings?: The Art of Good Business Communication. *Journal of Pension Benefits, 25*(2), 21–24.

Jack, L., Davison, J., & Craig, R. (Eds.). (2013). *The routledge companion to accounting communication.* London: Routledge. doi:10.4324/9780203593493

Jackson, D. (2010). An international profile of industry-relevant competencies and skill gaps in modern graduates. *International Journal of Management Education, 8*(3), 29–58. doi:10.3794/ijme.83.288

Jackson, D., & Chapman, E. (2012). Non-technical competencies in undergraduate business degree programs: Australian and UK perspectives. *Studies in Higher Education*, *37*(5), 541–567. doi:10.1080/03075079.2010.527935

Jackson, M., Watty, K., Yu, L., & Lowe, L. (2006). Inclusive assessment: improving learning for all: a manual for improving assessment in accounting education. RMIT University.

Jones, C. G. (2011). Written and Computer-Mediated Accounting Communication Skills: An Employer Prespective. *Business Communication Quarterly*, *74*(3), 247–271. doi:10.1177/1080569911413808

Kavanagh, M., & Drennan, L. (2008). What skills and attributes does an accounting graduate need? Evidence from student perceptions and employer expectations. *Accounting and Finance*, *48*(2), 279–300. doi:10.1111/j.1467-629X.2007.00245.x

Lu, V. N., Scholz, B., & Nguyen, L. T. (2018). Work integrated learning in international market: Student Insights. *Australasian Marketing Journal*, *26*(2), 132–139. doi:10.1016/j.ausmj.2018.05.002

Maupin, R. J., & May, C. A. (1993). Communication for Accounting Students. *International Journal of Educational Management*, *7*(3), 30–38. doi:10.1108/09513549310039918

McMurray, S., Dutton, M., McQuaid, R., & Richard, A. (2016). Employer demands from business graduates. *Education + Training*, *58*(1), 112–132. doi:10.1108/ET-02-2014-0017

McPherson, B. (1998). Student perceptions about business communication in their careers. *Business and Professional Communication Quarterly*, *61*(2), 68–79. doi:10.1177/108056999806100209

Meall, L. (2018). The Human Factor. *Accountancy Futures: Critical Issues for tomorrow's profession, 17*, 6-9.

Nguyen, T., White, S., Hall, K., Bell, R. L., & Ballentine, W. (2019). Emotional Intelligence and Managerial Communication. *American Journal of Management*, *19*(2), 54–63.

O'Connell, B., Carnegie, G. D., Carter, A. J., de Lange, P., Hancock, P., Helliar, C. V., & Watty, K. (2015). *Shaping the future of accounting in business education in Australia*. Melbourne: CPA.

Okoro, E. A., & Washington, M. C. (2012). Workforce Diversity and Organizational Communication: Analysis of Human Capital Performance and Productivity. *Journal of Diversity Management*, *7*(1), 57–62. doi:10.19030/jdm.v7i1.6936

Owen, G. A., & Gerfen, R. C. (1951). Can Junior Accountatns be Trained to write Better? *American Accounting Association*, *26*(3), 313–320.

Parker, L. D., Guthrie, J., & Linacre, S. (2011). The relationship between academic accounting research and professional practice. *Accounting. Auditing & Accountability*, *24*(1), 5–14. doi:10.1108/09513571111098036

Pennington, A., & Stanford, J. (2019). *The Future of Work for Australian Graduates: The Changing Landscape of University-Employment Transitions in Australia.* Retrieved from The Centre for Future Work at the Australia Institute: https://d3n8a8pro7vhmx.cloudfront.net/theausinstitute/pages/3083/attachments/original/1571640129/Future_of_Work_for_Australian_Graduates_GCA_Final_Formatted.pdf?1571640129

PwC. (2014). *The future of work: a journey to 2022.* Retrieved from https://www.pwc.com.au/pdf/future-of-work-report-v23.pdf

Riley, T. J., & Simons, K. A. (2016). The written communication skills that matter most for accountants. *Accounting Education, 25*(3), 239–255. doi:10.1080/09639284.2016.1164066

Roos, G. (2014). Intellectual capital in Australia- economic development in a high cost economy. In *11th International Conference on Intellectual Capital, Knowledge Management & Organisational Learning -ICICKM 2014.* Sydney: The University of Sydney Business School.

Salovey, P., & Mayer, J. (1990). Emotional Intelligence. *Imagination, Cognition and Personality, 9*(3), 185–211. doi:10.2190/DUGG-P24E-52WK-6CDG

Schartel Dunn, S., & Lane, P. (2019). Do interns know what they think they know? Assessing business communication skills in interns and recent graduates. *Business and Professional Communication Quarterly, 82*(2), 202–213. doi:10.1177/2329490619826258

Schwab, K. (2016). *The Fourth Industrial Revolution.* Geneva: World Economic Forum.

Sharp, M. R., & Brumberger, E. R. (2013). Business Communication Cirricula Today: Revisiting the Top 50 Undergraduate Business Schools. *Business Communication Quarterly, 76*(1), 5–27. doi:10.1177/1080569912471187

Stone, G., & Lightbody, M. (2012). The nature and significance of listening skills in accounting practice. *Accounting Education, 21*(4), 363–384. doi:10.1080/09639284.2011.617062

Stretcher Sigmar, L., Hynes, G., & Hill, K. L. (2012). Strategies for Teaching Social and Emotional Intelligence in Business Communication. *Business Communication Quarterly, 75*(3), 301–317. doi:10.1177/1080569912450312

Susskind, R., & Susskind, D. (2015). *The Future of the Professions: How Technology Will Transform the Work of Human Experts.* Oxford: Oxford University Press.

Swanson, J., & Swanson, N. (1990). The value of business communications as perceived by business administration graduates. *Journal of Education for Business, 64*(4), 168–171. doi:10.1080/08832323.1990.10117420

Thorndike, R. (1936). Factor analysis of social and abstract intelligence. *Journal of Educational Psychology, 27*(3), 231–233. doi:10.1037/h0059840

Thorndike, R., & Stein, S. (1937). An evaluation of the attempts to measure social intelligence. *Psychological Bulletin, 34*(5), 275–285. doi:10.1037/h0053850 von Hippel, E. (2005). *Democratising Innovation.* Cambridge: MIT Press. doi:10.7551/mit-press/2333.001.0001

Wardrope, W. J. (2002). Department Chairs' perceptions of the importance of business communication skills. *Business Communication Quarterly, 65*(4), 60–72. doi:10.1177/108056990206500406

Yong, J., Ryan, S., Yap, C., & Goela, N. (2011). A case study in the failiure of graduate attributes in accounting education. In K. Krause, M. Buckridge, C. Grimmer, & S. Purbrick-Illek (Eds.), *Research and development in higher education: reshaping higher education* (pp. 383–394). Gold Coast.

Zaid, O. A., Abraham, A., & Abraham, A. (1994). Communication Skills in accounting education: Perceptions of academics, employers and graduate accountants. *Accounting Education, 3*(3), 205–221. doi:10.1080/09639289400000020

KEY TERMS AND DEFINITIONS

Business Communication: The process of effective human interchange coupled with the ability to combine discipline-specific knowledge to create the desired impact on a relevant professional community.

Creativity: The ability to use imagination and ingenuity to solve complex or wicked problems.

Emotional Intelligence: The ability to regulate one's own emotions as well as the ability to recognise the emotions of others. It sometimes referred to as 'social intelligence'.

Fourth Industrial Revolution: The social and economic world change and disruption that has been driving by technologies and digital innovation.

Compilation of References

Aaker, D. A. (1991). *Managing Brand Equity*. New York: Maxweel Macmillan-Canada.

Aaker, D. A. (1996). Measuring brand equity across products and markets. *California Management Review, 38*(3), 102–120. doi:10.2307/41165845

Aalto, L., & Saari, A. (2009). Reengineering of the meal logistics in a sheltered house for elderly people. *Facilities, 27*(3/4), 120–137. doi:10.1108/02632770910933143

Abbad, M. M., Morris, D., & De Nahlik, C. (2009). Looking under the bonnet: Factors affecting student adoption of e-learning systems in Jordan. *The International Review of Research in Open and Distributed Learning, 10*(2). doi:10.19173/irrodl.v10i2.596

Abbasi, F. K., Ali, A., & Bibi, N. (2018). Analysis of skill gap for business graduates: Managerial perspective from banking industry. *Education + Training, 60*(4), 354–367. doi:10.1108/ET-08-2017-0120

Abdullateef, B. N., Elias, N. F., Mohamed, H., Zaidan, A., & Zaidan, B. (2016). An evaluation and selection problems of OSS-LMS packages. *SpringerPlus, 5*(1), 1. doi:10.118640064-016-1828-y PMID:27064567

Acharya. (2018). *How can Blockchain help in Background Check?* Harbinger Systems.

Achtenhagen, L., & Johannisson, B. (2018). Exploring conscientization in entrepreneurship education. In K. Berglund & K. Verdujin (Eds.), *Revitalizing Entrepreneurship Education: Adopting a Critical Approach in the Classroom* (p. 64). London: Routledge.

Adams, D. A., Nelson, R. R., & Todd, P. A. (1992). Perceived usefulness, ease of use, and usage of information technology: A replication. *Management Information Systems Quarterly, 16*(2), 227–247. doi:10.2307/249577

Adamyk, O., Adamyk, B., & Khorunzhak, N. (2018). *Auditing of the Software of Computer Accounting System*. Academic Press.

Addison, L. B. (1984). *Investigation of the leadership abilities of intellectually gifted students* (Unpublished dissertation). University of South Florida.

Adhikari, A., Lebow, M. I., & Zhang, H. (2004). Firm characteristics and selection of international accounting software. *Journal of International Accounting, Auditing & Taxation, 13*(1), 53–69. doi:10.1016/j.intaccaudtax.2004.02.001

Adi, A., & Grigore, G. (2015). Communicating CSR on social media: the case of Pfizer's social media communications in Europe. Corporate Social Responsibility in the Digital Age. doi:10.1108/S2043-052320150000007009

Aguinis, H., & Glavas, A. (2012). What we know and don't know about corporate social responsibility: A review and research agenda. *Journal of Management, 38*(4), 932–968. doi:10.1177/0149206311436079

Ahmad, F., Mahmud, S. A., & Yousaf, F. Z. (2016). Shortest processing time scheduling to reduce traffic congestion in dense urban areas. *IEEE Transactions on Systems, Man, and Cybernetics. Systems, 47*(5), 838–855. doi:10.1109/TSMC.2016.2521838

Ahmad, S. A., Chinade, U. B., Gambaki, A. M., Ibrahim, S., & Ala, N. A. (2012). The need for MOODLE as a learning management system in Nigerian Universities: Digesting University Utara Malaysia Learning Zone as a case study. *Academic Research International, 2*(3), 444.

Aktan, C., Sumer-Inci, B., & Ozgoren, F. (2009). Kurumsal sosyal sorumluluk faaliyetlerinde glokal yaklaşımlar: 100 değerli global markanın Türkiye'deki web sitelerinin içerik analizi. Ulusal Pazarlama Kongresi, 14.

Al Amoush, A. B., & Sandhu, K. (2019). *A New Model for Acceptance of Analytics in Learning Management Systems at Jordanian Universities (JLMS). In Modern Technologies for Teaching and Learning in Socio-Humanitarian Disciplines* (pp. 138–161). IGI Global.

Al Musawi, A., Ambusaidi, A., Al-Balushi, S., & Al-Balushi, K. (2015). Effectiveness of E-Lab Use in Science Teaching at the Omani Schools. *TOJET: The Turkish Online Journal of Educational Technology, 14*(1).

Alao, A. E., Diyaolu, G. O., & Afuape, A. M. (2014). The changing trend in marketing of financial services: An empirical study on bank performance in Nigeria. *International Journal of Business and Economic Development, 2*(2).

Alasadi, R., & Abdelrahim, A. (2008). Analysis of small business performance in Syria. *Education, Business and Society, 1*(1), 50–62. doi:10.1108/17537980810861510

Alawadhi, S., & Morris, A. (2008). The Use of the UTAUT Model in the Adoption of E-government Services in Kuwait. *Proceedings of the 41st Hawaii International Conference on System Sciences*, 219 - 230. 10.1109/HICSS.2008.452

Alawneh, A., Al-Refai, H., & Batiha, K. (2013). Measuring user satisfaction from e-Government services: Lessons from Jordan. *Government Information Quarterly, 30*(3), 277–288. doi:10.1016/j.giq.2013.03.001

Albrecht, W. S., & Sack, R. J. (2000). *Accounting education: Charting the course through a perilous future*. Sarasota: American Accounting Association.

Al-Dmour, R. (2014). *An integration model for identifying the determinants of the adoption and implementation level of HRIS applications and Its effectiveness in business organisations in Jordan* (Doctor of Philosophy). Brunel University. Retrieved from http://bura.brunel.ac.uk/handle/2438/9222

Al-Dmour, H., Zu'bi, M. F., & Kakeesh, D. (2013). The effect of services marketing mix elements on customer-based brand equity: An empirical study on mobile telecom service recipients in Jordan. *International Journal of Business and Management, 8*(11), 13. doi:10.5539/ijbm.v8n11p13

Aldrich, W., Smith, B., & Dong, F. (1998). Obtaining repeatability of natural extended upper body positions: Its use in comparisons of the functional comfort of garments. *Journal of Fashion Marketing and Management, 2*(4), 329–351. doi:10.1108/eb022538

Al-Gahtani, S., & King, M. (1999). Attitudes. Satisfaction and usage: Factors contributing to each in the acceptance of information technology. *Behaviour and Information Technology Studies: Special Issue on Research Methodology, 18*(4), 277–297. doi:10.1080/014492999119020

Al-Hujran, O., Al-Debei, M. M., Chatfield, A., & Migdadi, M. (2015). The imperative of influencing citizen attitude toward e-government adoption and use. *Computers in Human Behavior, 53*, 189–203. doi:10.1016/j.chb.2015.06.025

Ali, I., Jimenez-Zarco, A. I., & Bicho, M. (2015). Using social media for CSR communication and engaging stakeholders. Corporate Social Responsibility in the Digital Age. doi:10.1108/S2043-052320150000007010

Al-Kasasbeh, M. M., Dasgupta, S., & Al-Faouri, A. H. (2011). Factors Affecting E-Service Satisfaction. *Communications of the IBIMA*, *2011*, 12.

Almarabeh, T. (2014). Students' Perceptions of E-learning at the University of Jordan. *iJET, 9*(3), 31-35.

Alnsour, A., Muhsen, Z., Dababnah, M., Eljinini, M. A., & Barhoum, K. A. (2011). Implementing Moodle as a Tool to develop the Isra University e-learn system. *IJCSNS International Journal of Computer Science and Network Security*, *11*, 120–124.

AlQudah, A. A. (2014). Accepting Moodle by academic staff at the University of Jordan: Applying and extending TAM in technical support factors. *European Scientific Journal*, *10*(18).

Al-Shaikh, F. N. (2003). The practical reality theory and business ethics in non-Western context: Evidence from Jordan. *Journal of Management Development*, *22*(8), 679–693. doi:10.1108/02621710310487855

Al-Shboul, M. A., & Alsmadi, I. (2010). Challenges of Utilizing E-Learning Systems in Public Universities in Jordan. *iJET, 5*(1), 4-10.

Al-Shboul, M. (2011). Potential Use of Course Management Systems in Higher Education Institutions in Jordan. *Online Submission*, *8*(2), 220–232.

Al-Shboul, M. (2013). The Level of E-Learning Integration at the University of Jordan: Challenges and Opportunities. *International Education Studies*, *6*(4). doi:10.5539/ies.v6n4p93

Al-Zoubi, S. I., & Ali, M. (2019). *The Bearing of Culture upon Intention to Utilize D-learning Amongst Jordanian University Students: Modernizing with Emerging Technologies.* Paper presented at the International Conference for Emerging Technologies in Computing. 10.1007/978-3-030-23943-5_21

Amagoh, F. (2009). Leadership development and leadership effectiveness. *management. Decision (Washington, D.C.)*, *47*(6), 989–999.

American Accounting Association. (1968). *A Guide to Accounting Instruction: Concepts & Practices*. Cincinnati: South-Western Publishing.

Anandarajan, M., Igbaria, M., & Anakwe, U. P. (2000). Technology Acceptance in the Banking Industry: A prospective from a less developed country. *Information Technology & People*, *13*(4), 298–312. doi:10.1108/09593840010359491

Anderson, E. W., & Sullivan, M. W. (1993). The antecedents and consequences of customer satisfaction for firms. *Marketing Science*, *12*(2), 125–143. doi:10.1287/mksc.12.2.125

Anderson, J. C., & Gerbing, D. W. (1988). Structural equation modeling in practice: A review and recommended two-step approach. *Psychological Bulletin*, *103*(3), 411–423. doi:10.1037/0033-2909.103.3.411

Anderson, R. E., & Srinivasan, S. S. (2003). E-satisfaction and eloyalty: A contingency framework. *Psychology and Marketing*, *§§§*, 20.

Antal, A. B., Dierkies, M., MacMillan, K., & Marz, L. (2002). Corporate social reporting revisited. *Journal of General Management*, *28*(2), 22–42. doi:10.1177/030630700202800202

Anthopoulos, L. G., Siozos, P., & Tsoukalas, L. A. (2007). pplying Participatory Design and Collaboration in Digital Public Services for Discovering and Re-designing E-government Services. *Government Information Quarterly*, *24*(2), 353–376. doi:10.1016/j.giq.2006.07.018

Arai, M., Wanca-Thibault, M., & Shockley-Zalabak, P. (2001). Communication theory and training approaches for multiculturally diverse organizations: Have Academics and Practitioners Missed the Connection? *Public Personnel, 30*(4), 445–455. doi:10.1177/009102600103000402

Araujo, T., & Kollat, J. (2018). Communicating effectively about CSR on Twitter: The power of engaging strategies and storytelling elements. *Internet Research, 28*(2), 419–431. doi:10.1108/IntR-04-2017-0172

Arguel, A., Lockyer, L., Kennedy, G., Lodge, J. M., & Pachman, M. (2019). Seeking optimal confusion: A review on epistemic emotion management in interactive digital learning environments. *Interactive Learning Environments, 27*(2), 200–210. doi:10.1080/10494820.2018.1457544

Arham, A. F. (2014a). Leadership and Performance: The Case of Malaysian SMEs in the Services Sector. *International Journal of Asian Social Science, 4*(3), 343–355.

Arham, A. F. (2014b). *The Relationship between Leadership Behaviour, Entrepreneurial Orientation and Organisational Performance in Malaysian Small and Medium Enterprises (PhD)*. Royal Melbourne Institute of Technology University.

Arham, A. F., Boucher, C., & Muenjohn, N. (2013). Leadership and entrepreneurial success: A study of SMEs in Malaysia. *WORLD (Oakland, Calif.), 3*(5), 117–130.

Ariff, M. S. M., Yun, L. O., Zakuan, N., & Ismail, K. (2013). The Impacts of Service Quality and Customer Satisfaction on Customer Loyalty in Internet Banking. *Procedia: Social and Behavioral Sciences, 81*, 469–473. doi:10.1016/j.sbspro.2013.06.462

Arslan, A., & Staub, S. (2013). Theory X and Theory Y Type Leadership Behavior and its Impact on Organizational Performance: Small Business Owners in the Şishane Lighting and Chandelier District. *Procedia: Social and Behavioral Sciences, 75*, 102–111. doi:10.1016/j.sbspro.2013.04.012

Aslani, M., Seipel, S., & Wiering, M. (2018). Continuous residual reinforcement learning for traffic signal control optimization. *Canadian Journal of Civil Engineering, 45*(8), 690–702. doi:10.1139/cjce-2017-0408

Atilgan, E., Aksoy, Ş., & Akinci, S. (2005). Determinants of the brand equity: A verification approach in the beverage industry in Turkey. *Marketing Intelligence & Planning, 23*(3), 237–248. doi:10.1108/02634500510597283

Atoum, I., Otoom, A., & Ali, A. A. (2017). Holistic Cyber Security Implementation Frameworks: A Case Study of Jordan. *International Journal of Information. Business and Management, 9*(1), 108.

Autor, D. (2015). Why are there still so many jobs? The history and future of workplace automation. *The Journal of Economic Perspectives, 29*(3), 3–30. doi:10.1257/jep.29.3.3

Avolio, B. J., Bass, B. M., & Jung, D. I. (1999). Re-examining the components of transformational and transactional leadership using the Multifactor Leadership. *Journal of Occupational and Organizational Psychology, 72*(4), 441–462. doi:10.1348/096317999166789

Avolio, B. J., & Gardner, W. L. (2005). Authentic leadership development: Getting to the root of positive forms of leadership. *The Leadership Quarterly, 16*(3), 315–338. doi:10.1016/j.leaqua.2005.03.001

Avolio, B. J., Sosik, J. J., Jung, D. I., & Berson, Y. (2003). *Leadership models, methods, and applications*. Handbook of psychology. doi:10.1002/0471264385.wei1212

Axelrod, L., Fitzpatrick, G., Burridge, J., Mawson, S., Smith, P., Rodden, T., & Ricketts, I. (2009). The reality of homes fit for heroes: Design challenges for rehabilitation technology at home. *Journal of Assistive Technologies, 3*(2), 35–43. doi:10.1108/17549450200900014

Babić, S. (2012). Factors that influence academic teacher's acceptance of e-learning technology in blended learning environment. *E-Learning-Organizational Infrastructure and Tools for Specific Areas*, 3-18.

Badenoch and Clark. (2009). *Balancing act: is the accounting and finance profession ready to step up?* Retrieved from Badenoch and Clark: https://www.badenochandclark.com/

Bailey, J. E., & Pearson, S. W. (1983). Development of a tool for measuring and analyzing computer user satisfaction. *Management Science*, *29*(5), 530–544. doi:10.1287/mnsc.29.5.530

Baldwin, R. (2016). *The Great Convergence: Information Technology and the New Globalization*. Cambridge, MA: Harvard University Press.

Baliga. (2017). *Understanding Blockchain Consensus Models*. Corporate CTO Office Persistent Systems Ltd.

Ballantine, J., & McCourt Larres, P. (2009). Accounting undergraduates' perceptions of cooperative learning as a model for Enhancing their interpersonal and communication skills to interface successfully with professional accountancy education and training. *Accounting Education*, *18*(4-5), 387–402. doi:10.1080/09639280902719366

Balliester, T., & Elsheikhi, A. (2018). *The Future of Work: A Literature Review ILO Research Department* Working Paper No. 29. Geneva: International Labour Organisation.

Barber, S. J., & Tan, S. C. (2018). Ageism affects the future time perspective of older adults. *GeroPsych*, *31*(3), 115–126. doi:10.1024/1662-9647/a000189

Baroudi, J., & Orlikowski, W. J. (1988). A short-form measure of user information satisfaction: A psychometric evaluation and notes on use. *Journal of Management Information Systems*, *4*(4), 44–59. doi:10.1080/07421222.1988.11517807

Basil, D. Z., & Erlandson, J. (2008). Corporate social responsibility website representations: A longitudinal study of internal and external self-presentations. *Journal of Marketing Communications*, *14*(2), 125–137. doi:10.1080/13527260701858497

Bass, B. M. (1986). Leadership and performance beyond expectations (Vol. 25). New York: The Free Press.

Bass, B. M. (1985). *Leadership and performance beyond expectations*. Collier Macmillan.

Bass, B. M. (1985). Leadership: Good, better, best. *Organizational Dynamics*, *13*(3), 26–40. doi:10.1016/0090-2616(85)90028-2

Bass, B. M., & Riggio, R. E. (2006). *Transformational leadership*. Psychology Press. doi:10.4324/9781410617095

Bass, B. M., & Stogdill, R. M. (1990). *Bass & Stogdill's handbook of leadership: Theory, research, and managerial applications*. Simon and Schuster.

Batistic, S., & Tymon, A. (2017). Networking behaviour, graduate employability: A social capital perspective. *Education + Training*, *59*(4), 374–388. doi:10.1108/ET-06-2016-0100

Bazhair, A., & Sandhu, K. (2015). Factors influencing the acceptance of Enterprise Resource Planning System (ERP) and financial performance of Saudi Arabia listed companies: Multivariate data analysis using Structural Equation Modeling (SEM). *International Journal of Business and Management Review*, *3*(4), 93–118.

Beach, L. R., & Mitchell, T. R. (1978). A contingency model for the selection of decision strategies. *Academy of Management Review*, *3*(3), 439–449. doi:10.5465/amr.1978.4305717

Behrisch, M. (2011). SUMO–simulation of urban mobility: an overview. In *Proceedings of SIMUL 2011, The Third International Conference on Advances in System Simulation*. ThinkMind.

Bélanger, F., & Carter, L. (2008). Trust and risk in e-government adoption. *The Journal of Strategic Information Systems*, *17*(2), 165–176. doi:10.1016/j.jsis.2007.12.002

Beller, J., & Wagner, A. (2018). Loneliness, social isolation, their synergistic interaction, and mortality. *Health Psychology*, *37*(9), 808–813. doi:10.1037/hea0000605 PMID:30138019

Bennis, W., & Nanus, B. (1985). Leadership: The strategies for taking charge. New York.

Bennis, W. (1995). *Nanus (1985) Leaders: The Strategies for Taking Charge*. New York: Harper and Row.

Bennis, W. (2007). The challenges of leadership in the modern world: Introduction to the special issue. *The American Psychologist*, *62*(1), 2–5. doi:10.1037/0003-066X.62.1.2 PMID:17209674

Bentler, P. M. (1995). EQS structural equations program manual (Vol. 6). Encino, CA: Multivariate Software.

Berg, A., Buffie, E., & Zanna, L. (2018). *Should We Fear the Robot Revolution? (The Correct Answer is Yes)*. IMF Working Paper No. 18/116. Washington, DC: International Monetary Fund.

Berkley, B. J., & Gupta, A. (1994). Improving service quality with information technology. *International Journal of Information Management*, *14*(2), 109–121. doi:10.1016/0268-4012(94)90030-2

Berry, A. J., Sweeting, R., & Goto, J. (2006). The effect of business advisers on the performance of SMEs. *Journal of Small Business and Enterprise Development*, *13*(1), 33–47. doi:10.1108/14626000610645298

Bhardwaj, A. (2018). *Using Blockchain Can Do Wonders In Education Sector*. https://www.oodlestechnologies.com/blogs/Using-Blockchain-Can-Do-Wonders-In-Education-Sector

Bhatia, V., & Bhatia, A. (2011). Business communication. In J. Simpson (Ed.), *The routledge handbook of applied linguistics* (pp. 24–35). Oxfordshire: Routledge.

Bhattacherjee, A. (2001). An empirical analysis of the antecedents of electronic commerce service continuance. *Decision Support Systems*, *32*(2), 201–214. doi:10.1016/S0167-9236(01)00111-7

Bitner, M. J. (1990). Evaluating Service Encounters: The Effects of Physical Sur-roundings and Employee Responses. *Journal of Marketing*, *54*(2), 69–82. doi:10.1177/002224299005400206

BitRice. (2018). *Create the optimum data storage and content sharing eco-chain*. White Paper of Bit Rice (BTR), BitRice Foundation Singapore.

Blockchain News. (2018). How will blockchain technology affect higher education in the future? *Blog, 2017. Introduction to Blockchain Technology*. https://netsend.com/blog/introduction-to-blockchain-technology/

Block, J. H., Fisch, C. O., & van Praag, M. (2017). The Schumpeterian entrepreneur: A review of the empirical evidence on the antecedents, behaviour and consequences of innovative entrepreneurship. *Industry and Innovation*, *24*(1), 61–95. doi:10.1080/13662716.2016.1216397

Boal, K. B., & Hooijberg, R. (2001). Strategic leadership research: Moving on. *The Leadership Quarterly*, *11*(4), 515–549. doi:10.1016/S1048-9843(00)00057-6

Boulter, J. (2014). *How to build profitable customer relationships*. Academic Press.

Bowen, H. R. (1953). *Social responsibilities of the businessman*. New York: Harper and Row.

Brach, J. S., FitzGerald, S., Newman, A. B., Kelsey, S., Kuller, L., VanSwearingen, J. M., & Kriska, A. M. (2003). Physical activity and functional status in community-dwelling older women: A 14-year prospective study. *Archives of Internal Medicine*, *163*(21), 2565–2571. doi:10.1001/archinte.163.21.2565 PMID:14638556

Brecht, K., Swift, J. K., Worrall, J. M., & Parkin, S. R. (2017). A randomized controlled test of direct-to-consumer marketing using the American Psychological Association psychotherapy works videos. *Professional Psychology, Research and Practice*, *48*(6), 421–428. doi:10.1037/pro0000167

Brensinger, R. P., & Lambert, D. M. (1990). Can the SERVQUAL Scale be Generalized to Business-to-Business Services? *Knowledge Development in Marketing1990 AMA's Summer Educators' Conference Proceedings*, 289.

Bressler, L. A., & Bressler, M. S. (2006). How entrepreneurs choose and use accounting information systems. *Strategic Finance*, *87*(12), 56.

Bressolles, G., Durrieu, F. & Senecal, S. (2014). A consumer typology base done-service quality and e-satisfaction. *Journal of Retailing and Consumer Services, 21*, 889-896.

Broderick, A. J., & Vachirapornpuk, S. (2002). Service quality in internet banking: The importance of customer role. *Marketing Intelligence & Planning*, *20*(6), 327–335. doi:10.1108/02634500210445383

Brogowicz, A. A., Delene, L. M., & Lyth, D. M. (1990). A synthesised service quality model with managerial implications. *International Journal of Service Industry Management*, *1*(1), 27–44. doi:10.1108/09564239010001640

Brown, T., & Wyatt, J. (2010). Design thinking for social innovation. *Stanford Social Innovation Review*, (Winter): 31–35.

Bruce, M. (2009). Unleashing the creative potential of design in business. In T. Rickards, M. A. Runco, & S. Moger (Eds.), *The Routledge Companion to creativity*. Oxfordshire: Routledge.

Bruce, M., & Bessant, J. (2002). *Design in Business: Strategic Innovation through Design*. Englewood Cliffs: Prentice Hall.

Bryer, A. R. (2011). Accounting as learnt social practice: The case of the empresas recuperades in Argentina. *Accounting, Organizations and Society*, *36*(8), 478–495. doi:10.1016/j.aos.2011.09.002

Buchanan, T., Paine, C., Joinson, A. N., & Reips, U.-D. (2007). Development of measures of online privacy concern and protection for use on the internet. *Journal of the American Society for Information Science and Technology*, *58*(2), 157–165. doi:10.1002/asi.20459

Bui, B., & Porter, B. (2010). The expectation-performance gap in accounting education: An exploratory study. *Accounting Education*, *19*(1-2), 23–50. doi:10.1080/09639280902875556

Bujaki, M., Durocher, S., Brouard, F., Neilson, L., & Pyper, R. (2018). Protect, profit, profess, promote: Establishing legitimacy through logics of diversity in Canadian accounting firm recruitment documents. *Canadian Journal of Administrative Sciences*, *35*(1), 162–178. doi:10.1002/cjas.1392

Burt, S., & Gabbott, M. (1995). The elderly consumer and non-food purchase behaviour. *European Journal of Marketing*, *29*(2), 43–57. doi:10.1108/03090569510080941

Buyukkupcu, A., Atilgan, E., & Akinci, S. (2007). *Corporate social responsibility: Cases in Turkey*. In *Strategic Management Conference*, Antalya, Turkey.

Buzarna-Tihenea, A. (2019). Written business communication. Case study: Auditor's Report. *"Ovidus" University Annals, Economic Sciences Series, 19*(1).

Campopiano, G., & De Massis, A. (2015). Corporate social responsibility reporting: A content analysis in family and non-family firms. *Journal of Business Ethics*, *129*(3), 511–534. doi:10.100710551-014-2174-z

Carmines, E. G., & Zeller, R. A. (1979). *Reliability and validity assessment* (Vol. 17). Sage publications. doi:10.4135/9781412985642

Carnegie, G., & Napier, C. (2010). Traditional accountants and business professionals: Portraying the accounting profession after Enron. *Accounting, Organizations and Society*, *35*(3), 360–376. doi:10.1016/j.aos.2009.09.002

Carroll, A. B. (1979). A three-dimensional conceptual model of corporate performance. *Academy of Management Review*, *4*(4), 497–505. doi:10.5465/amr.1979.4498296

Carter, L., & Bélanger, F. (2005). The utilization of e-government services: Citizen trust, innovation and acceptance factors. *Information Systems Journal*, *15*(1), 5–26. doi:10.1111/j.1365-2575.2005.00183.x

Casanueva, C., Gallego, A., & Revilla, M. (2015). Access and mobilization of network resources and competitive advantage in hotels. *International Journal of Contemporary Hospitality Management*, *27*(6), 1279–1300. doi:10.1108/IJCHM-03-2013-0144

Castello, I., Morsing, M., & Schultz, F. (2013). Communicative dynamics and the polyphony of corporate social responsibility in the network society. *Journal of Business Ethics*, *118*(4), 683–694. doi:10.100710551-013-1954-1

Castro-Gonzales, S., Bande, B., Fernandez-Ferrin, P., & Kimura, T. (2019). Corporate social responsibility and consumer advocacy behaviors: The importance of emotions and moral virtues. *Journal of Cleaner Production*, *231*, 846–855. doi:10.1016/j.jclepro.2019.05.238

Chae, B. & Park, E. (2018). Corporate social responsibility (CSR): A survey of topics and trends using Twitter data and topic modelling. *Sustainability*, *10*(7), 22-31.

Chakraborty, S., & Sengupta, K. (2014). Structural equation modelling of determinants of customer satisfaction of mobile network providers: Case of Kolkata, India. *IIMB Management Review*, *§§§*, 1–15.

Chandra, R., & Gregory, C. (2010). *Insync adaptive traffic signal technology: Real-time artificial intelligence delivering real-world results*. Academic Press.

Chang, H. H., & Chen, S. W. (2008). The impact of customer interface quality, satisfaction and switching costs on e-loyalty: Internet experience as a moderator. *Computers in Human Behavior*, *24*(6), 2927–2944. doi:10.1016/j.chb.2008.04.014

Chang, S., Lin, R., Chen, J., & Huang, L. (2005). Manufacturing flexibility and manufacturing proactiveness. *Industrial Management & Data Systems*, *105*(8), 1115–1132. doi:10.1108/02635570510624482

Chaudhri, V., & Wang, J. (2007). Communicating corporate social responsibility on the internet: A case study of the top 100 information technology companies in India. *Management Communication Quarterly*, *21*(2), 232–247. doi:10.1177/0893318907308746

Che-Ha, N., & Hashim, S. (2007). Brand equity, customer satisfaction and loyalty: Malaysian banking sector. *International Review of Business Research Papers, 3*(5), 123-133.

Che-Ha, N., Nguyen, B., Yahya, W. K., Melewar, T. C., & Chen, Y. P. (2016). Country branding emerging from citizens' emotions and the perceptions of competitive advantage: The case of Malaysia. *Journal of Vacation Marketing*, *22*(1), 13–28. doi:10.1177/1356766715586454

Chen, R. R., Davison, R. M., & Qu, C. X. (2016). Using social media for business communication: A symbolic interaction perspective. In *Australasian Conference on Information Systems*, (pp. 1-11). Wollongong: Academic Press.

Chen, S.-C. (2012). The customersatisfaction–loyaltyrelationininaninteractivee-servicesetting: The mediators. *Journal of Retailing and Consumer Services, 19*, 202-210.

Chen, G., Xu, B., Lu, M., & Chen, N.-S. (2018). Exploring blockchain technology and its potential applications for education. *Smart Learning Environments*, *5*(1), 1. doi:10.118640561-017-0050-x

Chen, K., & Chan, A. H. (2013). Use or Non-Use of Gerontechnology—A Qualitative Study. *International Journal of Environmental Research and Public Health, 10*(10), 4645–4666. doi:10.3390/ijerph10104645

Chen, L. D., Soliman, K. S., Mao, E., & Frolick, M. N. (2000). Measuring user satisfaction with data warehouses: An exploratory study. *Information & Management, 37*(3), 103–110. doi:10.1016/S0378-7206(99)00042-7

Chen, Y. (2013). *Relationships Among Emotional Intelligence, Cultural Intelligence, Job Performance, and Leader Effectiveness: A Study of County Extension Directors in Ohio (Doctor of Philosophy)*. The Ohio State University.

Cho, M., Furey, L. D., & Mohr, T. (2016). Communicating corporate social responsibility on social media: Strategies, stakeholders, and public engagement on corporate Facebook. *Business and Professional Communication Quarterly, 80*(1), 52–69. doi:10.1177/2329490616663708

Cho, N., & Park, S. (2001). Development of Electronic Commerce User-Consumer Satisfaction Index (ECUSI) for Internet Shopping. *Industrial Management & Data Systems, 101*(8), 400–405. doi:10.1108/EUM0000000006170

Cho, S. K., & Berge, Z. L. (2002). Overcoming barriers to distance training and education. *USDLA Journal, 16*(1), 16–34.

Choudhary, A. I., Akhtar, S. A., & Zaheer, A. (2013). Impact of transformational and servant leadership on organizational performance: A comparative analysis. *Journal of Business Ethics, 116*(2), 433–440. doi:10.100710551-012-1470-8

Churchill, G. A. Jr. (1979). A paradigm for developing better measures of marketing constructs. *JMR, Journal of Marketing Research, 16*(1), 64–73. doi:10.1177/002224377901600110

Churchill, G. A. Jr, & Surprenant, C. (1982). An investigation into the determinants of customer satisfaction. *JMR, Journal of Marketing Research, 19*(4), 491–504. doi:10.1177/002224378201900410

Clark, D. (2016). *10 ways Blockchain could be used in education*. https://oeb.global/oeb-insights/10-ways-blockchain-could-be-used-in-education

Collier, J. E., & Bienstock, C. C. (2006). Measuring Service Quality in E-Retailing. *Journal of Service Research, 8*(3), 260–275. doi:10.1177/1094670505278867

Collins, J. C. (1999). How to select the right accounting software. *Journal of Accountancy, 188*(4), 67.

Coluccia, D., Fontana, S., & Solimene, S. (2016). Disclosure of corporate social responsibility: A comparison between traditional and digital reporting: an empirical analysis on Italian listed companies. *International Journal of Managerial and Financial Accounting, 8*(3-4), 230-246.

Colwell, S. R., Aung, M., Kanetkar, V., & Holden, A. L. (2008). Toward a measure of service convenience: Multiple-item scale development and empirical test. *Journal of Services Marketing, 22*(2), 160–169. doi:10.1108/08876040810862895

Conger, J. A. (1998). The dark side of leadership. *Leading organizations: Perspectives for a new era*, 250-260.

Conger, J., & Kanungo, R. (1998). *Charismatic leadership in organizations*. Sage Publications.

Copeland, M. K. (2013). *The Importance of Ethical Leadership in the Accounting Industry (Doctor of Philosophy in Organizational Leadership)*. Regent University.

Corredor, I., García, A., Martínez, J. F., & López, P. (2008). Wireless sensor network-based system for measuring and monitoring road traffic. 6th Collaborative Electronic Communications and eCommerce Technology and Research (CollECTeR 2008), Madrid, Spain.

Cox, A. (2009). Creating or destroying business value: understanding the opportunities and the limits of a win-win collaboration. In T. Rickards, M. A. Runco, & S. Moger (Eds.), *The Routledge companion to creativity*. Oxfordshire: Routledge.

Creswell, J. W. (2013). *Research design: Qualitative, quantitative, and mixed methods approaches*. Sage Publications.

Crisan, C., & Zbuchea, A. (2015). CSR and social media: Could online repositories become regulatory tools for CSR related activities reporting? In A. Adi, G. Grigore, & D. Crowther (Eds.), *Corporate Social Responsibility in the Digital Age* (pp. 197–220). Bingley: Emerald Publishing Group. doi:10.1108/S2043-052320150000007011

Cristobal, E., & Flavian, C. & GUINALIU, M. (2007). Perceived E-Service Quality: Measurement Validation and Effects on Consumer Satisfaction and Website Loyalty. *Managing Service Quality*, *17*, 317–340. doi:10.1108/09604520710744326

Cronin, J. J. Jr, & Taylor, S. A. (1992). Measuring service quality: A reexamination and extension. *Journal of Marketing*, *6*(July), 55–68. doi:10.1177/002224299205600304

Cronin, J. J. Jr, & Taylor, S. A. (1994). SERVPERF versus SERVQUAL: Reconciling performance-based and perception minus-expectations measurement of service quality. *Journal of Marketing*, *58*(1), 125–131. doi:10.1177/002224299405800110

Crosby, M., Nachiappan, P. P., Verma, S., & Kalyanaraman, V. (2015). Blockchain Technology, Beyond Bitcoin. Sutardja Center for Entrepreneurship & Technology Technical Report.

Crosby, P. B. (1979). *Quality is free: The art of making quality certain* (Vol. 94). New York: McGraw-hill.

Crossman, J., & Bordia, S. (2012). Piecing the puzzle. *Journal of International Education in Business*, *5*(1), 71–88. doi:10.1108/18363261211261773

Cummings, N. A. (2000). Psychology and the new entrepreneurship: Possibilities and opportunities. *The Psychologist Manager Journal*, *4*(1), 27–43. doi:10.1037/h0095877

Dabholkar, P. A. (1996). Consumer evaluations of new technology-based self-service operations: An investigation of alternative models. *International Journal of Research in Marketing*, *13*(1), 29–51. doi:10.1016/0167-8116(95)00027-5

Daff, L., de Lange, P., & Jackling, B. (2012). A comparison of generic skills and emotional intelligence in accounting education. *Issues in Accounting Education*, *27*(3), 627–645. doi:10.2308/iace-50145

Dale-Jones, G., Hancock, P., & Willey, K. (2015). Accounting Students in an Australian University Improve their Writing: But How did it Happen? In R. M. Wilson, F. E. Gray, & L. Hamilton (Eds.), *Communication in Accounting Education* (pp. 160–178). Oxfordshire: Routledge.

Daley, S. (2018). *Blockchain education companies earning straight A's*. https://builtin.com/blockchain/blockchain-in-education

Danisman, S., Tosuntas, S. B., & Karadag, E. (2015). The Effect of Leadership on Organizational Performance. *Leadership and Organizational Outcomes*, 143-168.

Das, D. (2011). An Empirical Study To Build A Theoretical Framework That Can Determine Customer Satisfaction In Terms Of People, Process & Physical Evidence. *Service Marketing Practices in India: Changing Paradigms*, 135-143.

Das, S., Nayyar, A., & Singh, I. (2019). *An assessment of forerunners for customer loyalty in the selected financial sector by SEM approach toward their effect on business*. Data Technologies and Applications. doi:10.1108/DTA-04-2019-0059

Dauletova, V. (2016). Innovating business communication courses in Oman: From design to implementation. *Innovations in Education and Teaching International*, *53*(5), 545–554. doi:10.1080/14703297.2015.1015594

Davis, F. D. (1989). Perceived usefulness, perceived ease of use, and user acceptance of information technology. *Management Information Systems Quarterly*, *13*(3), 319–340. doi:10.2307/249008

Davis, F. D., Bagozzi, R. P., & Warshaw, P. R. (1989). User Acceptance of Computer Technology: A Comparison of two Theoretical models. *Management Science*, *35*(8), 982–1003. doi:10.1287/mnsc.35.8.982

Dawson, R. (2015). What is the future of work? In E. Evans, R. Burritt, & J. Guthrie (Eds.), *Future proofing the profession: preparing business leaders andfinance professionalfor 2025*. Sydney: Chartered Accountants Australia and New Zealand.

Daymon, C., & Durkin, K. (2013). The impact of marketisation on postgraduate career prepardness in a high skills economy. *Studies in Higher Education*, *38*(4), 595–612. doi:10.1080/03075079.2011.590896

De Chernatony, L., & Harris, F. J. (2001). *Measuring the consumer-based equity of financial services brands. Birminghan Business Scholl*. The University of Birmingham.

De Rossi, L. M., Salviotti, G., & Abbatemarco, N. (2019). Towards a Comprehensive Blockchain Architecture Continuum. *Proc. of the 52nd Hawaii Intel. Conference on System Sciences*. 10.24251/HICSS.2019.557

Debons, A., Ramage, W., & Orien, J. (1978). Effectiveness Model of Productivity. Research on Productivity Measurement Systems for Administrative Services: Computing and Information Services. NSF Grant APR-20546.

Delone, W. H., & McLean, E. R. (1992). Information systems success: The quest for the dependent variable. *Information Systems Research*, *3*(1), 60–95. doi:10.1287/isre.3.1.60

Denison, D. R., Hooijberg, R., & Quinn, R. E. (1995). Paradox and performance: Toward a theory of behavioral complexity in managerial leadership. *Organization Science*, *6*(5), 524–540. doi:10.1287/orsc.6.5.524

Dey, D. W., Fitzsimons, S., Morris, A., & Ng, D. (2002). *Adaptive Traffic Signal Interconnect in Menlo Park and Sunnyvale*. Academic Press.

Dhar, R. L. (2016). Ethical leadership and its impact on service innovative behavior: The role of LMX and job autonomy. *Tourism Management*, *57*, 139–148. doi:10.1016/j.tourman.2016.05.011

Dhar, U., & Mishra, P. (2001). Leadership effectiveness: A study of constituent factors. *Journal of Management Research*, *1*(4), 254.

Dickel, P. (2017). The impact of protectability and proactiveness on the environmental performance of new ventures. *Corporate Governance*, *17*(1), 117–133. doi:10.1108/CG-03-2016-0055

Dickerson, M. D., & Gentry, J. W. (1983). Characteristics of adopters and non-adopters of home computers. *The Journal of Consumer Research*, *10*(2), 225–235. doi:10.1086/208961

Dino, R. N. (2015). Crossing boundaries: Toward integrating creativity, innovation, and entrepreneurship research through practice. *Psychology of Aesthetics, Creativity, and the Arts*, *9*(2), 139–146. doi:10.1037/aca0000015

Doane, D. (2005). Beyond corporate social responsibility: Minnows, mammoths and markets. *Futures*, *37*(2-3), 215–229. doi:10.1016/j.futures.2004.03.028

Doll, W. J., & Torkzadeh, G. (1988). The measure of end-user computing satisfaction. *Management Information Systems Quarterly*, *12*(2), 259–274. doi:10.2307/248851

Dong, Z., Luo, F., & Liang, G. (2018). Blockchain: A secure, decentralized, trusted cyberinfrastructure solution for future energy systems. *Journal of Mod. Power Syst. Clean Energy*, *6*(5), 958–967. doi:10.100740565-018-0418-0

Dritsas, S., Gymnopoulos, L., Karyda, M., Balopoulos, T., Kokolakis, S., Lambrinoudakis, C. & Katsikas, S. (2006). A knowledge-based approach to security requirements for e-health applications. *The electronic Journal on Emerging Tools and Applications, In the Special Issue: Emerging Security Paradigms in the Knowledge Era*, 2.

Drucker, P. F. (1974). *Management: Tasks, Responsibilities, Practices*. New York: Haper & Row.

Drucker, P. F. (2007). *Management challenges for the 21st century*. Routledge.

Dua, S., Chahal, R., & Sharma, A. (2013). Interrelationship of Aaker's customer based brand equity dimensions: Offering a model to banking sector. *Asian Journal of Management Research*, *4*(2), 297–307.

Du, S., Bhattacharya, C. B., & Sen, S. (2010). Maximising business returns to corporate social responsibility (CSR): The role of CSR communication. *International Journal of Management Reviews*, *12*(1), 1, 8–19. doi:10.1111/j.1468-2370.2009.00276.x

Dwivedi, Y. K., Choudrie, J., & Brinkman, W.-P. (2006). Development of a survey instrument to examine consumer adoption of broadband. *Industrial Management & Data Systems*, *106*(5), 700–718. doi:10.1108/02635570610666458

Dwyer, J. (2016). *Communication for Business and the Professions*. Melbourne: Pearson Australia.

Efanny, W., Haryanto, J., Kashif, M., & Widyanto, H. (2018). The relationship between marketing mix and retailer-perceived brand equity. *IMP Journal*, *12*(1), 192–208. doi:10.1108/IMP-12-2016-0019

Eismann, M., Verbeij, T., & Henkens, K. (2019). Older workers' plans for activities in retirement: The role of opportunities, spousal support, and time perception. *Psychology and Aging*, *34*(5), 738–749. doi:10.1037/pag0000377 PMID:31305089

Elden, M., Yeygel Cakir, S., & Bakir, U. (2011). Corporate social responsibility campaigns in the digital age: The case of Vodafone "Red light application/Between us". In *Conference on e-Business, e-Services and e-Society* (120-127). Springer.

Elikai, F., Ivancevich, D. M., & Ivancevich, S. H. (2007). Accounting software selection and user satisfaction. *The CPA Journal*, *77*(5), 26–31.

Empen, J., Loy, J., & Weiss, C. (2015). Price promotions and brand loyalty. *European Journal of Marketing*, *49*(5/6), 736–759. doi:10.1108/EJM-08-2013-0433

Esrock, S. L., & Leichty, G. B. (1998). Social responsibility and corporate web pages: Self presentation or agenda-setting? *Public Relations Review*, *24*(3), 305–319. doi:10.1016/S0363-8111(99)80142-8

Evans, C., Gbolahan, G., Wells, J., & Scott, I. (2012). Balancing the yin and yang: The role of universities in developing softer skills in accounting. *Industry and Higher Education*, *26*(1), 36–70. doi:10.5367/ihe.2012.0081

Evanschitzky, H., Iyer, G. R., Hesse, R. J., & Ahlert, D. (2004). E-satisfaction: A Re-Examination. *Journal of Retailing*, *80*(3), 239–247. doi:10.1016/j.jretai.2004.08.002

Fabrigar, L. R., Wegener, D. T., Maccallum, R. C., & Strahan, E. J. (1999). Evaluating the use of exploratory factor analysis in psychological research. *Psychological Methods*, *4*(3), 272–299. doi:10.1037/1082-989X.4.3.272

Farjam, S., & Hongyi, X. (2015). Reviewing the concept of brand equity and evaluating consumer-based brand equity (CBBE) models. *International Journal of Management Science and Business Administration*, *1*(8), 14–29. doi:10.18775/ijmsba.1849-5664-5419.2014.18.1002

Farquhar, P. H. (1989). *Managing Brand Equity Marketing Research*. Academic Press.

Faye, S., Chaudet, C., & Demeure, I. (2012a, October). *Un algorithme distribué de contrôle des feux de circulation sur plusieurs intersections par un réseau de capteurs sans fil*. Academic Press.

Faye, S., Chaudet, C., & Demeure, I. (2012b). *Contrôle du trafic routier urbain par un réseau fixe de capteurs sans fil*. Academic Press.

Fiedler, S. (2010). Managing resistance in an organizational transformation: A case study from a mobile operator company. *International Journal of Project Management, 28*, 370-383.

Filipe Lages, L., & Montgomery, D. (2004). Export performance as an antecedent of export commitment and marketing strategy adaptation. *European Journal of Marketing, 38*(9/10), 1186–1214. doi:10.1108/03090560410548933

Fletcher, D. (2018). Prologue Looking to the Future: How can we further develop critical pedagogies in entrepreneurship education? In K. Berglund & K. Verduijn (Eds.), *Revitalizing Entrepreneurship Education: Adopting a Critical Approach in the Classroom* (pp. xvii–xviii). London: Routledge.

Forum, W. E. (2016). *The Future of Jobs Employment, Skills and Workforce Strategy for the Fourth Industrial Revolution.* Retrieved from World Economic Forum: http://www3.weforum.org/docs/WEF_Future_of_Jobs.pdf

Forum, W. E. (2018). *The Future of Jobs Report.* Retrieved from World Economic Forum: http://www3.weforum.org/docs/WEF_Future_of_Jobs_2018.pdf

Forum, W. E. (2020). *Jobs of Tomorrow Mapping Opportunity in the new economy.* Retrieved from World Economic Forum: http://www3.weforum.org/docs/WEF_Jobs_of_Tomorrow_2020.pdf

Fraustino, J. D., & Connolly-Ahern, C. (2015). Corporate associations written on the wall: Publics' responses to Fortune 500 ability and social responsibility Facebook posts. *Journal of Public Relations Research, 27*(5), 452–474. doi:10.1080/1062726X.2015.1098543

Freeman, C. (1982). *The Economics of Industrial Innovation.* London: Frances Pinter.

Frey, C., & Osborne, M. (2013). *The Future of Employment: How susceptible Are Jobs to Computerisation.* Oxford: Oxford University Press.

Friedman, M. (1962). *Capitalism and Freedom.* Chicago: University of Chicago Press.

Frost, F. A., & Kumar, M. (2000). INTSERVQUAL: An internal adaptation of the GAP model in a large service organization. *Journal of Services Marketing, 14*(5), 358–377. doi:10.1108/08876040010340991

Galbreath, J., & Shum, P. (2012). Do customer satisfaction and reputation mediate the CSR-FP link? Evidence from Australia. *Australian Journal of Management, 37*(2), 211–229. doi:10.1177/0312896211432941

Gandhi, S., & Kang, L. S. (2011). Customer satisfaction, its antecedents and linkage between employee satisfaction and customer satisfaction: A study. *Asian Journal of Business and Management Sciences, 1*(1), 129–137.

Gao, K., Zhang, Y., Sadollah, A., & Su, R. (2016). Optimizing urban traffic light scheduling problem using harmony search with ensemble of local search. *Applied Soft Computing, 48*, 359–372. doi:10.1016/j.asoc.2016.07.029

Gardner, S., & Stohrer, H. (2018, March). *How intelligent transportation systems are changing the industry.* Retrieved from https://www.dxc.technology/digital_transformation/insights/141104-how_intelligent_transportation_systems_are_changing_the_industry.

Gardner, H. (1985). *The mind's new science: a history of the cognitive revolution.* New York: Basic Books.

Garriga, E., & Mele, D. (2004). Corporate social responsibility theories: Mapping the territory. *Journal of Business Ethics, 53*(1/2), 51–71. doi:10.1023/B:BUSI.0000039399.90587.34

Gartner, N. H., Pooran, F. J., & Andrews, C. M. (2001, August). Implementation of the OPAC adaptive control strategy in a traffic signal network. In ITSC 2001. 2001 IEEE Intelligent Transportation Systems. Proceedings (Cat. No. 01TH8585) (pp. 195-200). IEEE. doi:10.1109/ITSC.2001.948655

Garvin, D. A. (1986). Quality problems, policies, and attitudes in the United States and Japan: An exploratory study. *Academy of Management Journal*, *29*(4), 653–673.

Gefen, D., & Straub, D. W. (1997). Gender differences in the perception and use of e-mail: An extension to the technology acceptance model. *Management Information Systems Quarterly*, *21*(4), 389–400. doi:10.2307/249720

Ge, H., Song, Y., Wu, C., Ren, J., & Tan, G. (2019). Cooperative Deep Q-Learning With Q-Value Transfer for Multi-Intersection Signal Control. *IEEE Access : Practical Innovations, Open Solutions*, *7*, 40797–40809. doi:10.1109/ACCESS.2019.2907618

Geng, X., & Chu, X. (2012). A new importance–performance analysis approach for customer satisfaction evaluation supporting PSS design. *Expert Systems with Applications*, *39*(1), 1492–1502. doi:10.1016/j.eswa.2011.08.038

George, D., & Mallery, P. (2003). *SPSS for Windows step by step: A simple guide and reference*. Boston: Allyn & Bacon.

Ghaffar, A. M., Mokhtar, M. Z., Ismail, W. N. S. W., & Othman, M. R. (2019). Determinant of e-accounting (EA) adoption among Malaysian maritime SMES. *International Journal of Engineering & Technology, 8*(1.8), 102-105.

Ghasemi, M., Shafeiepour, V., Aslani, M., & Barvayeh, E. (2011). The impact of Information Technology (IT) on modern accounting systems. *Procedia: Social and Behavioral Sciences*, *28*, 112–116. doi:10.1016/j.sbspro.2011.11.023

Ghost, F. H., & Gnanadhas, M. E. (2011). Impact of service quality in commercial banks on the customers satisfaction: An empirical study. *International Journal of Multidisciplinary Research*, *1*(6), 19–37.

Goldspink, D. F. (2005). Ageing and activity: Their effects on the functional reserve capacities of the heart and vascular smooth and skeletal muscles. *Ergonomics*, *48*(11–14), 1334–1351. doi:10.1080/00140130500101247 PMID:16338704

Goleman, D. (2001). Issues in Paradigm Building. In C. Chermiss & D. Goleman (Eds.), *The emotionally intelligent workpalce: How to select for, measure, and improve emotional intelligence in individuals, groups, and organizations* (pp. 13–26). San Francisco: Jossey-Bass.

Goleman, D. (2005). *Emotional Intelligence*. New York: Bantam Dell.

Gonçalves, A. P. B., Tarrasconi, M. A., Holz, M. R., Kochhann, R., & Paz Fonseca, R. (2019). Cognitive flexibility and inhibition in single-versus multiple-domain mild cognitive impairment: A comparative and discriminative analysis. *Psychology & Neuroscience*, *12*(2), 209–223. doi:10.1037/pne0000160

Gorsuch, R. (1983). *Factor Analysis*. Hillsdale, NJ: Erlbaum.

Gray, F. E., Hamilton, L., & Wilson, R. M. (2015). Introduction: Communication in Accounting Education. In R. M. Wilson, F. E. Gray, & L. Hamilton (Eds.), *Communication in Accounting Education* (pp. 1–3). Oxfordshire: Routledge.

Grech, A., & Camilleri, A. F. (2017). Blockchain in Education. Joint Research Centre, the European Commission's Science and Knowledge Service.

Griffith, D. A., Lee, S., Seob, H., Yeo, C., & Calantone, R. (2014). Marketing process adaptation. *International Marketing Review*, *31*(3), 308–334. doi:10.1108/IMR-06-2013-0113

Grigore, G., Molesworth, M., & Watkins, R. (2016). New corporate responsibilities in the digital economy. In Corporate Social Responsibility in the Post-Financial Crisis Era. Palgrave Macmillan.

Gronroos, C. (1984). A service quality model and its marketing implications. *European Journal of Marketing*, *18*(4), 36–44. doi:10.1108/EUM0000000004784

Guay, R. P. (2013). The relationship between leader fit and transformational leadership. *Journal of Managerial Psychology, 28*(1), 55–73. doi:10.1108/02683941311298869

Gul, S., Ahmad, B., Rehman, S. U., Shabir, N., & Razzaq, N. (2012a). *Leadership styles, turnover intentions and the mediating role of organizational commitment.* Paper presented at the Information and Knowledge Management.

Gul, S., Ahmad, B., Rehman, S. U., Shabir, N., & Razzaq, N. (2012b). *Leadership styles, turnover intentions and the mediating role of organizational commitment.* Paper presented at the Information and Knowledge Management.

Gummerus, J., Liljander, V., Pura, M., & Riel, A. V. (2004). Customer loyalty to content-basedWeb sites: The case of an online healthcare service. *Journal of Services Marketing, 18*(3), 175–186. doi:10.1108/08876040410536486

Gummesson, E. (1979). The Marketing of Professional Services— An Organizational Dilemma. *European Journal of Marketing, 13*(5), 308–318. doi:10.1108/EUM0000000004951

Gupta, D. K., Jena, D., Samantaray, A. K., & Das, S. (2019). HRD climate in selected public sector banks in India. *Revista ESPACIOS, 40*(11).

Gupta, D., Das, A., Jain, V., Soneja, T., Dang, P., & Srivastava, P. (2013). Design of Ergonomic Garment for Elderly Indian Women. *Research Journal of Textile and Apparel, 17*(3), 118–127. doi:10.1108/RJTA-17-03-2013-B012

Gupta, S. K., & Rao, D. (2018). A case study on contemporary water management innovation (CWMI) in sustainable agriculture: Farmers joined hands for mutual survival and prosperity: The case of Kummarvandlapalli. *IJCS, 6*(6), 2283–2287.

Gwebu, K. L., & Wang, J. (2011). Adoption of Open Source Software: The role of social identification. *Decision Support Systems, 51*(1), 220–229. doi:10.1016/j.dss.2010.12.010

Hair, J. F., Anderson, R. E., Tatham, R. L., & Black, W. C. (1998). *Multivariate Data Analysis.* Upper Saddle River, NJ: Prentice Hall.

Hair, J., Anderson, R., Tatham, R., & Black, W. (1995a). *Multivariate data analysis.* New Jersey: Prentice-Hall Inc.

Hancock, P., Howieson, B. A., Kavanagh, M., Kent, J., Tempone, I., & Segal, N. (2009). *Accounting for the future: more than numbers: volume 1, Final Report.* Canberra: Australian Learning and Teaching Council.

Hancock, P., Watty, K., Birt, J., & Tyler, J. (2016). *Accounting learning standards.* Australian Business Deans Council (ABDC). Retrieved from https://abdc.edu.au/data/Accounting_LS/New_TLS_Final_2016.pdf

Harms, P. D., & Credé, M. (2010). Emotional intelligence and transformational and transactional leadership: A meta-analysis. *Journal of Leadership & Organizational Studies, 17*(1), 5–17. doi:10.1177/1548051809350894

Hartley, R. (2018). *What is the role of blockchain in education?* Cognizant Education Technology.

Ha, S.-T., Lo, M.-C., & Wang, Y.-C. (2016). Relationship between knowledge management and organizational performance: A test on SMEs in Malaysia. *Procedia: Social and Behavioral Sciences, 224*, 184–189. doi:10.1016/j.sbspro.2016.05.438

Hashim, M. K., Ahmad, S. a., & Zakaria, M. (2012). *A Study on Leadership Styles in SMEs.* Academic Press.

Hattie, J. (1985). Methodology review: Assessing unidimensionality of tests and ltenls. *Applied Psychological Measurement, 9*(2), 139–164. doi:10.1177/014662168500900204

Hattie, J., & Fraser, C. (1988). The constraining of parameters in restricted factor analysis. *Applied Psychological Measurement, 12*(2), 155–162. doi:10.1177/014662168801200204

Haywood-Farmer, J. (1988). A conceptual model of service quality. *International Journal of Operations & Production Management, 8*(6), 19–29. doi:10.1108/eb054839

Head, K. L., Mirchandani, P. B., & Sheppard, D. (1992). *Hierarchical framework for real-time traffic control* (No. 1360). Academic Press.

Henderson, S. (2001). The education of accountants- a comment. *Accounting Forum, 25*(4), 398–400. doi:10.1111/1467-6303.00074

Hernandez, B., Jimenez, J., & Martin, M. J. (2011). Age, gender and income: Do they really moderate online shopping behaviour? *Online Information Review, 35*(1), 113–133. doi:10.1108/14684521111113614

Hershfield, H. E., & Alter, A. L. (2019). On the naturalistic relationship between mood and entertainment choice. *Journal of Experimental Psychology. Applied, 25*(3), 458–476. doi:10.1037/xap0000220 PMID:31120264

Himann, J. E., Cunningham, D. A., Rechnitzer, P. A., & Paterson, D. H. (1988). Age-related changes in speed of walking. *Medicine and Science in Sports and Exercise, 20*(2), 161–166. doi:10.1249/00005768-198820020-00010 PMID:3367751

Hisrich, R. D. (1990). Entrepreneurship/intrapreneurship. *The American Psychologist, 45*(2), 209–222. doi:10.1037/0003-066X.45.2.209

Hoffman, K. D., & Bateson, J. E. G. (2010). *Services Marketing: Concepts, Strategies*. Cengage Learning.

Hofstede, G. (1983). National cultures in four dimensions: A research-based theory of cultural differences among nations. *International Studies of Management & Organization, 13*(1-2), 46–74. doi:10.1080/00208825.1983.11656358

Hooker, J. (2012). Cultural Differences in Business Communication. In C. B. Paulston, S. F. Kiesling, & E. S. Rangel (Eds.), *Handbook of intercultural discourse and communication*. Malden: John Wiley & Sons. doi:10.1002/9781118247273.ch19

Howieson, B. (2003). Accounting practice in the new millennium: Is accounting education ready to meet the challenge? *The British Accounting Review, 35*(2), 69–103. doi:10.1016/S0890-8389(03)00004-0

Hsbollah, H. M., & Idris, K. M. (2009). E-learning adoption: The role of relative advantages, trialability and academic specialisation. *Campus-Wide Information Systems, 26*(1), 54–70. doi:10.1108/10650740910921564

Hua Lu, M., Madu, C., Kuei, C., & Winokur, D. (1994). Integrating QFD, AHP and Benchmarking in Strategic Marketing. *Journal of Business and Industrial Marketing, 9*(1), 41–50. doi:10.1108/08858629410053470

Huang, J. H., Yang, C., Jin, B. H., & Chiu, H. (2004). Measuring satisfaction with business-to-employee systems. *Computers in Human Behavior, 20*(1), 17–35. doi:10.1016/S0747-5632(03)00047-5

Huck, G. E., Finnicum, C., Morrison, B., Kaseroff, A., & Umucu, E. (2018). Consumer perspectives on physical activity interventions within assertive community treatment programs. *Psychiatric Rehabilitation Journal, 41*(4), 312–318. doi:10.1037/prj0000311 PMID:29999334

Huck, S. W. (2007). *Reading Statistics and Research*. Allyn & Bacon.

Hu, L. T., & Bentler, P. M. (1999). Cutoff criteria for fit indexes in covariance structure analysis: Conventional criteria versus new alternatives. *Structural Equation Modeling, 6*(1), 1–55. doi:10.1080/10705519909540118

Hummer, R. L. (2018). Do You Want to Work in Tall Buildings?: The Art of Good Business Communication. *Journal of Pension Benefits, 25*(2), 21–24.

Hunt, P. B., Robertson, D. I., Bretherton, R. D., & Winton, R. I. (1981). *SCOOT-a traffic responsive method of coordinating signals* (No. LR 1014 Monograph). Academic Press.

Hussain, R., Nasser, A. A., & Hussain, Y. K. (2014). (in press). Service quality and customer satisfaction of a UAE-based airline: An empirical investigation. *Journal of Air Transport Management*, 1–9.

Hyvönen, T., Järvinen, J., & Pellinen, J. (2006). The role of standard software packages in mediating management accounting knowledge. *Qualitative Research in Accounting & Management*, *3*(2), 145–160. doi:10.1108/11766090610670677

Idowu, S. O. (2017). Current issues in corporate social responsibility: An introduction. In S. O. Idowu, C. Sitnikov, D. Simion & C. G. Bocean (Eds.), Current issues in corporate social responsibility: An international consideration (pp. 1-7). Springer.

Idowu, S. O. (2018). Current issues in corporate social responsibility: An introduction. In S. O. Idowu & R. Schmidpeter (Eds.), *Current Issues in Corporate Social Responsibility: An International Consideration*. Springer. doi:10.1007/978-3-319-70449-4_1

Igbaria, M., Zinatelli, N., Cragg, P., & Cavaye, A. L. (1997). Personal computing acceptance factors in small firms: A structural equation model. *Management Information Systems Quarterly*, *21*(3), 279–305. doi:10.2307/249498

Illia, L., Romenti, S., Rodriguez-Canavas, B., Murtarelli, G., & Carroll, C. E. (2017). Exploring corporations' dialogue about CSR in the digital era. *Journal of Business Ethics*, *146*(1), 39–58. doi:10.100710551-015-2924-6

Imlawi, J., Gregg, D., & Karimi, J. (2015). Student engagement in course-based social networks: The impact of instructor credibility and use of communication. *Computers & Education*, *88*, 84–96. doi:10.1016/j.compedu.2015.04.015

IS07498-2 (2004). Information Processing Systems – Open Systems Interconnection – Basic Reference Model – Part 2: Security Architecture. International Organization for Standardization.

Iskander, M. (2008). *Innovative techniques in instruction technology, e-learning, e-assessment and education*. Springer Science & Business Media. doi:10.1007/978-1-4020-8739-4

Ismail, N. A., & Mat Zin, R. (2009). Usage of accounting information among Malaysian Bumiputra small and medium non-manufacturing firms. *Journal of Enterprise Resource Planning Studies*.

Ismaila, S., & Samuel, T. (2014). Human-centered engineering: The challenges of Nigerian engineer. *Journal of Engineering. Design and Technology*, *12*(2), 195–208. doi:10.1108/JEDT-02-2011-0013

Ives, B., Olson, M. H., & Baroudi, J. J. (1983). The measurement of user information satisfaction. *Communications of the ACM*, *26*(10), 785–793. doi:10.1145/358413.358430

Jack, L., Davison, J., & Craig, R. (Eds.). (2013). *The routledge companion to accounting communication*. London: Routledge. doi:10.4324/9780203593493

Jackson, M., Watty, K., Yu, L., & Lowe, L. (2006). Inclusive assessment: improving learning for all: a manual for improving assessment in accounting education. RMIT University.

Jackson, D. (2010). An international profile of industry-relevant competencies and skill gaps in modern graduates. *International Journal of Management Education*, *8*(3), 29–58. doi:10.3794/ijme.83.288

Jackson, D., & Chapman, E. (2012). Non-technical competencies in undergraduate business degree programs: Australian and UK perspectives. *Studies in Higher Education*, *37*(5), 541–567. doi:10.1080/03075079.2010.527935

Jahdi, K. S., & Acikdilli, G. (2009). Marketing communications and corporate social responsibility (CSR): Marriage of convenience or short gun wedding? *Journal of Business Ethics*, *88*(1), 103–113. doi:10.100710551-009-0113-1

Jain, S., Jain, V., & Das, S. (2018). Relationship analysis between emotional intelligence and service quality with special evidences from Indian banking sector. *Revista ESPACIOS*, *39*(33).

Jain. (2018). *Blockchain Goes to School, Digital Solutions, Innovation & Domain Consulting.* Cognizant's Education Practice, Cognizant 20-20 Insights.

Jain, S. K., & Gupta, G. (2004). Measuring service quality: SERVQUAL vs. SERVPERF scales. *Vikalpa, 29*(2), 25–38. doi:10.1177/0256090920040203

Jalilvand, M. R., Esfahani, S. S., & Samiei, N. (2011). Electronic word-of-mouth: Challenges and opportunities. *Procedia Computer Science, 3*, 42–46. doi:10.1016/j.procs.2010.12.008

Janda, S., Trocchia, P. J., & Gwinner, K. P. (2002). Consumer perceptions of Internet retail service quality. *International Journal of Service Industry Management, 13*(5), 412–431. doi:10.1108/09564230210447913

Jeong, J. (2009). *Wireless sensor networking for intelligent transportation systems.* Academic Press.

Jiang, J. J., Klein, G., & Crampton, S. M. (2000a). A Note on SERVQUAL Reliability and Validity in Information System Service Quality Measurement. *Decision Sciences, 31*(3), 725–744. doi:10.1111/j.1540-5915.2000.tb00940.x

Johansen, S. K. (2018). *A comprehensive literature review on the Blockchain as a technological enabler for innovation.* Dept. of Information Systems, Mannheim University.

Johnson, M. D., Anderson, E. W., & Fornell, C. (1995). Rational and adaptive performance expectations in a customer satisfaction framework. *The Journal of Consumer Research, 21*(4), 128–140. doi:10.1086/209428

Johnston, R. (1997). Identifying the critical determinants of service quality in retail banking: Importance and effect. *International Journal of Bank Marketing, 15*(4), 111–116. doi:10.1108/02652329710189366

Jones, C. G. (2011). Written and Computer-Mediated Accounting Communication Skills: An Employer Prespective. *Business Communication Quarterly, 74*(3), 247–271. doi:10.1177/1080569911413808

Jones, T., & Taylor, S. F. (2007). The conceptual domain of service loyalty: How many dimensions? *Journal of Services Marketing, 21*(1), 36–51. doi:10.1108/08876040710726284

Joyner, M. J. (1993). Physiological limiting factors and distance running: Influence of gender and age on record performances. *Exercise and Sport Sciences Reviews, 21*(1), 103–133. doi:10.1249/00003677-199301000-00004 PMID:8504840

Jun, M., Yang, Z., & Kim, D. (2004). Customers' perceptions of online retailing service quality and their satisfaction. *International Journal of Quality & Reliability Management, 21*(8), 817–840. doi:10.1108/02656710410551728

Kallman, D. A., Plato, C. C., & Tobin, J. D. (1990). The role of muscle loss in the age-related decline of grip strength: Cross-sectional and longitudinal perspectives. *Journal of Gerontology, 45*(3), 82–88. doi:10.1093/geronj/45.3.M82 PMID:2335723

Kam Sing Wong, S. (2012). The influences of entrepreneurial orientation on product advantage and new product success. *Journal of Chinese Entrepreneurship, 4*(3), 243–262. doi:10.1108/17561391211262175

Kang, J., & Namkung, Y. (2018). The effect of corporate social responsibility on brand equity and the moderating role of ethical consumerism: The case of starbucks. *Journal of Hospitality & Tourism Research (Washington, D.C.), 42*(7), 1130–1151. doi:10.1177/1096348017727057

Kapferer, J. N. (2015). *Kapferer on luxury: How luxury brands can grow yet remain rare.* Kogan Page Publishers.

Kaplan, A. M., & Haenlein, M. (2010). Users of the world, unite! The challenges and opportunities of social media. *Business Horizons, 53*(1), 59–68. doi:10.1016/j.bushor.2009.09.003

Karamitsos, I., Papadaki, M., & Al Barghuthi, N. B. (2018). Design of the Blockchain Smart Contract: A Use Case for Real Estate. *Journal of Information Security*, *9*(03), 177–190. doi:10.4236/jis.2018.93013

Kats, Y. (2010). *Learning Management System Technologies and Software Solutions for Online Teaching: Tools and Applications: Tools and Applications*. IGI Global.

Kavanagh, M., & Drennan, L. (2008). What skills and attributes does an accounting graduate need? Evidence from student perceptions and employer expectations. *Accounting and Finance*, *48*(2), 279–300. doi:10.1111/j.1467-629X.2007.00245.x

Keller, K. L., Parameswaran, M. G., & Jacob, I. (2011). *Strategic brand management: Building, measuring, and managing brand equity*. Pearson Education India.

Khairuddin, H. M., Sa'ari, A., & Zakaria, M. (2012). A Study on Leadership Styles in SMEs. In *Proceeding: International Conference on Islamic Leadership-2 (ICIL), Nilai, Negeri Sembilan*. Penerbit Universiti Sains Islam Malaysia

Khorov, E., Lyakhov, A., Krotov, A., & Guschin, A. (2015). A survey on IEEE 802.11 ah: An enabling networking technology for smart cities. *Computer Communications*, *58*, 53–69. doi:10.1016/j.comcom.2014.08.008

Khorsandi, H., Mohammadi, A., Karimzadeh, S., & Khorsandi, J. (2016). Evaluation of corrosion and scaling potential in rural water distribution network of Urmia, Iran. *Desalination and Water Treatment*, *57*(23), 10585–10592. doi:10.1080/19443994.2015.1042058

Khwaldeh, S. M., Al-Hadid, I., Masa'deh, R. e., & Alrowwad, A. (2017). The Association between E-Services Web Portals Information Quality and ICT Competence in the Jordanian Universities. *Asian Social Science*, *13*(3), 156. doi:10.5539/ass.v13n3p156

Kim, H., Youn, S., & Lee, D. (2019). The effect of corporate social responsibility on consumer support for cause-related marketing. *Total Quality Management*, *30*(6), 682–707. doi:10.1080/14783363.2017.1332482

Kim, I., & Kuljis, J. (2010). Applying content analysis to web based content. *CIT. Journal of Computing and Information Technology*, *18*(4), 369–375. doi:10.2498/cit.1001924

Kirk-Smith, M., & Gault, W. (1995). Marketing Local Enterprise Agencies. *Journal of Small Business and Enterprise Development*, *2*(3), 142–148. doi:10.1108/eb020956

Kirmani, A., & Zeithaml, V. (1993). Advertising, perceived quality, and brand image. *Brand equity & advertising: Advertising's role in building strong brands*, 143-161.

Klein, J., & Dawar, N. (2004). Corporate social responsibility and consumers' attributions and brand evaluations in a product-harm crisis. *International Journal of Research in Marketing*, *21*(3), 203–217. doi:10.1016/j.ijresmar.2003.12.003

Klein, S. A., & Hilbig, B. E. (2019). On the lack of real consequences in consumer choice research: And its consequences. *Experimental Psychology*, *66*(1), 68–76. doi:10.1027/1618-3169/a000420 PMID:30777510

Kline, P. (1997). *An Easy Guide to Factor Analysis*. London: Routledge.

Knaian, A. N. (2000). *A wireless sensor network for smart roadbeds and intelligent transportation systems* (Dissertation). Massachusetts Institute of Technology.

Knaut, A. (2017). How CSR should understand digitalization. In S. O. Idowu & R. Schmidpeter (Eds.), *Sustainability in a Digital World*. Springer. doi:10.1007/978-3-319-54603-2_21

Ko, K. H. (1990). Promotion of IT Applications in Singapore: Policy Issues and Strategic Thrusts. In Information Technology and Singapore Society: Trends, Policies and Applications. Singapore: Singapore University Press.

Kochhann, R., & Wilson, M. A. (2019). Introduction: Special issue on neuropsychology of aging. *Psychology & Neuroscience*, *12*(2), 141–143. doi:10.1037/pne0000176

Kotler, P., Hayes, T., & Bloom, P. N. (2002). *Marketing professional services*. Prentice Hall.

Kotler, P., & Keller, K. L. (2006). *Marketing Management*. Twelefth Edition.

Kraiser, H. (1958). The varimax criterion for analytic rotation in factor analysis. *Psychometrika*, *23*(3), 187–200. doi:10.1007/BF02289233

Krishnan, B. C., & Hartline, M. D. (2001). Brand equity: Is it more important in services? *Journal of Services Marketing*, *15*(5), 328–342. doi:10.1108/EUM0000000005654

Kull, A. J., & Heath, T. B. (2016). You decide, we donate: Strengthening consumer-brand relationships through digitally co-created social responsibility. *International Journal of Research in Marketing*, *33*(1), 78–92. doi:10.1016/j.ijresmar.2015.04.005

Kumaran, S. K., Mohapatra, S., Dogra, D. P., Roy, P. P., & Kim, B. G. (2019). Computer Vision-guided Intelligent Traffic Signaling for Isolated Intersections. *Expert Systems with Applications*, *134*, 267–278. doi:10.1016/j.eswa.2019.05.049

Lacerda, T. M. R. D. O. C. d. (2015). *Understanding Leadership Effectiveness in Organizational Settings: An Integrative Approach (PhD)*. Universidade De Lisboa.

Lai, I. K. W., & Lai, D. C. F. (2013). User acceptance of mobile commerce: An empirical study in Macau. *International Journal of Systems Science*, *45*(6), 1321–1331. doi:10.1080/00207721.2012.761471

Lai, M.-L. (2008). Technology readiness, internet self-efficacy and computing experience of professional accounting students. *Campus-Wide Information Systems*, *25*(1), 18–29. doi:10.1108/10650740810849061

Larsson, L., Grimby, G., & Karlsson, J. (1979). Muscle strength and speed of movement in relation to age and muscle morphology. *Journal of Applied Physiology*, *46*(3), 451–456. doi:10.1152/jappl.1979.46.3.451 PMID:438011

Lassar, W., Mittal, B., & Sharma, A. (1995). Measuring customer-based brand equity. *Journal of Consumer Marketing*, *12*(4), 11–19. doi:10.1108/07363769510095270

Laurent, St., & Andrew, M. (2008). *Understanding Open Source and Free Software Licensing*. O'Reilly Media.

Lean, O. K., Zailani, S., Ramayah, T., & Fernando, Y. (2009). Factors influencing intention to use e-government services among citizens in Malaysia. *International Journal of Information Management*, *29*(6), 458–475. doi:10.1016/j.ijinfomgt.2009.03.012

Lederer, A. L., Maupin, D. J., Sena, M. P., & Zhuang, Y. (2000). The technology acceptance model and the World Wide Web. *Decision Support Systems*, *29*(3), 269–282. doi:10.1016/S0167-9236(00)00076-2

Leech, N., Barrett, K., & Morgan, G. A. (2005). SPSS for intermediate statistics: Use and interpretation. London: Lawrence Erlbaum Associates.

Leeflang, P. S. H., Verhoef, P. C., Dahlström, P., & Freundt, T. (2014). Challenges and solutions for marketing in the digital era. *European Management Journal*, *32*(1), 1–12. doi:10.1016/j.emj.2013.12.001

Lee, K., Oh, W., & Kim, N. (2013). Social media for socially responsible firms: Analysis of Fortune 500's Twitter profiles and their CSR/CSIR ratings. *Journal of Business Ethics*, *118*(4), 791–806. doi:10.100710551-013-1961-2

Lee, K., & Shin, D. (2010). Consumers' responses to CSR activities: The linkage between increased awareness and purchase intention. *Public Relations Review*, *36*(2), 193–195. doi:10.1016/j.pubrev.2009.10.014

Lee, L., Kerler, W., & Ivancevich, D. (2018). Beyond Excel: Software Tools and the Accounting Curriculum. *AIS Educator Journal, 13*(1), 44–61. doi:10.3194/1935-8156-13.1.44

Lee, M. P. (2008). A review of the theories of corporate social responsibility: Its evolutionary path and the road ahead. *International Journal of Management Reviews, 10*(1), 53–73. doi:10.1111/j.1468-2370.2007.00226.x

Legris, P., Ingham, J., & Collerette, P. (2003). Why do people use information technology? A critical review of the technology acceptance model. *Information & Management, 40*(3), 191–204. doi:10.1016/S0378-7206(01)00143-4

Leong, Y. L. (1997). ECH Programme Hits Its Stride. *Computerworld, §§§*, 3.

Lexell, J., Taylor, C. C., & Sjöström, M. (1988). What is the cause of the ageing atrophy? Total number, size and proportion of different fiber types studied in whole vastus lateralis muscle from 15- to 83-year-old men. *Journal of the Neurological Sciences, 84*(2–3), 275–294. doi:10.1016/0022-510X(88)90132-3 PMID:3379447

Li, L., Lv, Y., & Wang, F. Y. (2016). Traffic signal timing via deep reinforcement learning. *IEEE/CAA Journal of Automatica Sinica, 3*(3), 247-254.

Liang, X., Du, X., Wang, G., & Han, Z. (2019). A Deep Reinforcement Learning Network for Traffic Light Cycle Control. *IEEE Transactions on Vehicular Technology, 68*(2), 1243–1253. doi:10.1109/TVT.2018.2890726

Lin, C. (2017). A multi-level test for social regulatory focus and team member creativity. *Leadership and Organization Development Journal, 38*(8), 1057–1077. doi:10.1108/LODJ-05-2016-0125

Liu, B., & Liu, W. (2011, May). Evaluation of traffic control methods at traffic circles. In *2011 Chinese Control and Decision Conference (CCDC)* (pp. 3371-3377). IEEE. 10.1109/CCDC.2011.5968698

Li, X., Hess, T. J., & Valacich, J. S. (2006). Using Attitude and Social Influence to Develop an Extended Trust Model for Information Systems. *The Data Base for Advances in Information Systems, 37*(2-3), 108–124. doi:10.1145/1161345.1161359

Llopis, J., Gonzales, R., & Gasco, J. (2010). Web pages as a tool for a strategic description of the Spanish largest firms. *Information Processing & Management, 46*(3), 320–330. doi:10.1016/j.ipm.2009.06.004

Loonam, M., & O'Loughlin, D. (2008). Exploring e-service quality: A study of Irish online banking. *Marketing Intelligence & Planning, 26*(7), 759–780. doi:10.1108/02634500810916708

Lovelock, C. H. (1981). *Why marketing management needs to be different for services.*

Lu, J. (2001). Measuring cost/benefits of e-business applications and customer satisfaction. *Proceedings of the 2nd International Web Conference*, 139-147.

Lu, J., Yu, C. S., Liu, C., & Yao, J. E. (2003). Technology acceptance model for wireless Internet. *Internet Research, 13*(3), 206–222. doi:10.1108/10662240310478222

Lu, J., & Zhang, G. (2003). Cost benefit factor analysis in e-services. *International Journal of Service Industry Management, 14*(5), 570–595. doi:10.1108/09564230310500237

Luk, J. Y. K. (1984). Two traffic-responsive area traffic control methods: SCAT and SCOOT. *Traffic Engineering & Control, 25*(1).

Lumpkin, J. R., & Festervand, T. A. (1988). Purchase information sources of the elderly. *Journal of Advertising Research, 27*, 31–43.

Luo, M. M., Chea, S., & Chen, J.-S. (2011). Web-based information service adoption: A comparison of the motivational model and the uses and gratifications theory. *Decision Support Systems, 51*(1), 21–30. doi:10.1016/j.dss.2010.11.015

Luo, M. M.-L., Remus, W., & Chea, S. (2006). Technology Acceptance of Internet-based Information Services: An Integrated Model of TAM and U&G Theory. *Proceedings of the Twelfth Americas Conference on Information Systems*, 1139-1150.

Luo, X., & Bhattacharya, C. B. (2006). Corporate social responsibility, customer satisfaction and market value. *Journal of Marketing*, *70*(4), 1–18. doi:10.1509/jmkg.70.4.001

Lu, V. N., Scholz, B., & Nguyen, L. T. (2018). Work integrated learning in international market: Student Insights. *Australasian Marketing Journal*, *26*(2), 132–139. doi:10.1016/j.ausmj.2018.05.002

Madanchian, M., Hussein, N., & Noordin, F. (2016). *Effects of Leadership on Organizational Performance*. Paper presented at the 12th International Conference on Educational Technologies (EDUTE '16), Barcelona, Spain.

Madanchian, M., Hussein, N., Noordin, F., & Taherdoost, H. (2015a). *Effects of Leadership on Organizational Performance*. Academic Press.

Madanchian, M., Hussein, N., Noordin, F., & Taherdoost, H. (2015b). *Leadership Theories; an Overview of Early Stages*. Paper presented at the 4th International Conference on Management, Marketing, Tourism, Retail, Finance and Computer Applications, Venice, Italy.

Madanchian, M., Hussein, N., Noordin, F., & Taherdoost, H. (2016b). *The Relationship between Ethical Leadership, Leadership Effectiveness and Organizational Performance: A Review of Literature in SMEs Context*. Academic Press.

Madanchian, M., Hussein, N., Noordin, F., & Taherdoost, H. (2016c). *Review of Organizational Leadership Theories*. Paper presented at the 10th International Conference on Business Administration (ICBA '16), Barcelona, Spain.

Madanchian, M., Hussein, N., Noordin, F., & Taherdoost, H. (2015). The role of SMEs in economic development: Case study of Malaysia. *International Journal of Academic Research in Management*, *4*(3), 77–84.

Madanchian, M., Hussein, N., Noordin, F., & Taherdoost, H. (2016a). The Relationship between Ethical Leadership, Leadership Effectiveness and Organizational Performance: A Review of Literature in SMEs Context. *European Business & Management*, *2*(2), 17–21. doi:10.11648/j.ebm.20160202.11

Madanchian, M., Hussein, N., Noordin, F., & Taherdoost, H. (2017). Leadership Effectiveness Measurement and Its Effect on Organization Outcomes. *Procedia Engineering*, *181*, 1043–1048. doi:10.1016/j.proeng.2017.02.505

Madanchian, M., Hussein, N., Noordin, F., & Taherdoost, H. (2018). The Impact of Ethical Leadership on Leadership Effectiveness among SMES in Malaysia. *Procedia Manufacturing Journal*, *22*, 968–974. doi:10.1016/j.promfg.2018.03.138

Madanchian, M., & Taherdoost, H. (2017a). Role of leadership in small and medium enterprises (SMEs). *Journal of Economics and Management Systems*, *2*, 240–243.

Madanchian, M., & Taherdoost, H. (2017b). Role of Leadership in Small and Medium Enterprises (SMEs). *International Journal of Economics and Management Systems*, *2*, 240–243.

Madanchian, M., & Taherdoost, H. (2019). Assessment of Leadership Effectiveness Dimensions in Small & Medium Enterprises (SMEs). *Procedia Manufacturing*, *32*, 1035–1042. doi:10.1016/j.promfg.2019.02.318

Mahinda, E., & Whitworth, B. (2006). *Using The WOSP Model To Improve End-User Productivity Of Information Systems*. International Conference on Business IT (BIZIT 2006): Collaborating with ICT Innovations for Business Survival, Kuala Lumpur, Malaysia.

Maier, C. D., & Ravazzani, S. (2019). Bridging diversity management and CSR in online external communication. *Corporate Communications*, *24*(2), 269–286. doi:10.1108/CCIJ-01-2018-0015

Maignan, I., & Ralston, D. A. (2002). Corporate social responsibility in Europe and the U.S.: Insights from businesses' self-presentations. *Journal of International Business Studies*, *33*(3), 497–514. doi:10.1057/palgrave.jibs.8491028

Maio Mackay, M. (2001). Evaluation of brand equity measures: Further empirical results. *Journal of Product and Brand Management*, *10*(1), 38–51. doi:10.1108/10610420110382812

Makasi, A., Govender, K., & Madzorera, N. (2014). Re-branding and its effects on consumer perceptions: A case study of a Zimbabwean bank. *Mediterranean Journal of Social Sciences*, *5*(20), 2582.

Makasi, A., Govender, K., & Rukweza, C. (2015). Building brand equity through advertising. *Mediterranean Journal of Social Sciences*, *5*(20), 2613.

Malhotra, N. K., Mukhopadhyay, S., Liu, X., & Dash, S. (2012). One, few or many?: An integrated framework for identifying the items in measurement scales. *International Journal of Market Research*, *54*(6), 835–862. doi:10.2501/IJMR-54-6-835-862

Manasra, E. A. A., Zaid, M. K. S. A., & Taherqutaishat, F. (2013). Investigating the Impact of Website Quality on Consumers' Satisfaction in Jordanian Telecommunication Sector. *Arab Economic and Business Journal, 8*, 31-37.

Mannion, P., Talpaert, V., Sobh, I., Kiran, B. R., Yogamani, S., El-Sallab, A., & Perez, P. (2019). *Exploring applications of deep reinforcement learning for real-world autonomous driving systems*. Academic Press.

Mao, E., & Palvia, P. (2006). Testing an Extended Model of IT Acceptance in the Chinese Cultural Context. *The Data Base for Advances in Information Systems*, *37*(2-3), 20–32. doi:10.1145/1161345.1161351

Maon, F., Lindgreen, A., & Swaen, V. (2010). Organisational stage and cultural phases: A critical review and a consolidative model of corporate social responsibility development. *International Journal of Management Reviews*, *12*(1), 20–38. doi:10.1111/j.1468-2370.2009.00278.x

Martensen, A., & Grønholdt, L. (2003). Understanding and modelling brand equity. *Asian Journal on Quality, 4*(2), 73-100.

Martinez, P., & Nishiyama, N. (2017). Enhancing customer-based brand equity through CSR in the hospitality sector. *International Journal of Hospitality & Tourism Administration*, *20*(3), 329–353. doi:10.1080/15256480.2017.1397581

Mata, R., Schooler, L. J., & Rieskamp, J. (2007). The aging decision maker: Cognitive aging and the adaptive selection of decision strategies. *Psychology and Aging*, *22*(4), 796–810. doi:10.1037/0882-7974.22.4.796 PMID:18179298

Mathwick, C., Malhotra, N., & Rigdon, E. (2001). Experiential value: Conceptualization, measurement and application in the catalog and Internet shopping environment. *Journal of Retailing*, *77*(1), 39–56. doi:10.1016/S0022-4359(00)00045-2

Mattsson, J. (1992). A service quality model based on ideal value standard. *International Journal of Service Industry Management*, *3*(3), 18–33. doi:10.1108/09564239210015148

Maupin, R. J., & May, C. A. (1993). Communication for Accounting Students. *International Journal of Educational Management*, *7*(3), 30–38. doi:10.1108/09513549310039918

McConnell, J. D. (1968). The price-quality relationship in an experimental setting. *JMR, Journal of Marketing Research*, *5*(3), 300–303. doi:10.1177/002224376800500309

McDaniel, P. A., Cadman, B., & Malone, R. E. (2016). Shared vision, shared vulnerability: A content analysis of corporate social responsibility information on tobacco industry websites. *Preventive Medicine*, *89*, 337–344. doi:10.1016/j.ypmed.2016.05.033 PMID:27261411

McGuire, J. B., Sundgren, A., & Schneeweis, T. (1988). Corporate social responsibility and firm financial performance. *Academy of Management Journal*, *31*(4), 854–872.

Mchaney, R., & Cronan, T. P. (1998). Computer simulation success: on the use of the end-user computing satisfaction instrument: a comment. *Decision Sciences*, *29*(2), 525–534. doi:10.1111/j.1540-5915.1998.tb01589.x

McIntosh, J., & Torres, M. I. (2014). *Learning Management Systems: Revisiting Learning Management Systems at the University Level*. The University of Tampa.

Mcknight, D. H., Choudhury, V., & Kacmar, C. (2002b). Developing and Validating Trust Measures for e-Commerce: An Integrative Typology. *Information Systems Research*, *13*(3), 334–359. doi:10.1287/isre.13.3.334.81

McMurray, S., Dutton, M., McQuaid, R., & Richard, A. (2016). Employer demands from business graduates. *Education + Training*, *58*(1), 112–132. doi:10.1108/ET-02-2014-0017

McPherson, B. (1998). Student perceptions about business communication in their careers. *Business and Professional Communication Quarterly*, *61*(2), 68–79. doi:10.1177/108056999806100209

Meall, L. (2018). The Human Factor. *Accountancy Futures: Critical Issues for tomorrow's profession, 17*, 6-9.

Melnyk, V., van Herpen, E., Jak, S., & van Trijp, H. C. M. (2019). The mechanisms of social norms' influence on consumer decision making: A meta-analysis. *Zeitschrift fur Psychologie mit Zeitschrift fur Angewandte Psychologie*, *227*(1), 4–17. doi:10.1027/2151-2604/a000352

Metaxas, T., & Tsavdaridou, M. (2013). CSR in metallurgy sector in Greece: A content analysis. *Resources Policy*, *38*(3), 295–309. doi:10.1016/j.resourpol.2013.03.010

Metzger, M. (2004). Privacy, trust, and disclosure: Exploring barriers to electronic commerce. *Journal of Computer-Mediated Communication*, *9*(4), 9. doi:10.1111/j.1083-6101.2004.tb00292.x

Meyer, H. H., Walker, W. B., & Litwin, G. H. (1961). Motive patterns and risk preferences associated with entrepreneurship. *Journal of Abnormal and Social Psychology*, *63*(3), 570–574. doi:10.1037/h0043698 PMID:14473104

Mihelic, K. K., Lipicnik, B., & Tekavcic, M. (2010). Ethical leadership. *International Journal of Management & Information Systems*, *14*(5).

Mimbela, L. E. Y., & Klein, L. A. (2000). *Summary of vehicle detection and surveillance technologies used in intelligent transportation systems*. Academic Press.

Mishra, S., & Suar, D. (2010). Does corporate social responsibility influence firm performance of Indian companies? *Journal of Business Ethics*, *95*(4), 571–601. doi:10.100710551-010-0441-1

Mitseva, A. P., Peterson, C. B., Karamberi, C., Oikonomou, L. C., Ballis, A., Giannakakos, C., & Dafoulas, G. E. (2012). Gerontechnology: Providing a Helping Hand When Caring for Cognitively Impaired Older Adults—Intermediate Results from a Controlled Study on the Satisfaction and Acceptance of Informal Caregivers. *Current Gerontology and Geriatrics Research*, 1–19.

Mittal, V., & Tsiros, M. (2007). Customer Loyalty in Electronically Mediated Environments. *Journal of Value Chain Management*, *1*, 80–109.

Mkhize, P., Mtsweni, E. S., & Buthelezi, P. (2016). Diffusion of Innovations Approach to the Evaluation of Learning Management System Usage in an Open Distance Learning Institution. *The International Review of Research in Open and Distributed Learning*, *17*(3). doi:10.19173/irrodl.v17i3.2191

Mohr, L. A., & Webb, D. J. (2005). The effects of corporate social responsibility and price on consumer responses. *The Journal of Consumer Affairs*, *39*(1), 121–147. doi:10.1111/j.1745-6606.2005.00006.x

Mondal, S., Mall, M., Mishra, U. S., & Sahoo, K. (2017). Investigating the factors affecting customer purchase activity in retail stores. *Revista ESPACIOS, 38*(57).

Monroe, K. B., & Krishnan, R. (1983). *A procedure for integrating outcomes across studies*. ACR North American Advances.

Montesdioca, G. P. Z., & Maçada, A. C. G. (2014). Measuring User Satisfaction with Information Security Practices. *Computers & Security*.

Moore, N. (2006). *How to do research: a practical guide to designing and managing research projects*. London: Facet Publishing.

Mosbeh, R., & Soliman, K. S. (2008). An exploratory analysis of factors affecting users' adoption of corporate intranet; A Tunisian study. *Management Research News, 31*(5), 375–385. doi:10.1108/01409170810865172

Mougayar, W. (2016). *The business blockchain: promise, practise, and application of the next Internet technology*. Wiley.

Mumford, M. D., Zaccaro, S. J., Harding, F. D., Jacobs, T. O., & Fleishman, E. A. (2000). Leadership skills for a changing world: Solving complex social problems. *The Leadership Quarterly, 11*(1), 11–35. doi:10.1016/S1048-9843(99)00041-7

Mutlag, A. A., Ghani, M. K. A., Arunkumar, N., Mohamed, M. A., & Mohd, O. (2019). Enabling technologies for fog computing in healthcare IoT systems. *Future Generation Computer Systems, 90*, 62–78. doi:10.1016/j.future.2018.07.049

Muylle, S., Moenert, R., & Despontin, M. (2004). The conceptualization and empirical validation of website user satisfaction. *Information & Management, 41*(5), 543–560. doi:10.1016/S0378-7206(03)00089-2

Narici, M. V., Bordini, M., & Cerretelli, P. (1991). Effect of aging on human adductor pollicis muscle function. *Journal of Applied Physiology, 71*(4), 1277–1281. doi:10.1152/jappl.1991.71.4.1277 PMID:1757349

Nath Sanyal, S., & Datta, S. K. (2011). The effect of country of origin on brand equity: An empirical study on generic drugs. *Journal of Product and Brand Management, 20*(2), 130–140. doi:10.1108/10610421111121125

Neumann, W., Winkel, J., Medbo, L., Magneberg, R., & Mathiassen, S. (2006). Production system design elements influencing productivity and ergonomics. *International Journal of Operations & Production Management, 26*(8), 904–923. doi:10.1108/01443570610678666

Nguyen, T., White, S., Hall, K., Bell, R. L., & Ballentine, W. (2019). Emotional Intelligence and Managerial Communication. *American Journal of Management, 19*(2), 54–63.

Nicholls, R., & Gad Mohsen, M. (2015). Other customer age: Exploring customer age-difference related CCI. *Journal of Services Marketing, 29*(4), 255–267. doi:10.1108/JSM-04-2014-0144

NIST-SPECIAL-PUBLICATION-800-16. (1998). *Information Technology Security Training Requirements: A Role-and Performance-Based Model*. Gaithersburg: National Institute of Standards and Technology.

Noh, J., & Fitzsimmons, J. (1999). Effect of information technology on marketing performance of Korean service firms. *International Journal of Service Industry Management, 10*(3), 307–321. doi:10.1108/09564239910276908

Nunnally, J. (1978). *Psychometric Theory*. New York, NY: McGraw-Hill.

O'Connell, B., Carnegie, G. D., Carter, A. J., de Lange, P., Hancock, P., Helliar, C. V., & Watty, K. (2015). *Shaping the future of accounting in business education in Australia*. Melbourne: CPA.

Obschonka, M., Schmitt-Rodermund, E., Silbereisen, R. K., Gosling, S. D., & Potter, J. (2013). The regional distribution and correlates of an entrepreneurship-prone personality profile in the United States, Germany, and the United Kingdom: A socioecological perspective. *Journal of Personality and Social Psychology*, *105*(1), 104–122. doi:10.1037/a0032275 PMID:23586410

Ofori, G. (2009). Ethical leadership: Examining the relationships with full range leadership model, employee outcomes, and organizational culture. *Journal of Business Ethics*, *90*(4), 533–547. doi:10.100710551-009-0059-3

Ogbonna, E., & Harris, L. C. (2000). Leadership style, organizational culture and performance: Empirical evidence from UK companies. *International Journal of Human Resource Management*, *11*(4), 766–788. doi:10.1080/09585190050075114

Oh, H. (1999). Service quality, customer satisfaction and customer value: A holistic perspective. *International Journal of Hospitality Management*, *18*(1), 67–82. doi:10.1016/S0278-4319(98)00047-4

Ojokuku, R. M., Odetayo, T. A., & Sajuyigbe, A. S. (2012). Impact of leadership style on organizational performance: A case study of Nigerian Banks. *American Journal of Business and Management*, *1*(4), 202–207.

Ok, S.-J. & Shon, J.-H. (2006). The Determinant of Internet Banking Usage Behavior in Korea: A Comparison of Two Theoretical Models. *CollECTeR '06*.

Okazaki, S., Plangger, K., West, D., & Menendez, H. D. (2019). Exploring digital corporate social responsibility communications on Twitter. *Journal of Business Research*. doi:10.1016/j.jbusres.2019.09.006

Okoro, E. A., & Washington, M. C. (2012). Workforce Diversity and Organizational Communication: Analysis of Human Capital Performance and Productivity. *Journal of Diversity Management*, *7*(1), 57–62. doi:10.19030/jdm.v7i1.6936

Oliver, R. L. (1980). A cognitive model of the antecedents and consequences of satisfaction decisions. *JMR, Journal of Marketing Research*, *17*(4), 460–469. doi:10.1177/002224378001700405

Oliver, R. L. (1997). *Satisfaction: A Behavioral Perspective on the Consumer*. New York: McGraw-Hill.

Oliver, R. L. (2014). *Satisfaction: A behavioral perspective on the consumer: A behavioral perspective on the consumer*. Routledge. doi:10.4324/9781315700892

Oly Ndubisi, N. (2006). Effect of gender on customer loyalty: A relationship marketing approach. *Marketing Intelligence & Planning*, *24*(1), 48–61. doi:10.1108/02634500610641552

Orbik, Z., & Zozul'akova, V. (2019). Corporate social and digital responsibility. *Management Systems in Production Engineering*, *27*(2), 79–83. doi:10.1515/mspe-2019-0013

Orr, G. (2003). *Diffusion of innovations*. Everett Rogers.

Orr, S. (2019). Daring to tap external strategic resources: Competitive advantage in global industries. *The Journal of Business Strategy*, *40*(3), 25–35. doi:10.1108/JBS-03-2018-0032

Owen, G. A., & Gerfen, R. C. (1951). Can Junior Accountatns be Trained to write Better? *American Accounting Association*, *26*(3), 313–320.

Parasuraman, A., Berry, L. L., & Zeithaml, V. A. (1991). Refinement and reassessment of the SERVQUAL scale. *Journal of Retailing*, *67*(4), 420–450.

Parasuraman, A., Berry, L. L., & Zeithaml, V. A. (1991a). Refinement and Reassessment of the SERVQUAL Scale. *Journal of Retailing*, *67*, 420–450.

Parasuraman, A., Zeithaml, V. A., & Berry, L. L. (1985). A conceptual model of service quality and its implications for future research. *Journal of Marketing*, *49*(3), 41–50. doi:10.1177/002224298504900403

Parasuraman, A., Zeithaml, V. A., & Berry, L. L. (1988). SERVQUAL: A multi-item scale for measuring consumer perceptions of service quality. *Journal of Retailing*, *64*, 2–40.

Parasuraman, A., Zeithaml, V. A., & Berry, L. L. (1988). SERVQUAL: A multiple item scale for measuring consumer perception of service quality. *Journal of Retailing*, *64*(1), 12–37.

Parasuraman, A., Zeithaml, V. A., & Berry, L. L. (1988). Servqual: A multiple-item scale for measuring consumer perc. *Journal of Retailing*, *64*(1), 12.

Parasuraman, A., Zeithaml, V. A., & Berry, L. L. (1994). Reassessment of expectations as a comparison standard in measuring service quality: Implications for further research. *Journal of Marketing*, *58*(1), 111–124. doi:10.1177/002224299405800109

Park, C. W., Iyer, E. S., & Smith, D. C. (1989). The effects of situational factors on in-store grocery shopping behavior: The role of store environment and time available for shopping. *The Journal of Consumer Research*, *15*(4), 422–433. doi:10.1086/209182

Parker, C. M., Bellucci, E., Zutshi, A., Torlina, L., & Fraunholz, B. (2015). SME stakeholder relationship descriptions in website CSR communications. *Social Responsibility Journal*, *11*(2), 364–386. doi:10.1108/SRJ-09-2013-0114

Parker, L. D., Guthrie, J., & Linacre, S. (2011). The relationship between academic accounting research and professional practice. *Accounting. Auditing & Accountability*, *24*(1), 5–14. doi:10.1108/09513571111098036

Pavlou, P. (2003). Consumer acceptance of electronic commerce: Integrating trust and risk with the technology acceptance model. *International Journal of Electronic Commerce*, *7*, 69–103.

Pedersen, P. E. (2005). Adoption of mobile Internet services: An exploratory study of mobile commerce early adopters. *Journal of Organizational Computing and Electronic Commerce*, *15*(3), 203–222. doi:10.120715327744joce1503_2

Pelenk Ozel, A., & Yılmaz Sert, N. (2014). Corporate blogs as a tool of digital public relations: A research on Turkey's first 100 companies. *Global Media Journal: TR Edition*, *5*(9), 303–321.

Pennington, A., & Stanford, J. (2019). *The Future of Work for Australian Graduates: The Changing Landscape of University-Employment Transitions in Australia.* Retrieved from The Centre for Future Work at the Australia Institute: https://d3n8a8pro7vhmx.cloudfront.net/theausinstitute/pages/3083/attachments/original/1571640129/Future_of_Work_for_Australian_Graduates_GCA_Final_Formatted.pdf?1571640129

Peterson, R. S., Smith, D. B., Martorana, P. V., & Owens, P. D. (2003). The impact of chief executive officer personality on top management team dynamics: One mechanism by which leadership affects organizational performance. *The Journal of Applied Psychology*, *88*(5), 795–808. doi:10.1037/0021-9010.88.5.795 PMID:14516245

Petit, T., & McEnally, M. (1985). Putting Strategy Into Promotion Mix Decisions. *Journal of Consumer Marketing*, *2*(1), 41–47. doi:10.1108/eb038819

Petticrew, M., & Roberts, H. (2008). *Systematic reviews in the social sciences: A practical guide*. John Wiley & Sons.

Pett, M. A., Lackey, N. R., & Sullivan, J. J. (2003). *Making Sense of Factor Analysis: The use of factor analysis for instrument development in health care research.* Sage Publications Inc. doi:10.4135/9781412984898

Phillipo, J., & Krongard, S. (2012). *Learning Management System*. LMS.

Phillips, S. K., Rook, K. M., Siddle, N. C., Bruce, S. A., & Woledge, R. C. (1993). Muscle weakness in women occurs at an earlier age than in men, but strength is preserved by hormone replacement therapy. *Clinical Science*, *84*(1), 95–98. doi:10.1042/cs0840095 PMID:8382141

Pikkarainen, T., Pikkarainen, K., Karjaluoto, H., & Pahnila, S. (2004). Consumer acceptance of online banking: An extension of the technology acceptance model. *Internet Research*, *14*(3), 224–235. doi:10.1108/10662240410542652

Pinar, M., Girard, T., & Eser, Z. (2012). Consumer-based brand equity in banking industry: A comparison of local and global banks in Turkey. *International Journal of Bank Marketing*, *30*(5), 359–375. doi:10.1108/02652321211247417

Polat, A. F. (2018). *Social media reflections and consequences of corporate social responsibility projects: Samsung sample of hearing hands project* (Unpublished Master of Arts Thesis). The University of Fırat, Elazığ, Turkey.

Porter, M. M., Vandervoort, A. A., & Lexell, J. (1995). Aging of human muscle: Structure, function, and adaptability. *Scandinavian Journal of Medicine & Science in Sports*, *5*(3), 129–142. doi:10.1111/j.1600-0838.1995.tb00026.x PMID:7552755

Potter, L. E., & Thompson, A. (2019). Engaging with STEM Students: Successes and Challenges in Course Design. *Blended Learning Designs in STEM Higher Education*, 231–248.

Prado, M. A., & Giraldi, J. D. M. E. (2015). A Influência da Imagem do País de Origem no Brand Equity: Um Estudo com Bancos Espanhóis. *Revista Brasileira de Marketing*, *14*(3), 407–420. doi:10.5585/remark.v14i3.2890

Premkumar, G., & Bhattacherjee, A. (2008). Explaining information technology usage:Atest of competing models. *Omega*, *36*(1), 64–75. doi:10.1016/j.omega.2005.12.002

Pulakanam, V., & Suraweera, T. (2010). Implementing accounting software in small business in New Zealand: An exploratory investigation. *Accountancy Business and the Public Interest*, *9*(64), 98–124.

Putra, Y. M. (2019). Analysis of factors affecting the interests of SMEs using accounting applications. *Journal of Economics and Business*, *2*(3), 818–826. doi:10.31014/aior.1992.02.03.129

PwC. (2014). *The future of work: a journey to 2022.* Retrieved from https://www.pwc.com.au/pdf/future-of-work-report-v23.pdf

Rabin, J. H. (1983). Accent is on quality in consumer services this decade. *Marketing News*, *17*(4), 12.

Ramasubbu, N., Mithas, S., & Krishnan, M. (2008). High tech, high touch: The effect of employee skills and customer heterogeneity on customer satisfaction with enterprise system support services. *Decision Support Systems*, *44*(2), 509–523. doi:10.1016/j.dss.2007.06.005

Rank, u. U. (2019). *Jordanian University Ranking 2019.* Retrieved from https://www.4icu.org/jo/

Razak, R. A. (2011). Entrepreneurial Orientation as a Universal Remedy for the Receding Productivity in Malaysian Small and Medium Enterprises: A Theoretical Perspective. *International Journal of Business and Social Science*, *2*(19).

Rida, N., Ouadoud, M., Hasbi, A., & Chebli, S. (2018, October). Adaptive Traffic Light Control System Using Wireless Sensors Networks. In *2018 IEEE 5th International Congress on Information Science and Technology (CiSt)* (pp. 552-556). IEEE. 10.1109/CIST.2018.8596620

Rida, N., & Hasbi, A. (2018, October). Dynamic Traffic Lights Control for Isolated Intersection Based Wireless Sensor Network. In *The Proceedings of the Third International Conference on Smart City Applications* (pp. 1036-1044). Springer.

Rida, N., & Hasbi, A. (2018, October). Traffic Lights Control using Wireless Sensors Networks. In *Proceedings of the 3rd International Conference on Smart City Applications* (p. 14). ACM. 10.1145/3286606.3286791

Ridder, H.-G. (2017). The theory contribution of case study research designs. *Business Research*, *10*(2), 281–305. doi:10.100740685-017-0045-z

Riebe, D., Blissmer, B. J., Greaney, M. L., Garber, C. E., Lees, F. D., & Clark, P. G. (2009). The relationship between obesity, physical activity, and physical function in older adults. *Journal of Aging and Health*, *21*(8), 1159–1178. doi:10.1177/0898264309350076 PMID:19897781

Riel, A. C. R. V., Semeijn, J., & Pauwels, P. (2003). Online Travel Service Quality: The Importance of Pre-transaction Services. METEOR, Maastricht research school of Economics of Technology and Organizations.

Riley, T. J., & Simons, K. A. (2016). The written communication skills that matter most for accountants. *Accounting Education*, *25*(3), 239–255. doi:10.1080/09639284.2016.1164066

Rios, R. (2007). *Sources and antecedents of brand equity for online companies*. Academic Press.

Robertson, D. I. (1969). 'Tansyt' method for area traffic control. *Traffic Engineering & Control*, *8*(8).

Robertson, D. I., & Bretherton, R. D. (1991). Optimizing networks of traffic signals in real time-the SCOOT method. *IEEE Transactions on Vehicular Technology*, *40*(1), 11–15. doi:10.1109/25.69966

Robertson, D. I., & Hunt, P. B. (1982). Method of estimating the benefits of co-ordinating signals by TRANSYT and SCOOT. *Traffic Engineering & Control*, *23*, 527–531.

Robinson, J. (2009). Triandis theory of interpersonal behaviour in understanding software privace behaviour in the South African context (Masters degree). University of the Witwatersrand.

Robinson, P., & Lowe, J. (2015). Literature reviews vs systematic reviews. *Australian and New Zealand Journal of Public Health*, *39*(2), 103–103. doi:10.1111/1753-6405.12393 PMID:25827181

Roedder John, D., & Cole, C. A. (1986). Age differences in information processing: Understanding deficits in young and elderly consumers. *The Journal of Consumer Research*, *13*(3), 297–315. doi:10.1086/209070

Rogers, E. (1995). *Diffusion of Innovations*. The Free Press.

Rogers, E. (1995). *Diffusion of Innovations* (4th ed.). The Free Press.

Rogers, M. A., & Evans, W. J. (1993). Changes in skeletal muscle with aging: Effects of exercise training. *Exercise and Sport Sciences Reviews*, *21*(1), 65–102. doi:10.1249/00003677-199301000-00003 PMID:8504850

Roos, G. (2014). Intellectual capital in Australia- economic development in a high cost economy. In *11th International Conference on Intellectual Capital, Knowledge Management & Organisational Learning -ICICKM 2014*. Sydney: The University of Sydney Business School.

Roper, K., & Yeh, D. (2007). Ergonomic solutions for an aging workforce. *Journal of Facilities Management*, *5*(3), 172–178. doi:10.1108/14725960710775054

Roşca, M. I., Sarău, A. C., & Vonţea, A. A. (2015). Classifying social causes derived from the communication of CSR initiatives online: A theoretical and practical approach. Corporate Social Responsibility in the Digital Age.

Rowe, G. (2012). Performance measurement. *Introduction to Nonprofit Management: Text and Cases*, 129.

Rowe, J. W., & Kahn, R. L. (1987). Human aging: Usual and successful. *Science*, *237*(4811), 143–149. doi:10.1126cience.3299702 PMID:3299702

Rowe, W. G. (2001). Creating wealth in organizations: The role of strategic leadership. *The Academy of Management Executive*, *15*(1), 81–94. doi:10.5465/ame.2001.4251395

Rowley, J. (2002). Using case studies in research. *Management Research News*, *25*(1), 16–27. doi:10.1108/01409170210782990

Rushinek, A., & Rushinek, S. F. (1995). Accounting software evaluation: Hardware, audit trails, backup, error recovery and security. *Managerial Auditing Journal*, *10*(9), 29–37. doi:10.1108/02686909510100887

Ruyter, K. D., Wetzels, M., & Kleijnen, M. (2001). Customer adoption of e-service: An experimental study. *International Journal of Service Industry Management*, *12*(2), 184–207. doi:10.1108/09564230110387542

Ryan Nelson, R., Michael, W. K., & Cheney, P. H. (1991). An Empirical Re-Examination of the Relationship among Training, Ability, and the Acceptance of Information Technology. *SIGCPR '91 Proceedings of the 1991 conference on SIGCPR*, 177-186.

Rybalko, S., & Seltzer, T. (2010). Dialogic communication in 140 characters or less: How Fortune 500 companies engage stakeholders using Twitter. *Public Relations Review*, *36*(4), 336–341. doi:10.1016/j.pubrev.2010.08.004

Saadé, R., & Bahli, B. (2005). The impact of cognitive absorption on perceived usefulness and perceived ease of use in on-line learning: An extension of the technology acceptance model. *Information & Management*, *42*(2), 317–327. doi:10.1016/j.im.2003.12.013

Saaty, T. L. (1980). *The Analytic Hierarchy Process: Planning, Priority Setting, Resources Allocation*. London: McGraw-Hill.

Salisbury, W. D., Pearson, R. A., Pearson, A. W., & Miller, D. W. (2001). Perceived security and World Wide Web purchase intention. *Industrial Management & Data Systems*, *101*(4), 165–176. doi:10.1108/02635570110390071

Salovey, P., & Mayer, J. (1990). Emotional Intelligence. *Imagination, Cognition and Personality*, *9*(3), 185–211. doi:10.2190/DUGG-P24E-52WK-6CDG

Samak, A., & Tawfik, Z. (2017). *Exploration of Jordanian English Language Teachers' Attitudes*. Skills, and Access as Indicator of Information and Communication Technology Integration in Jordan.

Sam, M., Fazli, M., Tahir, M. N. H., & Abu Bakar, K. (2012). Owner-managers of SMEs in it sector: Leadership and company performance. *International Journal of Business and Social Science*, *3*(14), 1–11.

Sandberg, B. (2007). Customer-related proactiveness in the radical innovation development process. *European Journal of Innovation Management*, *10*(2), 252–267. doi:10.1108/14601060710745288

Sandhu, K., & Terdpaopong, K. (2018). *New research findings from a university web-based information systems*. Asia-Pacific Management Accounting Association. (14th) Annual Conf., Waseda Uni, Tokyo, Japan.

Sandhu, K., & Terdpaopong, K. (2019). *Digital Transformation of Accounting Systems*. Asia-Pacific Management Accounting Association (APMAA) 15th Annual Conference, at Qatar University, Doha, Qatar.

Sandhu, K. (2008). *Information quality for a university accounting information system*. Elsevier. doi:10.2139srn.1289508

Sandhu, K., & Corbitt, B. (2007). Framework for Electronic Services System. In *The Fifth International Conference on Supply Chain Management and Information Systems (SCMIS)*. Monash University.

Santos, J. (2003). E-service quality: A model of virtual service quality dimensions. *Managing Service Quality*, *13*(3), 233–246. doi:10.1108/09604520310476490

Saraph, J. V., Benson, P. G., & Schroeder, R. G. (1989). An instrument for measuring the critical factors of quality management. *Decision Sciences*, *20*(4), 810–829. doi:10.1111/j.1540-5915.1989.tb01421.x

Saryazdi, R., Bannon, J., & Chambers, C. G. (2019). Age-related differences in referential production: A multiple-measures study. *Psychology and Aging*, *34*(6), 791–804. doi:10.1037/pag0000372 PMID:31204834

Saxe, R., & Weitx, B. A. (1982). The SOCO Scale: A Measure of the Customer Orientation of Sales people. *Journal of Marketing, 19*(3), 343–351. doi:10.1177/002224378201900307

Scemama, G., & Laffont, P. (2013). CLAIRE-SITI Système pour la supervision intelligente, intermodale, intégrée des réseaux de transport de surface. *TEC Transport environnement circulation*, (219), 11.

Schartel Dunn, S., & Lane, P. (2019). Do interns know what they think they know? Assessing business communication skills in interns and recent graduates. *Business and Professional Communication Quarterly, 82*(2), 202–213. doi:10.1177/2329490619826258

Schewe, C. D. (1984). Buying and Consuming Behavior of the Elderly Findings From Behavioral Research. NA - Advances in Consumer Research, 11, 558-562.

Schoon, I., & Duckworth, K. (2012). Who becomes an entrepreneur? Early life experiences as predictors of entrepreneurship. *Developmental Psychology, 48*(6), 1719–1726. doi:10.1037/a0029168 PMID:22746220

Schumpeter, J. A. (1965). Economic Theory and Entrepreneurial History. In H. G. Aitken (Ed.), *Explorations in enterprise*. Cambridge, MA: Harvard University Press. doi:10.4159/harvard.9780674594470.c5

Schwab, K. (2016). *The Fourth Industrial Revolution.* Geneva: World Economic Forum.

Seebacher, S., & Schüritz, R. (2017). Blockchain Technology as an Enabler of Service Systems: A Structured Literature Review. *Springer International Publishing AG, 2017*, 12–23. doi:10.1007/978-3-319-56925-3_2

Selinger, M., & Schmidt, L. (2009). *A review of the cost, maintenance and reliability of popular adaptive traffic control technologies.* Adaptive Traffic Control Systems in the United States.

Semeijn, J., Riel, A. C. R. V., Birgelen, M. J. H. V., & Streukens, S. (2005). E-services and offline fulfilment: How e-loyalty is created. *Managing Service Quality, 15*(2), 182–194. doi:10.1108/09604520510585361

Shachaf, P., & Oltmann, S. M. (2007). E-quality and e-service equality. *Proceedings of the 40th Hawaii International Conference on System Sciences.*

Shapiro, S. S., & Francia, R. S. (1972). An approximate analysis of variance test for normality. *Journal of the American Statistical Association, 67*(337), 215–216. doi:10.1080/01621459.1972.10481232

Shareef, M. A., Kumar, U., Kumar, V., & Dwivedi, Y. K. (2009). Identifying critical factors for adoption of e-government. *Electronic Government: An International Journal, 6*(1), 70–96. doi:10.1504/EG.2009.022594

Shareef, M. A., Kumar, V., Kumar, U., & Dwivedi, Y. K. (2011). e-Government Adoption Model (GAM): Differing service maturity levels. *Government Information Quarterly, 28*(1), 17–35. doi:10.1016/j.giq.2010.05.006

Sharp, M. R., & Brumberger, E. R. (2013). Business Communication Cirricula Today: Revisiting the Top 50 Undergraduate Business Schools. *Business Communication Quarterly, 76*(1), 5–27. doi:10.1177/1080569912471187

Sheikh, S., & Beise-Zee, R. (2011). Corporate social responsibility or cause-related marketing? The role of cause specificity of CSR. *Journal of Consumer Marketing, 28*(1), 27–39. doi:10.1108/07363761111101921

Sheikhshoaei, F., & Oloumi, T. (2011). Applying the technology acceptance model to Iranian engineering faculty libraries. *The Electronic Library, 29*(3), 367–378. doi:10.1108/02640471111141106

Sheldon, O. (1923). *The Philosophy of Management.* Sir Isaac Pitman & Sons.

Shi, M. K., Jiang, H., & Li, S. H. (2016, November). An intelligent traffic-flow-based real-time vehicles scheduling algorithm at intersection. In *2016 14th International Conference on Control, Automation, Robotics and Vision (ICARCV)* (pp. 1-5). IEEE. 10.1109/ICARCV.2016.7838779

Shih, H.-P. (2004). Extended technology acceptance model of Internet utilization behavior. *Information & Management*, *41*(6), 719–729. doi:10.1016/j.im.2003.08.009

Shinar, D. (2017). Driver Information Processing: Attention, Perception, Reaction Time, and Comprehension. *Traffic Safety and Human Behavior*, 189-256.

Shin, D.-H. (2010). The effects of trust, security and privacy in social networking: A security-based approach to understand the pattern of adoption. *Interacting with Computers*, *22*(5), 428–438. doi:10.1016/j.intcom.2010.05.001

Singh, I., Nayyar, A., & Das, S. (2019). A study of antecedents of customer loyalty in banking & insurance sector and their impact on business performance. *Revista ESPACIOS, 40*(6).

Singh, I., Nayyar, A., Le, D. H., & Das, S. (2019). A conceptual analysis of internet banking users' perceptions. An Indian perceptive. *Revista ESPACIOS, 40*(14).

Singh, S., & Das, S. (2018). Impact of post-merger and acquisition activities on the financial performance of banks: A study of Indian private sector and public sector banks. *Revista Espacios Magazine*, *39*(26), 25.

Skelton, D. A., Greig, C. A., Davies, J. M., & Young, A. (1994). Strength, power and related functional ability of healthy people aged 65–89 years. *Age and Ageing*, *23*(5), 371–377. doi:10.1093/ageing/23.5.371 PMID:7825481

Smith, A. G. (2001). Applying evaluation criteria to New Zealand government Web sites. *International Journal of Information Management*, *21*(2), 137–149. doi:10.1016/S0268-4012(01)00006-8

Spreng, R. A., Mackenzie, S. B., & Olshavsky, R. W. (1996). A re-examination of the determinants of consumer research. *Journal of Marketing*, *60*(3), 15–32. doi:10.2307/1251839

Spreng, R. A., & Mackoy, R. D. (1996). An empirical examination of a model of perceived service quality and satisfaction. *Journal of Retailing*, *722*(2), 201–214. doi:10.1016/S0022-4359(96)90014-7

Srinivasan, S. S., Anderson, R., & Ponnavolu, K. (2002). Customer loyalty in e-commerce: An exploration of its antecedents and consequences. *Journal of Retailing*, *78*(1), 41–50. doi:10.1016/S0022-4359(01)00065-3

Steers, R. M., Meyer, A. D., & Sanchez-Runde, C. J. (2008). National culture and the adoption of new technologies. *Journal of World Business*, *43*(3), 255–260. doi:10.1016/j.jwb.2008.03.007

Steffens, N. K., Yang, J., Jetten, J., Haslam, S. A., & Lipponen, J. (2018). The unfolding impact of leader identity entrepreneurship on burnout, work engagement, and turnover intentions. *Journal of Occupational Health Psychology*, *23*(3), 373–387. doi:10.1037/ocp0000090 PMID:28749160

Stephanie, A. J., Abdul Nasir, Z., & Nur Fadziana, F. M. (2008). A Study on the Acceptance of E-Ticketing in Universiti Utara *Malaysia Bus Service. Knowledge Management International Conference*. Langkawi, Malaysia.

Stevens, J. (2001). *Applied multivariate statistics for the social sciences*. Mahwah, NJ: Lawrence Erlbaum.

St-Hilaire, W., & Boisselier, P. (2018). Evaluating profitability strategies and the determinants of the risk performance of sectoral and banking institutions. *Journal of Economic and Administrative Sciences*, *34*(3), 174–186. doi:10.1108/JEAS-08-2017-0078

Stohl, C., Etter, M., Banghart, S., & Woo, D. (2017). Social media policies: Implications for contemporary notions of corporate social responsibility. *Journal of Business Ethics*, *142*(3), 413–436. doi:10.100710551-015-2743-9

Stone, G., & Lightbody, M. (2012). The nature and significance of listening skills in accounting practice. *Accounting Education, 21*(4), 363–384. doi:10.1080/09639284.2011.617062

Straub, D., Boudreau, M.-C., & Gefen, D. (2004). Validation guidelines for IS positivist research. *Communications of the Association for Information Systems, 13*, 380–427. doi:10.17705/1CAIS.01324

Stretcher Sigmar, L., Hynes, G., & Hill, K. L. (2012). Strategies for Teaching Social and Emotional Intelligence in Business Communication. *Business Communication Quarterly, 75*(3), 301–317. doi:10.1177/1080569912450312

Subhankar, D., & Anand, N. (2019, May). Digital sustainability in social media innovation: a microscopic analysis of Instagram advertising & its demographic reflection for buying activity with R. In *1st International Scientific Conference" Modern Management Trends and the Digital Economy: from Regional Development to Global Economic Growth"(MTDE 2019)*. Atlantis Press. 10.2991/mtde-19.2019.72

Sultan, K., Ruhi, U., & Lakhani, R. (2018). Conceptualizing Blockchains: Characteristics & Applications. *11th IADIS Intel. Conference Information Systems.*

Sun, W., & Price, J. M. (2016). The impact of environmental uncertainty on increasing customer satisfaction through corporate social responsibility. *European Journal of Marketing, 50*(7/8), 1209–1238. doi:10.1108/EJM-02-2015-0077

Susskind, R., & Susskind, D. (2015). *The Future of the Professions: How Technology Will Transform the Work of Human Experts*. Oxford: Oxford University Press.

Swanson, J., & Swanson, N. (1990). The value of business communications as perceived by business administration graduates. *Journal of Education for Business, 64*(4), 168–171. doi:10.1080/08832323.1990.10117420

Sweeney, J. C., Soutar, G. N., & Johnson, L. W. (1997). Retail service quality and perceived value. *Journal of Consumer Services, 4*(1), 39–48. doi:10.1016/S0969-6989(96)00017-3

Syafrudin, V. (2012). An empirical study of Accounting software Acceptance among Bengkulu City students. *Asian Journal of Accounting and Governance, 3*, 99-112.

Szajna, B. (1996). Empirical evaluation of the revised technology acceptance model. *Management Science, 42*(1), 85–92. doi:10.1287/mnsc.42.1.85

Szymanski, D. M., & Hise, R. T. (2000). E-satisfaction: An initial examination. *Journal of Retailing, 76*(3), 309–322. doi:10.1016/S0022-4359(00)00035-X

Taherdoost, H. (2019). Electronic Service Quality Measurement (eSQM); Development of a Survey Instrument to Measure the Quality of E-Service. *International Journal of Intelligent Engineering Informatics.*

Taherdoost, H., & Hassan, A. (2020). Development of An E-Service Quality Model (eSQM) to Assess the Quality of E-Service. In Strategies and Tools for Managing Connected Customers. IGI Global. Doi:10.4018/978-1-5225-9697-4.ch011

Taherdoost, H. (2017a). Decision Making Using the Analytic Hierarchy Process (AHP); A Step by Step Approach. *International Journal of Economics and Management Systems, 2*, 244–246.

Taherdoost, H. (2017b). Understanding of e-service security dimensions and its effect on quality and intention to use. *Information & Computer Security, 25*(5), 535–559. doi:10.1108/ICS-09-2016-0074

Taherdoost, H. (2018a). Development of an adoption model to assess user acceptance of e-service technology: E-Service Technology Acceptance Model. *Behaviour & Information Technology, 37*(2), 173–197. doi:10.1080/0144929X.2018.1427793

Taherdoost, H. (2018b). A Review of Technology Acceptance and Adoption Models and Theories. *Procedia Manufacturing Journal, 22*, 960–967. doi:10.1016/j.promfg.2018.03.137

Tahseen Arshi, A., & Al Lawati Jassim, M. (2013). *Customer satisfaction in banking sector in Oman: what do they care for?* Advances in Management.

Takeuchi, H., & Quelch, J. (1983). *Quality is more than making a good product.* Academic Press.

Tanaka, H., & Higuchi, M. (1998). Age, exercise performance, and physiological functional capacities. *Advances in Exercise and Sports Physiology, 4*, 51–56.

Tanaka, H., & Seals, D. R. (1997). Age and gender interactions in physiological functional capacity: Insight from swimming performance. *Journal of Applied Physiology, 82*(3), 846–851. doi:10.1152/jappl.1997.82.3.846 PMID:9074973

Tan, K. C., Xie, M., & Li, Y. N. (2003). A service quality framework for Web-based information systems. *The TQM Magazine, 15*(3), 164–172. doi:10.1108/09544780310469262

Taragola, N., Van Lierde, D., & Van Huylenbroeck, G. (2001). *Adoption of computers, internet and accounting software at the glasshouse holdings of the Belgian farm accountancy data network.* Paper presented at the Proc. 3rd EFITA Conference, Montpellier, France.

Tasca, P., & Tessone, C. J. (2019). A Taxonomy of Blockchain Technologies: Principles of Identification and Classification. *Ledger, 4*, 1–39. doi:10.5195/ledger.2019.140

Taylor, S., & Todd, P. (1995a). Understanding information technology usage: A Test of Competing Models. *Information Systems Research, 6*(2), 144–176. doi:10.1287/isre.6.2.144

Terdpaopong, K., Visedsun, N., Nitirojntanad, K., & Sandhu, K. (2018). Advancement of the Management Accounting Practices of Large Thai Manufacturing Companies. In *Asia-Pacific Management Accounting Association (14th) Annual Conference.* Waseda University.

Thomas, B., Basil, M., Christina, M., Fedra, K., & Manuela, T. (2013). Measuring Users Satisfaction of an e-Government portal. *Procedia Technology, 8*, 371–377. doi:10.1016/j.protcy.2013.11.049

Thompson, B. (2004). *Exploratory and confirmatory factor analysis: understanding concepts and applications.* Washington, DC: American Psychological Association. doi:10.1037/10694-000

Thorndike, R. (1936). Factor analysis of social and abstract intelligence. *Journal of Educational Psychology, 27*(3), 231–233. doi:10.1037/h0059840

Thorndike, R., & Stein, S. (1937). An evaluation of the attempts to measure social intelligence. *Psychological Bulletin, 34*(5), 275–285. doi:10.1037/h0053850

Tien, T. A. D., Wang, J., Chen, G., Liu, R., Ooi, B. C., & Tan, K.-L. (2017). *Blockbench: A Framework for Analyzing Private Blockchains.* SIGMOD.

Tojib, D. R., Sugianto, L.-F., & Sendjaya, S. (2006). A Conceptual Model for B2E Portal User Satisfaction. *Proceedings of the International Conference on Business and Information.*

Torkzadeh, G., & Dhillon, G. (2002). Measuring factors that influence the success of Internet commerce. *Information Systems Research, 13*(2), 187–204. doi:10.1287/isre.13.2.187.87

Tsai, H.-T., Huang, H.-C., Jaw, Y.-L., & Chen, W.-K. (2006). Why on-line customers remain with a particular e-retailer: An integrative model and empirical evidence. *Psychology and Marketing, 23*(5), 447–464. doi:10.1002/mar.20121

Tuna, H. D., Edeer, A. O., Malkoc, M., & Aksakoglu, G. (2009). Effect of age and physical activity level on functional fitness in older adults. *European Review of Aging and Physical Activity*, *6*(2), 99–106. doi:10.100711556-009-0051-z

Turkanović, M., Hölbl, M., Košič, K., Heričko, M., & Kamišalić, A. (2018). EduCTX: A Blockchain-Based Higher Education Credit Platform. *IEEE Access : Practical Innovations, Open Solutions*, *6*, 2018. doi:10.1109/ACCESS.2018.2789929

Uchenwamgbe, B. (2013). Effects of leadership style on organizational performance in small and medium scale enterprises (SMEs) in Nigeria. *European Journal of Business and Management*, *5*(23), 53–73.

Uman L. S. (2011). Systematic reviews and meta-analyses. *Journal of the Canadian Academy of Child and Adolescent Psychiatry = Journal de l'Academie canadienne de psychiatrie de l'enfant et de l'adolescent, 20*(1), 57–59.

Uman, L. S., Chambers, C. T., McGrath, P. J., & Kisely, S. (2008). A systematic review of randomized controlled trials examining psychological interventions for needle-related procedural pain and distress in children and adolescents: An abbreviated Cochrane review. *Journal of Pediatric Psychology*, *33*(8), 842–854. doi:10.1093/jpepsy/jsn031 PMID:18387963

UNIDO (United Nations International Development Organization). (2019). https://www.unido.org/our-focus/advancing-economic-competitiveness/competitive-trade-capacities-and-corporate-responsibility/corporate-social-responsibility-market-integration/what-csr

Unwin, T., Kleessen, B., Hollow, D., Williams, J. B., Oloo, L. M., Alwala, J., . . . Muianga, X. (2010). Digital learning management systems in Africa: myths and realities. *Open Learning: The Journal of Open, Distance and e-Learning, 25*(1), 5-23.

Van der Pol, E., & Oliehoek, F. A. (2016). Coordinated deep reinforcement learners for traffic light control. *Proceedings of Learning, Inference and Control of Multi-Agent Systems (at NIPS 2016).*

Van Hasselt, H. (2012). Reinforcement learning in continuous state and action spaces. In *Reinforcement learning* (pp. 207–251). Berlin: Springer. doi:10.1007/978-3-642-27645-3_7

Varis, T., & Al-Agtash, S. (2008). *Ubiquitous ICT for sustainable education and cultural literacy*. Citeseer.

Venkatesh, V. (1999). Creation of favorable user perceptions: Exploring the role of intrinsic motivation. *Management Information Systems Quarterly*, *23*(2), 239–260. doi:10.2307/249753

Venkatesh, V., & Davis, F. D. (2000). A theoretical extension of the technology acceptance model: Four longitudinal field studies. *Management Science*, *46*(2), 186–204. doi:10.1287/mnsc.46.2.186.11926

Venkatesh, V., Morris, M. G., Davis, G. B., & Davis, E. D. (2003). User acceptance of information technology: Towards a unified view. *Management Information Systems Quarterly*, *27*(3), 425–478. doi:10.2307/30036540

Verdegem, P., & Verleye, G. (2009). User-centered e-Government in practice: A comprehensive model for measuring user satisfaction. *Government Information Quarterly*, *26*(3), 487–497. doi:10.1016/j.giq.2009.03.005

Verhoef, P., & Langerak, J. (2001). Possible determinants of consumers' adoption of electronic grocery shopping in the Netherlands. *Journal of Retailing and Consumer Services*, *8*(5), 275–285. doi:10.1016/S0969-6989(00)00033-3

Vijayasarathy, L. R. (2004). Predicting consumer intentions to use on-line shopping: The case for an augmented technology acceptance model. *Information & Management*, *41*(6), 747–762. doi:10.1016/j.im.2003.08.011

Visser, W. (2014). *CSR 2.0 Transforming Corporate Sustainability and Responsibility*. Springer.

von Hippel, E. (2005). *Democratising Innovation*. Cambridge: MIT Press. doi:10.7551/mitpress/2333.001.0001

Wang, D. H., Chen, P., Yu, T. H., & Hsiao, C. (2015). The effects of corporate social responsibility on brand equity and firm performance. *Journal of Business Research, 68*(11), 2232–2236. doi:10.1016/j.jbusres.2015.06.003

Wang, J. (2009). A study of resiliency characteristics in the adjustment of international graduate students at American universities. *Journal of Studies in International Education, 13*(1), 22–45. doi:10.1177/1028315307308139

Wardrope, W. J. (2002). Department Chairs' perceptions of the importance of business communication skills. *Business Communication Quarterly, 65*(4), 60–72. doi:10.1177/108056990206500406

Warrier, M. M., & Kumar, A. (2016). An energy efficient approach for routing in wireless sensor networks. *Procedia Technology, 25*, 520–527. doi:10.1016/j.protcy.2016.08.140

Wasiuzzaman, S. (2019). Resource sharing in interfirm alliances between SMEs and large firms and SME access to finance. *Management Research Review, 42*(12), 1375–1399. doi:10.1108/MRR-10-2018-0369

Watters, A. (2016). *The Blockchain for Education: An Introduction, 2016.* http://hackeducation.com/2016/04/07/blockchain-education-guide

Wei, W., & Zhang, Y. (2002, May). FL-FN based traffic signal control. In *2002 IEEE World Congress on Computational Intelligence. 2002 IEEE International Conference on Fuzzy Systems. FUZZ-IEEE'02. Proceedings* (Cat. No. 02CH37291) (Vol. 1, pp. 296-300). IEEE. 10.1109/FUZZ.2002.1005004

Wei, H., Zheng, G., Yao, H., & Li, Z. (2018, July). Intellilight: A reinforcement learning approach for intelligent traffic light control. In *Proceedings of the 24th ACM SIGKDD International Conference on Knowledge Discovery & Data Mining* (pp. 2496-2505). ACM. 10.1145/3219819.3220096

Westerterp, K. R. (2000). Daily physical activity and ageing. *Current Opinion in Clinical Nutrition and Metabolic Care, 3*(6), 485–488. doi:10.1097/00075197-200011000-00011 PMID:11085835

Whelan, R., & Bhartu, D. (2007). Factors in the deployment of a learning management system at the University of the South Pacific. *Proceedings Ascilite Singapore*, 1053-1062.

White, D. A., McGuire, A. B., Luther, L., Anderson, A. I., Phalen, P., & McGrew, J. H. (2017). Consumer factors predicting level of treatment response to illness management and recovery. *Psychiatric Rehabilitation Journal, 40*(4), 344–353. doi:10.1037/prj0000284 PMID:28910123

Whitley, B. E. (2002). *Principals of Research and Behavioural Science.* Boston: McGraw-Hill.

Williams, P. (2002). The learning web: The development, implementation and evaluation of internet-based undergraduate materials for the teaching of key skills. *Active Learning in Higher Education, 3*(1), 40–53. doi:10.1177/1469787402003001004

Wimpenny, K., Adefila, A., & DeWinter, A. (2018). *Jordan Opportunity for Virtual Innovative Teaching and Learning: A Needs Analysis Report Contextualising the State of the Art in International Online Teaching and Learning, with Particular Attention to the Jordanian Case.* Academic Press.

Winsted, K. F. (1997). The service experience in two cultures: A behavioral perspective. *Journal of Retailing, 73*(3), 337–360. doi:10.1016/S0022-4359(97)90022-1

Wixom, B. H., & Todd, P. A. (2005). A theoretical integration of user satisfaction and technology acceptance. *Information Systems Research, 16*(1), 85–102. doi:10.1287/isre.1050.0042

Wolfinbarger, M., & Gilly, M. C. (2003). Etailq: Dimensionalizing, Measuring and Predicting Etail Quality. *Journal of Retailing, 79*(3), 183–198. doi:10.1016/S0022-4359(03)00034-4

Wright, C. R. (1986). *Mass communication: A sociological perspective* (3rd ed.). New York: Random House.

Wu, Y.-L., Tao, Y.-H., & Yang, P.-C. (2008). The use of unified theory of acceptance and use of technology to confer the behavioral model of 3G mobile telecommunication users. *Journal of Statistics & Management Systems*, *11*(5), 919–949. doi:10.1080/09720510.2008.10701351

Xu, X., Weber, I., Staples, M., Zhu, L., Bosch, J., Bass, L., ... Rimba, P. (2017). A Taxonomy of Blockchain-Based Systems for Architecture Design. *IEEE International Conference on Software Architecture (ICSA)*, 243-252. 10.1109/ICSA.2017.33

Yaga, Mell, Roby, & Scarfone. (2018). *Blockchain Technology Overview*. National Institute of Standards and Technology, Internal Report 8202.

Yang, Z., & Jun, M. (2002). Consumer perception of e-service quality: From Internet purchaser and non-purchaser perspectives. *Journal of Business Strategies Huntsville*, *19*, 19–41.

Yang, Z., Peterson, R. T., & Cai, S. (2003). Services quality dimension of Internet retailing: An exploratory analysis. *Journal of Services Marketing Science*, *17*(7), 685–690. doi:10.1108/08876040310501241

Yen, C. C., Ghosal, D., Zhang, M., Chuah, C. N., & Chen, H. (2018, December). Falsified Data Attack on Backpressure-based Traffic Signal Control Algorithms. In *2018 IEEE Vehicular Networking Conference (VNC)* (pp. 1-8). IEEE. 10.1109/VNC.2018.8628334

Yenisey, M. M., Ozok, A. A., & Salvendy, G. (2005). Perceived security determinants in ecommerce among Turkish University students. *Behaviour & Information Technology*, *24*(4), 259–274. doi:10.1080/0144929042000320992

Yin, R. K. (2012). A (very) brief refresher on the case study method. *Applications of Case Study Research*, 3-20.

Yin, R. K. (1981). The case study crisis: Some answers. *Administrative Science Quarterly*, *26*(1), 58–65. doi:10.2307/2392599

Yin, R. K. (2015). *Qualitative research from start to finish*. Guilford Publications.

Yong, J., Ryan, S., Yap, C., & Goela, N. (2011). A case study in the failiure of graduate attributes in accounting education. In K. Krause, M. Buckridge, C. Grimmer, & S. Purbrick-Illek (Eds.), *Research and development in higher education: reshaping higher education* (pp. 383–394). Gold Coast.

Yoo, B., & Donthu, N. (2001). Developing a scale to measure perceived quality of an Internet shopping site (SITEQUAL). *Quarterly Journal of Electronic Commerce*, *2*, 31–46.

Yoo, B., & Donthu, N. (2001). Developing and validating a multidimensional consumer-based brand equity scale. *Journal of Business Research*, *52*(1), 1–14. doi:10.1016/S0148-2963(99)00098-3

Yoo, B., & Donthu, N. (2002). Testing cross-cultural invariance of the brand equity creation process. *Journal of Product and Brand Management*, *11*(6), 380–398. doi:10.1108/10610420210445505

Yoon, C. (2010). Antecedents of customer satisfaction with online banking in China: The effects of experience. *Computers in Human Behavior*, *26*(6), 1296–1304. doi:10.1016/j.chb.2010.04.001

Yoon, C., Feinberg, F., & Schwarz, N. (2010). Older consumers and satisfaction. In A. Drolet, N. Schwarz, & C. Yoon (Eds.), *The Aging Consumer: Perspectives from Psychology and Economics* (pp. 209–227). London: Taylor and Francis.

Younes, M. B., & Boukerche, A. (2018). An efficient dynamic traffic light scheduling algorithm considering emergency vehicles for intelligent transportation systems. *Wireless Networks*, *24*(7), 2451–2463. doi:10.100711276-017-1482-5

Younes, M. B., Boukerche, A., & Mammeri, A. (2016, April). Context-aware traffic light self-scheduling algorithm for intelligent transportation systems. In *2016 IEEE Wireless Communications and Networking Conference* (pp. 1-6). IEEE. 10.1109/WCNC.2016.7564924

Yousef, K. M., Al-Karaki, M. N., & Shatnawi, A. M. (2010). Intelligent traffic light flow control system using wireless sensors networks. *Journal of Information Science and Engineering*, *26*(3), 753–768.

Yu, J., Ha, I., Choi, M., & Rho, J. (2005). Extending the TAM for a t-commerce. *Information & Management*, *42*(7), 965–976. doi:10.1016/j.im.2004.11.001

Yukl, G. (2008). How leaders influence organizational effectiveness. *The Leadership Quarterly*, *19*(6), 708–722. doi:10.1016/j.leaqua.2008.09.008

Zadek, S. (2004). The path to corporate responsibility. *Harvard Business Review*, *82*(12), 125–132. PMID:15605571

Zahodne, L. B., Ajrouch, K. J., Sharifian, N., & Antonucci, T. C. (2019). Social relations and age-related change in memory. *Psychology and Aging*, *34*(6), 751–765. doi:10.1037/pag0000369 PMID:31180697

Zaid, O. A., Abraham, A., & Abraham, A. (1994). Communication Skills in accounting education: Perceptions of academics, employers and graduate accountants. *Accounting Education*, *3*(3), 205–221. doi:10.1080/09639289400000020

Zarowin, S. (1998). Accounting software: The road ahead. *Journal of Accountancy*, *185*(1), 67.

Zavareh, F. B., Ariff, M. S. M., Jusoh, A., Zakuan, N., Bahari, A. Z., & Ashourian, M. (2012). e-Service quality dimensions and their effects on e-Customer satisfaction in internet banking services. *Procedia: Social and Behavioral Sciences*, *40*, 441–445. doi:10.1016/j.sbspro.2012.03.213

Zhang, X., & Prybutok, V. (2005). A consumer perspective of e-service quality. *IEEE Transactions on Engineering Management*, *52*(4), 461–477. doi:10.1109/TEM.2005.856568

Zhang, X., Prybutok, V., & Huang, A. (2006). An empirical study of factors affecting e-service satisfaction. *Human Systems Management*, *25*, 279–291.

Zhou, B., Cao, J., Zeng, X., & Wu, H. (2010, September). Adaptive traffic light control in wireless sensor network-based intelligent transportation system. In *2010 IEEE 72nd Vehicular Technology Conference-Fall* (pp. 1-5). IEEE.

Zhou, P., Braud, T., Alhilal, A., Hui, P., & Kangasharju, J. (2019, March). ERL: Edge based Reinforcement Learning for optimized urban Traffic light control. In *2019 IEEE International Conference on Pervasive Computing and Communications Workshops (PerCom Workshops)* (pp. 849-854). IEEE.

Zou, F., Yang, B., & Cao, Y. (2009, August). Traffic light control for a single intersection based on wireless sensor network. In *2009 9th International Conference on Electronic Measurement & Instruments* (pp. 1-1040). IEEE. 10.1109/ICEMI.2009.5273994

About the Contributors

Kamaljeet Sandhu is an active scholar, experienced & passionate about research in Digital Innovation & Strategy, Business Data Analytics, Digital Health, AI, IoT, Cryptocurrency, Blockchain, Cloud Computing, IT Startups, FinTech, Cybersecurity, Accounting, Corporate Governance & CSR, Supply Chain, ERP, SMEs, & Entrepreneurship. Editor of 3 Books & published internationally over 180 articles in peer-reviewed (refereed) journals, conferences, & book chapters. Having held multiple Leadership positions including Professor at the University of Northern British Columbia Canada, Senior Research Fellow at the University of South Australia, and other Senior Academic positions at: University of Wollongong, Charles Darwin University, Deakin University, & at the University of South Pacific, Fiji. As a PhD Principal Supervisor (Advisor), he has supervised & mentored several PhD Research students to successful completion & students have successfully gained academic & research appointments at leading international universities & other organizations. His PhD students research are funded by international government & industry scholarships. New scientific discoveries from supervising doctoral research have been implemented by government, private institutions and universities in Australia, Canada, USA, UK, Europe, China, India, Saudi Arabia, Jordan, & UAE. He has multidisciplinary experience working across different Faculties such as Business, Accounting, Finance, Management, Economics, IT & IS, Software, & Computer Science.

* * *

Abdeleh Al Amoush is a PhD Candidate in Business School at University of New England; M.S. degree in Computer Information System from AABFS; BSc degree in Computer Science from PSUT.

Subhankar Das is currently working at Duy Tan University, Vietnam as a Researcher & Professor. He is a UGC NET qualified Ph.D. in Marketing Management from SoA University. He has 13 SSCI and SCOPUS indexed publications. He is a winner of 4 International Awards in the field of management study & research from reputed organizations. He is an IIM Lucknow alumni and has certifications from University of British Columbia & IIM Bangalore, Manipal & Google certified faculty in Case-based pedagogy and digital branding. He is also acting as Member of Center of Excellence for TISS-SVE for 'Management & Entrepreneurship and Professional Skills' Vertical, Mumbai. He is having 14 years of progressive teaching experience across with proven abilities in classroom teaching, management of departmental activity & 3 years of Industry experience in production and research. He is associated with nine associations with various International & national governing bodies.

Abderrahim Hasbi has a PhD degree in computer science from the University Mohammed V of Rabat Morocco. He's full Professor in Computer Science at the Mohammadia School of Engineering of the University Mohammed V Rabat, Morocco. He's member of the Network and Intelligent systems Group and he has a lot of contributions researches.

Gomathi Sankar Jeganathan is a member of SSM since 2015. Prior to this, he served as full time research scholar in Department of International Business at Pondicherry University. Dr. Sankar develops and teaches a course on Marketing Management, Services Marketing, Advertising and Sales Promotion, Sales Management, and Consumer Behaviour for post graduate students. A pure educationist by choice, he has been involved with teaching and research in marketing field. His wider areas of research include Internal Marketing, Services quality, Information diffusion, ICT, and MOOCs. His work has been published in scopus indexed and UGC listed journals. Dr. Sankar holds a PhD from Pondicherry University, Masters in Business Administration from Anna University, Thirunelveli. Bachelors in Electronics and Communication Engineering from Anna University Chennai.

Aslihan Kiymalioglu (Ph.D., Akdeniz University), Assistant Professor at Akdeniz University Serik Faculty of Business Administration. Her research interests include advertising and marketing research. She has published articles as well as various conference proceedings.

Palanivel Kuppusamy received his Master Degree in Computer Science & Engineering from Pondicherry University, Pondicherry, India. Prior to this, he received his Bachelor Degree in Computer Science & Engineering from Bharathiar University, India. His research coverage includes software architecture, e-Learning and data analytics. He is responsible for driving the institution network establishment, monitoring and presence.

Mitra Madanchian is a PhD of Business Management from University Technology Mara (UiTM). Currently, she was a former employee of KPMG Management & Risk Consulting- Malaysia, holding Assistant Manager of Business Development role and Lead of Events and also Business Development Manager of Hamta Group | Hamta Business Solution Sdn Bhd. She is an enthusiastic extensive experience in academic research, in area of Management, Leadership and Business Development. She has published over fifteen articles in the field of Management and Leadership in authentic journals and conferences and is a member of some International Management Associations. Currently, she is Research Assistant at Research Club and Business Consultant at Hamta Group.

Fahri Özsungur graduated from Ataturk University Faculty of Law, Hacettepe University Department of Family and Consumer Sciences PhD. and Aksaray University Department of Business Ph.D. He is a Eurostars Technical Expert (EUREKA Secretariat). He is affiliated to Adana Chamber of Commerce Department of Trade Registry Office in the province of Adana in Turkey, Adana Science and Technology University, Rotary International, Osmaniye Korkut Ata University, Çağ University, WEGATE- European Gateway for Women's Entrepreneurship and Canadian Institute for International Law Expertise (CIFILE). He has four books, 6 book chapters and more than 70 (4 SSCI/SCI/SCI-Expanded,9 ESCI) published articles. He is the editor of 9 Journals (1 SSCI/SCI/SCI-Expanded), and the reviewer of 28 Journals (8 SSCI/SCI/SCI-Expanded,5 ESCI).

Nouha Rida is currently a Ph.D. Student at Computer Networks, Modeling and ELearning Research Laboratory at Mohammadia School of Engineer, Mohammed V University, Morocco. She received her degree in engineering in computer science by "Ecole Nationale Superieur de Mine of Rabat". Her main research interests are related to the intelligent transportation system,road traffic optimization and ELearning.

Siranjeevi Sivakumar is experienced logistics professional who got rich experience in the field of logistics and supply chain. He completed his under graduation in B.Tech petrol chemical technology from Bharathidasan university Trichy,a nd post-graduation from Amet University Chennai, he topped his batch. completed UGC NET in 2010. Worked with logistics major companies like FedEx, all cargo global logistics.

Hamed Taherdoost holds a PhD of Computer Science from UTM, Master of Information Security, and Bachelor degree in the field of Science of Power Electricity. With over 19 years of work experience in both industry and academic sectors, he has been involved in development of several projects in different industries including oil and gas, laboratory, hospital, transportation and IT development as a project manager, business manager, technology head, R&D head, and team leader. Apart from his experience in industry background, he also has numerous experiences in academic environment. He has authored over 120 scientific articles in authentic journals and conference proceedings, seven book chapters and six books in the field of technology and research methodology. His current papers published in Behaviour & Information Technology, Information and Computer Security, Annual Data Science, Cogent Business & Management, Procedia Manufacturing & International Journal of Intelligent Engineering Informatics. Currently, he is the Team Leader & Supervisor - Research & Development Manager of Research Club and Team Leader & Business Advisor of Hamta Academy | Hamta Group, Canada, Hamta Business Solution Sdn Bhd, Malaysia, and R&D Head at Tablokar Co | Switchgear Manufacturer, Iran.

Andrea Wallace is a lecturer in Management and Business Communication at the University of New England. Her research has been published in the International Journal of Public Administration, the Australasian Journal of Regional Studies and the Australian Journal of Social Issues.

Index

www.ingramcontent.com/pod-product-compliance
Lightning Source LLC
LaVergne TN
LVHW080526300926
849162LV00007B/1544